THE LETTERS OF

Charles Armitage Brown

THE LETTERS OF

Charles Armitage Brown

EDITED BY

Jack Stillinger

HARVARD UNIVERSITY PRESS

Cambridge, Massachusetts

1966

Distributed in Great Britain by Oxford University Press, London

Publication of this book has been aided by a grant from the
Hyder Edward Rollins Fund

Library of Congress Catalog Card Number 66–10809

Printed in the United States of America

Preface

In 1848 W. S. Landor suggested to Charles Brown's son Carlino "that he should collect, and publish, a collection of Brown's writings, but when it was mentioned to Trelawny, the latter said that they were only of interest at the time, and not worth republishing." Although Charles Brown was a respectable contributor to the periodicals, a playwright, a translator, and a critic of Shakespeare, what was true of his published writings in 1848, six years after his death, still holds today. But E. J. Trelawny's words would not apply to a book about Brown's life and friendships. As a "friend of Keats" (like J. H. Reynolds', his gravestone proclaims that honor) Brown's fame is secure, and he has already received some attention from students of the poet. He was the closest friend of Keats during the two most important years of the poet's life, spent more time with him, played a greater role in the transmission of his texts, and did more to advance his fame than anyone else in the Keats circle. The facts that Brown was for some years a close associate of Leigh Hunt, Landor, and Trelawny, that he knew and befriended William Hazlitt, that he was acquainted with Byron, who invited him to contribute to the *Liberal*, further recommend him for study.

The present edition, containing 142 letters by Brown, thirteen letters to him or otherwise associated with his letters, and two documents related to topics discussed in his letters, offers, first of all, abundant information about Brown himself. The letters are fairly well distributed over a period of twenty-five years — from the Scottish tour with Keats in 1818 to the year of his death — and as supplemented by the Introduction and notes they present a full account of his interests, activities, and character. The letters also provide new facts about Keats, various members of the Keats circle, Hunt, Landor, Hazlitt, Trelawny, and many lesser figures in whom individual readers for one reason or another will be interested. Finally, though some of the letters (especially those concerned with the proprietorship of the *Examiner*) make dull reading, many others are good purely, as Brown would say, from a

v

literary point of view, apart from their value as source material. As early as September 14, 1817, after describing the "precious havoc" that he would make on Mrs. Dilke's house, furniture, and garden, Keats commented that he would rather see Brown's "Letter to her [Mrs. Dilke] on these events . . . than the original copy of the Book of Genesis." William Sharp, Joseph Severn's biographer, says that Brown "was a good *raconteur*, and a shepherd of all the vagrant amusing stories of his day," and these characteristics (which he shared with Keats) enrich many of his letters. Brown himself, who once wrote an article on "Letter-Writing," took pleasure in them, and his friends' enjoyment in the best of them can still be shared. Elizabeth Nitchie's remark, "Brown is a sprightly letter writer: his lively anecdotes and his comments are worth quoting," applies well to the letters to Severn, Thomas Richards, Robert Finch, and the later letters to Hunt. Even in those to his son Carlino, which too frequently lack the racy wit, anecdote, and gossip of letters to friends, Edmund Blunden has found "Great eccentricity and talent."

I have included all letters by Brown that could be located, whether in holograph or in printed source, regardless of their availability elsewhere. To the extent that I have been a diligent searcher the edition is "complete," though it of course represents only a small fraction of the letters that Brown wrote during his lifetime.* About half the letters have been printed before, in periodicals and books ranging from the *New Monthly Magazine* of 1823 to Joanna Richardson's recent study, *The Everlasting Spell* (1963). Sixty-six of the letters are entirely new or have been known hitherto only by a few words or sentences extracted by

---

* While including many fragmentary letters, I have omitted Brown's dozen words on Keats's letter to C. W. Dilke, July 31, 1819 (*Letters*, II, 136); his short note to Nathan Benjamin, September 1819, as reported by Keats (*Letters*, II, 216); a sentence from a letter to Dilke, late 1822, quoted in *Papers of a Critic*, I, 15; a sentence from a letter to Severn, September 30, 1828, quoted by Sharp, p. 157; two words from a letter to Landor, April 27, 1838, quoted by John Forster, *Walter Savage Landor* (London, 1869), II, 388; a sentence from a letter to Hunt, November 8, 1838, quoted in *The Correspondence of Leigh Hunt* (London, 1862), II, 326; four words from a letter to Seymour Kirkup, early 1841, quoted by Sharp, p. 191; and the shorthand notes, on a flyleaf of his logbook of the voyage to New Zealand (Keats House, Hampstead), for a letter that he wrote sometime after leaving England in June 1841. I have also omitted Brown's articles in the form of letters published in the *Examiner*, October 3, 24, 1824, pp. 626–628, 674–676, and *New Monthly Magazine*, 14 (1825): 261–266, 346–352, 463–469.

writers on Keats, Severn, Hunt, or Landor. Sixteen letters are about half new in the present edition, and the texts of three others add a few sentences to versions already in print.

Of letters written to Brown I have included only those for which substantially better texts could be made than have so far been available.* Seven letters from Severn (numbers 30, 37, 45, 48, 100, 104, 109, formerly owned by T. J. Wise and now in the British Museum) fit this category. Numbers 60 and 72 (from C. W. Dilke and Hazlitt) have been printed before only in part, and numbers 87 and 135 (from C. C. Clarke and William Brown) are entirely new. Numbers 62 and 131 (Hunt to Vincent Novello, and William Brown to Carlino), both hitherto unpublished, have been included because they were written on letters by Brown. (They are given as separate letters because they were written at a later date than Brown's; additions to Brown's letters written on the same day, as in numbers 5, 52, 53, 141, are considered parts of single letters.) The two documents, numbers 91 and 108, are new in their present form, though a portion of the latter has previously appeared in both facsimile and transcript and its remaining contents have been known from other sources.

My editorial methods in most details follow those established by Hyder Rollins in *The Keats Circle* and his edition of Keats's *Letters*. The transcriptions of the 133 holographs reproduce the spelling, capitalization, and punctuation of the originals. I have silently (1) omitted dots and dashes under superscript letters, and lines and flourishes beneath signatures; (2) printed interlineations and marginal additions as if they were written currently; (3) ignored all deleted words and parts of words; (4) placed postscripts always at the end of the letters, regardless of where they were actually written; and (5) substituted "per," "at," and "to" for the commercial symbols that Brown sometimes used for these words. All other changes are either recorded in the notes or indicated by brackets. Square brackets enclose initial dates for the letters, whenever these have been omitted or are missing from the beginning of the text, and also a few other editorial additions —

---

* Hence most of the published letters to Brown (their originals either well edited in *KC* or *Letters* or now lost) are omitted, though they are of course frequently cited in my notes.

for example, question marks to indicate doubtful readings, and occasionally missing letters or words owing to slips of the pen where the writer's error might momentarily obscure his meaning. Many simple misspellings like "thats," "apreciated," "cherished," "harrased" (especially common in the letters of Severn, whose number 30 provides these examples) have been left uncorrected, and I do not employ *sic* to defend my own or the printer's reliability.

Braces ({ }) enclose editorial attempts to replace text lost through damage to the manuscript. Three dots within braces indicate a gap that could not be filled conjecturally; for such gaps the extent of damage is noted except where (through the conjunction of tears or mutilations with some special arrangement of lines on the page) it could not be determined. Three asterisks mark the beginning or end of fragmentary pages in holograph letters that survive only in part as well as the beginning or end of extracts from printed sources. I would emphasize that three or four dots unbracketed always indicate a gap in a printed source, not in a holograph.

In the texts of the twenty-four letters taken from printed sources I have silently corrected a few obvious misprints, and have occasionally departed from the typography of my source (for example, from Sharp's frequent italics in the first line of the date, and his use of large and small capitals for salutations and signatures). Where damage to the manuscript is reported, I have sometimes emended within braces, as with holographs. Restoration of lost text in these letters is, of course, purely conjectural, since the extent of damage to the now lost manuscript underlying the printed source is unknown.

Headnotes (used mainly for holograph letters) provide addresses, postmarks, and endorsements by the recipient whenever a letter has them; the present location of each holograph; and a selection of details about previous printings of the letters. If a letter has been wholly or in large part printed before, that fact is given, though for letters printed many times I usually cite only recent standard works, like *The Keats Circle* or *Letters*. In reproducing addresses I have ignored all slashes and underlines. Postmarks in series and disconnected items of endorsements are separated by semicolons; and defective postmarks are emended always within square brackets, regardless of whether the loss was caused by tears, blurring, fading, or improper inking.

The first footnote of every letter taken from a printed source refers to that source and, where appropriate, gives details of its context. Generally the notes are explanatory rather than textual. I have followed the convention of identifying even the best known quotations from Shakespeare, and in notes to three letters (numbers 133, 141, 142) I have translated passages of Italian and French for those Dilkes "who cannot afford to be puzzled with outlandish jargon" (see number 56).

The Introduction is a brief factual account of Brown's life, emphasizing his relationships with certain friends and correspondents and discussing some topics frequently mentioned in the letters. I have omitted biographical notices of Dilke, Hunt, Keats, Landor, Severn, and Trelawny, because their lives are well known either in the standard literary histories or in the sketches given in *The Keats Circle* and *Letters*. For the same reason I have nowhere formally identified Richard Abbey, Benjamin Bailey, the Brawnes, Charles Cowden Clarke, William Haslam, Benjamin Robert Haydon, William Hazlitt, James Augustus Hessey, Keats's brothers and sister, Richard Monckton Milnes, John Hamilton Reynolds, James Rice, Jr., John Taylor, Richard Woodhouse, Jr., and a few others familiar to students of Keats's life.

I gratefully acknowledge the generosity of the following individuals and institutions in granting me permission to print or quote from letters and other original manuscripts in their collections: Mr. William R. Maidment and the Libraries and Arts Committee of the London Borough of Camden for letters at Keats House, Hampstead; Dr. W. H. Bond and the late Mabel A. E. Steele for letters and manuscripts in the Harvard Keats Collection; Mr. David I. Masson for letters in the Brotherton Collection, University of Leeds; Mr. Frank Paluka for manuscripts in the Brewer–Leigh Hunt Collection, University of Iowa; and the librarians and trustees of the British Museum, London, the Bodleian Library, Oxford, the Pierpont Morgan Library, New York, the Historical Society of Pennsylvania, Philadelphia, and Dr. Williams's Library, London.

ACKNOWLEDGMENTS

I am of course under obligation to earlier researchers into the life of Brown — most notably William Sharp, Maurice Buxton Forman, Hyder Edward Rollins, Mrs. Dorothy Hyde Bodurtha, Professor Willard B. Pope, and Miss Joanna Richardson — and to many individuals who gave me various kinds of help, among whom I would single out the late Rainforth Armitage Walker, grandson of Brown's nephew James Armitage Brown, who answered a number of queries, and Mrs. Enid D. Nixon, who did some last-minute checking for me at the British Museum.

The presider over this edition is the late Hyder Rollins, who read it in an earlier form as a Harvard doctoral thesis. Professor Herschel Baker, as second reader of the thesis, made several good suggestions, and more recently both he and Professor W. J. Bate have been very kind in urging me to complete my revisions and turn the manuscript over to the press. Principally to these three, and to my wife, an invaluable helper from the beginning, this book owes its existence.

Harvard University provided a postdoctoral Charles Dexter Traveling Scholarship that enabled me to search out additional manuscript material in England in the summer of 1958. The John Simon Guggenheim Memorial Foundation and the Trustees of the University of Illinois made possible between them a year's leave of absence (1964–65) during which, at one end, I put the finishing touches to the manuscript and, at the other, read the proofs.

J. S.

Urbana, Illinois

CONTENTS

THE LETTERS OF

Charles Armitage Brown

ABBREVIATIONS USED IN NOTES

Bodurtha and Pope	*Life of John Keats by Charles Armitage Brown*, ed. Dorothy Hyde Bodurtha and Willard Bissell Pope, London, 1937
Forman (1883)	*The Poetical Works and Other Writings of John Keats*, ed. Harry Buxton Forman, 4 vols., London, 1883
Forman (1952)	*The Letters of John Keats*, ed. Maurice Buxton Forman, 4th edn., London, 1952
KC	*The Keats Circle: Letters and Papers*, ed. Hyder Edward Rollins, 2 vols., Cambridge, Mass., 1948
Letters	*The Letters of John Keats*, ed. Hyder Edward Rollins, 2 vols., Cambridge, Mass., 1958
Papers of a Critic	*The Papers of a Critic. Selected from the Writings of the Late Charles Wentworth Dilke*, 2 vols., London, 1875
PDWJ	*The Plymouth and Devonport Weekly Journal*
Sharp	William Sharp, *The Life and Letters of Joseph Severn*, London, 1892
Some Letters	*Some Letters & Miscellanea of Charles Brown the Friend of John Keats & Thomas Richards*, ed. Maurice Buxton Forman, London, 1937
TLS	*The Times Literary Supplement*
Williamson	*The Keats Letters, Papers, and Other Relics Forming the Dilke Bequest in the Hampstead Public Library*, ed. George C. Williamson, London, 1914

Introduction

When Charles Brown first met Keats, on the Hampstead Road late in the summer of 1817, he was thirty years old. No "melancholy Carle / Thin in the waist, with bushy head of hair," [1] he was instead a convivial, corpulent, bearded, balding gentleman of property and leisure, an epicure, and something of a ladies' man. Among reckonable achievements he had to his credit only the libretto of a comic opera, but he had traveled and read widely, gathered experience, and witnessed life from several points of view.

He was born in Lambeth on April 14, 1787, and baptized at the church of Saint Mary-at-Lambeth on August 25, the sixth of seven sons of William and Jane Brown.[2] His father was a Scottish stockbroker and owner of a landed estate in Grey's Walk that later provided property for 140 houses. His mother was the only daughter of Hugh Davis, a Welsh clockmaker established in London. By 1816 William had died, and Jane had taken as a second husband Joseph Rennock Browne.[3] Nothing else is known of the parents, except that his mother was still alive in 1829 (she is mentioned by Brown in letter number 94). The oldest of the brothers, John Armitage, like Charles first a merchant's clerk and then a "Russia-merchant," in 1806 married Jane Elizabeth Mavor, by whom he had four children, two of them the "little Browns" mentioned in Keats's letters.[4] He died in London on March 8, 1823, and his widow later lived with one of her sons in Plymouth (number 111). The next brother, William, became a doctor, and

[1] See Keats's verses in *Letters*, II, 89–90.

[2] So the parish register, of which the Reverend Harry Hedley kindly supplied me a copy. Much of the following information about Brown's family is derived from letters of Brown's great-grandnephew R. A. Walker and a genealogy compiled by his son A. F. Walker; from James Brown's will at Somerset House; from obituary notices in *The Times*; and from Carlino's memoirs of his father at Keats House, Hampstead, and at Harvard. Where Carlino is cited without a specific reference, the source is the latter of these memoirs, published in *KC*, I, liv–lxii.

[3] She is described as "Wife of Joseph Rennock Brown" by the court clerk who recorded the admission of James Brown's will on January 5, 1816. William Dilke (see *TLS*, August 29, 1952, p. 565) noted that "Chs. Brown's mother married a second time to a Browne with an e which used to be emphasized by way of distinction."

[4] See number 2, n. 4.

1

by 1839, when Carlino came to stay with him for a year, was settled with a wife, née Mary Sparks, in Midhurst, Sussex. The third brother, Henry, went to sea, and died of a fever in the West Indies before he was twenty.[5] The fourth, James, was an East India Company resident in Sumatra, where he owned a house and two nutmeg plantations, fathered a natural daughter by a native woman, and amassed some £40,000 before coming to England to die, at the age of thirty-five, on October 22, 1815.[6] A fifth brother did not survive infancy. Charles's only younger brother, aptly named Septimus, whose wife Keats met in February 1819, died at Ramsgate, aged thirty-seven, on August 31, 1828.

Charles early attended school with Charles Wentworth Dilke, who became a nearly lifelong friend. At fourteen,[7] however, he entered a merchant's office as a clerk at £40 a year, and at eighteen he followed his brother John to Russia to become a partner in an export business that the latter had founded. John returned to manage the firm in London (at 138 Leadenhall Street), leaving Charles as its representative in St. Petersburg. But after three or four years, having accumulated some £20,000 of capital, the partners invested too heavily in bristles just when a cheap (though, as it proved too late, worthless) substitute was being introduced on the market. The devaluation of their goods bankrupted them, and Brown returned to England almost penniless.

The commercial career that ended thus abruptly when he was twenty-one or twenty-two had a lasting effect on his character. More than one writer has called him "methodical Brown" from Keats's description of his preparations for writing: "[Brown] affronts my indolence and Luxury by pulling out of his knapsack 1st his paper — 2ndy his pens and last his ink — Now I would not care if he would change about a little — I say now, why not . . . take out his pens first sometimes — But I might as well tell a hen

---

[5] Joanna Richardson, *The Everlasting Spell: A Study of Keats and His Friends* (London, 1963), p. 233.

[6] The natural daughter, Mary, born around 1802, later came to England and frequently visited or lived with the widow of John Armitage Brown, according to William Dilke (*TLS*, August 29, 1952, p. 565), who mistakenly thought she was Keats's "Charmian" (*Letters*, I, 394–396).

[7] In one memoir Carlino says fourteen, in another sixteen, perhaps influenced in the latter by the fact that Brown's fictional hero Walter Hazlebourn joined his uncle's firm at the age of sixteen.

to hold up her head before she drinks instead of afterwards." [8]
The penchant for method was only a part of his immense practicality, a quality suggested by Keats's remark of September 18,
1819, when he discovered one of his earlier "scotch Letters" and
began copying it for his brother and sister-in-law: "I did not know
the day of the month for I find I have not dated it — Brown must
have been asleep." [9] Brown also had a legalistic mind, and in the
letters that follow we see him arguing against George Keats and
John Hunt like a prosecuting attorney. "I have been very much
occupied in Mrs. Medwin's affairs," he tells Severn, "battling with
bankers, and lawyers, with my hands day after day full of documents in Courts of Law" (number 102), and he adds in a letter
to Hunt, "I was battling in a Court of Law for her against that
banker, and gained my point!" (number 106). His frequent concern with financial accounts — Keats's with Brown, Keats's with
Abbey, Hunt's with Brown, the *Examiner* accounts — shows that
he was all his life, among other things, a bookkeeper at heart. The
qualities deriving from what Dilke called "the commercial kennel" [10] make up only one side of Brown's character, but they
should not be minimized. They in part made him a mainstay to
Keats, Severn, Hunt, and others who looked to him as an oracle of
practical wisdom.

In London around 1809 he concluded the business of bankruptcy ("I am well aware of the power a creditor possesses over
his debtor," he later wrote from experience in number 66), and
then, according to Dilke, "for many years had a *very hard struggle.*"
Carlino adds that he "suffered great privations . . . as he was too
independant to ask for any assistance, often living on one meal a
day, where he got it for four pence, and the knives and forks were
chained to the table." It was not only from his favorite Rousseau
but from firsthand acquaintance with poverty that he learned
benevolence, generosity, and some democratic principles that
made him later vow never to put his legs under a lord's table.

---

[8] *Letters*, I, 344.
[9] *Letters*, II, 196.
[10] Forman (1952), p. li. This and the quotation near the beginning of the next
paragraph are from Dilke's notes in his copy of R. M. Milnes's *Life, Letters, and
Literary Remains, of John Keats* (London, 1848), now in the Pierpont Morgan
Library.

His adversity lasted perhaps four years before a succession of events brought remedy. First he became his East Indian brother James's London agent. Then in January 1814 his comic opera *Narensky*, written nearly five years earlier, just after he had returned from Russia, was produced at Drury Lane, where, on the strength of its music, by John Braham and William Reeve, and Braham's singing, it ran for ten nights, winning him £300 and free lifetime admission to that theater.[11] And in October of the following year James died, leaving "to my Brother Charles Brown the sum of Ten thousand pounds sterling & to him & his heirs for ever all & every part of a Landed Estate in the parish of Lambeth County of Surry Great Britain which may devolve to me or to my Assigns on the decease of my Mother"[12] — "the competence," says Carlino, "which allowed him to lead a life of literary leisure afterwards." Shortly after James's death, and more than a year before the will was actually proved, he began building with Dilke a double house in Hampstead to be called Wentworth Place, now the Keats House.

II

Apparently Reynolds introduced Brown to Keats,[13] who, living with his brothers at 1 Well Walk, Hampstead, in 1817 was Brown's neighbor. In his "Life" of Keats, Brown tells that he succeeded in making the poet "come often to my house by never asking him

[11] Brown's share in it was mentioned indifferently by *The Times*, January 12, and unfavorably by the *Champion* (see Richardson, *The Everlasting Spell*, p. 21) and the *Examiner*, January 16, p. 43, which said, "The only way in which . . . [*Narensky*] differs from all the rest is, that it is exceedingly duller, not being enlivened with even one attempt at a joke . . . . The story . . . is unintelligible." Brown's libretto was published by John Cawthorn early in 1814. A manuscript version submitted to the Examiner of Plays in December 1813 (under the title "The Russian Village") is extant in the Larpent Collection of the Huntington Library.

[12] James Brown's will (Somerset House). Dilke (Forman, 1952, p. li) calls Brown's inheritance a "small share of James's property" and a "moderate, very moderate, independence." In number 7 (August 23, 1819) Brown speaks of "locked up" property sending him "quarterly & half yearly driblets" insufficient for the support of himself and Keats. It is difficult to determine exactly how much money he had after James's death. References to his finances in the letters generally suggest that he had enough to live on but never any great surplus.

[13] In 1846 Reynolds told Milnes (*KC*, II, 177) that Brown "knew Keats through me," and in early references in *Letters*, I, 169, 171, Brown's and Reynolds' names are mentioned together. Carlino, however, says that Brown "made the acquaintance of Keats . . . through . . . Dilke."

to come oftener; and I let him feel himself at perfect liberty there, chiefly by avoiding to assure him of the fact. We quickly became intimate." [14] Frequent references in Keats's letters after September 1817 confirm this last remark: "Yesterday Morning . . . I was at Brown's"; "we are going to dine at Brown's"; "Brown & Dilke walked with me"; "I dined with Brown lately." By the following February 21 Keats was "a good deal" with Brown and "very thick," [15] and by early April they were planning to see Scotland together.

Their famous tour, described by Keats in his letters, by Brown in letters and later in "Walks in the North," [16] and more recently by Nelson S. Bushnell in *A Walk after John Keats* (New York, 1936), began late in June and took them through the English Lake District to the western coast of Scotland, into Ireland and the Island of Mull, and then across the Highlands to Inverness and Cromarty, where Keats's illness forced him to return home. They were well suited as walking companions. The older, more-traveled Brown pretended to introduce Keats, who "had witnessed nothing superior to Devonshire," [17] to the mountains, but both were awed by the beauty of the scenery. They spent their days tramping and sightseeing, their nights writing "volumes of adventures" — Keats chiefly the letters to his brothers and sister; Brown his journal and the letters to Dilke containing "every little circumstance." [18] Stared at and "taken for Spectacle venders, Razor sellers, Jewellers, travelling linnen drapers, Spies, Excisemen, & many things else," [19] they thoroughly enjoyed themselves. "We

[14] *KC*, II, 57. In 1841 Dilke (*KC*, II, 104–105) commented spitefully, "At that time Brown & myself lived in adjoining cottages at Hampstead, & the Keats, John George & Tom, were with me three times a week, often three times a day, & Brown & Keats were *drawn together* by force of circumstances & position." By then (for reasons given in a later section of this introduction) Dilke was Brown's enemy, and he made many such remarks attempting to show that Brown was no more than Keats's landlord.

[15] *Letters*, I, 169, 171, 193, 214, 237.

[16] An unfinished revision of his "pains-taking journal, written at the conclusion of each several stage." Four chapters of it were published in *PDWJ* in 1840 (see numbers 146, 147). They are reprinted in *Letters*, I, 421–442.

[17] "Walks in the North," ch. I (*Letters*, I, 425). According to his notes on a tour of the industrial cities of England in the spring of 1809 (Keats House, Hampstead), Brown had seen the mountains of South Wales from the highest part of Clifton, in Bristol.

[18] *Letters*, I, 344, 351. Of Brown's Scottish letters to Dilke only a single brief extract (number 1) is known. But see numbers 2, 3.

[19] *Letters*, I, 332, 360 (see also I, 310).

have been as happy as possible together," wrote Brown (number 3), and the dominant note of both their accounts is mutual pleasure in good-humored observations. "O scenery that thou shouldst be crush'd between two Puns," says Keats, the "rascalliest" punner "in the Scotch Region," who recorded some of Brown's worst in the opening of a letter to Tom on July 17.[20] But Brown had to write from Inverness on August 7, "Mr. Keats will leave me here, and I am full of sorrow about it; he is not well enough to go on; a violent cold and an ulcerated throat make it a matter of prudence that he should go to London in the Packet" (number 2). Brown continued alone, reaching Edinburgh around September 1, and after a visit with Benjamin Bailey at Carlisle returned to Hampstead in late September or early October.

When Tom Keats died on the morning of December 1, 1818, it was to Brown that Keats turned for comfort, awakening him with the unhappy news. "From that moment he was my inmate," says Brown,[21] and within a few days Keats was established in Brown's half of Wentworth Place — he taking the front parlor, Brown the back — where he lived for the next seventeen months, except for visits to Hampshire in January and to the Isle of Wight and Winchester in July–October of the following year. The harmony of opinions and activities of the Scottish tour continued between them. They disliked being outpunned at Novello's, agreed on Miss Robinson's ugliness, were bored by Davenport's chatter, cursed like Mandeville and Lisle over the stoppage of mail, and damned parsons. They played cards, held claret feasts, railed at one another over making "more feet for little stockings,"

---

[20] *Letters*, I, 324, 333–334.

[21] *KC*, II, 64–65. Keats says that "Brown detained me at his House," but the stay was at first intended to be temporary, if Mrs. Dilke's statement on December 18 — "[Keats] is staying with Mr Brown" — was news to Fanny Keats, who had seen her brother around the tenth and again on the thirteenth. At any rate, Keats wrote from Brown's on the sixteenth that he was "going to domesticate" with Brown, and on the next day his landlord brought his belongings to Wentworth Place (*Letters*, II, 4, 11–12; Forman, 1952, p. 268).

On the passage cited above from Brown's "Life" of Keats, Dilke commented to Severn in 1841 (*KC*, II, 105): "as to the 'come live with me' scene — why Brown . . . was accustomed to have people live with him — it helped him to eke out a small income. When therefore Tom died, John was glad, both for economy & company, to board with Brown — but he was charged for his board" (see also *KC*, II, 336). The fact that Brown charged Keats for board — £5 per month, as number 84 shows — has disturbed others besides Dilke.

engaged in drawing contests, wrote Spenserian stanzas against one another, visited Wordsworth,[22] attended the theater, read together, and often sat opposite one another all day "authorizing."

At Wentworth Place Keats "authorized" the poems that put him among the English poets, while Brown puttered with such things as a story of Alice and the Devil, fairy tales, and a "Life of David." They collaborated on the maligned *Otho the Great*, "a joint money speculation" from which they hoped to earn £200 each.[23] As half of "this Beaumont & Fletcher pair," Brown provided "the fable, characters, and dramatic conduct" of the play, while Keats "acted as Midwife to his plot." [24] Brown had a hand in other writings of Keats by suggesting the subjects of "King Stephen," "The Cap and Bells," and a few shorter poems, and by persuading him, when he was about to give up poetry, to "try the press once more" with the *Lamia* volume.[25]

His most important connection with Keats's poems lies in his transcripts of them. After telling in his "Life" of Keats how one day in the spring of 1819 he rescued the Nightingale ode and other "fugitive pieces" that were "used as a mark to a book, or thrust any where aside," Brown says, "From that day he gave me permission to copy any verses he might write, and I fully availed myself of it." [26] Actually he had begun copying Keats's poems during the Scottish tour of 1818, and by the end of 1820 had collected "four Ms books in my hand writing of Mr Keats' poems," each containing a poem "of an exceptionable kind" to ward off bluestocking borrowers (numbers 31, 152). After Keats's death Brown lent these volumes through Taylor to Woodhouse, who copied poems that he did not have and noted variants in others (hence the frequent "from C.B." in his transcripts). Brown published poems and parts of poems from time to time,[27] and then in 1841 gave the four

[22] So Brown told Landor in 1837 (R. H. Super, *Walter Savage Landor: A Biography*, New York, 1954, p. 282).

[23] *KC*, II, 105; *Letters of Fanny Brawne to Fanny Keats*, ed. Fred Edgcumbe (New York, 1937), p. 34.

[24] *KC*, I, 86, and II, 66; *Letters*, II, 157.

[25] *KC*, II, 67, 72; *Letters*, II, 121.

[26] *KC*, II, 65. Against Milnes's paraphrase of this passage (*Life*, I, 245) Dilke noted, "Brown had slowly and doubtingly grown into a high admiration of Keats, and began therefore to collect every scrap of his writing" (Bodurtha and Pope, p. 107).

[27] Poems in the *New Monthly Magazine*, 4 (1822): 47–48, 252, and 5 (1822): 47–48; in the *Examiner*, July 14, 1822, p. 445; and in the Plymouth newspapers, 1836, 1838–

manuscript volumes to Milnes, who printed the new poems in 1848. His transcripts preserved at Harvard and references in Keats's and his own letters and elsewhere identify some fifty poems that he copied, a number of them known only through his texts or texts deriving from them. His statement to Milnes in October 1840 — "most of the originals were scrambled away to America by his brother, after I had made copies of them for the press" (number 146) — illuminates Keats's remark to James Elmes, "I have but just received the Book which contains the only copy of the verses in question [the Nightingale ode]," [28] and, along with the presence of Keats's holograph revisions here and there on the transcripts, suggests that for some poems Brown's copy became the principal manuscript version, while the first draft was discarded as no longer useful.

Soon after joining Brown in Wentworth Place Keats mentioned to his sister (March 13, 1819) Brown's kindness "to me in many things when I most wanted his assistance," and about the same time described him to his brother and sister-in-law as "always one's friend in a disaster." In the fall of 1819 he wrote that the interval between February and September "has been completely filled with generous & most friendly actions of Brown towards me," and that without Brown "I should have been in, perhaps, personal distress." [29] Such references are frequent. In 1833 George Keats, who by then disliked Brown ("with cause," he thought), told Dilke, "I have been looking over John's correspondence, in which he dwells so much on his [Brown's] kindness that I must perforce acquit, and *try* to like him." [30] To Brown himself Keats wrote on September 22, 1819, speaking of their friendship, "You have been living for others more than any man I know. . . . if you can go over, day by day, any month of the last year, — you will know what I mean." He gave Brown the highest praise in mentioning his "disinterested character." [31]

Brown's kindness consisted partly in being a good companion.

1840 (see number 111, n. 2, number 117, n. 5, number 146, n. 2). Extracts in Trelawny's *Adventures of a Younger Son* (1831) and elsewhere.

[28] *Letters*, II, 118.

[29] *Letters*, II, 46, 78, 71, 225.

[30] *KC*, II, 4, 16.

[31] *Letters*, II, 176, 279.

Some of the liveliest passages in Keats's letters, like the account of the hoax he played on Brown and Nathan Benjamin,[32] testify to the high spirits that Brown could excite. Brown's exuberant "society" was not always welcome, as when at Shanklin in August 1819 his return from two days' "gadding" broke in upon Keats's dream of Fanny Brawne "like a Thunderbolt." [33] But as much as any friend could, he provided sympathy and encouragement to ease the loss of Tom and to keep the poet from despondency over his future and the harshness of the reviewers. His kindness also took practical forms. After Keats's severe hemorrhage of February 3, 1820, Brown nursed him day and night and handled all his business affairs, paying bills, writing letters for him, continuing to lend him money (as he had since June 1819, more than once borrowing money to lend him and offering to stand as surety for a loan to him). They remained together until May 1820, when Brown, following his usual practice of renting his house for the summer, went again to Scotland. Keats had planned, and his doctor had advised him, to accompany Brown, but at the last minute he decided not to go. Brown found him lodgings in Kentish Town, and then took leave of him at Gravesend on May 6, sailing on the smack for Scotland alone. He did not see Keats again.

Only concerning Fanny Brawne was there discord between them. While he and Brown were still together at Hampstead Keats told Fanny, "I think you had better not make any long stay with me when Mr Brown is at home," and after Brown's departure Keats spoke bitterly to Fanny about her conduct with Brown: "When you were in the habit of flirting with Brown you would have left off, could your own heart have felt one half of one pang mine did. Brown is a good sort of Man — he did not know he was doing me to death by inches. I feel the effect of every one of those hours in my side now; and for that cause, though he has done me many services, though I know his love and friendship for me, though at this moment I should be without pence were it not for his assistance, I will never see or speak to him until we are both old men, if we are to be." "I see nothing but thorns for the future — wherever I may be next winter in Italy or nowhere Brown will

[32] *Letters*, II, 215–216.
[33] *Letters*, II, 138.

be living near you with his indecencies." [34] His words are mitigated by George's later remark that Keats's "nervous morbid temperament at times led him to misconstrue the motives of his best Friends," by Keats's own remark to Brown, "Imaginary grievances have always been more my torment than real ones," [35] and by the fact that Keats wrote soon afterward to ask Brown to accompany him to Italy. When Brown remained behind, Keats urged him to "be a friend to Miss Brawne when I am dead," and to "be her advocate for ever." "I should think of — you in my last moments," he added in a letter written aboard the *Maria Crowther,* and in his only known letter from Rome he mentions his love for Brown. [36]

When Brown received Keats's request to go to Italy he turned his steps (he says in his "Life" of Keats) "undeviatingly homewards," [37] arriving at Hampstead only hours after the *Maria Crowther* sailed from Gravesend. Once there, however, learning that Severn had gone in his stead ("Keats could not be in more affectionate hands"), he contented himself "with preparing to follow him very early in the spring, and not return, should he prefer to live there." [38] By "very early in the spring" Keats was dead, and Milnes changed Brown's words in paraphrase to read "following Keats as speedily as possible," causing Dilke to comment tartly: "What are the facts? . . . Keats *died* Feby 1821 and

---

[34] *Letters,* II, 269, 303, 312. Nothing supports the statement of Brown's granddaughter Mona Osborne (see Joanna Richardson, *Fanny Brawne: A Biography,* London, 1952, p. 31), "My grandfather did not like Fanny Brawne; he thought her superficial and vain, and he considered that her flirtatious manner, in the company of every man she met, accounted for Keats's jealousy." On the other hand, there is no known basis — certainly not Brown's fragmentary valentine to Fanny, printed in *Some Letters,* pp. xiii–xiv — for the intensity of Keats's bitterness toward Brown in the letters just cited.

[35] *KC,* I, 284; *Letters,* II, 181 (see also II, 185–186, 210). Hunt, too (*Autobiography,* ed. J. E. Morpurgo, London, 1949, p. 274), speaks of "an irritable morbidity" that drove Keats's "suspicions to excess," and Amy Lowell, while researching for her biography of Keats, learned "that one of the signs of tuberculosis is what is called 'suspicionism,' attacks not only of melancholy but of violent suspicion against people" (H. E. Rollins and S. M. Parrish, *Keats and the Bostonians,* Cambridge, Mass., 1951, p. 155).

[36] *Letters,* II, 345, 352, 346, 360.

[37] *KC,* II, 77. The request sent by Keats around August 18 reached Brown, with other "letters forwarded from various parts of the Highlands," on September 9 at Dunkeld. He arrived home nine days later, on the eighteenth.

[38] *KC,* II, 80.

Brown *started* for Italy in July or August 1822! fifteen or sixteen months after he was *dead!*" [39] The facts are that Brown believed Keats's "disease is on his *mind*" (number 13), and "thought of nothing but his recovery; for all the medical men who attended him were constant in their assertions that his lungs were ininjured," [40] and that going to Italy "not [to] return" required time to arrange affairs. In replying to another request by Keats — "so you still wish me to follow you to Rome? and truly I wish to go, — nothing detains me but prudence" [41] — Brown had no idea of the "most unlooked for relapse" that Keats had suffered eleven days earlier, or of the imminence of his death, which occurred two months later, on February 23, 1821. That death was a great shock to Brown. His early "cruel charge" against George Keats and his lifelong belief that Keats "was destroyed by hirelings, under the imposing name of Reviewers" [42] stem from the idea that Keats's disease was mentally rather than physically based, and from an unwillingness to accept the fact that Keats was mortally ill when he left England.

"Keats never had a more zealous, a firmer, or more practical friend and adviser than . . . Brown," wrote Charles Cowden Clarke,[43] who was no authority, but whose words are apt. Keats's and Brown's letters are ample evidence of the sincerity of Brown's devotion to the younger man, of the importance of his help to Keats as companion, counselor, nurse, and financial agent, and of the goodness of his intentions, whether or not he bungled his responsibilities, during the last months of Keats's life.

III

The news of Keats's death reached London on March 17, 1821. In his reply to Severn six days later Brown wrote, "what I am now most anxious about . . . [is] your health. My solicitude

---

[39] Milnes, *Life*, II, 71; Bodurtha and Pope, p. 116.

[40] *KC*, II, 80. See number 12, n. 3.

[41] Number 20. Brown answers a letter in which Keats had told him (*Letters*, II, 360), "Dr Clarke . . . says, there is very little the matter with my lungs."

[42] *KC*, II, 95.

[43] Charles and Mary Cowden Clarke, *Recollections of Writers* (London, 1878), p. 146.

seems transfered from him [Keats] to you" (number 29). He sent cheerful letters of encouragement to Rome, urged other friends to write, advised the artist about his career, consoled him (and busied himself "from house to house") over the disappearance of the prize picture, "The Death of Alcibiades," and drafted an inscription to be used on Keats's gravestone. As a kind of unofficial executor, he distributed Keats's books among the poet's friends, and set about retrieving his transcripts of poems from Taylor. In August or September he received Keats's papers from Rome, followed by Severn's suggestion that he write Keats's life.[44] A projected memoir had already been announced by Taylor, who with Reynolds sought Brown's help and the use of his papers; but Brown would not "consent to be a party in a bookseller's job" without the right to approve the memoir (number 35; see also number 33). Discord among the surviving friends, for many years a major obstacle to the writing of Keats's biography, quickly arose.

Dilke, Hunt, and Thomas Richards, all of whom supported his opposition to Taylor's "bookseller's job," were Brown's closest friends at the time. As Hunt's health grew increasingly bad in the spring of 1821, Brown took over in his place partial responsibility for the weekly theatricals in the *Examiner*. After Taylor and Hessey rejected an article submitted by him to their *London Magazine*, it was probably either Hunt or Dilke who secured him entry into the *New Monthly Magazine*, where in 1821–1822 he published three articles based on his trips to Scotland and two poems written with Keats.[45] Richards, another writer of *Examiner* theatricals for Hunt, a clerk in the Ordnance Department, and brother to the printer of Keats's 1817 *Poems*, appears to have been Brown's most frequent companion. Brown stood godfather to his son Sidney in 1821, and Richards in turn supported Brown in his somewhat unconventional domestic affairs, which in the months after Keats's death became a troublesome concern.

Sometime in 1819, certainly by October, Brown had formed a liaison with their Irish servant Abigail O'Donaghue, who is de-

[44] Forman (1883), IV, 365–366; Sharp, p. 110.

[45] 2 (1821): 561–571; 4 (1822): 47–48, 247–252, 329–333; 5 (1822): 47–48. See Richardson, *The Everlasting Spell*, pp. 236–237, for a list of some other writings possibly by Brown in the *New Monthly Magazine* during 1821–1824.

scribed [46] as "something of a firebrand . . . a good-looking woman" with "a great gift of repartee." The affair produced a son, Carlino (Charles, Jr.), born on July 16, 1820,[47] while Brown was in Scotland. There is no evidence that Keats, who knew about the affair, thought any more of it than he did about the news that "Severn has got a little Baby." [48] Whether Brown really chose Abby "for her splendid physique, for the sake of the offspring," as Carlino told F. H. Day, or went through a form of marriage with her to salve her conscience, or did not marry her at all,[49] he did acknowledge the child; and after Keats had gone to Italy both Abby and Carlino, to the distress of James Rice and others, came to live with Brown in Wentworth Place: "she keeps to her own bed, & I keep myself continent. Any more nonsense of the former kind would put me in an awkward predicament with her. One child is very well. . . . The fact is I could not afford to allow her a seperate establishment" (number 20). In November 1821 Brown complained that Carlino "is kept aloof from me by his obstinate Mother" (number 36), but by March 1822 he had Carlino in his charge again, and was trying to decide whether to take him to Italy or leave him with the Richardses (number 38) — though he wished to keep him from Abby's hands in any case.

Brown's move to Italy is variously explained. Carlino says that he feared Abby "might appeal to Chancery to give her legal custody of the boy, on the same grounds that Shelley had been deprived of his children. He therefore transferred himself, with his boy to Italy." Carlino's daughter Mrs. Jessie Brown tells that

[46] By Brown's granddaughter Mona Osborne (Betty Askwith, *Keats*, London, 1941, p. 278). On the spelling of Abby's name see *KC*, I, lxiv n.

[47] The date is given by Dorothy Hewlett, *A Life of John Keats* (New York, 1950), p. 276.

[48] *Letters*, II, 205.

[49] See *KC*, I, lxvii. Most of the evidence concerning Brown's supposed marriage comes from Carlino, either directly or through his descendants. Mona Osborne, however, saw a birth certificate on which Carlino is described as the "son of Charles Brown and Abigail Brown," and a letter written by Abby to Carlino in the 1870's signed "A. Brown"; she also tells that in 1840 or 1841, when Carlino jokingly suggested that Brown take a wife along to New Zealand, the latter replied "very shortly" that he was already married (Askwith, *Keats*, pp. 278–279). Carlino says that a "marriage was performed by a catholic priest, and therefore [was] not legal, but as she was a bigoted catholic, and Irish, she was satisfied." Brown's remark to Carlino in number 145, "Disguise it as you will, I see you wince under the circumstances of your birth," shows that not everyone was satisfied.

"when C.A.B. discovered that she [Abby] had (unknown to him) had my Father christened a Roman Catholic, he took my Father . . . to Italy." [50] Whatever the reliability of these accounts, the fact is that Hampstead had changed drastically since the days when Brown first kept house with Keats. Dilke had moved away in April 1819, Keats was dead, Severn remained in Rome, Hunt had departed for Pisa in November 1821, Richards was tied down by family cares and business, and the affair with Abby had lost him various other friends. In addition, Severn had pointed out to him the cheapness of living in Italy. After some delay in finding a buyer, he sold his half of Wentworth Place, and in August 1822 took Carlino across the Channel and thence overland to Italy, where he lived for the next thirteen years.

IV

At Pisa Brown joined Hunt, who within three or four days introduced him to Byron. "I was prejudiced against him," Brown told Severn about the meeting, "but somehow he got the better of my prejudice, and I hear he has taken a liking to me." [51] Byron had also taken a liking to Keats's "Hyperion," and his unlordly political views satisfied all Brown's "qualms": "There never was a poor creature in rags a greater Radical than Byron," he wrote to Dilke (number 44). Before Hunt and Byron left Pisa for Genoa at the end of September they invited Brown to write for the *Liberal,* to which he subsequently contributed three essays. For eight months Brown remained at Pisa, and then, having settled Carlino there with an Italian family named Gordini, he removed to Florence, where Severn joined him in June 1823. With Severn he visited Venice for a month in September, returning briefly to Florence to see Hunt, who had just taken a villa at Maiano, outside Florence. Then he and Severn, with Hunt's problem child John, set off to Rome, where they kept house together for seven

[50] Letter to L. A. Holman, July 11, 1913 (Harvard). Compare number 38, in which Brown says that Abby "rather *entreated* I would take him abroad."

[51] Number 41. Fanny Brawne wrote to Fanny Keats on October 15, 1822 (*Letters of Fanny Brawne,* p. 78), "Mr Brown is safely arrived at Pisa and in spite of his vow [never to put legs under a lord's table] has made an acquaintance with Lord Byron, he liked him very much." On December 7 Severn (*ibid.,* p. 80) told his father that Brown had promised to introduce him to Byron.

months. He returned to Florence by way of Pisa, bringing Carlino back with him, and settled in a nunnery near Maiano in May 1824.

Anticipating Brown's arrival, Hunt wrote on April 20, 1824, to Robert Finch, who had just seen Brown in Rome, "As you have had a jubilee . . . in Rome, so are we going to have one here at Maiano, for Mr. Brown is coming; and a new regiment of hussars in a country town could not have a sound with it, to us recluses, more gay & multitudinous." [52] Shortly after Brown's return Richard Westmacott, Jr., having passed through Florence and spent a day with Hunt and Brown, told Severn on May 20, "Mr. Brown is just the man to be happy with," and he recalled that at Severn's in Rome "Mr. Brown made us all merry." [53] Brown's abundant good spirits seem always to have had a happy effect on others. He met many people and made friends in short space: John Taaffe, Jr., who had known Shelley and Byron; Robert Finch, through whom Shelley had learned of Keats's death; the artists William Etty, Richard Evans, Westmacott, William Edward West, James Giles, Seymour Kirkup (who later with his mistress came to live with Brown), George Hayter, William Bewick; Shelley's schoolmate Thomas Jefferson Hogg; and others. Through Kirkup he met Landor, who had been living at Florence since 1821, and he renewed acquaintance with Hazlitt when the latter came with his second wife through Florence on his way to Rome early in 1825.

During his first few years in Italy Brown was above all the "admirable friend of Leigh Hunt," [54] who described him in *Lord Byron* and later in his *Autobiography*: "My friend, Mr. Brown, occupied for a time the little convent of St. Baldassare, near Maiano, where he represented the body corporate of the former possessors, with all the joviality of a comfortable natural piety. The closet in his study, where the church treasures had most likely been kept, was filled with the humanities of modern literature, not less Christian for being a little sceptical: and we had a zest in fancying that we discoursed of love and wine in the apartments of

[52] Elizabeth Nitchie, *The Reverend Colonel Finch* (New York, 1940), p. 97.
[53] Sharp, pp. 142–143.
[54] Thornton Hunt's phrase, in *The Correspondence of Leigh Hunt* (London, 1862), I, 273.

the Lady Abbess." [55] Until Hunt returned to England in September 1825 Brown was his regular companion. He introduced Hunt to friends like Landor, Kirkup, Finch, and Westmacott; relieved him of the care of his most troublesome son for several months; advised him in his household expenditures; twice wrote "Wishing-Caps" for the *Examiner*; and contributed his finest story, "La Bella Tabaccaia," to Hunt's *Literary Examiner*. He also acted as Hunt's advocate in a dispute with his brother John Hunt over the *Examiner* property. That dispute, a frequent subject of Brown's letters, should be explained briefly.

Sometime after John and Leigh Hunt were imprisoned in 1813–1815 for libeling the Prince Regent in the *Examiner*, which they owned in partnership with the printer James Whiting, Leigh Hunt withdrew from public proprietorship of the paper — by John Hunt's "particular wish," Hunt later told Shelley, "in order that Government might not be able to imprison both of us at once. I consented . . . not only because my health was the more precarious, but because my brother's name is obliged to be at the bottom of the paper as printer, and printers, though not editors, are indictable, like proprietors." [56] Hunt continued as a partner by private agreement with John, who regularly paid him a share of the profits from the paper. By July 1821, however, when Hunt's illness had forced him to stop writing for several months, and John Hunt had just begun a year's prison sentence for libeling the House of Commons, the *Examiner* was "lamentably falling off," and the brothers "feared for its very existence." [57] Then in November, while John was still in prison, though with his approval (and financial assistance), Hunt took his family to Italy to join Byron and Shelley. From their projected *Liberal* he expected large profits for himself and John, who was to be its publisher.

While Hunt was delayed in Plymouth, en route to Pisa, Shelley inquired of him on January 25, 1822, "Pray tell me . . . what arrangement you have made about the receipt of a regular income from the profits of the Examiner. You ought not to leave England

---

[55] Hunt, *Lord Byron and Some of His Contemporaries*, 2nd edn. (London, 1828), II, 374–375.
[56] *Correspondence of Leigh Hunt*, I, 162.
[57] *Ibid.*, I, 163, 167.

without having the assurance of an independence in this particular." [58] Probably Hunt made no arrangement. In Italy, finding that he could not write for two periodicals at once, he ceased work altogether on the *Examiner* to devote his meager energies to the *Liberal*, a step to which John Hunt apparently assented by not objecting. When the *Examiner* sales further diminished and the *Liberal* proved a financial failure, John no longer credited his brother with profits from the newspaper, and on September 19, 1823, he startled him with a letter mentioning "your entire secession" from the *Examiner*.[59] Though Hunt quickly replied that he would resume work on the paper,[60] John on October 21 reaffirmed his declaration that Hunt had forfeited his share of the partnership and proposed a settlement by allowance, the terms to be decided by arbitration.

Vincent Novello temporarily ended the dispute by December 15: John Hunt agreed to pay his brother an annuity of £100, and two guineas each for his articles. "All will now proceed amicably," Hunt wrote confidently to Novello on January 9, 1824; in March he told his sister-in-law Elizabeth Kent, "All my present energy goes to the manufacture of *Wishing Caps*, and to the endeavour to raise the sale of the *Examiner* all I can." [61] In the course of 1824, however, John Hunt began omitting "Wishing-Caps." On July 20 he informed Hunt that only eight of his articles had been printed in twelve weeks,[62] and in the same letter asked him to draw no longer upon the *Examiner* for money. Terrified by the unexpected further reduction of his income, on August 19 Hunt placed his financial affairs in Brown's hands.

Brown quickly sent off to Hunt (to be forwarded to Novello and John Hunt) an eight-page, closely written account of the dispute (number 61), urging Hunt's right to have an article printed weekly and exposing serious errors in the *Examiner* accounts. (Charles Ollier read the letter and was "filled with wonder at the

[58] *The Letters of Percy Bysshe Shelley*, ed. Frederick L. Jones (Oxford, 1964), II, 382.

[59] Edmund Blunden, *Leigh Hunt: A Biography* (London, 1930), p. 203. This letter and that of October 21 are abstracted in number 91.

[60] Luther A. Brewer, *My Leigh Hunt Library: The Holograph Letters* (Iowa City, 1938), pp. 157–160 — hereafter cited as Brewer, *Holograph Letters*.

[61] Clarke, *Recollections of Writers*, p. 223; *Correspondence of Leigh Hunt*, I, 214.

[62] See the first paragraph of number 61.

conduct of the party opposed to" Hunt.) [63] Then for two more years, in letters to Leigh Hunt, John Hunt, and John's son and printing partner Henry Leigh Hunt,[64] Brown debated the problem, maintaining Hunt's claim to a share in the partnership, refuting arguments against that claim, and showing further lapses on the part of John Hunt and his son. He sought the opinions of Hazlitt, Kirkup, and an English attorney in Florence named Reader.

When he ordered his main points into a formal statement to be submitted to arbitrators (number 91) the opposition was crushed. The award went to Leigh Hunt, and a mutual release between the brothers was signed at the end of 1827.[65] Through no fault of Brown — since Hunt was clearly imposed upon, and Brown had merely corrected the injustice — the brothers were estranged. When Hunt returned to England at the end of 1825 his brother, who had already retired from business, refused to see him. "It afterwards turned out," says Hunt's son Thornton, that John Hunt "had acted on advices which misled him in his own affairs." (Probably the wrongdoer was John's son Henry Leigh Hunt, who appears meddlesome and intemperate in the affair.) The brothers were later reunited "by the sheer prompting of natural affection, to find that the grounds of quarrel had been the result of misconstruction on both sides." [66]

V

After Hunt took leave of Brown's "grave face" on September 10, 1825, "obliged," as he departed for England, "to gulp down a sensation in the throat, such as men cannot very well afford to confess," [67] Brown rented a house on the Piazza del Duomo (he had already moved from Maiano into the city in the fall of 1824), and then went "gadding" — to Milan in the following February, to Pisa in June, to Rome and Naples in September. In Hunt's absence he became a good friend of Landor, whom he had met probably in 1824. It is a pity that Brown does not say more about

[63] Brewer, *Holograph Letters*, p. 160.
[64] Notably numbers 65, 66, 69, 70, 73–75, 78, 83.
[65] Brewer, *Holograph Letters*, p. 164.
[66] *Correspondence of Leigh Hunt*, II, 167; I, 245.
[67] Hunt, *Lord Byron*, II, 388.

Landor in his letters, for it is clear that they were together frequently in Italy and later in England, and we have Kirkup's word that Brown was "the most intimate and confidential friend of Landor for many years." [68] Brown discussed Shelley and Keats with him, lent him periodicals and probably books (Hunt had been surprised by the smallness of Landor's library),[69] witnessed Mrs. Landor's hysterical tirade against her husband, and wrote a statement testifying to Landor's good character (number 110). Most significantly, he discussed his "strange discovery into the character of Shakespear" with Landor, who by daily visits spurred him on in the study that became *Shakespeare's Autobiographical Poems.* "Landor swears, out and out," Brown told Hunt, "that no man ever understood Shakespear like myself; this is the greatest compliment, true or not, that ever I have received" (number 106).

Intimacy with writers inspired continued literary activity. Brown concentrated his efforts toward the *New Monthly*, where he had published articles before leaving England and a poem and another article since arriving in Italy. In 1825–1826 four of his essays — on his walks in Italy, on the Misericordia, and on Bandello's court fool Gonnella — appeared in that periodical, and he sent off several others that were not printed. Through Hunt, now living in England and writing for the *New Monthly*, he sought an agreement with Henry Colburn, its publisher, for a regular series of articles; but Colburn apparently was not interested in Brown's topic, "Italian Chat." Brown also planned and may have begun a novel about Bianca Capello, wife of Francesco de' Medici, and it was probably about this time that he did the "many translations, and a long and exhaustive critical study of the Venetian dramatist" Carlo Goldoni and the "complete and admirable" translation of five cantos of Boiardo's *Orlando innamorato* that were seen by Sharp and Milnes but are now lost.[70]

In September 1826 Dilke and his son visited Brown, and the

---

[68] John Forster, *Walter Savage Landor. A Biography* (London, 1869), II, 204. Carlino says that the "friendship . . . between Brown and Landor, lasted for the remainder of their lives."

[69] Hunt, *Lord Byron*, II, 380.

[70] Sharp, p. viii; Milnes, *Life*, II, 50. Forty-eight stanzas of Brown's translation of *Orlando innamorato*, Canto I, were published in the *West of England Magazine* in 1838.

old friends traveled together to Rome, where they saw Severn. Returning to England, Dilke left his son to stay with Brown for several months. Kirkup and his mistress moved in with Brown at the beginning of 1827 to stay for nearly two years, the mistress being established as Carlino's governess (a position, as we learn from number 79, into which Brown had earlier tried to entice a certain "Euphemia," with whom he was "in love" for all of a week in 1825). In October 1828 Severn arrived to marry a ward of the eccentric Lady Westmorland. In an unpublished passage of "My tedious Life," Severn recalls that "Seymour Kirkup & Charles Brown my old & devoted friends received me at Florence & the last communication with Lady W. asked who & what was my friend Charles Brown, I answerd that he was a very independant man '& would be most unhappy to know Lady Westmorland' this expression upset her & she went the next day all over Florence telling people that Mr Brown would be most unhappy to know her." [71]

In 1829 Trelawny, whom Brown had known briefly in 1823, came to live with him in Florence, where Brown now occupied a house that he thought had once belonged to Petrarch. For half the profits from its publication Brown rewrote Trelawny's *Adventures of a Younger Son,* a work that Milnes described excitedly to his father in 1833: "For mere power of expression I think it is the most wonderful thing I know. Landor says it is like nothing but the Iliad." [72] Brown provided Trelawny with passages from Keats's unpublished poems to be used among its chapter headings. To Mary Shelley, Trelawny characterized Brown as "a plain downright Cockney critic, learned in the trade of authorship . . . [who] has served his time as a literary scribe." [73] He later (April 19, 1849) explained to Carlino the nature of Brown's criticism: "my own vanity & conseit . . . [have] been so very troublesome to me during my career in life . . . . your Father checked it many times by his plain dealings & calling things by their proper names & I had sense to like him all the more for it." [74]

---

[71] Severn's manuscript (1873) is at Harvard.

[72] T. Wemyss Reid, *The Life, Letters, and Friendships of Richard Monckton Milnes* (London, 1890), I, 145.

[73] *Letters of Edward John Trelawny,* ed. H. Buxton Forman (London, 1910), p. 140.

[74] Trelawny's letter (sent by Carlino to F. H. Day in 1890) is at Harvard.

Toward the end of 1829 Brown received a request from the Galignanis, of Paris, who were about to issue Keats's poems with a memoir, for an autograph of the poet. Already dissatisfied with Hunt's portrayal of Keats in *Lord Byron*, published in the year before — "worse than disappointing," he told Fanny Brawne, "I cannot bear it" (number 98) — he resolved to write Keats's life himself, and immediately sent off to Dilke, Fanny Brawne, Severn, Richards, and others for help. The resolution quickly involved him in a serious controversy with Dilke over the honesty of George Keats in his financial dealings with his brother.

VI

Gathering materials for the memoir, Brown found documents among Keats's papers that he thought "gave the lie direct" (number 102) to a letter sent by George Keats to Dilke in 1824 as an explanation of his money transactions with John. Dilke had then forwarded a summary of its details to Brown, who, since he had been the loudest critic of George's conduct in the two or three months just before Keats's death, felt that his integrity was called in question by the explanation. It was mainly as a defense of his own character that he reopened the question on the basis of the newly discovered documents. Like the Hunts' *Examiner* dispute, the controversy is a frequent subject of Brown's letters, and it merits some detailed discussion.

When George Keats returned to America in January 1820, after a quick visit to England to raise cash, he took with him, according to Brown, so much of John's money that the poet was left in debt. The amount actually received from John (Brown said at first £700, later £425, while George calculated £170) cannot be determined, though it is clear that after George's departure John had only £60 or £70 remaining to him, some £20 or £10 less than the amount of his debts at the time.[75] It similarly cannot be determined whether the money was borrowed by George, or received by him as the partial repayment of an earlier loan to John. The brothers kept no accounts, and the few facts (though they

[75] See number 63; *Letters of Fanny Brawne*, p. 33; *KC*, I, 217–218. Later Brown put the figure even lower, saying in number 101 (see also number 108) that George left John £40. The account in number 84 records Brown's receipt of £40 from John, but the date of the entry is February 6, 1820, nine days after George's departure.

do not support George's side) are inconclusive: that Keats's letter to Haslam of August 23, 1820, mentions a loan to George; [76] that Abbey wrote to Keats on the same day, "it was very much against my will that you lent your money to George," [77] and told Brown early in 1822 that John had lent George between £350 and £400; [78] that George wrote to John on November 8, 1820, "I hope to be able to send you money soon"; [79] and that when Taylor in February 1821 indirectly accused him of borrowing £700 and leaving John in financial distress,[80] George offered no reply before his defense of 1824.

What is clear, however, is that Keats, quite possibly in the state of "nervous morbid temperament" that, ironically enough, helps explain his bitter outburst against Brown, believed that George had treated him unfairly. After George's departure he told Brown that his "brother did not act rightly in leaving him so," [81] and he remarked to Fanny Brawne, "George ought not to have done this." [82] As a result, nearly all Keats's friends turned against George. Brown asked Haslam, "What is to be done with George? Will he ever dare to come among his brother's friends?" (number 19), and he informed Severn that he was planning "schemes of vengeance upon his [George's] head. . . . I knew not, till after he quitted us the second time for America, how cruel he had been" (number 22). On opening a letter from George to John that contained no "notice of a present remittance," Brown called George "a canting, selfish, heartless swindler," who (since Brown persisted in thinking Keats's illness psychologically based) "shall have to answer for the death of his brother, — if it must be so" (number 23). He and Haslam, who thought George "a scoundrel," [83] sent letters to America demanding remittances, and Taylor and Hessey, convinced by Brown of George's indebtedness,

---

[76] *Letters*, II, 330. His fragmentary letter to Abbey, July 16, 1819 (*Letters*, II, 131), also seems to mention a loan.

[77] *Letters*, II, 331.

[78] Number 63. Three years later Abbey decided that George's explanation of his dealings was correct (*KC*, I, 285–286), but his earlier testimony is more reliable.

[79] *Letters*, II, 356.

[80] *KC*, I, 217–219.

[81] "These were his words," says Brown, quoting them in number 63.

[82] *Letters of Fanny Brawne*, p. 34.

[83] Sharp, p. 72.

tried to draw upon him for £150 to repay some of the money advanced for Keats's trip to Italy.[84] Fanny Keats (who heard of George's supposed ill conduct from someone other than Brown or Fanny Brawne) refused to write to George when Keats died and for a year afterward.[85] Fanny Brawne, though she thought George "more blamed than he should be," since he could not have foreseen Keats's illness, said that "his behaviour has been very selfish and I may say shuffling," and that he could not "have supposed it would be in his power to return the money [borrowed from John], at the best not for many years." [86] Brown's indignation apparently was short-lived, however, and when he heard of Keats's death he wrote to Severn, "no one could know him [Keats] and treat him unkindly, — so convinced am I of this that I acquit his brother of malevolence" (number 29). Though he subsequently dunned George for £75 that Keats owed him, he did not thereafter mention George uncharitably until the summer of 1824.

On April 10, 1824, George finally defended himself, sending to Dilke, as "least likely to be influenced by those reports so injurious to my honor," what he called "proof that I not only did not wrong my Brother in money concerns, but that I owed him little or nothing." [87] His letter contends that when he first went to America (June 1818) he left nearly £300 with John, who had no money of his own; that on leaving England for the second time (January 1820), although he did take £700 with him, only £170 of that sum belonged to John; and that since John was already indebted to him for a larger amount, the £170 was not a loan but a partial repayment to him from John. At least one detail of the defense, that £160 (or possibly £260) of his £700 consisted of a gift and a loan from Abbey ("in consideration of what I had done for Tom"), must certainly be wrong; for Keats wrote to George on November 12, 1819, "You urg'd me to get Mr Abbey to advance you money — that he will by no means do." [88] But Dilke for-

[84] *KC*, I, 214–219. Taylor wrote to his brother and to Severn about George's indebtedness to John — Olive M. Taylor in *London Mercury*, 12 (1925): 259; Sharp, p. 99.
[85] Marie Adami, *Fanny Keats* (London, 1937), p. 107.
[86] *Letters of Fanny Brawne*, pp. 33–34.
[87] The letter is printed in *KC*, I, 276–281.
[88] *Letters*, II, 231.

warded the letter to Fanny Keats, who was convinced by it that "George is still and ever will be an honourable man," [89] and he sent a summary of it (number 60) to Brown, requesting him to "convey the spirit of [George's defense] . . . to Mr Hunt & any other likely to have heard of the charge."

Brown thought the defense weak, resting only on George's assertions, and he contested several of its points in his reply to Dilke (number 63): Keats was not penniless when George first went to America in June 1818, and in fact thought he had some £700 when he tried to procure £500 to lend to Haydon in 1819; the money left him by George in June 1818 was a partial settlement of a debt, not a gift or a loan; and, according to Richard Abbey, John had lent George between £350 and £400 on the latter's second departure for America in January 1820. Realizing, however, that he countered George's assertions merely with assertions of his own, he informed Hunt, Severn, and others of the defense, as Dilke had requested, and let the matter rest. In the fall of 1826, when Dilke came to see Brown in Italy, there were no ill feelings between them.

At the end of 1829, with factual evidence to support his earlier arguments, Brown reopened the dispute with a mild letter to Dilke (number 97), describing the newly discovered documents and asking for a copy of George's defense of 1824. "Fact is," he wrote, "your account of the business was, as I thought at the time, though I was willing to take the best side, lame in the extreme. I think his may be a better story, and therefore wish to see it." Dilke was now in the position of a lawyer who has exposed his entire case in a preliminary hearing. Between George in America and Brown in Italy, each with conflicting facts and recollections, he stood in ignorance. Since April 1819, when he left Hampstead to enroll his son in Westminster School, Dilke had been on the periphery of the Keats circle, and Keats's letters show an increasing coolness toward him after that date.[90] Though he had later become the protector and advocate of Fanny Keats, he never really knew much about Keats's personal financial affairs, and George had offered no new information beyond the defense of 1824. It is quite prob-

[89] Adami, *Fanny Keats*, p. 108.
[90] See Keats's comments on Dilke in *Letters*, II, 84, 190, 213, 244, 312.

able, since he had sent it to Fanny Keats upon receiving it, that he no longer even had George's defense to refer to. He at least should have heard his old schoolfellow; but George had recently written to him, "*I* . . . look upon y{ou} as the best Friend I have in the world," "you have proved my friend when (perhaps) *all others* have deserted me," and to Mrs. Dilke, "I look to Mr Dilke as my anchor in my native sod." [91] Dilke tried, therefore, to brush off Brown's fresh attack by threatening a "mass . . . of facts, documents, and writings" that supported George.[92]

The bluff did not work, and on January 20, 1830, Brown sent a lengthy refutation (number 101) of George's 1824 defense. He had a letter (George to John, March 18, 1818, mentioning his indebtedness to John) that he thought denied the claim that John owed George money when the latter first departed for America. As for George's assertion that John then had no money of his own, Brown had a copy of John's account with Abbey crediting him with several hundred pounds at the very time. He had also discovered Abbey's letter of August 23, 1820, mentioning John's loan to George, and he sharpened his memory to recall other facts differing from George's: that George had repaid John £70 or £80 in June 1818 rather than given or lent him £300, and that John had been left with a smaller sum in January 1820 than George admitted.[93] "I compel George," he wrote, "to accuse himself of a vile falsehood. . . . I have proved that George, for a second time, is guilty of falsehood in his defence. . . . For the third time I accuse George of falsehood . . . . as I am weary of charging him with falsehood, I now leave that to you."

Brown called his refutation "the most unpleasant letter I ever sent you," but when Dilke replied that it was "unintelligible" that Brown should "inflict" the refutation on him, "unasked for, unnecessary," stirring up his "gall and bitterness with facts and figures," that Brown's documents were "ingenious, quite conclu-

---

[91] *KC*, I, 315, 316, 318–319.
[92] See the opening of number 101.
[93] Brown also makes the point that George would have had £440, not £700, if he took only £170 of John's money. But he could charge George only with faulty arithmetic, since Dilke had not clearly explained the supposed source of the additional money (either £260 from Abbey, or £160 plus a rather ambiguous "£100 before mentioned" — see *KC*, I, 278).

sive to those who do not know they are erroneous," that "to build up an error *solidly*, there is nothing like facts, dates, and figures," Brown sent a much more unpleasant one: [94] "You have wounded me to the quick. I could not have believed that any one I am acquainted with, far less you, would treat me, both in matter and manner, with such injustice. To make these words good, I must use many more." By the time Brown finished saying what he thought of Dilke's "enigmatical positiveness" and "sheer rudeness" their correspondence and their friendship of more than thirty years were ended.

It is debatable whether Brown's documents prove George wrong, because each, with a little ingenuity, can be interpreted to agree, or at least not conflict, with the details of George's defense.[95] It is less debatable whether Brown represented the truth in his recollections of Keats's and Abbey's words. He sought (if he did not achieve) objectivity in his attitude toward George, and his honesty, as even Dilke later admitted, was unquestionable.[96] Whether or not George was guilty, Brown acted reasonably and presented detailed argument and factual evidence. Dilke, on the other hand, offered not a single point of rebuttal — nothing, in fact, but evasion and hardheaded obstinacy.

During a brief visit to England in 1833 Brown (perhaps with Dilke) took the controversy to Dilke's brother William, who made notes of the charges and countercharges (number 108) but settled nothing. When Brown came to London in May 1838 to publish *Shakespeare's Autobiographical Poems*, he called on Dilke and found him "unpleasant . . . dogmatical, conceited, and rude" (number 116). Dilke repaid him publicly with a nasty attack on the Shakespeare book in the *Athenaeum* (July 21, 1838), and Brown, considering the review "infamous treachery" (number 125), wrote Dilke "a declaration of war," calling him "a dilkish blockhead" (see number 117), after which even their formal civility ceased.

[94] Number 103, in which Dilke's words above are quoted.

[95] The latest discussion in support of George's probity is that by Robert Gittings, *The Keats Inheritance* (London, 1964), pp. 45–51.

[96] Fred Edgcumbe wrote to L. A. Holman on September 4, 1933 (the letter is at Harvard), "After reading [Brown's letters] . . . one must conclude that Charles Brown was a man of sterling qualities. Naturally he had his peccadillos, otherwise he would not have been human. But he never let a friend down, and his quarrel with George Keats was justified."

Brown does not mention the "cruel charge" against George in his "Life" of Keats.[97] He had told Dilke in 1829, on reopening the controversy, "be not fearful that I will make a cruel use of the letter from George; quite the contrary; all that I want is authority for stating that Keats's generosity to Tom when under age, and to George after 21, diminished his fortune, or rather finished it, — or something to that effect, — I mean that it shall not be a stigma on George." [98] But his remark to Carlino on March 15, 1839, is unhappily crude: "If he [Dilke] should accidentally meet with you . . . spit in his face" (number 125). It may be more to Dilke's credit that his summary of Brown's character in the margin of his copy of Milnes's *Life* is in some ways a generous tribute: "He was the most scrupulously honest man I ever knew." [99] His other comments on Brown are petty and sometimes, as when he reiterates the assertion that Brown charged George interest on the amount owed him by John, wrong.

VII

Having fired broadsides at George Keats and Dilke early in 1830, Brown returned to his work on Trelawny's *Adventures*, and began writing Keats's life and the study of Shakespeare's poems. In the spring of 1832 he "cut the town" for the seclusion of a villa (perhaps once Galileo's) outside Florence, where Richard Woodhouse visited him for seven weeks in August and September. He made a brief trip to England in the following year. Back in Italy, he wrote to Severn early in 1834, giving what Sharp calls "the first warning of that disastrous change in . . . [his] fortunes as well as in his bodily health, which was the indirect cause of his leaving Italy," and sometime afterward he suffered an apoplectic seizure in Vieusseux's Library in Florence.[100] (Trelawny later recalled that "Our old friend Brown was subject to those attacks for many years — but then he was a huge feeder . . . he took

[97] Brown (*KC*, II, 72) says merely that Keats's "patrimony . . . might have upheld him through the storm, had he not imprudently lost a part of it in generous loans." See numbers 149, 152.

[98] Number 97. George's letter to Dilke of May 7, 1830 (*KC*, I, 325) — "The threatened life of poor John by Brown, involving the sacrifice of my good name is most unwelcome" — shows that Dilke paid no attention to Brown's assurance.

[99] See Forman (1952), p. li.

[100] Sharp, p. 175 (Brown's letter has since been lost). Sharp also says that after his attack at Vieusseux's Brown was "more or less an invalid."

2 7

little exercise, was a book-worm.") [101] In the following spring, whether for reasons of health and economy, as Sharp suggests, or for his son's education [102] — Carlino was now nearly fifteen — Brown and his son returned to England, settling first in Plymouth and then in Laira Green, a small village just outside Plymouth.

Soon after his return Brown joined the Plymouth Institution, an organization "for the promotion of Literature, Science, and the Fine Arts, in the town and neighbourhood," [103] in which he supervised art exhibitions, served as vice-president, and lectured on literary subjects — the intellectual history of Florence, Shakespeare, the influence of Italian on English literature, and "The Life and Poems of John Keats." In spite of repeated urging by Severn ("*The time has come,* AND I FEAR THE TIME MAY PASS" — number 109) and a promise exacted from him by Woodhouse in 1832, he had done little work on his memoir of Keats since 1830. Division among the Keats circle was always a great hindrance to the gathering of information, and Brown's late controversy with Dilke had caused George Keats to threaten an injunction against the publication of the poems in Brown's possession. But in the summer of 1836, "to compel me to my duty," as Brown told Severn (number 112), "I boldly put down my name at our Institution for a lecture" on the poet, and he finally began writing seriously. That lecture, delivered on December 29, 1836, slightly revised in 1841, is the "Life" as we now have it.

Disappointing [104] though it may be at this late date, when its materials have been well known for over a century, Brown's "plain unvarnished tale, and rather short" (number 113) gave Keats's fame the boost that Brown and Severn desired, though in a way that they had not envisioned. On it — after Brown tried unsuccessfully to publish it himself and then gave it, with his copies of Keats's unpublished poems, to Milnes when he was about to leave England for New Zealand — was based the first major life of Keats, Milnes's *Life, Letters, and Literary Remains* of 1848, a date after which Keats has always been "among the English Poets." Though

[101] *Letters of Trelawny*, p. 215.
[102] So Carlino, *KC*, I, lix.
[103] *Transactions of the Plymouth Institution* (Plymouth, 1830), p. iii.
[104] It is so termed by Bodurtha and Pope, p. 24; by Rollins, *KC*, I, lxix, and II, 53n; and by a writer in *TLS*, February 24, 1950, p. 120.

Milnes's biography is seven or eight times as long as Brown's, and contains considerable additional matter, it owes much of its form and essential portrayal of Keats to the earlier work, and its very existence, of course, to Brown's original gift of materials. Exhausted by later writers, the "Life" remains the primary source for eight of Keats's letters and for valuable information about Keats's quitting surgery, his reaction to Tom Keats's death, his hemorrhage of February 1820, the writing of the Nightingale ode, and other incidents.

Brown provided between three fourths and five sixths of the "literary remains" in Milnes's second volume. Before giving the poems to Milnes he published a number of them in the *Plymouth and Devonport Weekly Journal*, for which by 1838 he was a regular writer.[105] His letters show how seriously he took journalism: "I have no high opinion of my Articles, but May [the proprietor of the *Journal*] is delighted . . . . I don't trouble my head about them till Sunday night when the *Examiner* appears, and on the Monday my *Article* is finished" (number 123). He filled columns of the paper with reprints of some of his earlier periodical writings, and with book reviews, which he wrote mainly to add the review copies to his library. But he also supported liberal politicians, and by August 1839 had "silenced the Tory press here, — it is quiet and civil" (number 132). When the rejection of one of his articles attacking "the Parsons" led to a break with the proprietor of the *Journal* in April 1840, he quickly found outlets for his radical writings in two other weeklies. While contributing to local newspapers he kept trying the London periodicals, and began an autobiographical novel, "Walter Hazlebourn."

In the summer of 1838 he gave to the world what Sir Sidney Lee generously calls his "best-known literary work," [106] *Shakespeare's Autobiographical Poems*, the product of his conferences with Landor (to whom it is dedicated) and his lectures on Shakespeare at the Plymouth Institution. Attempting what has since

---

[105] According to L. A. Holman's notes at Harvard, Brown's writings first appeared in *PDWJ* in 1836. The only complete file of the paper for this year (the British Museum's) was destroyed during World War II.

[106] *Dictionary of National Biography*. In publishing it Brown assumed the middle name Armitage, "bearing in mind," explains Carlino, "what Trelawny said to him, 'Brown, your name is that of a tribe, not of a family.'"

become impossible, it advanced a new theory about the Sonnets — that they were written as six poems in sonnet stanzas, and that, when read as such, they provide "nothing but pure uninterrupted biography." "It cannot be said that the author has clearly educed his theory," wrote Charles Cowden Clarke, about to issue his own *Shakespeare Key* (1879), "but, in the face of his failure upon the main point, the book is interesting for the heart-whole zeal and homage with which he has gone into his subject." [107] Though Brown's arrangement wins no new adherents, it met approval in its own day, and the book shows Brown to have had the instincts of a scholar. He strongly defended the 1609 quarto order of the Sonnets, and with James Boaden, whom he supported in identifying "Mr. W. H." with the third Earl of Pembroke, he initiated what Rollins, surveying the vogue of the poems, calls a "new era in study and criticism" of the Sonnets in England: "Henceforth, it became almost impossible . . . to dodge a consideration of the sonnet 'problems,' and henceforth, too, 'discoveries' and interpretations abounded." [108] At the end of Brown's book is the announcement, "Preparing for the Press, Shakespeare's Poems, edited by the author of this volume," but the edition never appeared.

VIII

A major topic in Brown's letters of 1838–1840 is the problem of his son's future. Carlino had had only four years of formal education (1825–1828) before Brown took him under his own tuition on the theory that "long walks upon the hills are of more use than books" (number 94). The diarist Henry Crabb Robinson, who visited Florence in October 1830, noted that Brown "was a speculator in education and brought up his boy on the principle of letting him do what he liked," and that as a result Landor thought Carlino "the wickedest boy he had ever known." [109] Carlino was not the "wickedest" in September 1838, when he went up to London in search of employment, but thanks to Brown's

[107] Clarke, *Recollections of Writers*, p. 146.
[108] Hyder E. Rollins, *A New Variorum Edition of Shakespeare: The Sonnets* (Philadelphia, 1944), II, 358. On the critical reception of Brown's book see II, 77–78.
[109] *Henry Crabb Robinson on Books and Their Writers*, ed. Edith J. Morley (London, 1938), I, 387–388.

speculation he may well have been the least prepared to enter a career. With almost nothing to recommend him in the way of talent, training, or personal character, he made motions toward engineering and civil service, wasted much time, and finally apprenticed himself unsatisfactorily to a Midhurst millwright. All the while Brown approved now this inclination, now that, offered moral advice, but gave no practical help.

Then Brown took a bold step for his son. As Carlino tells it, "In 1840 he decided to emigrate to New Zealand, his health had been failing for some years, he felt annoyed at the fancied or real, clerical intolerance of a provincial town, as an avowed freethinker and liberal; several severe accidents had happened in the factory where his son was working in Sussex, to whom he was much attached; he felt his growing loneliness, and determined on becoming a settler under the Plymouth Co^y of New Zealand, from whom he purchased land orders in their settlement of New Plymouth . . . in the Taranaki district." Having severed his connection with the Plymouth *Journal* in April 1840, and a month later having resigned from the Plymouth Institution in a petty quarrel with its secretary, Brown was ready for another move. But his decision to go to New Zealand, against the advice of his friends, only a year after the first boatload of emigrants under the Plymouth Company had sailed, must have been made, as he told Milnes and Severn (numbers 148, 150), for Carlino's "sake, not for mine." He sold his house in Laira Green, bought equipment for a sawmill, sent Carlino off to New Plymouth in March 1841, made last-minute revisions in the "Life" of Keats, which he sent with the poems to Milnes, and then sailed for New Plymouth in June.

Emigration made a man of Carlino, who "went through the whole gamut of the colonist, pioneering, business, journalism and public affairs, and speedily took a leading part in the life of the province." [110] When the sawmill venture proved a failure, Carlino, "by the force of circumstances in New Zealand, had to abandon his engineering experience, and for many years, to make use of his

[110] G. H. Scholefield, *A Dictionary of New Zealand Biography* (Wellington, N.Z., 1940), I, 99 — the source of many of the details in this paragraph. There is also considerable information about Carlino in *The Richmond-Atkinson Papers*, ed. Scholefield, 2 vols. (Wellington, 1960).

pen." [111] From journalism it was but a short step to public office. In 1852 he was elected New Plymouth's representative in the Legislative Council of New Ulster, and in 1853 he became the first superintendent of Taranaki, holding the office until 1857 and again from 1861 to 1865. He served in the New Zealand parliament (1856, 1858, 1864–1865, 1868–1870), and was appointed colonial treasurer (1856), a member of the Provincial Council (1866–1869), and civil commissioner (1875). A captain in the militia from 1855 to 1860, he headed the Taranaki Rifle Volunteers beginning in 1859, and retired as a major after seeing action in 1860–1861, 1869, against the Maoris. Twice married, by his first wife, Margaret Horne,[112] who died in 1875, he had four daughters and a son, and by his second, a daughter of William Northcroft, whom he married at sixty, he had twin sons and a daughter. When he died at the age of eighty-one, on September 2, 1901, he had achieved a career of public service that his years in Italy and England scarcely hint at.

Brown shared none of his son's success. Arriving at New Plymouth in November 1841, on the third ship to sail under the Plymouth Company's charter, he found wilderness instead of farm plots, treacherous coast instead of a harbor or a roadstead, and none of the "probable great advantages" that the "best report" of the country had promised (number 150). He planned an early return to England, spent a few months organizing protests against the Plymouth Company, sending public letters to England denouncing its fraudulence, and writing — a New Zealand Handbook, "not 'New Zealand Guide,' because I cannot conscientiously guide any one to it" (number 154) — before he suffered a final apoplectic stroke and died, aged fifty-five, on June 5, 1842. He was buried on Marsland Hill, overlooking New Plymouth and the sea, with his son and John George Cooke as mourners.[113] His grave was covered in the 1860's when the hill was leveled for military

---

[111] *KC*, I, lx.

[112] Her name may be inferred from the inscription in a copy of Albert Smith's *The Story of Mont Blanc* (1853) now at Keats House, Hampstead: "Julie Horne from her loving brother and sister Charles & Margaret Brown 5th Sepr 1854." She was seventeen when Carlino married her in 1851 (*The Richmond-Atkinson Papers*, I, 96, 104).

[113] Sharp, p. 265.

barracks, but relocated in 1921 and marked by a stone bearing the inscription, "Charles Armitage Brown. The Friend of Keats."

Severn, who on hearing of his friend's death felt "as though his sense of youth had gone for ever," characterized Brown as "One of the best fellows who ever lived; a creditable writer; a natural wit; a man of the world in the best sense; and possessed with a happy genius for friendship." [114] He was what Keats would have given "a guinea to be" on September 21, 1819, "a reasonable man — good sound sense — a says what he thinks, and does what he says man." Earlier, on April 24, 1818, Keats had found that "there is no worthy pursuit but the idea of doing some good for the world — some do it with their society — some with their wit — some with their benevolence — some with a sort of power of conferring pleasure and good humour on all they meet." [115] Intentionally or not, he described Brown, who had that power. As businessman, playwright, essayist, critic, translator, biographer, and emigrant, a man who lived in England, Russia, Italy, and New Zealand, Brown is interesting in the mere variety of his activities. But it is by virtue of his character and his friendships with important literary men that he deserves attention. They are the subjects of the letters that follow.

[114] Sharp, pp. 201, ix.
[115] *Letters*, II, 168, and I, 271.

LETTERS AND PAPERS

1818 — 1842

TO C. W. DILKE [1]

[July 1818]

*   *   *

Keats has been these five hours abusing the Scotch and their
country. He says that the women have large splay feet, which is
too true to be controverted,[2] and that he thanks Providence he is
not related to a Scot, nor any way connected with them.

*   *   *

TO HENRY SNOOK [1]

My dear Henry,   Inverness, 7th August 1818.

Yesterday I had a letter from your Uncle.[2] He told me you
had been for a day at Wentworth Place. Why did he not say how
you got on at Eton? I am very — very anxious to hear of your

---

[1] From *Papers of a Critic*, I, 2–3, where it is headed, "July, 1818, Brown writes
to Mr. Dilke." The letter may have been written at Dumfries on July 1, after Keats
and Brown had "met numbers of men & women on the road, the women nearly all
barefoot." From Dumfries Keats wrote to his brother Tom of endeavoring "to get
rid of my prejudices" (*Letters*, I, 309). Brown called the town "a befitting place
wherein to write a libel on the Scotch" ("Walks in the North," ch. IV; *Letters*, I,
439).

[2] Brown later recalled that the women's "neatness of attire . . . made me the
more object to their not wearing shoes and stockings. Keats was of an opposite opinion, and expatiated on the beauty of a human foot, that had grown without an
unnatural restraint" ("Walks in the North," ch. IV; *Letters*, I, 439).

[1] From Forman (1883), III, 354–359. A "fragmentary copy," giving the address "To
Master Henry Snook, care of Mr. Snook, opposite the College, Eton, Windsor," is
printed by Joanna Richardson in *TLS*, August 29, 1952, p. 565. Henry Snook (1805–
1879) was the elder son of Brown's friends John Snook (1780–1863), farmer, miller,
and baker of Bedhampton, and his wife Letitia (1784–1865), Dilke's sister. For information about the Snooks see Guy Murchie in *Keats-Shelley Journal*, 3 (1954): 1–6.

[2] C. W. Dilke.

success in the Classics. I have thought of you, and your brother,[3] and my two nephews,[4] every day on my walk. To have left you all, after so long having been your companion,[5] sometimes comes across my mind in a painful manner, and the farther I have travelled away the stronger has been the feeling. There may be many who cannot understand why I should think of you so much, but my dear boys know how much I have loved them, and they must likewise know it is not in my nature to be changeable with them. But let the proof of this remain till some future day, that is, the proof of my unchangeableness for in the meanwhile I can have nothing to offer but assurances of affection. It gives me delight to think I have friends growing round me.

Do you want to hear about my journey? I think you do; and what else can I have to write about? Come, — listen! You shall have an abridgement of the history of Charles Brown's adventures, first part. We set out from Lancaster [6] and went to Windermere Lake, then to Keswick and Derwent Water, and up Mount Skiddaw; these Lakes like all fresh water ones must be in the neighbourhood of great mountains, for they are fed by the springs and rain from the sides of them; it is for this reason they are so beautiful; imagine if you can a large piece of clear, smooth water not round or square like a pond in a Garden but winding about to and fro with parts of the rocks jutting forward in them, and with several little islands peeping up here and there, all wooded with different kinds of trees, while the view upwards rests on grand mountains, one rising above another, with the clouds sailing beneath their summits, and sometimes spreading downwards into the valleys. When we had seen many of these scenes in Cumberland and Westmoreland, we trudged to Carlisle, from which City we took the stage to Dumfries, which was an uninteresting dis-

[3] John Snook, Jr. (1807–1887), called "Jack" at the end of this letter and in numbers 11 and 15.

[4] John Mavor Brown (b. 1807 or 1808) and James Armitage Brown (1809–1896), sons of Brown's eldest brother, John Armitage Brown. They came to see Brown at least twice while Keats lived with him (*Letters*, II, 12, 83, 90).

[5] Brown had visited the Snooks in January (*Letters*, I, 206), though this sentence seems to refer to a longer stay, perhaps before he and Dilke built Wentworth Place in the winter of 1815–1816.

[6] On June 25. For dates of events mentioned in this letter and the next see the chronology in *Letters*, I, 42–44.

tance of 36 miles. We travelled all over the coast of Kircudbright with great pleasure; the country there is very fruitful, and the views delightful. It was our intention to see the Giant's Causeway in Ireland, and we took the packet from Port Patrick to Donaghadee, but did not proceed further than Belfast and returned back again, for the Irish people did not please us, and the expence was enormous. You must now follow me, up the coast to Ayr, and I heartily wish I had time to detain you on the road, for it's worth admiring, even at second hand. Near Ayr, we paid a visit to the Cottage in which Burns was born, — thousands go there for no other purpose but the happiness of being under the roof, and I was not the least among them in that happiness; we likewise took a survey of the Ruins of Kirk Alloway, where, you will remember, Tam o'Shanter saw the Witches dancing as he peeped thro' the west window, and we saw the "banks and braes o' bonny Doon," and the "auld Brig" and the "new Brig" in the Town; and every thing we could think of that was connected with Burns' poetry.[7] I ought to tell you Burns had as charming a country to live in, as he himself has described, — indeed the sight of it is almost enough to make a man a Poet. In a little time after, we entered the City of Glasgow, — the largest City in all Scotland, and a noble place it is. Then journeying by the banks of the Clyde, we reached Dumbarton, and turned northwards by the side of Loch Lomond, the famous Lake that people go in such crowds to have a sight of. Who shall attempt to describe such scenery? I believe I must pass it over, and take you across the country to the top of Loch Awe, where we had one of our pleasantest days in walking by its side to the south end. We afterwards went to the coast, — a rough and mountainous coast, where the sea breaks in between the hills, twenty and thirty miles up the Country, forming what they call salt water Lakes. At last we arrived at Oban, and took the ferries, first to the Island of Kerrera, and then to the Island of Mull. Here a Guide led us thro' the Country; no stranger could possibly find the road — for in fact *road there was none,* nearly for the whole journey of 37 miles, — sometimes it was over smooth rock, then we had for miles to hop from one stone to another, up hill and

[7] "Tam o' Shanter," ll. 119–120 (Tam saw "Auld Nick" across the church in a "winnock-bunker in the east"); "The Banks o' Doon," l. 1; "The Brigs of Ayr."

down hill, then to cross rivers up to our knees, and, what was worst of all, to walk thro' bogs. At the extremity of Mull, we crossed to the little Island of Iona or Ikolmkill, which is only three miles long, but it was here that Christianity was first taught in Scotland, and for that reason perhaps it was thought a more sacred ground, and it became the burial place of Kings; 48 Scotch Kings have been buried here, 8 Irish, 4 Norwegian, and 1 French; besides there are very interesting ruins of the Cathedral, the College, a Nunnery, Monasteries, and Chapels. We hired a Boat at Iona to take us to Staffa, — that astonishing island of Basaltic Pillars, which you know I so much desired to look at. We went into the cave, nearly to the end, and I shall never forget the solemn impression it made on me; — the pillars on each side, the waves beneath, and the beautiful roof, — all surpassed the work of man, — it seemed like a Cathedral,[8] built by the Almighty to raise the minds of his creatures to the purest and the grandest devotion, — no one could have an evil thought in such a place. We returned to Oban by a different road, and I ought to tell you of the strange sight we had of a swarm of sea gulls attacking a shoal of herrings, with now and then a porpoise heaving about among them for a supper, — I assure you that as our boat passed the spot, the water was literally spangled with herring scales, so great had been the destruction by these Gulls. And now come on with me to Fort William, near Ben Nevis, the highest mountain in Great Britain. We went to the very top of it, and we had to toil up a prodigious steep, chiefly over large loose stones, for eight miles, before we could boast of being above all His Majesty's subjects, and as for the coming down, it was worse than the ascent. It is 4,370 feet above the level of the sea; there is always snow upon it in the hollows of the mountain, where the sun never shines; I walked about on snow, which they said was 100 feet deep; the air is very cold, and there is no vegetation near the top, — not even so much as a little moss on the edges of the stones. I went near, — not *too near* you may be sure, — to some most frightful precipices, they were most tremendous places perhaps 1500 feet deep, — if you holla over them the voice is echoed all the way down till it dies away, and the effect of

---

[8] Keats wrote to Tom that "it far surpasses the finest Cathedrall," and in "Not Aladin magian" he called it "This Cathedral of the Sea" (*Letters*, I, 349–350).

throwing stones down is extraordinary. I won't trouble you much in my travels to Inverness, along the banks of Loch Lochy and Loch Ness, but I must mention my having seen the grandest fall of water in Europe, — called the Falls of Foyers. — As for the natives, — the Highlanders, — I like them very well; they are very civil, kind, and attentive; I think they are always sincere in what they say; they are much more civilised than I expected to find them in the wild places I have visited. But oh! what a poor Country it is; mountains are fine to look at, but they will not bear corn, and even the valleys afford very scanty crops. We have sometimes been nearly starved; for 3 or 4 days together we have not been able to procure a morsel of meat, and their oat-bread I thought my dainty stomach never would accept of, but I contrive to eat it now; — all this is hard work in such long walks. I have stumped my ten toes over 642 miles, and shall have twice as much more to accomplish if I can, but Mr. Keats will leave me here, and I am full of sorrow about it; he is not well enough to go on; a violent cold and an ulcerated throat make it a matter of prudence that he should go to London in the Packet; [9] he has been unwell for some time, and the Physician here is of opinion he will not recover if he journeys on foot, thro' all weathers, and under so many privations. Give my compliments to Mrs. Woods and Mrs. Snook if they will accept of them from one in a tartan dress and with a Highland plaid thrown across my shoulder; — Keats calls me the Red Cross Knight, and declares my own shadow laughs at me! As for cousin John, remember me to him, I have wanted both of you with me, but you are both too young yet, and you must first get learning in wholesale. If you write to me before 20th August, addressed *"Mr Charles Brown, from London, Post Office, Edinburgh,"* I shall receive the letter.[10] When you write to Jack, give my true love to him, — and to your father and mother, my sincere friendship. God keep you well, my dear Boy, and believe me your more than brother-friend,

Chas. Brown.

[9] Keats sailed from Cromarty on the next day, reaching London on August 18.

[10] From this Bodurtha and Pope, p. 104, infer that he planned to reach Edinburgh about September 1. He spent "some days" with Benjamin Bailey at Carlisle on the return trip (*KC*, II, 285), and arrived home at the end of September or the beginning of October (Bodurtha and Pope, p. 106).

· 3 ·

TO C. W. DILKE, SR.[1]

AL: Keats House, Hampstead. Printed in *Papers of a Critic*, I, 3–5, by Williamson, pp. 57–58 (with a facsimile, plates XVII, XVIII), and in *Letters*, I, 361–363.

My dear Sir,   Inverness. 7th August 1818.

What shall I write about? I am resolved to send you a letter, but where is the subject? I have already stumped away on my ten toes 642 miles, and seen many fine sights, but I am puzzled to know what to make choice of. Suppose I begin with myself, — there must be a pleasure in that, — and, by way of variety, I must bring in Mr Keats. Then, be it known, in the first place, we are in as continued a bustle as an old Dowager at Home. Always moving — moving from one place to another, like Dante's inhabitants of the Sulphur Kingdom in search of cold ground, — prosing over the Map, — calculating distances, — packing up knapsacks, — and paying bills. There's so much for yourself, my dear. "Thank'ye, Sir." How many miles to the next Town? "Seventeen lucky miles, Sir." That must be at least twenty; come along, Keats; here's your stick; why, we forgot the map! — now for it; seventeen lucky miles! I must have another hole taken up in the strap of my Knapsack. Oh, the misery of coming to the meeting of three roads without a finger post! There's an old woman coming, — God bless her! she'll tell us all about it. Eh! she can't speak English! Repeat the name of the town over in all ways, but the true spelling way, and possibly she may understand. No, we have not got the brogue. Then toss up heads or tails for right and left, and fortune send us the right road! Here's a soaking shower coming! ecod! it rolls between the mountains as if it would drown us. At last we come wet and weary to the long wished for Inn. What have you for

---

[1] Dilke's father (1742–1826), who in 1814 had retired from the Navy Pay Office to live in Chichester. The opening mention of 642 miles and the early reference to Keats's illness, topics of the close of number 2, suggest that this is the later letter of August 7. About this date Brown wrote a third letter (now lost), which the Hampstead Dilkes received on August 14 (*Papers of a Critic*, I, 5).

Dinner? "Truly nothing." No Eggs? "We have two." Any loaf bread? "No, Sir, but we've nice oat-cakes." Any bacon? any dried fish? "No, no, no, Sir!" But you've plenty of Whiskey? "O yes, Sir, plenty of Whiskey!" This is melancholy. Why should so beautiful a Country be poor? Why can't craggy mountains, and granite rocks, bear corn, wine, and oil? These are our misfortunes, — these are what make me "an Eagle's talon in the waist." [2] But I am well repaid for my sufferings. We came out to endure, and to be gratified with scenery, and lo! we have not been disappointed either way. As for the Oat-cakes, I was once in despair about them. I was not only too dainty, but they absolutely made me sick. With a little gulping, I can manage them now. Mr Keats however is too unwell for fatigue and privation. I am waiting here to see him off in the Smack for London. He caught a violent cold in the Island of Mull, which far from leaving him, has become worse, and the Physician here thinks him too thin and fevered to proceed on our journey. It is a cruel disappointment. We have been as happy as possible together. Alas! I shall have to travel thro' Perthshire and all the Counties round in solitude! But my disappointment is nothing to his; he not only loses my company, (and that's a great loss,) but he loses the Country. Poor Charles Brown will have to trudge by himself, — an odd fellow, and moreover an odd figure; — imagine me with a thick stick in my hand, the knapsack on my back, "with spectacles on nose," [3] a white hat, a tartan coat and trowsers, and a Highland plaid thrown over my shoulders! Don't laugh at me, there's a good fellow, — altho' Mr Keats calls me the Red Cross Knight, and declares my own shadow is ready to split its sides as it follows me. This dress is the best possible dress, as Dr Pangloss would say. It is light and not easily penetrated by the wet, and when it is, it is not cold, — it has little more than a kind of heavy smoky sensation about it. I must not think of the wind, and the sun, and the rain, after my journey thro' the island of Mull. There's a wild place! Thirty seven miles of jumping and flinging over great stones along no path at all, up the steep and down the steep, and wading thro' rivulets up to the knees, and crossing a bog, a mile long, up to the ancles. I should like to give

[2] *1 Henry IV*, II.iv.363.
[3] *As You Like It*, II.vii.159.

you a whole and particular account of the many — many wonderful places I have visited, — but why should I ask a man to pay vigentiple postage? In one word then, — that is to the end of the letter, — let me tell you I have seen one half of the Lakes in Westmoreland & Cumberland, — I have travelled over the whole of the coast of Kirkcudbrightshire, and skudded over to Donaghadee. But I did not like Ireland, — at least that part, — and would go no farther than Belfast. So back came I in a whirligig, — that is in a hurry, — and trotted up to Ayr; where I had the happiness of drinking Whiskey in the very house that Robin Burns was born, — and I saw the banks of bonny Doon, — and the brigs of Ayr, — and Kirk Alloway, — I saw it all! After this we went to Glasgow, & then to Loch Lomond, — but you can read all about that place in one of the fashionable guide-books. Then to Loch Awe and down to the foot of it, — oh, what a glen we went thro' to get at it! At the top of the glen my Itinerary mentioned a place called "Rest and be thankful" nine miles off; now we had set out without breakfast, intending to take our meal there, when, horror and starvation! "Rest and be thankful" was not an Inn, but a stone seat! [4]

*   *   *

---

[4] So, says Keats, they "were cheated into 5 more Miles to Breakfast" (*Letters*, I, 334). The present letter consists of a single sheet written on both sides. The remainder is lost.

· 4 ·

TO RICHARD WOODHOUSE

Address: — Woodhouse Esqr

ALS: Harvard. Printed in *KC*, I, 66–67, and *Letters*, I, 409.

　　　　　　　　　　　　　　Hampstead
Sir,　　　　　　　　　　　　Tuesday 1st Dec^r [1818]
　　Mr Keats requests me to inform you his brother Thomas died this morning at 8 o'Clock quietly & without pain — Mr Keats is pretty well & desires to be remembered to you — [1]
　　　　　　　　　　　　　I am, Sir,
　　　　　　　　　　　　　Your obed^t hum Servt
　　　　　　　　　　　　　Chas Brown.

· 5 ·

(WITH JOHN KEATS) TO C. W. AND MARIA DILKE

Address: To, / Chas W: Dilke Esqr / Navy Pay Office / Somerset house / London.

Postmarks: HAVANT; F 25 JA 25 1819

ALS: Keats House, Hampstead. Printed by Williamson, pp. 63–65 (with a facsimile, plates XXII–XXV), and in *Letters*, II, 34–36.

Dear Dilke,　　　　　　　　Bedhampton. 24th Jany 1819.
　　This letter is for your Wife, and if you are a Gentleman, you will deliver it to her, without reading one word further. 'read thou Squire.[1] There is a wager depending on this.

My charming dear Mrs Dilke,
　　It was delightful to receive a letter from you; — but such a letter! What presumption in me to attempt to answer it! Where

---

[1] The famous account of Keats's awakening Brown "one morning . . . to tell me his brother was no more" is in *KC*, II, 64. Shortly afterward Keats moved in with Brown at Wentworth Place (*KC*, II, 65; *Letters*, II, 4–5).

[1] Throughout this letter Keats's words are indicated by underlines.

shall I find, in my poor brain, such gibes, such jeers, such flashes of merriment? Alas! you will say, as you read me, Alas! poor Brown! quite chop fallen! [2] But that's not true; my chops have been beautifully plumped out since I came here; my dinners have been good & nourishing, & my inside never washed by a red herring broth. Then my mind has been so happy! I have been smiled on by the fair ones, the Lacy's,[3] the Prices, & the Mullings's,[4] but not by the Richards's; Old Dicky has not called here during my visit, — I have not seen him; the whole of the family are *shuffling* to carriage folks for acquaintances, *cutting* their old friends, and *dealing* out pride & folly, while we allow they have got the *odd trick*, but dispute their *honours*. I was determined to be beforehand with them, & behaved cavalierly & neglectingly to the family, & passed the girls in Havant with a slight bow. — Keats is much better, owing to a strict forbearance from a third glass of wine. He & I walked from Chichester yesterday; we were here at 3, but the Dinner was finished; a brace of Muir fowl had been dressed; I ate a piece of the breast cold, & it was not tainted; I dared not venture further. Mr Snook was nearly turned sick by being merely asked to take a mouthful. The other brace was so *high*, that the Cook declined preparing them for the spit, & they were thrown away. I see your husband declared them to be in excellent order; I suppose he enjoyed them in a disgusting manner, — sucking the rotten flesh off the bones, & crunching the putrid bones. Did you eat any? I hope not, for an *ooman* should be delicate in her food. — O you Jezabel! to sit quietly in your room, while the thieves were ransacking my house! No doubt poor Ann's throat was cut; has the Coroner sat on her yet? [5] — Mrs Snook says she knows how to hold a pen very well, & wants no lessons from me; only think of the vanity of the *ooman*! She tells me to make honourable mention of your letter which she received at Breakfast time, but how can I do so? I have not read it; & I'll lay my life

---

[2] *Hamlet*, V.i.209–212, "gibes . . . flashes of merriment . . . Quite chop-fallen."

[3] According to Robert Gittings, *John Keats: The Living Year* (Cambridge, Mass., 1954), pp. 69–70, Mrs. Mary Lacy (1749?–1823) was "one of the card-playing circle" at Chichester, which Brown and Keats had left on the preceding day.

[4] See n. 9 below.

[5] *Hamlet*, V.i.4, "The crowner hath sat on her." Keats mentions "ann the mai{d}" in *Letters*, II, 29.

it is not a tenth part so good as mine, — pshaw on your letter to her! — On Tuesday night I think you'll see me. In the mean time I'll not say a word about spasms in the way of my profession, tho' as your friend I must profess myself very sorry. Keats & I are going to call on Mr Butler & Mr Burton this morning, & to-morrow we shall go to Sanstead to see Mr Way's Chapel consecrated by the two Big-wigs of Gloucester & St Davids.[6] If that vile Carver & Gilder does not do me justice, I'll annoy him all his life with legal expences at every quarter, if my rent is not sent to the day, & that will not be revenge enough for the trouble & confusion he has put me to. — Mrs Dilke [7] is remarkably well for Mrs Dilke in winter. — Have you heard any thing of John Blagden; [8] he is off! want of business has made him play the fool, — I am sorry. that Brown and you are getting so very witty — my modest feathered Pen frizzles like baby roast beef at making its entrance among such tantrum sentences — or rather ten senses. Brown *super* or *supper* sirnamed the Sleek has been getting thinner a little by pining opposite Miss Muggins [9] — (Brown says Mullins but I beg leave to differ from him) — we sit it out till ten o'Clock — Miss M. has persuaded Brown to shave his Whiskers — he came down to Breakfast like the Sign of the full Moon — his Profile is quite alter'd — He looks more like an oman than I ever could think it possible — and on putting on M^rs D's Calash the deception was complete especially as his voice is trebbld by making love in the draught of a door way — I too am metamorphosed — a young oman here in Bed – – – hampton has over persuaded me to wear my Shirtcollar up to my eyes. Mrs Snook I catch smoking it every now and then and

---

[6] Lewis Way (1772–1840), "a great Jew converter — who in that line has spent one hundred thousand Pounds," wrote Keats three weeks later when he described to his brother and sister-in-law the dedication ceremonies at Stansted (*Letters*, II, 62). Butler and Burton remain unidentified. The "Big-wigs" were Henry Ryder (1777–1836), bishop of Gloucester, and Thomas Burgess (1756–1837), bishop of St. David's. See Gittings, *John Keats*, pp. 75–82.

[7] Mrs. C. W. Dilke, Sr.

[8] A former mayor of Chichester, who in 1819 was a bankrupt (*Letters*, II, 35n).

[9] Miss Sarah Mullins (b. 1747?), the daughter of a former mayor of Chichester, who, like Mrs. Lacy, was a card-playing septuagenarian (Gittings, *John Keats*, pp. 66–67).

I believe Brown does — but I cannot now look sideways — Brown wants to scribble more so I will finish with a marginal note — Viz — Remember me to Wentworth Place and Elm Cottage — not forgetting Millamant [10] — Your's if possible J. Keats —

This is abominable! I did but go up stairs to put on a clean & starched hand-kerchief, & that over weening rogue read my letter, & scrawled over one of my sheets, and given him a counterpain, — I wish I could blank-it all over and beat him with a $\left\{ \begin{array}{l} \text{k} \\ \overline{\text{certain}} \end{array} \right.$ rod, — & have a fresh one bolstered up, Ah! he may dress me as he likes but he shan't ticlke me pillow the feathers, — I would not give a tester for such puns, let us *ope* brown erratum — a large *B* a Bumble B.[11] will go no further in the Bedroom & not call Mat Snook a relation to Matt-rass — This is grown to a conclusion — I had excellent puns in my head but one bad one from Brown has quite upset me but I am quite set-up for more, but I'm content to be conqueror. Your's in love, Chas Brown.

N. B. I beg leaf to withdraw all my Puns — they are all wash, an base uns —

. 6 .

TO C. W. DILKE [1]

[August 12, 1819]

* * *

Keats is very industrious, but I swear by the prompter's whistle, and by the bangs of stage-doors, he is obstinately monstrous. What think you of Otho's threatening cold pig [2] to the new-married couple? He says the Emperor must have a spice of drollery.

---

[10] Fanny Brawne, who had moved from Wentworth Place to Elm Cottage in the fall of 1818.

[11] The words "erratum . . . B." are added in the margin.

[1] From *Papers of a Critic*, I, 9, where it is headed, "On August 12, 1819, Brown writes from the Isle of Wight, to Mr. Dilke."

[2] "Give cold pig" is defined by Eric Partridge, *A Dictionary of Slang and Uncon-*

His introduction of Grimm's adventure, lying three days on his back for love,[3] though it spoils the unity of time, is not out of the way for the character of Ludolf, so I have consented to it; but I cannot endure his fancy of making the princess blow up her hair-dresser, for smearing her cheek with pomatum, and spoiling her rouge. It may be natural, as he observes, but so might many things. However, such as it is, it has advanced to nearly the end of the fourth act.[4]

*   *   *

· 7 ·

TO JOHN TAYLOR

Address (in Keats's hand): John Taylor Esq[re] / Taylor and Hessey / Fleet Street / London

Postmarks: WINCHESTER 23 AU 23 1819; E 24 AU 24 1819

ALS: Harvard. Printed in *Letters*, II, 145.

Dear Sir,   [August 23, 1819]

Keats has told me the purport of this letter.[1] Had it been in my power to have prevented this application to you, I would have

---

ventional English (London, 1949), p. 169, as "To awaken by sluicing with cold water or by pulling off the bed-clothes."

[3] The memoir of Friedrich Melchior Grimm (1723–1807) prefixed to *Historical & Literary Memoirs and Anecdotes . . . from the Correspondence of Baron de Grimm*, 2nd edn. (London, 1815), I, viii, tells that when a "Mademoiselle Fel" rejected his advances he "fell into a sort of catalepsy which continued for several days. He remained stretched on his bed, with his eyes fixed and all his limbs stiffened . . . [until one morning he] rose suddenly from his bed, dressed himself, went about his business and never thought more of his chaste Lucretia." This incident, like the others of this letter and the elephant mentioned by Keats in *Letters*, II, 135, was omitted from *Otho*.

[4] Act IV was completed by August 14, Act V by the twenty-third (*Letters*, II, 139, 143).

[1] Brown's note is written on the fourth page of a letter in which Keats told Taylor (*Letters*, II, 143), "Being thus far connected [in *Otho*, from which they expected "moderate Profits"], Brown proposed to me, to stand with me responsible for any money you may advance . . . . I offer a Bill . . . as a relief to myself from a too lax sensation of Life." Woodhouse, whom Taylor asked for an opinion of the letter, offered the publisher £50 to lend to Keats, and agreed with him that Brown's name and the note should not be used. Perhaps these are "Brown's few lines" that Woodhouse liked "much" (*Letters*, II, 151–152).

done so. What property I have is locked up, sending me quarterly & half yearly driblets, insufficient for the support of both of us. I am fully acquainted with his circumstances, — the monies owing to him amount to £230, — the Chancery Suit will not I think eventually be injurious to him, — and his perseverance in the employment of his talents, — will, in my opinion, in a short time, place him in a situation more pleasant to his feelings as far as his pocket is considered. Yet, for all this, I am aware, a man of business should have every security in his power, and Keats especially would be uncomfortable at borrowing unless he gave all *in his power*; besides his own name to a Bill he has none to offer but mine, which I readily agree to, and (speaking in a business-like way) consider I possess ample security for doing so. It is therefore to be considered as a matter of right on your part to demand my name in conju[n]ction with his; and if you should be inclined to judge otherwise, still it would be painful to him not to give you a double security when he can do so, & painful to me to have it withheld when it ought to be given.

Your's sincerely Chas Brown.

. 8 .

TO B. R. HAYDON [1]

Address (in Keats's hand): B. R. Haydon Esqre / Lisson-Grove North / Paddington

Postmarks: WINCHESTER 3 OC 3 1819; 10 o'Clock OC [3] 1819 F[Nⁿ]; E 4 OC 4 1819

ALS: Harvard. Printed in *Letters*, II, 221.

[October 3, 1819]

My dear Sir, I heard yesterday you had written to me at Hampstead. I have not rec^d your letter. You must, I think, accuse me of neglect, but indeed I do not merit it. This many worded Keats

---

[1] Begun in the left-hand margin and written vertically across the second page of a letter from Keats to Haydon (*Letters*, II, 219–221). Brown had recently (perhaps on October 1) rejoined Keats in Winchester after visiting Chichester and Bedhampton.

has left me no room to say more. — I shall be in Town in a few
days —

Your's truly

Chas Brown.

· 9 ·

TO JOHN TAYLOR [1]

Address: To Mr. Taylor

[January 17, 1820]

My dear Sir. — Mr. Dilke & I have wagered which would write
the better fairy tale, — or fairy and chivalrous, as we pleased. The
wager is a Supper for Judges & selves. Four critics were chosen,
and it was settled that, in case the votes were divided, I was to
request you to give the casting vote.[2] It happens we have two on
each side. Will you therefore have the kindness to settle the con-
tention? You will see they are written on two distinct models, —
one after the style of *Prince Arthur*, — the other after that of the
comic Faery Tales, — the question is — which is the better of its
kind, and which the better tale, — and the preference is to be de-
cisively in favor of one of them.

Here's a thaw at last! — I congratulate you.

Your's sincerely,

Chas. Brown.

[1] From *TLS*, December 6, 1941, p. 624, where M. B. Forman says it was "written
by Brown at Wentworth Place two days earlier" than number 10.

[2] Maria Dilke thus described the wager to Dilke's father (*Papers of a Critic*, I,
14): "It was made on Christmas Day. The conversation turned on fairy tales —
Brown's forte — Dilke not liking them. Brown said he was sure he could beat Dilke,
and to let him try, they betted a beef-steak supper, and an allotted time was given."
Keats, Reynolds, and Rice were three of the "Four critics"; Forman thinks the
fourth was Thomas Richards. Taylor, who lacked "Taste for such Subjects as Fairy
Tales" (*Letters*, II, 183), replied on the same day in favor of Dilke and the tale of
chivalry (see *TLS*, as cited above). For Brown's payment of the wager see the next
letter.

· 10 ·

TO JOHN TAYLOR [1]

Address: To Mr. Taylor, No. 93 Fleet Street, London

Postmark: JA.19 1820

[January 19, 1820]

Mr. Charles Brown requests the favor of Mr. Taylor's Company to Supper on Saturday next at 8 o'clock, at No. 3 Great Smith Street, Westminster.[2]

Hampstead, Wednesday Morng.

· 11 ·

TO HENRY SNOOK [1]

Address: Master Henry Snook, at Mr. Lord's Academy, Tooting, Surrey

[February 11, 1820]

*   *   *

Mr. Keats fell very ill yesterday week,[2] and my office of head Nurse has too much employed me to allow of my answering your letter immediately; he is somewhat better, but I'm in a very anxious state about him. — I was in hopes of you and Jack [3] being able, during Easter, to go to the Theatre to witness our Tragedy; [4] but no, — at Drury Lane they engaged to play it *next* Season, and I, not liking the delay, took it home. — Here, to amuse myself, I began to copy some of my favorite Hogarth's heads; [5] they were in

---

[1] From *TLS*, December 6, 1941, p. 624.

[2] Though Brown lost the fairy-tale wager (see the preceding letter) he gave the supper of beefsteaks and punch at the Dilkes'.

[1] From Forman (1883), IV, 62–63n.

[2] See Brown's account in *KC*, II, 73–74.

[3] John Snook, Jr., Henry's brother.

[4] *Otho the Great.*

[5] "Brown . . . has just made a purchace of the methodist meeting Picture, which gave me a horrid dream a few nights ago," "A damn'd melancholy picture," wrote

Indian ink as usual; when Mr. Severn (I think you know him) put me on another plan, and I hope to succeed. I must tell you about Mr. Severn, whether you know him or not: he is a young Artist, who lately strove with his fellow students for a gold medal, which the Royal Academy gives annually for the best historical painting; the subject was fixed to be the Cave of Despair as described in Spencer's poem; [6] it was Mr. Severn's *second* attempt [7] in *oil* colours, and therefore it might have been supposed he stood no chance of success, and yet he won it! — it has been so much approved of that he will have his expenses paid for three years during his travels on the Continent, and his Majesty is to furnish him with letters of recommendation. What think you of this? I tell it you as a proof there is still some good reward in the world for superior talent; now and then a man of talent is disregarded, but it is an error to believe that such is the common fate of true desert. This does not apply solely to genius in the arts, but to you and me and all of us, as to our general character and capability.

*   *   *

Keats on February 14 and March 4 (*Letters*, II, 260, 271). It was either "Credulity, Superstition, and Fanaticism: A Medley" (see number 49) or "The Sleeping Congregation."

[6] *The Faerie Queene*, I.ix.52. Severn won the medal on December 10 (see Sharp, pp. 22–27).

[7] "Hermia and Helena," exhibited with the famous miniature of Keats at the Royal Academy in May 1819, was his first.

· 12 ·

TO JOHN TAYLOR

Address: To / Mr Taylor, / N° 93 Fleet Street.

Postmarks: Two Py Post Unpaid SO Hampstead; 7 o'Clock MR 8 1820 N^T

ALS: Pierpont Morgan Library. Printed in *KC*, I, 103, and *Letters*, II, 273–274.

Hampstead.

Dear Taylor,   Wednesday 8th March [1820]

   Poor Keats will be unable to prepare his Poems [1] for the Press for a long time. He was taken on Monday evening with violent palpitations at the heart, and has since remained too weak to get up. I expect Dr Bree [2] every hour. I am wretchedly depressed.

Your's sincerely,
Chas Brown.

If you come, do not let him hear your voice, as the slightest circumstance tending to create surprise, or any other emotion, must be avoided. [3]

CB

P. S.

   Since writing the above, Dr Bree has been here, and I am rejoiced to say, gives very favourable hopes.

CB

---

[1] The *Lamia* volume.

[2] Robert Bree (1759–1839), of George Street, Hanover Square, a specialist in respiratory diseases. He had attended Brown's brother James in 1815, and witnessed the signing of a codicil to his will.

[3] See similar remarks in numbers 13 and 15, and in *Letters*, II, 314, 315, 321. It is not surprising that Brown and others believed "poor Keats' disease is in the mind" (number 22). Keats himself told his sister on August 23, 1820 (*Letters*, II, 329), that dwelling "on unpleasant reflections . . . has been the destruction of my health," and his physician in Rome, Dr. James Clark, wrote on November 27, 1820 (*Letters*, II, 358), "His mental exertions and application have I think been the sources of his complaints — If I can put his mind at ease I think he'll do well . . . . I fear much there is something operating on his mind . . . . Let every thing be done to relieve his mind."

· 13 ·

TO JOHN TAYLOR

Address: To / Mr Taylor / N° 93 Fleet Street / London.

ALS: Pierpont Morgan Library. Printed in *KC*, I, 104, and *Letters*, II, 274–275.

                                                    Hampstead.
Dear Taylor,   Friday 10 March [1820].
    After my dismal note [1] I am glad to be able to give you good news. Keats is so well as to be out of danger. We intend, if the weather remain kindly, to go to the coast of Hants.[2] He walked in the Garden to-day. You will suspect I gave you a useless alarm, but I wrote at the time I was told that it was possible he might suddenly be lost to us in one of those fits. Hessey's letter came, & I opened it, for Keats could not endure even the circumstance of a letter being put in his hands, — nor can he bear it even yet, tho' I consider him perfectly out of danger, & I am happy to tell you that we are now assured there is no pulmonary affection, no organic defect whatever, — the disease is on his *mind*,[3] and there I hope he will soon be cured.

                                        Your's sincerely
                                        Chas Brown.
Remember me to Mr Hessey.

[1] Number 12.
[2] They did not go.
[3] Rollins (*Letters*, II, 275n) cites Sir William Hale-White, *Keats as Doctor and Patient* (London, 1938), p. 54: "To us this seems incredible, when we remember the bleeding from the lungs a month earlier." See the third note to the preceding letter.

· 14 ·

TO JOHN TAYLOR

Address: To / Mr Taylor.

ALS: Pierpont Morgan Library. Printed in *KC*, I, 105, and *Letters*, II, 276.

Dear Sir,   [March 13 (?), 1820] [1]

Keats has been slowly recovering; yesterday and to-day however he has been greatly altered for the better. He wishes his Poems to be published as soon as convenient to yourself, — the volume to commence with St Agnes' Eve. He was occupied yesterday in revising Lamia. It is not his intention at present to have a Preface,[2] — at least so we talked together to-day. He desires to be remembered. When will you come? for *he* must not venture to Town before we have mild weather, — & when? It is very pleasant at Hampstead — *in our parlour*.

Your's sincerely
Chas Brown.

Don't let any one take a Copy of Otho. — [3]

· 15 ·

TO HENRY SNOOK [1]

My dear Harry,   Hampstead. 24th March 1820.

Your absence and Jack's will be much felt at Easter, but I would rather you should cheer your mother in her sickness, than contribute to my pleasure, and I know you are of the same mind. I

---

[1] Rollins' tentative dating (*Letters*, II, 276), based on the fact that Keats felt well enough to dine with Taylor on March 14 — Edmund Blunden in *London Mercury*, 4 (1921): 141.

[2] Against the brief "Advertisement" printed at the beginning of the volume Keats wrote (in Burridge Davenport's copy, now at Harvard), "This is none of my doing — I w{as} ill at the time." "The Eve of St. Agnes" was the third poem in the volume.

[3] Severn told Brown on August 21, 1838 (Sharp, p. 166), that Woodhouse "had the tragedy copied . . . from the love he bore Keats."

[1] From Forman (1883), IV, 73–74n. A copy found among Dilke's papers is printed by Joanna Richardson in *TLS*, August 29, 1952, p. 565.

sincerely hope you will find her better, and that you will leave her quite well. Write to me how she is. Every body is ill, or has been. I am rejoiced to learn that your Grandfather [2] is well at last. Your Aunt [3] has not quite recovered her strength. I have been nurse, night and day, to Mr. Keats for 7 weeks, — no, — only 12 nights.[4] He will get well by degrees. This Nurseship of mine prevented my writing to you, or indeed to any one else, for tho' *I* had time enough, *he* could not endure to see me sit down to pen and ink, even now he has begun to feel quite nervous at the sight of this scrawl going on. The consequence was, I was compelled to betake myself to some other occupation, and as a man can't read from morning till bed-time, I have employed myself in drawing, — besides, too much reading before him was forbidden, — it is well I could do something inoffensive! You shall have one of his bits of comic verses, — I met with them only yesterday, but they have been written long ago, — it is a song on the City of Oxford. — [5]

Remembrance to Jack.

Your sincere friend
Chas. Brown.

On Oxford.

1

The Gothic looks solemn,
The plain Doric column
Supports an old Bishop and Crosier;
The mouldering arch,
Shaded o'er by a larch
Stands next door to Wilson the Hosier.

2

Vicè — that is, by turns, —
O'er pale faces mourns

---

[2] C. W. Dilke, Sr.
[3] Maria Dilke.
[4] Actually Keats suffered "violent palpitations at the heart" eighteen days earlier, on March 6 (number 12), and around the beginning of Brown's "12 nights" was "greatly altered for the better" (number 14).
[5] Keats visited Bailey at Oxford in September 1817, and sent these lines to Reynolds as a parody of Wordsworth's "Written in March" (*Letters*, I, 151–152).

The black tassell'd trencher and common hat;
The Chantry boy sings,
The Steeple-bell rings,
And as for the Chancellor — *dominat.*

3

There are plenty of trees,
And plenty of ease,
And plenty of fat deer for Parsons;
And when it is venison,
Short is the benison, —
Then each on a leg or thigh fastens.

· 16 ·

TO WILLIAM HASLAM

Address: To / Mr Wm Haslam, / Messrs Frampton & Sons, / Leadenhall Street / London. / Post paid

Postmark: F PAID 2 OC 2 1820

ALS: Harvard. Printed in *KC*, I, 159.

Dear Haslam,   Chichester. 30th Septr 1820.
    Pray direct this letter [1] properly and forward it. If a letter
from George [2] to me should come into your hands, I hereby duly
& truly authorise you to open it with said hands, as it is possible
the contents may be important, and I shall not be in my own
house till 21st Oct^r, whither you can forward it at that time.
    I'll not trouble you with much chatter, — so present my re-
spects to your wife's picture,[3] — that being all I have seen of her
fair face, — & believe me,
                    Your's truly,
                    Chas Brown.

    [1] Brown's lost letter, which "followed [Keats] . . . from Naples to Rome" (*Let-
ters*, II, 360), is mentioned again at the end of number 18.
    [2] Brown had written to George Keats in March (*Letters*, II, 284, 295–296).
    [3] Severn first painted Mary Haslam (1795?–1822) before September 17, 1819, and
then again, perhaps reworking the first portrait, in July 1820 (*Letters*, II, 187, 307).

· 17 ·

TO JOHN TAYLOR

Address: To / Messrs Taylor & Hessey / N° 93 Fleet Street / London. (*readdressed twice*[1] *to*: Mr John Taylor / Mesd^s Taylor & Hunt / Leicester)

Postmarks: CHICHESTER OC 5 1820; F 6 OC 6 1820; A OC 6 820

ALS: Pierpont Morgan Library. Printed in *KC*, I, 160–161, and *Letters*, II, 346–347.

Dear Taylor,   Chichester. 5th Sept^r [*for* October] 1820.

If neither Keats nor Severn has written from Portsmouth, and I believe neither of them has,[2] I have some news gratifying to you & to our friends in London. They landed at Portsmouth after having been tossed about in the Channel for ten days. This was on Thursday 28th. Having a day to spare, they went to Bedhampton, a distance of 7 miles, to visit M^r & Mrs Snook, who were here yesterday afternoon & gave me the following particulars. His health was better than they expected from the accounts they had previously heard, and Severn talked cheeringly of him. On the following morning (Friday) his spirits were excellent. He abuses the Captain,[3] tho' he acknowledges him to be civil & accommodating. He likes one of the Ladies, and has an aversion for the other,[4] whom he ridiculed with all the bustling wit of a man in saucy health. He was so sick of the voyage, that a word might have sent him back to London. Unknown to Severn he put on a blister (on his chest) soon after he went on board, c{onv}inced it would relieve him, and it appears he {belie}ves it has relieved him. Still however he is full of his old apprehensions. He knew I was here (within ten miles) but did not dare to come, lest the wind should

---

[1] By Hessey, who added the note of October 6 printed in *KC*, I, 161–162.

[2] Keats did write from Portsmouth, but did not send Brown the letter (*Letters*, II, 350).

[3] Thomas Walsh, who, according to Severn (*Letters*, II, 355), "has behaved with great kindness to us all — but more particularly [to] Keats . . . he is a good-natured man to his own injury."

[4] Miss Cotterell and Mrs. Pidgeon.

59

change; — how strangely unlucky that we should *twice* have been so near a meeting & yet not met![5] Had he known where I was at an earlier hour on Thursday, I think he would have come no! — I am mistaken, — he could not.[6] I tell you every thing — trifles & all — that you may form your opinion of him. Neither the boisterous weather, nor his antipathies, nor his anger, will do him harm; — on the contrary they will be of service, — they are good physic to his mind, & will help to purge away his apprehensions. He wrote to me in Scotland he was confident the indulgence of his friends injured him, & a letter from me to the same effect crossed on the road.[7] He sailed from Portsmouth on Friday afternoon, with a fair wind, which has continued ever since. Both he & Severn said they should not write; I suppose they relied on my doing so. I send this account to none but yourself, & leave you to disseminate it as you please. Comp^ts to Mr Hessey. I shall direct this to both of you, lest you should be out of Town, & have too much postage to pay for my scrawl.

Your's most truly,
Chas Brown.

[5] Earlier Brown had missed Keats at Gravesend on the night of September 17–18 (*KC*, II, 79).

[6] The words "no! . . . not" are added above the line.

[7] Rollins refers to *Letters*, I, 298: "Fact is, I have had so many kindnesses done me by so many people, that I am cheveaux-de-frised with benefits, which I must jump over or break down." Brown's letter "to the same effect" is lost.

· 18 ·

TO WILLIAM HASLAM

Address: To / Mr Haslam, / (Messrs Frampton & Co) / Leadenhall Street / London.

Postmarks: Two Py Post Unpaid SO Hampstead; [1]2 o'Clock DE 2 1820 N^n

ALS: Harvard. Printed in *KC*, I, 173.

Dear Haslam,   Hampstead. 1st Decr 1820.

This afternoon I had a letter from Keats, dated Naples, first Wednesday in Nov^r, the day after their quarantine was over.[1] It required an immediate answer, which I have complied with, & send it you to forward with all speed. He says — "write to *Rome*, (post restant)" — but I am afraid to give that address, — he is liable to strange errors of this sort, — Severn is the surer man, & I suppose you have heard from him giving reliable directions. Both to Mrs Brawne & to me he says "I refer you to Severn's letter to Haslam about my health", — now, if you have rec^d such letter, pray send it us,[2] — for this fortnight we have been impatiently expecting it, — do not fear it will be kept a day longer than you mention. I give you great trouble, — but in a matter relating to Keats I need scarce make an apology. I sent you a letter from Chichester to be forwarded to him.[3] With respects to M^rs H,

& best wishes,

I am always your's

Chas Brown.

[1] See *Letters*, II, 351–352. Brown's "immediate answer," which Haslam forwarded to Keats on December 4 (Sharp, p. 73), is lost.

[2] Keats refers Brown to Severn's letter of November 1, 2 (*Letters*, II, 353–355), which Haslam received on this day (Sharp, p. 72) and forwarded to Brown on December 2 or 3 (see the next letter). In his latest extant letter to Mrs. Brawne, Keats probably refers to Severn's of October 22, which had arrived in London on November 11 (*Letters*, II, 350, 348).

[3] See the opening of number 16.

· 19 ·

TO WILLIAM HASLAM

Address: To / Mr Haslam, / (Messrs Frampton & Co) / Leadenhall
Street / London.

Postmarks: Hampstead NO; [1]2 o'Clock [D]E 4 1820 N^n

ALS: Harvard. Printed in *KC*, I, 174–175.

Dear Haslam,   [December 3, 1820]
    Thank you for the enclosed.[1] I read it next door, skipping &
adding, without the slightest suspicion on their part. You call
Severn's letter a heavy narrative! — what would you say to Keats'
letter of despair to me? But I ascribe much of the dreary feelings
of both to that damned quarantine. Yet the spitting of blood is a
fact, that came upon me distressingly. In a few days we shall know
the truth. I am glad he unburthened his mind to Severn, — that
is good. I still have cheering hopes, — but I am afraid, — very
afraid. Keats' letter to me *I must not show*, — I wish I might, —
the showing it would even relieve me, for the thoughts of it quite
weigh me down. What is to be done with George? Will he ever
dare to come among his brother's friends?[2]
                            Your's most truly,
                            Chas Brown.
                            Hampstead. Sunday.

[1] Severn's letter to Haslam of November 1, 2, which Brown read ("next door") to
the Brawnes. For this and "Keats' letter of despair" to Brown, see the notes to
number 18.
[2] See section VI of the Introduction.

· 20 ·

TO JOHN KEATS

Address: To / John Keats Esqr / Poste Restante / à Rome, / en Italie.

Postmarks: F 20 145; ANGLETERRE; CHAMBERY; 9 GEN-NAIO

ALS: Harvard. Printed in *Letters*, II, 364–366.

My dear Keats,   Hampstead. 21st Decr 1820.

Not two hours since your letter from Rome 30th Novr came to me,[1] — and as to-morrow is post night, you shall have the answer in due course. And so you still wish me to follow you to Rome? and truly I wish to go, — nothing detains me but prudence. Little could be gained, if any thing, by letting my house at this time of the year, and the consequence would be a heavy additional ex-pence which I cannot possibly afford, — unless it were a matter of necessity, and I see none while you are in such good hands as Severn's. As for my appropriating any part of remittances from George, that is out of the question, while you continue disabled from writing. Thank God, you are getting better! [2] Your last letter, which I so gravely answered about 4th Dec^r,[3] showed how much you had suffered by the voyage & the cursed quarantine. Keep your mind easy, my dear fellow, & no fear of your body. Your sister I hear is in remarkably good health, — the last news from George (already given to you) was so far favorable that there were no complaints. Every body next door [4] is quite well. Taylor has just returned to Town, — I saw him for a few minutes the other day, & had not time to put some questions which I wished, — but I understand your poems [5] encrease in sale. Hunt has been very ill, but is now recovered. All other friends are well. I know

---

[1] See *Letters*, II, 359–360.

[2] Unknown to Brown, Keats had suffered "a most unlooked for relapse" on De-cember 10 (*Letters*, II, 361), from which he never recovered.

[3] See the first two sentences of number 18 and note.

[4] The Brawnes.

[5] The *Lamia* volume, published around July 1.

you don't like John Scott,[6] but he is doing a thing that tickles me to the heart's core,[7] and you will like to hear of it, if you have any revenge in your composition. By some means (crooked enough I dare say) he has got possession of one of Blackwood's gang, who has turned King's evidence, and month after month he belabours them with the most damning facts that can be conceived; — if they are indeed facts, I know not how the rogues can stand up against them. This virulent attack has made me like the London Magazine, & I sent the 1st chapter of my tour [8] for Scott to publish, if he would pay me 10 Gns per sheet, & print the whole chapters monthly, without my forfeiting the copyright in the end. This would have answered my purpose famously, — but he won't agree to my stipulations. He praises my writing wondrously, — will pay the 10 Gns & so on, — but the fellow forsooth must have the chapters somewhat converted into the usual style of magazine articles, & so the treaty is at an end. O, — I must tell you Abby [9] is living with me again, but not in the same capacity, — she keeps to her own bed, & I keep myself continent. Any more nonsense of the former kind would put me in an awkward predicament with her. One child is very well. She behaves extremely well, and, by what I hear from Sam,[10] my arrangements prevent the affair from giving pain next door. The fact is I could not afford to allow her a seperate establishment. Mrs Brown [11] at first (I thought) behaved tolerably well, — I can't say so much for her now; — her husband knows nothing of the matter yet, as she says. In the mean time the child thrives gloriously, — but I'm not going to be fondly parental, for, between you & me, I think an infant is disagreeable, — it is all gut and squall. I dined with Richards on

<hr />

[6] Scott (1783–1821), editor of the *London Magazine*. For the outcome of his attacks (in the issues of May, November, December, January) on *Blackwood's* see numbers 24, 26, 29.

[7] *The Wife of Bath's Prologue*, l. 471, "It tikleth me aboute myn herte roote."

[8] "Walks in the North," which remained entirely unpublished until 1840 (see number 146). One of Brown's contributions was rejected by the *London* in August 1821, and in January 1825 he told Richards that he "never wrote an Article in the London" (see numbers 34, 68).

[9] Abigail O'Donaghue, with their son Carlino, born on July 16 (see section III of the Introduction).

[10] Samuel Brawne, Jr.

[11] Either Brown's mother (now remarried to Joseph Rennock Browne) or one of his sisters-in-law.

his wedding day, — he had just recovered from breaking his leg, — how could he be so brittle? — and it was done in a game at romps with his children! — Now I've something to make you 'spit fire, spout flame',[12] — the batch of Brag players asked me to town, hoping to fleece me, — it was at Reynolds' lodging, — & I carried of[f] £2. 10/–, — when will they be sick of these vain attempts? Mrs Dilke was next door yesterday, — she had a sad tumble in the mud, — (you must not laugh,) — her news was that Martin[13] is to be married this year, — that Reynolds & Mrs Montague correspond sentimentally, — & that Barry Cornwall is to have Miss Montague,[14] — there's some interesting small talk for you. Oh! Barry C: has a tragedy coming forth at the Theatre, — christened Mirandola,[15] — Mire and O la! — What an odd being you are, — because you & I were so near meeting twice, yet missed each other both times, you cry out "there was *my* star predominant!" — why not *mine* (CB's) as well? But this is the way you argue yourself into fits of the spleen. If I were in Severn's place, & you insisted on ever gnawing a bone, I'd lead you the life of a dog. What the devil should you grumble for? Do you recollect my anagram on your name? — how pat it comes now to Severn! — my love to him & the said anagram. — *"Thanks Joe!"* If I have a right guess, a certain person next door is a little disappointed at not receiving a letter from you, but not a word has dropped. She wrote to you lately, & so did your sister. Your's most faithfully,

Chas Brown.

[12] *King Lear*, III.ii.14.

[13] John Martin (1791–1855), bibliographer, bookseller, librarian. Brown's *Narensky* (1814) was "Sold by John Martin, 23, Holles-Street, Cavendish-Square."

[14] Mrs. Basil Montagu and her daughter, Anne Skepper (1799–1888), who married "Barry Cornwall" (Bryan Waller Procter, 1787–1874) in 1824.

[15] Produced at Covent Garden on January 9, 1821.

· 21 ·

TO WILLIAM HASLAM

Address: Mr William Haslam / Messrs Frampton & Sons / N° 34 Leadenhall Street. / London.

Postmarks: Hampstead NO; JA 6 1821

ALS: Harvard. Printed in *KC*, I, 186–187.

My dear Haslam,　　　　　　　　　　　　　　　[January 5, 1821]

Severn's letter [1] is more satisfactory than any Keats would deign to write, — it enters into those particulars which friends are always anxious about. I carried it next door with your Comp^ts. When I *travelled* into the City, to Frampton & Sons,[2] it was merely to show you how much better Keats appeared to be, and, provokingly, you were away. You have heard, or may hear, of my letter to George,[3] — I read a copy of it to Taylor; — should you hear news of that *money brother* pray let me know, — as for remittances from him, — we must dream about them. — Wait a month, and if George remains still silent, give him such a sting as he has had from me, — it will pierce deeper from you than from me. The return of this letter has been delayed a day, — I'll be a good boy & do so no more.

　　　　　　　　　　　　　　　　Your's sincerely,
　　　　　　　　　　　　　　　　　Chas Brown.
　　　　　　　　　　　　Hampstead. 5th Jany 1821.

[1] Apparently lost (see *Letters*, II, 363).

[2] Wholesale grocers, Haslam's employers since March 1819 (*Letters*, I, 75).

[3] Of December 21, now lost (George's reply of March 3, 1821, is quoted in number 108).

· 22 ·

TO JOSEPH SEVERN

Address: Joseph Severn Esqr / Poste Restante / à Rome / en Italie.

Postmarks: SO Hampstead 2py P Paid; 7 o'Clock Night JA 16 1821 Two PENNY P PAID; Paid; F 21 310; CHAMBERY; 5 FEB[BRAIO] (*twice*)

ALS: Harvard. Printed by Sharp, pp. 75–76, and, from a transcript in an unidentified hand, in *KC*, I, 200–201.

My dear Severn,   Hampstead. 15th Jany 1821.
    Your letter of 17th Decr arrived here last Tuesday the 9th.[1] I cannot dwell on the subject of it. Either I am shortly to receive more favorable accounts, or to suffer the bitterest news. I feel — and I cannot help it — all your attentions to my unhappy Keats as if they were shown to myself, — yet how difficult I have found it to return you thanks, — until this morning it has been utterly out of my power to write on so melancholy a story. He is present to me every where and at all times, — he now seems sitting by my side and looking hard in my face, — though I have taken the opportunity of writing this in company, — for I scarcely believe I could do it alone. So much as I have loved him, I never knew how closely he was wound about my heart. Mrs Brawne was greatly agitated when I told her of —— and her daughter — I don't know how, — for I was not present, — yet she bears it with great firmness, — mournfully but without affectation, — I understand she says to her mother, 'I believe he must soon die, — when you hear of his death, tell me immediately, — I am not a fool!' Poor girl! she does not know how desolate her heart will be when she learns there is no hope, and how wretched she will feel, — without being a fool. The only hope I have rests on Dr Clarke [2] not considering the case in so gloomy a light as you do, — for his kindness ask him to receive a stranger's thanks. But you and I well know poor Keats'

[1] See *Letters*, II, 361–363.
[2] Dr. (later Sir) James Clark (1788–1870), to whom Keats carried an introduction when he went to Rome (*Letters*, II, 327).

disease is in the mind,[3] — he is dying broken hearted. You know much of his grief, but do you know how George has treated him? I sit planning schemes of vengeance upon his head. Should his brother die, exposure and infamy shall consign him to perpetual exile. I will have no mercy, — the world will cry aloud for the cause of their Keats' untimely death, and I will give it. O Severn, nothing on my part could stop that cruel brother's hand, — indeed I knew not, till after he quitted us the second time for America, how cruel he had been. I have already written to him.[4] Not a penny remitted yet! — not a word in excuse for not remitting! — I authorise you to open my letters to Keats, — if he is still alive, you may perhaps cull out something to cheer him, — if not it is no matter, — but take care you do not open a letter with *my* hand writing on the address which *contains another* hand writing, — there *is* such a letter, & you can avoid opening it by peeping inside.[5] I hear your family are well, but I suppose you are by this time satisfied on that score. Take care of your own health. While attending a sick bed, I know, by experience, we can bear up for a long long time, — but in the end we feel it severely.

God bless you!
Your's sincerely,
Chas Brown.

[3] See number 12, n. 3.

[4] See the preceding letter.

[5] This letter from Fanny Brawne and the one mentioned in number 23 were buried with Keats unopened (Sharp, p. 92).

· 23 ·

TO JOSEPH SEVERN

Address: à Joseph Severn Esqr / Poste restante / à Rome / en Italie.

Postmarks: Hampstead NO 2py P Paid; 7 o'Clock Night JA 30 1821 T[WO P]ENNY P PAID; Paid; F 21 71; CHAMBERY; 19 FEBRAIO (*twice*)

ALS: Harvard. Printed by Sharp, p. 76.

My dear Severn,   Hampstead. 30th January 1821.
This morning a letter from Mr G. Keats, dated Louisville Novr 8th, addressed to Keats, arrived.[1] I took the liberty of opening it, for it might have contained notice of a present remittance. It however does not, tho' he says "I hope to be able to send you money soon." As for the rest he writes very cheeringly, — every one is in good health, — and there is this sentence, "By next Autumn I hope to live in a house and on ground of my own, with returns at least three times my expences; my gain now is double my expences." It appears the only hindrance against remitting is a perverse want of the circulating medium. Tell Keats all this, — as for the remainder of the letter, it is full of happy prospects and good hopes.

So far, my dear Severn, you may read to our poor friend, — if yet alive, — it may do him more good than any thing else. Though the above extracts are really culled from the Louisville letter, and tho' the whole of it is composed of the kindest expressions, my opinion of the writer remains unaltered. He is a canting, selfish, heartless swindler, and shall have to answer for the death of his brother, — if it must be so. Three days since we heard, by a letter from Dr Clarke to one of his friends,[2] that there was no hope, and no fear of a lingering illness. I have no comfort except in my indignant feelings against Mr G. Keats, — they keep me up. Miss B— does not actually know there is no hope, — she looks more sad every day. She has insisted on writing to him by this post, —

[1] See *Letters*, II, 356–357.
[2] To a Mr. Gray, January 13 (*KC*, I, 193–195).

take care of the letter, — if too late, let it be returned unopened, together with the one with *my* hand writing on the address & *her's* inside, to Mrs Brawne.[3] God bless you! take care of your own health, — so much do I feel for your kindness towards Keats, that I cannot bear the thought of your being a sufferer by it, and therefore regret I did not, at all hazards, & in spite of apparent difficulties, follow you both to Italy, & relieve you in your distressing attentions.

Your's truly & affectionately,
Chas Brown.

· 24 ·

TO THOMAS RICHARDS

Address: To / T. Richards Esqr / Ordnance Office / Tower.

Postmark: FE [. . .] 1821 (*another illegible*)

Endorsement: 1821 / C Brown / 18 Feb^y

ALS: Keats House, Hampstead. Printed (with a facing facsimile) in *Some Letters*, p. 3.

Dear Richards,　　　　　　　　　　　[February 18, 1821]

I am very sorry Scott was the man to fall.[1] I have heard nothing further.

On Friday, between 12 & 3 I will be with you.

Taylor rec^d a letter yesterday from Severn.[2] Keats could not exist longer than a fortnight, — it is all over. Severn is ill.

Your's most truly,
Chas Brown
Hampstead. Sunday.

Miss Brawne has just told me she has heard that the ball has been extracted, & that Scott is likely to recover.

[3] See the end of the preceding letter.

[1] See numbers 20, 26, 29. Scott was wounded by J. G. Lockhart's friend, Jonathan Henry Christie (1792?–1876), at Chalk Farm, near London, on the night of February 16. He died on February 27.

[2] Dated January 25, 26 (see *Letters*, II, 371–373). Keats died on February 23.

· 25 ·

TO JOHN TAYLOR AND J. A. HESSEY

Address: To / Mess[rs] Taylor & Hessey / 93 Fleet Street / London.

Postmarks: Hampstead NO; 7 o'Clock MR 7 1821 N[T]

ALS: Harvard. Printed in *KC*, I, 228–229.

Dear Sirs,   [March 7, 1821]

I found a letter from Severn [1] on my return home last night.
Poor Keats was yet alive & calm. I tell you this before you begin
the letter, that you may read on without fear. Tho' I talked so
much about wishing his sufferings at an end, I confess I blundered
thro' the letter in a horror lest my wishes should have been real-
ised. Comp[ts] to M[r] Haslam when you see him, — you can send the
enclosed to him, — for I do not want it before Saturday.[2]

Your's sincerely,
Cha[s] Brown
Hampstead.
Wednesday Morn[g]

On Saturday I shall want it, as M[r] Richards will be here.

· 26 ·

TO JOSEPH SEVERN [1]

Wentworth Place,
9th March, 1821.

My dear Severn, —

Upon the whole your letter ending 14th and 15th Feb. gave
comfortable news.[2] Keats, though without hope of recovery, was

---

[1] Of February 8, 14, 15 (see *KC*, II, 90–94).

[2] Hessey forwarded this note and Severn's letter to Haslam on March 9 (*KC*, I,
229).

[1] From Sharp, pp. 87–88. An outside page contained Hunt's letter to Severn of
March 8, first printed by Milnes, *Life*, II, 95–97, and subsequently in *Correspondence of Leigh Hunt*, I, 107–108, in Forman (1883), IV, 220–222, and by Sharp, pp.
86–87.

[2] See the preceding letter and notes.

calm; and your health was reinstated. Ever since I first read your account of his dreadful relapse, I have never been able to hope. It was then his death took place in my mind — and inwardly I mourned for him as lost. That he should have so long lingered, and in pain of body, and in irritation of mind, was a new distress. The hearing of his sufferings was worse than of his hopeless state. I have sat and eagerly wished and prayed to learn he was no more. Yet I was full of fears as I read over your letter, that my wishes had become realized. Let me have a lock of his hair — should it end as my despair tells me it will. Taylor and Haslam have had your letter. I expect it back again to-morrow, when Mr. and Mrs. Richards will be here. You refer to Keats's enemies, cursing them as his friend, — I suppose you mean the villains of the "Quarterly" and "Blackwood." I understand (as indeed Keats told me) how he intended to treat Lockhart.[3] Now Lockhart was violently attacked in the "London" by John Scott for his atrocious libels on Keats and others. Lockhart challenged Scott, but was (it seems to me) afraid to fight. From this affair arose a quarrel between Scott and one Christie, Lockhart's second. They fought near Chalk Farm, and Scott is killed. Keats never liked Scott, but in such a cause, how hard that he should die.[4] I tell you this, as it is in a degree part of Keats's history, and possibly you have not heard it. They are in good health next door. Mrs. Brawne saw your letter, but her daughter did not, from whom the worst is kept back, in (to my mind) a very ill-judged way. Meanwhile she fears perhaps worse than is supposed. I observe her gaiety is become boisterous, — fitt{er to make}[5] one start rather than laugh; and, at {times she} seems sinking under apprehension. {Leigh Hunt is} getting better,

[3] John Gibson Lockhart (1794–1854), author of the "Cockney School of Poetry" articles in *Blackwood's* (October, November 1817; July, August 1818). Neither in these letters nor in his "Life" of Keats does Brown tell how Keats "intended to treat" him, though in number 101 he names "revenge against . . . Lockhart" as a motive for writing the "Life." According to C. L. Finney, *The Evolution of Keats's Poetry* (Cambridge, Mass., 1936), II, 746, Keats's remark noted by Woodhouse, "If I die you must ruin Lockhart," was addressed to Brown. The "villain" of the *Quarterly Review*, for its attack on *Endymion* in the April 1818 issue, was John Wilson Croker (1780–1857), though Brown, like Keats, Shelley, Hunt, Woodhouse, and others, always believed him to be William Gifford (1756–1826), editor of the *Quarterly* (see numbers 98, 101, and *KC*, II, 59).

[4] See numbers 24, 29.

[5] Sharp says that the "third page is much torn at the width-margin." The emendations here are purely conjectural.

— he has been extremely {ill. He} asked to fill a page,[6] and you will be {glad to have it.} I heard of your friend Holmes [7] two days {ago. I went} about to meet him (hearing he was walking {with} Hunt on the heath), to ask what he had to {say} to you, and how your family are; but I {unfortunately} missed him. I have just been next {door, and} Mrs. Brawne sends her remembrance to you — Miss Brawne said not a word, and looked so incapable of speaking, that I regretted having mentioned my writing to you before her. I have so many dull thoughts coming across me at every line, that I confess it is an irksome task to write [even] to Severn. Yet had I anything more to say, I would not spare myself for your sake; for, my dear Severn, I feel towards you as a brother for your kindness to our brother Keats.

Yours most sincerely,
Chas. Brown.

P.S. — Dilke is at my elbow, and desires to be remembered to you.

· 27 ·

TO JOHN TAYLOR

Address: To / M͏ʳ Taylor, / N° 93 Fleet Street, / London.

ALS: Pierpont Morgan Library. Printed in *KC*, I, 230, and *Letters*, II, 380.

Dear Taylor,   [March 18, 1821]
      Read the enclosed [1] — it is all over. I leave to you the care of inserting his death in the papers,[2] — word it as *you* please, — you will do it better than I can, — in fact I can't do it.

---

[6] See n. 1 above.
[7] Edward Holmes (1797–1859), musician, composer, author, schoolfellow of Keats, and, according to Sharp, p. 126, one of Severn's "oldest and most intimate acquaintances."
[1] Severn's letter to Brown of February 27 (*KC*, II, 94–95).
[2] *The Times* printed a notice on March 23: "DIED. At Rome, on the 23d of Feb., of a decline, John Keats, the poet, aged 25." See *Letters*, II, 380n, and J. R. MacGillivray, *Keats: A Bibliography and Reference Guide* (Toronto, 1949), pp. 73–74, for notices in some other periodicals.

I have sent this sad news to Rice & Dilke & to Mr Abbey, — not to Haslam, for you can send him the letter. On second thoughts I will destroy the note to Mr Abbey, & write to Haslam to call & inform him of it.

Your's most truly,

Chas Brown.

Hampstead. Sunday. 18 March.

· 28 ·

TO WILLIAM HASLAM

Address: To / Mr Haslam / Messrs Frampton & Sons / Leadenhall Street / London.

ALS: Harvard. Printed in *KC*, I, 231, and *Letters*, II, 381.

Hampstead.

Dear Haslam,   Sunday. 18 March [1821].

It is all over, — I had a letter from Severn last night, telling me poor Keats died on 23^d Feb^y, — the letter is forwarded to Taylor.[1] I was about to write to Mr Abbey, to inform him of this sad news, but request you will without delay call on him for that purpose, — I say *without delay*, — lest Miss Keats should hear of it by the papers or thro' some other means. Taylor will show you the letter. I can't write more.

Your's most truly

Chas Brown.

[1] See the preceding letter.

· 29 ·

TO JOSEPH SEVERN

Address: à Joseph Severn Esqr / Poste restante / à Rome / en Italie.

Postmarks: F 21 130; ANGLETERRE; CHAMBERY; 9 APRILE

ALS: Harvard. Printed by Sharp, pp. 97–98.

Dear Severn,   Hampstead. 23^d March 1821.

From the first account you gave of Keats' relapse in December,[1] I never had a hope, as you may have perceived by the constant strain of despair in my letters. At last your news from bad to worse, from worse to worst, (I will confess it) became too distressing to make me congratulate myself he was yet alive. Had I been with him I could have borne all this with an equal mind, and — perhaps — as you did — hoped. Still when the blow actually came, I felt at the moment utterly unprepared for it. Then *she*,[2] — she was to have it told her; and the worst had been concealed from her knowledge, ever since your December letter. It is now five days since she heard it. I shall not speak of the first shock, nor of the following days, — it is enough she is now pretty well, — and thro'out she has shown a firmness of mind which I little expected from one so young, and under such a load of grief. To-morrow I shall be expecting the promised letter of mournful particulars;[3] and, what I am now most anxious about, a true account of your health. My solicitude seems transfered from him to you. Under Dr Clarke's friendly care every thing I feel confident will be done towards reinstating your strength of body as soon as possible. Ah, I write this idly, — for before you read these lines you will be well and cheerful, — you ought to be so. The hand of God took our friend away, and to God, in all his behests, am I ever resigned. I never have yet lost any one by the hand of man, — tho' that (you will say) is still by the will of God, but certainly with a difference, — I mean by a violent death, and know not how I could bear the

[1] See the opening of number 22.
[2] Fanny Brawne.
[3] See number 30, n. 1.

loss of any one in that manner, — but here, tho' enemies have preyed upon him, I am quite resigned, for those very enemies knew not what they were doing, whose heart they were breaking; — the highest praise that mortal can have belonged to Keats, — no one ever saw him without loving him, — no one could know him and treat him unkindly, — so convinced am I of this that I acquit his brother of malevolence. There is no more news from that same brother. I wrote to Haslam to call on Abbey, — and, if Abbey will permit it, Mrs Brawne & Mrs Dilke will call on Miss Keats. They are in mourning next door. As for myself, tho' such things are a mere form, I mourn for him, outwardly as well as inwardly, as for a brother. My last letter was dated either ten or fourteen days ago,[4] — one side had a letter from Hunt. Mr Richards called on your Sister [5] nine days ago, and gave the good account you had then written of yourself. When I hear you are cheerily again, she shall again hear of you. All our friends in common are well. John [6] Scott's death has made some noise, and seems to threaten Mr Christie & the seconds seriously,[7] — they certainly behaved most foolishly. What is melancholy, and almost incomprehensible, is that Mrs Scott advertises for a subscription.[8] Hazlitt is to be chief man of the London Magazine, — Hunt will likewise write for it, — he has put a stop to his Indicator.[9] I have not yet seen Haydon's Agony in the Garden, — it does not appear to create a very great enthusiasm, — some find fault with it for being a little melo-dramatic. It is surely a great mistake to repre-

---

[4] Number 26.

[5] Maria Severn (b. 1798?).

[6] *Written* John's.

[7] See numbers 24, 26. On March 2 Christie, his second, James Traill, and Scott's second, Peter George Patmore (1786–1855), were charged with "*Wilful Murder*," but at their trial, April 13, "The Jury, after a deliberation of 25 minutes, returned a verdict of — *Not Guilty*" (*Examiner*, March 4, April 15, pp. 143, 239).

[8] According to the *Dictionary of National Biography*, citing the *London Magazine*, 3 (1821): 359, Scott's "family was left penniless. A subscription was raised for their benefit, and Sir James Mackintosh, [Sir Francis Legatt] Chantrey, Horace Smith, and John Murray were on the committee." Byron contributed £30.

[9] Hazlitt was "chief man of the London" only in March and April. Apparently he declined its editorship when Taylor and Hessey bought the magazine from Robert Baldwin in May, and Taylor himself edited it until the end of 1824 (P. P. Howe, *The Life of William Hazlitt*, London, 1947, pp. 285–286, 295–296; Edmund Blunden, *Keats's Publisher*, London, 1936, p. 125). Hunt did not write in the *London* after 1820. His *Indicator* ran from October 13, 1819, to March 21, 1821.

sent Judas as a palpable villain in his countenance, which I understand he has done in the extreme, — he ought to possess a good
taking face, one whom an honest man might trust.[10] There! I
have given you a page of chit chat — such as it is. God love you,
my dear fellow,

and believe me ever

Your's sincerely,

Cha[s] Brown.

· 30 ·

FROM JOSEPH SEVERN

Address: Charles Brown Esq[r] / Wentworth Place / Hampstead /
or elswhere / London — / Inghilterra / from J Severn Rome —

Postmarks: ROMA; FPO AU 11 1821; 4 o'Clock AU 11 1821 EV

Endorsement: Joseph Severn

ALS: British Museum. Long extracts are printed in the *Athenaeum*,
August 23, 1879, p. 238, in Forman (1883), IV, 363–365, and (from
the *Athenaeum*) by Sharp, pp. 106–107.

My dear Brown   Rome July 17th 1821 —
    I begin to be sadly anxious to hear from you — I have written
to you — and about you in full 3 Letters [1] — yet the long looked
for answer does not come — I fear the Post is jilting me — You
see on the approach of the hot and dangerous weather I shall be

---

[10] "Christ's Agony in the Garden," on exhibition at the Great Room, 29 St.
James's Street, since March 1, was praised in the *Examiner*, March 4, pp. 141–142,
but called "a comparative failure, both in execution and probable effect" by Hazlitt
in the *London Magazine* for May (*Complete Works*, ed. P. P. Howe, XVIII, London,
1933, 141). A correspondent in *Blackwood's*, 10 (1821): 681, felt that it had "been
unjustly depreciated; for the figure of Judas is original, and so much the better for
verging towards grimace." Haydon himself wrote of it (*Autobiography*, ed. Malcolm
Elwin, London, 1950, p. 345), "I took a great deal of money at this exhibition, but
. . . it was wrong so to strain public enthusiasm. This particular picture was
severely handled. . . . it was the worst picture ever escaped from my pencil."

[1] On July 12 Severn told his father (ALS, Keats House, Hampstead) that he was
"most anxiously waiting answers to 3 Letters" written to Haslam, Brown, and
Taylor. Between the announcement of Keats's death (see number 27) and number
30 only one letter from Severn to Brown is extant (see n. 16 below), unless Severn's
unaddressed note of March 3 (Sharp, pp. 95–96) was written to him.

77

obliged to go away — and thats without placing a Stone on poor Keats's Grave. — All his papers I have sent to you — packed for safety in a Case of divers things belonging to my old friend and Master Mr Bond [2] — I chose this from many as the safest way — they will arrive in London about August or Septembre —

Mr Taylor has written me of his intention to write some remembrances of our Keats [3] — this is a kind thought of his — & I reverence this good man — nothing can be more interesting than to have the beautiful character of Keats — described and apreciated. — If it can be made known to the English his memory will be cherised by them — not more for his Genius than for his English nature — I begin to think of him without pain — all the harsh horror of his death is fast subsiding from my mind — sometimes a delightfull glance of his life about the time when I first knew him — will take possession of me and keep me speculating on and on to some passage in the Endymion — (I am fortunate to have a Copy of this — it is Dr Clarks) — the last also) here I find many admirers — (Aye — real ones) of his Poetry. — this is a very great pleasure to me — I have many most agreable conversations about him — but that only with Classical Scholars [4] — The "Lamia" is the greatest favorite —

I have been most sadly harrased about my picture for the Royal Academy [5] — for this reason. I have received notice to send

[2] William Bond, of 87 Newman Street, Oxford Street, "an engraver in the chalk manner" and a governor of the Society of Engravers, to whom Severn was apprenticed from 1808 to 1815 or 1816 (Sharp, pp. 6–8, 10; Samuel Redgrave, *A Dictionary of Artists*, London, 1874, p. 46).

[3] Taylor's letter to Severn of April 3 (now at Harvard) is printed by Sharp, pp. 99–100. Even earlier, on March 28, Taylor had written to his brother James (Bodurtha and Pope, p. 5), "I believe I shall try to write his life." The project is mentioned in numbers 33–35 and 45, but though its completion was still a possibility late in 1823 (numbers 48, 56) it never appeared. Taylor's grandniece Olive M. Taylor, in *London Mercury*, 12 (1925): 260, says that a "short account" was written, "but by the writer's own desire . . . was never published, as he thought it would give pain to people then living." In her youth she "read this manuscript, but . . . it has now been lost sight of."

[4] Because, as Severn says in number 104, Keats "was so profound in the Greek Mythology."

[5] "The Death of Alcibiades" (see numbers 32–34, and *KC*, I, 250–251, 262–263), which after its tardy arrival at the Academy was lost. Only in November, when a search was ordered "and a tin case, all bent double and without any direction or intimation as to whom it belonged, was found," did the Academicians see it — whereupon, following "influential recommendations" (see nn. 7, 11 below), they awarded Severn a pension of £130 annually for three years and paid his traveling

it by the 10th of August — now this is a month sooner than I expected — in the last letter I received from Mr Taylor — he had been so kind as to consult his friend Mr Hilton — who sent me word that I must send the picture in Septembre for the inspection of the Council — and I had in that view been certain — when a week since my Sister Maria wrote that she had seen a Notice in the Hall of the R.A. requiring the picture by the 10th of next Month — so that I have sent it unfinished without any delay — Now this has been an unfortunate point — more particularly as I am ill — out of spirits — and friendless — most of the kind fellows here — have gone to Naples or elsewhere [6] — so that I am left to brood over the loss of poor Keats's company and above [all] — his advice — You will recollect my dear Brown a mention of me (not with the greatest kindness or charity) at Mr Hiltons house.[7] — Keats spoke several times of this with very great pain from the fear that something of the same spirit might keep back my Pension — he told me it was one of the meanest said things he ever knew — and at the same time made me promise that I would explain to Mr Taylor — the whole affair — that I would write in such a manner as to persuade Mr Taylor to use his greatest influence in my behalf with Mr Hilton. — he said — "I am sure Hilton will take up your case on my account — now promise me you will do this — I have been long brooding over it and think this damned H— will keep you without your Pension — or try to do so — I know he will — so that this cu[r]sed dying of mine — will have been to your loss" — this was but a short time before his death I have written to Mr Taylor about my present concern but not of the affair past — I have still thought it better not mentioned — nor [8] would I say about it now but it seems hard I must run the risk of my picture's non-arrival in time — from the notice

---

expenses to Rome (Sharp, p. 113). For William Hilton (1786–1839), historical painter and a friend of most of the members of the Keats circle, see *KC*, I, lxxvi–lxxx.

   [6] *Written* eslwhere.

   [7] Actually at the house of Hilton's brother-in-law, the artist Peter De Wint (1784–1849), in 1819 (see Severn's account in Sharp, pp. 65–66). Severn credited Hilton with saying "many things to better my unfortunate cause" and having "done much to my final success" in winning the pension, but partly attributed his support to "the lesson Ke{ats} gave by leaving the table" in this incident (*KC*, I, 266; II, 233).

   [8] *Written* not.

sent me by Hilton. — Keats foresaw most keenly and his words come strong upon me. — How my Dear Brown shall I do in this — I can remember your mention of the same affair without names — so that I can ask your advice in this on a thing you have already thought on — My Picture may arrive in time — it is coming by the Kings Messenger — owing to the kindness of the British Consul here [9] — who is much interested about me — but even should it arrive in time its unfinished state may be an objection — so that every way I am unfortunate — yet not without hope — I have certainly gain'd much in my Painting from coming here — I have taken a liking to this Rome — which I cannot forego — I hope to God I may be able to stay here — until I have made my gain — as yet I have done little else than look — altho I have worked very hard — yet my only time has been occupied on this picture and illness and [10] — But dont say a word but that which is approved by your own judgment in this affair — Above all things pray answer my letters — tell me how the sad finish of poor Keats affected his enemies — tell me about his friends — tell me about Miss B — I have been once or twice almost writing to her — Only think my dear Brown I have known nothing from England since poor Keats's death — O yes one very kind letter from Mr Taylor — which I answered — Haslam does not write me

Respecting my money affairs — I have not yet exhausted the money gained here from my Miniatures — it will hold me out another 6 weeks or more — after I hope to get more the same way — for Lady Westmorland [11] has taken me up most warmly — she has written to Sr T. Lawrence about — and has on two or three occasions talked me into very good spirits. — I wait the answer to a favor from Mr Taylor — I have by me 34£ the remainder (after all payings) from the last 50£ — now if Mr Taylor will permit me

[9] John Parke (*The Royal Kalendar*, London, 1821, p. 142; *KC*, I, 251).

[10] A doubtful reading, though Severn ends his postscript in a similar way.

[11] Jane Huck-Saunders (1783?–1857), second wife of John Fane, tenth Earl of Westmorland (1759–1841), "a most superior woman," wrote Severn to his sister Sarah, June 6, 1821 (Sheila Birkenhead, *Against Oblivion*, London, 1943, p. 115), "having all the really English nobility in her and with much learning — she is about thirty-eight and is a very noble looking lady." She wrote twice to Sir Thomas Lawrence (1769–1830), president of the Royal Academy, about Severn's "The Death of Alcibiades," and Birkenhead, p. 116, thinks that it was "greatly due to her efforts that he was in fact awarded the pension."

to have this remain at the Bankers [12] until after my affair is settled — or the English arrived here — it will be [a] source of
comfort to me. as I may be taken ill. seriously — since I began to
write this I have consulted the expence of visiting Florence — and
find it will be too great — so that I must remain in Rome — I am
now stud[y]ing in the Vatican from the "Stanza di Raffaele." — I
hope to bring a great number of large studies to Englan[d] from
these wonderful pictures — I am likewise preparing for another
picture [13] — it is to be a single figure the size of Life — I shall rest
very much on this — I have likewise got in a small whole length
of my poor Keats [14] — it is from a recollection of him at your
house — I think the last time I saw him there — he was reading —
the book on his knee Remember me to Mrs Brawn — how I should
like to receive another letter from this kind Lady — present my
Respects to Miss B. — and speak of me to any of the fine fellows
who visit you — if they would write me it would be an English
treat — superior to your gorg[e]ous Coronation [15] have you seen
Mr Ewing [16] a Gentleman from Rome —

believe me your anxious
Friend — Joseph Severn

I conclude both Mr Taylor and your self are in the Country —
luxuriating in your English comforts — memember [17] to Mr Taylor — and pray him to write me to my last — how does Richards.
— pray him to write me — I would go without a dinner a day to
pay for Letters — it is well that Rome is such a delicious place for
my studies — or —

[12] The Torlonias.

[13] "Alexander the Great Reading Homer" (see number 37).

[14] This famous picture (Donald Parson, *Portraits of Keats*, Cleveland and New
York, 1954, p. 73) is now in the National Portrait Gallery.

[15] George IV was crowned on July 19.

[16] William Ewing, sculptor, who, as Severn said when he introduced him to
Brown by letter on May 2 (Forman, 1883, IV, 362–363; Sharp, p. 103n), "gave us all
the attention of an old friend, and . . . saw more of Keats than any one." He
called on Brown and dined with him twice in September (Sharp, pp. 112–113).

[17] Apparently Severn's own coinage for "remember me." At the end of number
109 he twice writes "rember."

· 31 ·

TO J. A. HESSEY

Address: To / Mr Hessey / Fleet Street.

ALS: Pierpont Morgan Library. Printed in *KC*, I, 261.

Dear Sir,   Hampstead. 24th July 1821.

I return with many thanks the two vols of Letters from Scotland, which you had the kindness to lend me. They would not have been detained so long, as I told you two months since, had I known what books belonged to your house in Mr Keats' trunk, as I wished to send them all together. The Ancient Drama and Palmerin of England I understand are your property, and therefore I can add those to the parcel.[1]

Mr Taylor promised me some time ago to let me speedily have the four Ms books in my hand writing of Mr Keats' poems. I suppose they are copied by this time. It will be a great gratification both to myself and {to} my friends to have them returned as soon as convenient; — pray ask Mr Taylor to have the goodness to forward them by the Coach.

Your's truly,
Chas Brown.

[1] Rollins (*KC*, I, 261nn) suggests that these books were *Letters from an Officer in the North of Scotland to His Friend in London*, 2 vols. (1815), and two items from Brown's "List of Mr John Keats' Books" (*KC*, I, 258): Dilke's *Old English Plays*, 6 vols. (1814–1815), and Robert Southey's translation of *Palmerin of England*, 4 vols. (1817).

· 32 ·

TO JOHN TAYLOR

Address: To / Mr Taylor / 93 Fleet Street / London.

ALS: Pierpont Morgan Library. Printed in *KC*, I, 263–264.

Wentworth Place.

Dear Sir,   12th Aug^t [1821] Sunday.

Yesterday evening I received a letter from Mr Severn.[1] It is dated Rome 17th July. Among other matters he menti{on}s his great anxiety about his Picture. He says you had been so kind as to consult with your friend Mr Hilton respecting the time of its arrival for the inspection of the Council, and that he understood *September*, and then adds — "when a week since my Sister Maria wrote that she had seen a notice in the Hall of the R A requiring the Picture by the 10th of August." Fearful of a mistake in your letter, — and, at all events, resolved if possible to be on the safe side, — he intrusted it without delay to the King's Messenger. The worst is that in his hurry he has sent it in an unfinished state. He seems much worried at the idea of its not arriving in time; — and in the midst of his perplexities he is not in a good state of health. I shall write to him by Tuesday's post,[2] and if you have any thing to say on this subject I shall be happy to send it. He desires me to present his remembrance to you and to request {you} will have the goodness to answer his last letter, the subject of which he talks of as another source of anxiety.[3] He {i}ntends to remain at Rome during the bad season, not deeming it prudent with his means to travel elsewhere, tho' he fears he may yet suffer more in his health.

About three weeks ago (I think) I sent to Mr Hessey the books he had the kindness to lend me, together with the Old Drama and Palmerin of England which you mentioned as some of those books which belonged to you.[4] Have they arrived safe?

I have again to request that the Mss in my hand writing of

[1] Number 30.
[2] See the next letter.
[3] Taylor replied to Severn late in August (Sharp, p. 107).
[4] See the preceding letter.

Keats' poetry may at your earliest convenience be returned. They would prove, especially at this time, most gratifying to me, and to one more,[5] otherwise I would not urge the Copyist [6] to finish them.

Your's truly,
Cha[s] Brown.

· 33 ·

TO JOSEPH SEVERN [1]

[August 13, 1821]

*   *   *

As affairs stand, look to the worst. Believe that your pension is lost,[2] and if the contrary happens to be the case, it will be a joy. And supposing it to be lost, let it not fret you. Take heart, and laugh at an irreparable misfortune. I would do so were it my own case, better than if it were my friend's. Place your regret chiefly on the disappointment of others, and, surely, with your abilities, you can put your shoulder cheerfully to the wheel, and retrieve the loss. I am a fit one to give you comfort on this score. Over and over again have I to Keats and others lamented your reliance on a band of Academicians, where there is nothing but envy, jealousy, intrigues, and squabbles, in preference to the pursuit of the art on your own account, independently, and at freedom from all conventional laws. The English like to be flattered, but in fact they are not enthusiasts in art, — they neither understand it, nor are they generous enough to reward a man during his life. Can you not read a lesson in the fate of our unhappy Keats? The English are too proud and selfish to acknowledge living merit in art and literature. If you continue to study portraits, both in min-

[5] Presumably Fanny Brawne.

[6] Perhaps a slighting reference to Richard Woodhouse, "at whom Brown . . . [took] one of his funny odd dislikes" in September 1819 (*Letters*, II, 180).

[1] From Sharp, pp. 108–110. Though undated by Sharp, the first part of this letter (a reply to number 30) was almost certainly written on the night of August 13, after Brown had unsuccessfully busied himself "from house to house" seeking Severn's picture (number 34).

[2] See number 30, n. 5.

iature and in oil, crowds will be led by vanity to your door, and you be rich and at ease in your mind; but if you were to paint a work like the "Transfiguration," [3] lo! now — you must be poor in purse, and (what is worse) poor in spirit, and kick your heels in a great man's antechamber, and be fevered thro' your life with broils and anxieties. Look to facts. Who has succeeded in historical painting since Sir J. Reynolds? None, save West, and he most undeservedly.[4] I repeat, the English understand it not. Think of this, my dear Severn — think of the choice you are now to make. Do not let hopes destroy your happiness. What was Sir T. Lawrence's advice? [5] Truly, it was wise. You are now the best miniature-painter we have. This is no compliment; you know it yourself. Still, you need not debar yourself from the pursuit of the historical, — only make portraits your sheet-anchor for profit, and when your purse is swollen, sit down for awhile to the other. I could write a quire full on this theme — but enough.

14th Aug. — If my memory does not deceive me, I have sent three letters since I received your last; one of them had a page filled by Leigh Hunt; none of them, however, is of late date.[6] Mr. Ewing has not yet called, nor sent the letter from you which, I understand, is in his hands; I shall be glad to see him. You asked Mr. Taylor to consult with me about Keats's epitaph — or, I believe, to let you know what epitaph I wished. He did not allow me to see that letter for a long time; I then talked to him about it, and he behaved as if he thought it was no concern of mine, changing the topic as soon as he could. It was not till the other day that I discovered he bears me no goodwill for claiming, in return for MSS. and information, a sight of his memoir before it went to press. I confess I could not trust him entirely; now and then he is a mere bookseller — somewhat vain of his talents, and consequently self-willed. My anxiety for poor Keats's fame compelled me to make this request; for, in my opinion, Taylor neither

---

[3] Raphael's painting, in the Vatican.

[4] Sir Joshua Reynolds (1723–1792) and the American-born painter Benjamin West (1738–1820), the first and second presidents of the Royal Academy.

[5] Severn had called on Lawrence just before he left England (Sharp, pp. 48, 50).

[6] Numbers 23, 26 (containing "a page filled by Leigh Hunt"), and 29 are the three most recent known letters from Brown to Severn before number 33, though two of them were written before Brown received Severn's letter of February 27. See number 30, n. 1.

comprehended him nor his poetry. I shall always be the first to acknowledge Taylor's kindness to Keats; but towards me his conduct has been ungracious and even unmannerly. Reynolds is the secret spring; it is wished he should shine as the dear friend of poor Keats — (at least I suspect so) — when the fact is, he was no dear friend to Keats, nor did Keats think him so.[7] This, however, might be borne, but there are other points where I fear Taylor may do Keats an injustice — not knowingly, but from the want of knowing his character. He has sent no answer to my yesterday's note.[8] Either by the next or the next but one post I will write again, and give you my ideas of an epitaph for our beloved Keats.[9] The health of every one of your family is excellent, but they are sadly perplexed about this R.A. business. Mr. Bond sends his remembrances, and desired me to say his brother is in better health, and will soon arrive here from Paris.[10] Richards is well, and asks continually about you; I shall insist upon his writing. I thank you for intrusting me with Keats's papers — the sight of them will renew many painful thoughts. My next-door neighbours are quite well; Miss Brawne had been growing (I thought alarmingly) thin, but of late she has looked more cheerful and better. I delivered your messages to them, and they sent some of the same nature. Do not imagine I am in a peevish mood about Taylor; to give my aid to a thing of so momentous a description as the fame of Keats without being satisfied on every point is more than I can do in duty to the memory of the dearest friend I ever had. Still I promised Taylor my aid, provided I might be allowed to approve or condemn in particular passages, which he assented to, and praised my solicitude; but lately I have heard that having got the chief things from me, he resolved to laugh at my opinion. I am afraid it will be made a job — a mere trading job — and *that*

---

[7] There is ample testimony in *Letters* that Reynolds was a "dear friend to Keats," who, however, as early as December 1817 named him among the "acquaintance [that] will never do for me," and in 1820 no doubt included him in the tirade against "tattlers, and inquisitors" who disapproved of Fanny Brawne (*Letters*, I, 193, and II, 293; see also *KC*, I, cxx, 156).

[8] The preceding letter, written two days earlier.

[9] See number 35.

[10] William Bond's brother was named John. Possibly he was Henry John Hayles Bond (1801–1883), later a professor of physic at Cambridge, who about this time was a medical student in Paris.

I will lend no hand to, further than what I have done. You must feel with me that I should be culpable, as Keats's friend, even to run a risk. If Taylor choose, on my conditions (which he himself has approved of) my assistance will be given most willingly. I heard yesterday that Clark is thinking of writing a memoir [11] — to tell the truth, I would rather join him, but at present I am (conditionally) bound. God bless you, my dear Severn.

Yours truly,
Chas. Brown.

· 34 ·

TO THOMAS RICHARDS

Address: To / Thoˢ Richards Esqʳ / Storekeeper's Office / Ordnance Department / Tower.

Postmarks: Hampstead NO; 12 o'Clock AU 16 1821 Nⁿ

Endorsement: Mʳ Brown

ALS: Keats House, Hampstead. Printed in *Some Letters*, pp. 4–6.

Wentworth Place.

My dear Richards,   15ᵗʰ Augᵗ 1821.

On Saturday evening I received a letter from Severn, dated Rome 17ᵗʰ July.[1] He was harrassed and perplexed about his picture, and not very well in health. Mʳ Hilton sent him word, thro' Mʳ Taylor, that his picture, in order to obtain the pension, must be in the Academy on some particular day in September. Severn therefore worked and laid his plans accordingly. All at once his Sister wrote him word that the latest day appointed for its reception was 10ᵗʰ Augᵗ. Poor fellow! he instantly despatched it, partly unfinished, for London by the King's Messenger, and time enough for the purpose, but some untoward chances have detained the Messenger or the Picture, so that it had not arrived on 13ᵗʰ, when

---

[11] Charles Cowden Clarke, who had written on Keats in a letter to the *Morning Chronicle*, July 27 (see MacGillivray, *Keats*, p. 101), did not produce a memoir until January 1861, when his "Recollections of Keats" appeared in the *Atlantic Monthly* (7: 86–100).

[1] Number 30.

I was busying myself from house to house about it. It is feared that from this circumstance he never can get the pension, which is £130 per ann: for three years, & his travelling expences to Italy and back. Public bodies never make allowances, — they talk of precedents, — say a rule is a rule, — and pass on to the next, glad enough in all probability of an excuse for illiberality, as it may tend to the advantage of one of their more especial creatures. Now, Richards, write to Severn as soon as you can, to cheer him. I did what I could yesterday, & will try again next post.[2] My plan is (supposing the worst) to make him hate all Academies, to excite his spirit of independence, and to urge him to make portrait painting, in which he excels, his sheet anchor, leaving the historical in the back ground, as a study that will keep him poor all his life, and, at the best, only give him a good name when he shall be nothing but a name. We all know how difficult it is to stifle young ambition, but I have tried to do so, and a second in my cause may avail much. I want him to be reconciled & quiet in mind after this cruel disappointment. He complains seriously of the neglect of his friends in England, and, among the rest, your name is not forgotten. Mark that! Write, an you love him, with all speed. Keats' papers, in the destruction after his death,[3] were fortunately saved, and Severn has confided them to my care; they are not yet arrived. This I am rejoiced at. I gave him a hint that I feared Mr Taylor's Memoir would be a bookseller's job, — this I wrote yesterday. Indeed I have great reason to think so, from what has been buzzed abroad since I saw you. It appears that any interference on my part is conceived to be ridiculous. Putting these rumours together with Mr Taylor's late conduct I find my eyes beginning to open. Still he has my *conditional* promise of assistance, to which I must abide, but I guess he will not accept it under such conditions, *believing he has got out of me every thing essential for his purpose.* So I hear. My article [4] was returned last

---

[2] See numbers 33, 35.

[3] Roman law, as Severn told Mrs. Brawne on January 11 (Sharp, p. 78), required "that every individual thing, even to the paper on the walls in each room the patient has been in, shall without reserve be destroyed by fire." See Sharp, pp. 95–96, and *KC*, I, 196, 223, and II, 94.

[4] Probably one of the articles later printed in Colburn's *New Monthly Magazine*. In a letter to his father, January 31, 1822, Taylor discusses "the namby pamby of Colburn . . . [which] is supported by only such Writers as are scarcely able to get

night with a note from Mr *Hessey*, saying "it will not *do*", — I quote his words & the dash into the bargain; you shall read it. It may be bad enough, but I'll take my oath it's worth better treatment. Oh! here is Severn's address, — à Joseph Severn Esqr, Poste Restante, à Rome, en Italie. Your friend, Mr Peachy,[5] did me the favour of a call; we chatted for a long time, but he never once hinted at residing here, so I conjecture he has changed his mind; there would have been an impropriety in my proposing it to him. I am told that Clarke is thinking of writing a memoir of Keats.[6] Give my Comp^ts to Mrs Richards & my love to the Children, & believe me,

Your's most truly,
Chas Brown.

· 35 ·

TO JOSEPH SEVERN [1]

[August 21, 1821]

*   *   *

When I mentioned to you my fears about Mr. Taylor's memoir, I omitted to make known the original cause of those fears. It was this. Immediately on receipt of your letter announcing poor Keats's death, almost in the same newspapers where there was a notice of his death, even before Mrs. Brawne's family and myself had got our mourning, in those very newspapers was advertised "speedily will be published, a biographical memoir of the late John Keats, &c.," and I, among others, was applied to by Reynolds to collect with all haste, papers, letters, and so on, in order to assist Mr. Taylor.[2] This indecent bustle over (as it were) the

---

an engagement with us," among whom he names "Charles Brown of Hampstead, an Acquaintance, but in spite of that rejected by us" — Olive M. Taylor in *London Mercury*, 12 (1925): 264.

[5] Perhaps James Peachey, solicitor, of 17 Salisbury Square, Fleet Street, a schoolfellow of Keats (Robert Gittings in *TLS*, January 17, 1958, p. 36).

[6] See the end of the preceding letter.

[1] From Sharp, pp. 111–112.

[2] See numbers 30, 33. The announcement appeared in the *New Times*, March 29, April 9, and in the *Morning Chronicle*, June 4 (Bodurtha and Pope, p. 7n).

newly covered grave of my dear friend shocked me excessively. I told Mr. Taylor it looked as if his friends had been collecting information about his life in expectation of his death. This, indeed, was the fact. I believe I spoke warmly, and probably gave offence. However, as I was jealous of my own feelings upon such a subject, I took the precaution to sound those of Hunt, Dilke, and Richards, who were all equally hurt with myself at such an in-decorous haste. I then came to this conclusion, that Messrs. Taylor and Reynolds, who could show such a want of feeling at such a moment, ought not to be confided in by me unreservedly, and since I came to that conclusion, I have had cause to believe myself correct. I will not consent to be a party in a bookseller's job. Perhaps it may turn out otherwise, but in justice to the memory of Keats, I dare not run a risk. Mr. Taylor expected to be trusted implicitly, and takes dudgeon. Now, on such a point I know of none whom I could trust implicitly. He says no one understood Keats's character so well as himself; if so, I who knew him tolerably well, and others of his friends, greatly mistook him, judging from what has dropped from Mr. Taylor — for he is one from whom things *drop* — he cannot utter them boldly and hon-estly, at least he never did to me, and I have heard Keats say the same of him. What I have written, I have written, and I leave you to judge if you think me right or wrong. I rejoice you sent *me* the papers, and under the circumstances, I think you will rejoice likewise. He is welcome, according to *my* promise, to any infor-mation I can afford, provided he, according to *his* promise, allows me a voice on the occasion. In my opinion, Taylor would rather decline the information. If you differ from me in my claim of having a voice, still I have Dilke, Richards, and Hunt on my side. Hunt has some poems, &c., of Keats, and offers them unreservedly to *me*, stipulating, however, that Taylor must not be possessed of them without the memoirs passing under my eye. Why should it be denied to me? Any sort of hesitation will make the business suspicious. Hunt was very kind to Keats last summer, and I cannot forget it. If Keats could not like his wife,[3] that is nothing to the purpose. . . .

[3] Keats wrote to Reynolds, September 21, 1817 (*Letters*, I, 162), "What Evenings we might pass with him [Hunt], could we have him from Mrs H."

I [4] had written thus far on 21st, expecting every minute a knock by Hunt at the door with an epitaph for Keats. He did not come till the evening, and then with an apology, promising, however, to let me have it on the following post-day (Friday last), and then he again disappointed me. I can wait no longer, but am resolved to send you this letter without it. Why, you will ask, set Hunt about this affair? The truth is, I have tried, but can do nothing for the epitaph to my own satisfaction, and Hunt is one, if I am not mistaken, who could word it with feeling and elegance. He has sadly disappointed me, but the trouble he is in must be his excuse. I like your idea of the lyre with broken strings. Mr. Taylor sets his face against that, and against any words except what Keats himself desired to be put on his tombstone, viz.: "Here lies one whose name was writ in water." This I contend is scarcely proper, insomuch as an epitaph must necessarily be considered as the act of the deceased's friends and not of the deceased himself. Still, in obedience to his (Keats) will, I would have his own words engraven there, and *not* his name, letting the stranger read the cause of his friend's placing such words as "Here lies one, &c.," somewhat in the following manner: — "This grave contains all that was mortal of a young English poet, who, on his death-bed, in bitter anguish at the neglect of his countrymen, desired these words to be engraven on his tomb-stone: 'HERE LIES ONE WHOSE NAME WAS WRIT IN WATER.' " [5] Something expressive of this, and surmounted by your emblem of a Grecian lyre, I think would be

---

[4] This section was written after Hunt "disappointed" Brown on Friday, August 24, and probably just before the next post left for Rome, on Tuesday, August 28.

[5] On the inscription see numbers 37, 43, 45, and *KC*, I, 242, 250, 252, 273, and II, 91. About this time Taylor wrote to Severn (Sharp, p. 107), "I can conceive none better than our poor friend's melancholy sentiment . . . . It is very simple and affecting, and tells so much of the story that none need be told." Severn, however, as Brown later regretted (number 112), followed Brown's advice and, up to a point, his wording for the stone that was erected in 1823: *"This Grave / contains all that was Mortal, / of a /* YOUNG ENGLISH POET, / *Who, / on his Death Bed, / in the Bitterness of his Heart, / at the Malicious Power of his Enemies, / Desired / these Words to be engraven on his Tomb Stone /* 'Here lies One / Whose Name was writ in Water.' " To Rollins' collection of "sources" for Keats's words (*KC*, II, 91n) may be added Shakespeare's *Henry VIII*, IV.ii.45–46, "Men's evil manners live in brass; their virtues / We write in water" (suggested by H. W. Garrod in *TLS*, May 27, 1949, p. 353), and Philip Massinger's *The Maid of Honour*, V.ii: ". . . all that I had done, / My benefits, in sand or water written, / As they had never been, no more remember'd!" (*Plays*, ed. William Gifford, London, 1805, III, 99).

proper. But mind, I am not satisfied with *my* wording, and therefore pray delay the epitaph for a while. If, however, you are of the same opinion as Mr. Taylor, I give up mine instantly. I find it a difficult subject. Two or three days ago Richards called. He and family are very well. He was in the midst of a long letter to you.

*   *   *

· 36 ·

TO THOMAS RICHARDS

Address: T. Richards Esqr / Storekeeper's Office / Ordnance Department / Tower.

Postmarks: Hamp[stead]; 12 o'Clock NO 16 1821 Nⁿ

Endorsement: Mr Brown

ALS: Keats House, Hampstead. Printed in *Some Letters*, pp. 7–8.

Hampstead.

Dear Richards,   15 Nov 1821.

I would rather not, I thank you. If it is all the same to your worship, I will wait on you any day you please, (the Lord's day excepted,) *after* the business is over,[1] and when Mrs Richards is as well as can be expected. Truth is I prefer being out of the way, — M^{rs} I A Brown to wit.[2]

Hunt & his wife (the latter very weak & ill from blood-spitting) & their six children, left Hampstead yesterday for Pisa. The name of the Vessel is the Jane.[3] He left a message for you, and a present,

---

[1] Presumably the birth of Brown's godson, Sidney Richards, who in July 1824 (number 59) was "going on for three years old."

[2] M. B. Forman (*Some Letters*, p. 7n) thinks Brown is referring "to his wife." A better guess is his sister-in-law, Mrs. John Armitage Brown, though the meaning is still unclear.

[3] For the record, the children were Thornton (b. 1810), John (b. 1812), Mary Florimel (b. 1814), Swinburne (b. 1816?), Percy Shelley (b. 1817), and Henry Sylvan (b. 1819). The *Jane* sailed on November 15, but was forced by bad weather to put in at Dartmouth on December 22, whereupon the Hunts spent nearly five months in Plymouth, boarded a second ship, the *David Walter*, on May 13, 1822, and reached Pisa at the beginning of July.

both which are in my custody. I thought it a melancholy sight to see the whole of the family stuffed into a Hackney Coach, in search of a more favourable climate and more favourable friends, though I believe they will meet with both those good things at Pisa.

My house still remains unlet.[4] In all probability I shall be detained in England till March. No, — my poor boy is kept aloof from me by his obstinate Mother. I must teach myself to be content with imagining how good a father I should be, if circumstances would permit it.

Will your Son [5] come to my house, during the difficulties of your family?

Hunt's *message* & *present* need not be riddles to you. The first is an explanatory compliment, and the other is a Napoleon-Medal, — one of them, at least, is valuable.

I have no letter from Honble G Lamb,[6] — no news from Campbell,[7] — and I utterly give up the whole g{ang} now & for evermore. So I care not about putting {my} *design* into execution aga{inst} any of the aforesaid gang{ — it is} not worth while, I have d{one with} them, — I could snarl & b{ite,[8] but} I'll do neither, and then r{un} away, — I drive my disapp{ointment} to the winds, — and will lay {me} down in the sun at Pisa.

Your's sincerely,

Chas Brown.

[4] Brown had advertised it, "To be LET, on Lease," in *The Times* of October 26 (Richardson, *The Everlasting Spell*, pp. 51, 237). See number 41.

[5] Thomas Richards, Jr. (b. 1810).

[6] George Lamb (1784–1834), politician and writer. Since he managed Drury Lane with Byron and Douglas Kinnaird in 1815–1816 and urged Moore to make a play of *Lallah Rookh* in 1821, possibly Brown here refers to new negotiations for the production of *Otho*.

[7] Thomas Campbell (1777–1844), at least nominally the editor of the *New Monthly Magazine*.

[8] *3 Henry VI*, V.vi.77, "That I should snarl and bite and play the dog."

· 37 ·

FROM JOSEPH SEVERN

Address: Charles Brown Esqr / Wentworth Place / Hampstead / London / Inghilterra

Postmarks: ROMA; FPO JA 22 1822; 4 o'Clock JA 22 1822 EV

Endorsement: Joseph Severn

ALS: British Museum. Extracts are printed in the *Athenaeum*, August 23, 1879, p. 239, in Forman (1883), IV, 367, and (from the *Athenaeum*) by Sharp, p. 119.

My dear Brown   Rome 1st Jany 1822
    Pardon me that I have not written before — I have been so low in spirits with the Academy Affair [1] and so much occupied in Painting to keep away these Blue devils — that I could not lift a pen to you. — But now I do it with heart — I know you will be most glad at my pension coming to me here. — So I shall have the delight to meet you here? — you are really coming? — God I shall look at you as another Appollo Belvedere. — if you come soon you will do best to come on to Rome. — but not unless you could be here by March or April. — you would come to the fountain head first and see the noble things here in a beatiful Spring. — but I suppose you wont. — then I will hope to meet you in Florence. — it is my intention to visit Venice in the next Summer [2] — I hope by May to compleat my Alexander [3] — so that it will be June before I can be in Florence — and I should recon [?] you will be there about that time as my Sisters letter tells you will set off soon. —
    Why what a capital idea this is of yours. — you will satisfy all that Classical appetite of yours and live as the saying is dirt cheap. — I think it will be a 4 in hand change for you. — 100£ a year will be to you all the comforts you have in England — and you

---

[1] See numbers 30, 32–34.
[2] He did not go (see number 45).
[3] "Alexander the Great Reading Homer" (see the fourth paragraph below). Severn did not complete it until January 1824.

will be living in the midst of the Arts — where every thing bends to them. — I take it to be an expensive thing to have many servants and an open house — perhaps more so than in England. — the reason is every kind of hiring is enormously dear — they will serve a capital dinner from the best Hotel at 6s a head I would not return on any score. — I find such quietness — such time and desire. since every thing help it — to proceed in my occupations. — that I shall ever bless the day I came here. — We have not many Newspapers — or books — but what of that. — I rather think it an advantage to be out of that damn'd paper war carried on by the Newspapers — in London — it comes to nothing — I think of it with quite a whiss in my ears — In Rome we get all the main points — but they come so quietly — that you may judge them fairly — without becoming a Ranter [4] — We have famous society if you want to go into it. — that nasty stiffneck Rank is laid aside here. — and all associate together —

I have received a Copy of the Monody on Keats.[5] — I find many beauties in it — but is it not a pity so much beauty should be scattered about — without the balancing of lights and shades — or the oppositions of Colours. — in this poem there is such a want of repose. — you are continually longing to know what he will be at. — It gave me great pleasure as a tribute to poor Keats's memory. —

The picture of poor Keats. — is in a fair way — I have put in your accurate drawing — but I seem to want that beautiful Cast of him there is in London [6] — I cannot finish — without — and have named it amongst many things to be sent out to me —

I think now my dear Brown I am really advancing — my picture of Alexander is 9 Feet by 7. — the figure is a little larger than life. — an English nobleman is on a treaty for it — I dont know his name — but if I can sell and clear the way I shall improve greatly — for I have in contemplation to paint a large picture. —

---

[4] A doubtful reading. One word is written over another ("Politician"?) in such a way that both are virtually illegible.

[5] Shelley had sent him *Adonais* from Pisa on November 29, 1821 (*Letters of Shelley*, ed. Jones, II, 366).

[6] For Severn's picture see the end of number 30. Brown's "accurate drawing" is probably the pencil drawing of Keats that he made at Shanklin in July 1819 (*Letters*, II, 135; Parson, *Portraits of Keats*, pp. 107–108). The "Cast" is the life mask executed by Haydon late in 1816 (Parson, p. 4).

"Ah well a day" — says my well-wishing friend. — "he has that large picture still upon him well-well. — I gave him my adavice." [7] — I know you did and I had begun very chearily to paint my Miniatures — I had painted 2 whe[n] lo! and behold — my pension arrives — You see my dear Brown it will be expected from me to paint a grand Historical picture — whilst I am here — with the 500£ given I can do it. — and another strong reason is the immence desire I have to do it. — I remember once telling you and you told me to keep it to myself which I have done [8] it was (and is) my intention to paint a Series of [9] English pictures — 4 in number.[10] — illustrating the rise and power of England. — I am now painting in my "minds eye" [11] — these pictures. — and shall hope before I leave Rome to produce this 1st and large sketches of the others (— in the Rubens style) — You see what my notion has been — to unite the Composition and pure expression of Raffaele to Romantic Subjects — it has been done in Poetry with great success — but not in Painting. — it will be an easier way — to encouragement — and to the teaching painting to the "mob" — I have had this many Years in mind. — but never until I saw the Divine Frescoes of Raffaele — was I able to collect my stragling ideas — I am now far advanced in my 1st Composition — you will remember the subject — "The Britons proclaiming Arthur — King — when the Romans took their final leave of Britain." — I have the Romans (unarmed & crest fallen) crossing to their ships — in the distance. — whilst the Britons breaking the line rush to Arthur with Crowns of Oak — and make him King. — Arthur is comanding a Roman Officer to release an Old man from Chains — the Roman is sulkily delivering the key The Druids are sacrificing with cutting the Myseltoe — and imploring the protectors of Heaven — In the foreground also I have a Briton breaking the Roman standard under his foot. — You see this will be a fine subject to paint here. — The Britons in skins with their Golden

[7] See numbers 33, 34.

[8] The words "and you . . . done" are inserted above the line.

[9] *Written* of of.

[10] Severn described one of the four in a letter of February 19, 1821 (Birkenhead, *Against Oblivion*, p. 108): "the Golden Age of England, the Court of Queen Elizabeth, with portraits of all the distinguished folk of her time, Sir W. Raleigh, Shakespeare, etc. etc."

[11] *Hamlet*, I.ii.185.

Hair — will make a fine contrast with the Romans — in Armour — and with Black hair. — Now my good friend I bore you with all this — because I want to have your advice and learning. — Tell me any Facts about Arthur. — I know he is a doubtful hero — but I take him as the hero of English antiquity. — it is supposed by many he began to reign about the time the Romans left. — Another thing I have to trouble you — is this — I lay my scene at Dover. — as the best known — and thought to be where the Romans landed. — Now as you come through there if you would just make me a Sketch of the shore with the Sea to the left with the Castle if possible. — slight — just to give me an idea for I never was there. — I will be very thankfull to you for it — so now farewell. — I shall not send [12] a Drawing of poor Keats I intend for you [13] but reserve it until I have the happiness to meet you

Your obligd friend   Joseph Severn

bring all the books you will want — for English Books are most scarce and valuable here — I gave a Dinner on the 1st to 12 English Artists — the consequence of my Pension — they are all noble fellows — we had a jolly set out — there are 25 here. — Richards did not write me [14] — remember me to him —

The Grave stone is advanced but not up yet — I cannot well recollect the Greek Lyre so that they wait for the Drawg from London [15] — I liked the Inscription much — and it shall be done exacttly. — [16]

I have some hair of our poor Keats and have been waiting for a friend to bring it to London. — I have thought of a little conceit. — as a present to poor Miss Brawn — To make a Broach in form of my Greek Lyre — and make the strings of poor Keats's hair — but I cannot find any workman to do it — [17]

---

[12] *Written* sent.

[13] Probably a copy of the deathbed portrait (Parson, *Portraits of Keats*, pp. 65, 67–68). Brown himself later made a copy, which he hung in the Plymouth Institution in 1836 (see numbers 102, 111) and which Carlino subsequently gave to Alfred Domett (Sharp, pp. 262–263).

[14] See the end of number 35.

[15] Severn told Haslam on May 5, 1821 (*KC*, I, 242), that the "Greek Lyre . . . was Keats's idea a long time back in England — Brown will find a drawing of mine in his Copy of Endymion — done at Keatss request."

[16] See number 35, n. 5.

[17] "The brooch was ultimately made, though it was never given to Fanny Brawne. In 1861 Severn gave it as a wedding present to his daughter Mary." It is now at

· 38 ·

TO THOMAS RICHARDS

Endorsement: Mr Brown

ALS: Keats House, Hampstead. Printed in *Some Letters*, pp. 9–11.

Dear Richards,   Hampstead. 24th March 1822.
    Your kind offer to take charge of my child gave me no more than a sincere feeling of thankfulness till within the last week. Whether I accept it or not, is yet undetermined; and do you and Mrs Richards reflect upon it more deeply than perhaps you have done hitherto, before you clench the offer. Nothing is on my mind against leaving him with you except the losing of his company, and I am unwilling to be quite solitary when abroad. At all events I shall look forward to having him in Italy in the space of three or four years; — either sent with some family, or carried thither by myself. It is almost entirely on account of the child that I waver in my determination to take him with me now; for it appears to me it will be more advantageous for him to be with you, and your children, than with me alone, — tho', had any other person said so, I should have denied it, having so good an opinion of my own governorship. Without a compliment I say you and your wife are the only couple to whom I would intrust him. Let him be like Tom [1] and I am satisfied. As for the expences, we must agree about that as we can, taking care that you are fully covered, — in this I cannot conceive a hindrance. I will mention what, I think, are the chief objections against your taking him. 1st Abby; — she may annoy you; she was here a few days since, and rather *entreated* I would take him abroad. I told her I either should do so, or leave him with your family. She willingly agreed to the alternative, but still preferred his being under my own controul and management. In all this, I confess, she astonishes me. Her idea is to advertise for a place abroad and follow me; this I explained was stark folly. We

---

Keats House (*Keats House, Historical and Descriptive Guide*, 4th edn., revised, Hampstead, n.d., p. 20).
  [1] Thomas Richards, Jr.

must, as far as possible, *tie* down her consent, — perhaps by a witness to her agreement with you and me, before I go, but without
letting her know our purpose, for that would answer no end with
one so ignorant, and to let her know our purpose can do her
neither a kindness nor a good, nor the concealment an injury.
2nd Your feeling of responsibility. On that score you may be quite
at ease. If I hear of his death, the news would not be mixed with
any painful reflections against yourself, even without a word of
explanation on your part. If, on my return, I find him with a
wooden leg, or blind, or on crutches, or in any other awful situation, arising from the accidents of this life, I should look upon the
misfortune as accident and no more, even if you accused yourself
of wilful carelessness. 3d objection; — the extreme trouble in rear-
ing a child, whom you are to lose at a certain period, unless I
myself die, & then you & Dilke may settle him as you please. His
temper & disposition are, I suppose, bad or good, according to the
folks about him. I have already made him tolerably good, merely
by talking, and behaving with firmness. After you left us I saw
two apologies in his mouth for his fretfulness; for, on the day you
were here, he had cut his *eye teeth*. But to talk to you about so
young a child's conduct is superfluous, — it will rest with yourself,
and you know it. The remaining objections I leave to you and
Mrs R. You will see I have written this letter in a very grave mood,
for it is with me a weighty consideration. To lose him for 3 or 4
years is no trifle, especially while I am away from all my old
friends. Think of it, and write me word, and by that time I may
have set my seal on my resolve, one way or the other. You must
know from what I said to you a fortnight ago, it never was my
intention to leave the child with Mrs Dilke, and she knew it. I
must now end my letter, with Compts to your Wife.

Your's most truly,
Chas Brown.

· 39 ·

TO THOMAS RICHARDS

Address: To / Tho⁵ Richards Esqʳ / 9 Providence Place / near Vauxhall Gardens

Postmarks: Two Py Post Unpaid SO Hampstead; 7 o'Clock AP 2 1822 Nᵀ

Endorsement: 1822 / Apˡ 1 [?] / C Brown / (Palindromes)

ALS: Keats House, Hampstead. Printed in *Some Letters*, pp. 12–13.

Dear Richards,   2ⁿᵈ April [1822]. Tuesday.

Is Good Friday a Holy-day with you? If so, shall I come and dine with you? Then I intend, if convenient, to sleep at your house on that night, to dine at Camberwell on Saturday, to sleep a second time at your house, and on Sunday Morning to drag you hither neck & heels, giving you arguments for cribbaging you as thus, — two for your heels & one for your knob, — for what are you but a knave to the Duke of Wellington? — heavens preserve me! it never struck me before that my friend Richards was such low company. Since you were here last I have had inflamed eyes, a misery which I was rather a stranger to, & being unable to read or write or walk out in the cold air, I sauntered about my rooms making Palindrome verses, which, says the New Monthly,[1] cannot possibly be composed in the English language. I have made one tolerable line, and one excellent line (tho' I say it), & these furnish matter for a short article, — indeed shorter than I intended. If they do not please you, I am sure your daughter Harriet will be delighted with their oddity, — so I send them:

Evil is a name of foeman, as I live!
Madam is an Eve, even as I'm Adam.

---

[1] In an article — 2 (1821): 170–173 — beginning, "Among the fopperies . . . which in the dark ages supplied the place of learning and taste, there were none more remarkable, none on which more labour was wasted to less useful purpose, than the Palindromes, or Canorine, or recurrent verses, as they were called, from their reading the same, letter by letter, backwards and forwards." For the writer's view of the impossibility of palindromes in English see n. 3 to the next letter, which is all that Brown made of his "matter for a short article."

I made a third line which is bad:

Now, Sir, even Hannah never is won.

And, for your further amusement, I give you all my little sentences, which were beyond my ability to work up into heroic or any other kind of line: — (Rail at a liar. Repel a leper. Deny me no lad alone, my Ned! Name no one man. Lived as a Devil. Fled as a sad elf. No, it is opposition.) This last is extremely strange. It must be confessed these are curiosities in the language, but no more, and I know of no apology for making them except my bad eyes. Give my loving Comp^ts to M^rs R.

Your's very truly,

Chas Brown.

· 40 ·

TO THE EDITOR OF THE *New Monthly Magazine* [1]

[April (?) 1822]

O! Mr. Editor, what constant occupation has the Essay on Palindromes afforded me, (see vol. II. p. 170,) and what immortal fame shall I acquire! Since you set me upon this study, I have diligently read all my books backwards, in order to discover every Palindrome word, or combination of words, in the language, and, in this respect, I found "Locke on the Human Understanding," (which I had been often advised to read,) a particularly useful work. My ambition is to write a poem in this style, of at least 456 lines, that I may surpass Ambrosius himself.[2] I have fixed on the subject, — "a Satire on War." The very first line will give you no mean opinion of my versification and energy of expression. Here it is: —

Evil is a name of foeman, as I live!

---

[1] From the *New Monthly Magazine*, 9 (1823): 25, where the editor of the correspondence column heads it, "Let B. O. B. speak for himself." Presumably it was written shortly after the preceding letter.

[2] The writer of the essay had reserved for his climax "a poem . . . written in ancient Greek, by a modern Greek named Ambrosius, printed in Vienna in 1802, and dedicated to the Emperor Alexander. It contains 455 lines, every one of which is a literal Palindrome" (p. 172 of the article cited in the note to the preceding letter).

Now, Sir, what say you? And what says the writer of the Essay, who talked of a perfect Palindrome line in the English language as an impossibility! Between you and me, Mr. Editor, neither he nor James Harris before him, had a genius capable of the task.[3] It was reserved for me, and lo! I have achieved it. As I must confess I have gained much knowledge from the New Monthly Magazine, by my retrograde mode of reading, and as I hate ingratitude, you shall have one more of my lines. No doubt you recollect the old song beginning with —

"The busy world we leave

"For Paradise, dear Madam,

"Where you shall be my Eve,

"And I will be your Adam."

Well! I have adopted the idea in a Palindrome, as thus: —

Madam is an Eve, even as I'm Adam.

Surely this ought to satisfy both you and your readers until the publication of my long poem. In the mean while may no one else attempt to make a Palindrome, — it will be so useless!

· 41 ·

TO JOSEPH SEVERN

Address: à / Joseph Severn Esqre / Poste Restante / à Naples.

Postmarks: Pisa; [NAP.] 1822 12 SET

ALS: Harvard. Printed in part by Sharp, p. 129.

My dear Severn,　　　　　　　　　　　　Pisa. 5th Septr 1822.

Here I am at last. I arrived here six days ago with my little boy. In London I could not learn in what part of Italy you intended to pass the summer, and one of my first questions with

---

[3] "In English but one Palindrome line is known; at least, James Harris [1709–1780, grammarian], who had deeply studied our language, could discover no more; and that one is only procured by a quaintness of spelling in one word, and the substitution of a figure for another: —

Lewd did I live, & evil I did *dwel*.

"Our own observation confirms the difficulty of composing them in our own language, which this rarity implies" (*ibid.*, pp. 171–172).

Leigh Hunt was touching your present abode.[1] He believes you to be at Naples, so at Naples I address this letter. Yet I will not venture, till I hear from you, to send three letters from Holmes Ewing and Richards, which were intrusted to my care. I called on your Sister a few days before I packed up; she was not at home; we then entered into a correspondence, which ended in her not letting me be the bearer of any thing, on account of the difficulty of forwarding things from Pisa to Rome. Why letters were given to me for you I know not, for surely unless we were shortly to meet, the post would be ten times better. All your family were very well. I travelled as far as Turin with an English Lady & Child, by post,[2] which was as agreeable as possible. But from Turin to Genoa I had a tedious process to go through, and in the felucca, which was to carry us to Leghorn, we were favoured with a storm, & contrary winds, & every thing that was abominable, till my patience at the end of 4 days was exhausted, and landing at Lerici, I came here, by Carriage, with an English Gentleman.[3] You have heard, I suppose, of Shelley being drowned near Lerici, — I am really grieved for him, — I believe he was a good man, and certainly he was a good friend to Keats, and to his memory. His body has been burnt, and I understand his ashes are to be deposited near his child at Rome. A Capt[n] Williams was also drowned with him.[4] Lord Byron is moving off to Genoa, and so is Hunt with his family. Hunt introduced me to his Lordship two or three days ago, which is considered (not by me) as a prodigious favour. I was prejudiced against him, but somehow he got the better of my prejudice, and I hear he has taken a liking to me.[5]

[1] The Hunts had arrived in Pisa in July. Severn was in Naples from May to October (Sharp, pp. 128–129).

[2] In number 84 Brown says that he bought a carriage at Calais. Carlino (*KC*, I, lvii) identifies the "English Lady & Child" as "M[rs] Edwards and her boy, who was going to join her husband, Capt Edwards, in Turkey or Egypt. M[rs] Edwards was a daughter of Hope." For Thomas Hope (1770?–1831) see number 56, n. 7, and number 59, n. 14. *The Annual Biography and Obituary*, 16 (1832): 264, records that he had three sons, but fails to mention a daughter.

[3] Lord Charles Murray (1799–1824), on whom see *KC*, I, lvii n.

[4] Shelley and his friend Edward Ellerker Williams (b. 1793) were drowned on July 8. On the interment of Shelley's ashes see numbers 45, 47. "His child," William Shelley, who died on June 7, 1819, was buried in the Protestant Cemetery at Rome.

[5] See number 44. Carlino (*KC*, I, lviii) says that "at Pisa, Brown became acquainted with . . . Lord Byron, [whom] on one occassion he had to thank . . . for setting something right in reference to the 'Liberal,' when Brown for the first and

Oh! Severn, how I wish to sit with you for an hour! To Rome I cannot go this winter; my child is too young, and I wish to remain here, learning the language, till next summer, and then I think of moving to Florence, — will you be there next summer? Pisa can have no attractions for you, as it contains no works of art. How are your works of art going on? What a nuisance my house at Hampstead became! I could not let it, — there was not even a bidder for eight months, — and then, angry at its detaining me in England, I sold it outright, and (would you believe it?) it was let in five days after.[6] Here I am in Lodgings, but for the present you had better address your letters Poste Restante. I want a servant to attend on the child. What think you of my playing the nurse? — washing, combing, dressing &c a marmoset of 2 years old, ever since I quitted London. Yesterday while I was standing on the opposite side of the Lung'arno, a house fell down while the workmen were in it; the house was old, and they must have disturbed the foundation; to see the bodies brought away was a dreadful sight; only three were saved, and (some say) nineteen were killed. After telling you this story I ought to close my letter. Thus much however I must add, — I should like to keep house with you at Florence for a twelvemonth, — my brat, in the hands of a servant, will not annoy either of us. Now I wait for an answer,[7] and then I shall send your letters. Good b'ye, my dear Severn, and believe me ever,

Your's sincerely,
Chas Brown.

---

only time, gave him his title, which Byron immediately noticed by a quick glance." Brown once said (*KC*, I, lxii) that he "Would never put his legs under a Lord's table."

[6] On June 18 Brown "signed the final agreement transferring his part of Wentworth Place to old Mr Dilke of Chichester" (Richardson, *The Everlasting Spell*, p. 52). According to Adami, *Fanny Keats*, p. 125n, a Miss Steel was the tenant of Brown's half of the house from 1822 to 1828.

[7] "Severn wrote at once in reply, and though regretting his inability to go to Pisa, promised to meet his friend the following year in Florence, if not in Rome" (Sharp, p. 130).

· 42 ·

TO JOSEPH SEVERN

Address: To / Joseph Severn Esqr / Care of Messrs Cotterill & Freeborn,[1] / Palazzo Coscia / Napoli.

Postmarks: PISA; NAP. 1822 29 SET

ALS: Harvard.

My dear Severn,   Pisa. 23^d Septr 1822.

I had your letter five minutes since,[2] and I hasten to enclose the English news for you. One of the seals, or rather the only one sealed, I was compelled to break, lest I should be subject to a fine for cheating the Post Office. Your health gives me real concern, and I long to be with you, but fear it is not in my power to go to Rome this winter. Travelling with my bambino is no joke. A year hence he will be less trouble. Again I cannot afford to move about yet. My purse is sadly drained by my journey from England. Then what a heap of books &c have I! and how are they to be trundled? To tell you the truth Pisa is not a place to my taste; but I must remain here till the Spring, and the winter climate of Pisa is always represented as extremely beautiful. I must earn a little money by scribbling, & Lord Byron, with some compliments, has invited me to write with him & Hunt in their new periodical work.[3] The heats have attacked my Carlino with a bowel complaint, & I have been obliged to have a Physician, but he is now better. I can't write much to-day, but this shall shortly be followed by another scrawl,[4] & then I will give you an account of poor

---

[1] Charles Cotterell, a former naval officer, now a banker in Naples, was brother of the Miss Cotterell who sailed to Italy with Keats and Severn on the *Maria Crowther* (*Letters*, II, 353–354n; Sharp, p. 60). Apparently he was in business with the Roman wine merchant, commissioner, and consular agent John Freeborn, who helped make the arrangements for the burial of Shelley's ashes (*The Letters of Mary W. Shelley*, ed. Frederick L. Jones, Norman, Okla., 1944, I, 190n). Severn had been staying with Cotterell (whose house, he says, was always open to him in Naples) at least since July (ALS to his brother Tom, July 5, Keats House, Hampstead).

[2] See the last note to the preceding letter.

[3] The *Liberal*.

[4] It is lost, since in the next letter Brown says, "I told you all I could . . . about Shelley's ashes."

Shelley. I shall see Hunt to-day & will mention your having written, for I know he never rec^d such a letter, — he & his family leave
this for Genoa the day after tomorrow. I will also mention your
offer concerning Shelley's grave.[5] For God's sake take care of
yourself.

Your's most faithfully

Chas Brown.

· 43 ·

TO JOSEPH SEVERN [1]

Pisa,

Nov. 7th, 1822.

I got your letter yesterday.[2] If not too late pray reflect a little
more on the inscription for our Keats. Remember it was his dying
request that his *name* should *not* be on his tombstone, and that
the words "Here lies one whose name was writ in water" should
be there. I thought you liked my inscription, for you said so. All
his friends, Hunt, Richards, Dilke, and every one I showed it to,
were greatly pleased with it. You seem to imagine it does not
honour him enough, but, to our minds, it says more in his praise
than if his name were mentioned. You have done right in not
accepting of any assistance from strangers to his worth, in erecting
this gravestone; but I insist on bearing my share, and I will pay
it you when we meet in Florence — you shall not have all the
pleasure — a mournful one — but still a pleasure.[3] I told you all I
could, all that Hunt could tell me, about Shelley's ashes — Mrs.
Shelley had then set off to Genoa. As for Mr. Taylor, I have no
correspondence with him whatever. When we meet, if it live in

[5] See number 45, n. 14.

[1] From Sharp, pp. 131–132.

[2] Dated October 26 (Forman, 1883, IV, 368–369; Sharp, pp. 119–120). Severn had
decided to include Keats's "name, the date when he died, and his age," but wanted
Brown's approval, though "I fear it will be accomplished before you write." His
reply to this letter (see number 45) shows that he was easily persuaded to Brown's
opinion.

[3] Severn finally came to Florence in the middle of June 1823. Sir Charles W.
Dilke, *Papers of a Critic*, I, 17, says that Severn "never would allow Brown to pay
part of the expense" of Keats's gravestone.

my remembrance so long, and it is hardly worth it, I will tell you the whole story. Even my friends allow, and that I have found a rare thing, that he has behaved badly towards me, and, to my mind, unfeelingly towards the memory of Keats. . . .

I cannot give you any account of Lord Byron's and Leigh Hunt's work, except that it is called "The Liberal," and that the first number came out on the 14th of October.[4] To write in such good company I feel a great honour. What I shall be paid I know not; but it can't be less than what the "New Monthly" paid me, twelve guineas per sheet. I hear they are much pleased with my article "Les Charmettes and Rousseau";[5] and they have another[6] which Hunt saw in Pisa, and said was very good indeed.

*   *   *

· 44 ·

TO C. W. DILKE [1]

[November 12, 1822]

*   *   *

When Lord Byron talked to me of the "Vision of Judgment,"[2] I interrupted him, for a Blackwoodish idea came across my mind with "I hope you have not attacked Southey at his fire-side," when he expressed quite an abhorrence of such an attack, and declared he had not.

There never was a poor creature in rags a greater Radical than Byron. My qualms were satisfied much in the same *reasonable*

[4] Though originally advertised for the fourteenth, the first number was issued on October 15 (William H. Marshall, *Byron, Shelley, Hunt, and "The Liberal,"* Philadelphia, 1960, p. 81).

[5] Published in the second number of the *Liberal*, 1 (1822): 327–345, on January 1, 1823. Brown received £18 18s. for it, at the rate of about a guinea per page, or sixteen guineas per sheet (Marshall, p. 148).

[6] "Shakespear's Fools," which appeared in the third number, 2 (1823): 85–95, on April 26, 1823. Brown also contributed an article to the fourth number (see the opening of number 49).

[1] From *Papers of a Critic*, I, 15–16, where it is headed, "On the 12th November, 1822, Mr. Charles Brown writes . . . from Florence."

[2] Published a month earlier in the first number of the *Liberal*.

way as they were excited, and my satisfaction will appear to you just as unreasonable. I was angry at him, not for expressing an opinion on Keats' poetry, but for joining in the ridicule against him. He did so, in a note to a poem, forwarded to Murray;[3] but soon afterwards, when he learnt Keats' situation, and saw more of his works (for he had only read his first volume of poems, and flew out at the passage about Boileau),[4] he ordered the note to be erased, and this, foolish soul that I am, quite satisfied me, together with his eulogium on Hyperion,[5] for he's no great admirer of the others.

* * *

· 45 ·

FROM JOSEPH SEVERN

Address: Al Signore / Il Signor Carlo Brown / Gentiluomo Inglese / Poste Restante / Pisa / from Rome

Postmarks: ROMA; 13 DECEMBRE

Endorsement: Joseph Severn

ALS: British Museum. Brief extracts are printed in the *Athenaeum*, August 23, 1879, p. 239, in Forman (1883), IV, 369–370, and (from the *Athenaeum*) by Sharp, p. 131.

My dear Brown   Rome Decr 7th 1822
    Unlucky Dog — I am just risen from a 13 days illness in bed. — which stoped me from writing to you. — I fear this has again

---

[3] Perhaps Brown is thinking of the passage printed in Byron's *Letters and Journals*, ed. R. E. Prothero, V (London, 1901), 588–589, which was to have been inserted in his *Second Letter* against Bowles. Byron ordered it "erased" in a letter to Murray of July 30, 1821 (*ibid.*, p. 331): "as he is dead, omit *all* that is said *about him* in any *MSS.* of mine, or publication."

[4] "Sleep and Poetry," ll. 193–206.

[5] In the letter cited in n. 3 Byron called it "a fine monument," and in a note to "Some Observations upon an Article in *Blackwood's Magazine*," *Letters and Journals*, IV (1900), 491, he said that the "fragment of *Hyperion* seems actually inspired by the Titans, and is as sublime as Æschylus." The famous *Don Juan* stanza on Keats (XI.lx), which Hunt urged him in vain to alter (see Hunt's *Lord Byron*, I, 133, 227, 438–439), had been written by this time but not yet published. Other details of Byron's attitude toward Keats are summarized by Willis W. Pratt in *Byron's "Don Juan": A Variorum Edition* (Austin, 1957), IV, 227.

been entirely my own imprudence — I will tell you about it and you shall judge — I have been constirpated in bowels all the last Summer so that 3 days scarce went without Physic. — when the other Summer I had a diarrhea all the time. — was not this a change — Well soon after my return here from Naples [1] — I was taken day after day with a swimming in my head — my evacuations were a Clay colour — so I took a half tumbler of Epsom Salts — twice the quantity I had taken every 4 or 5 other days. — this seem'd to go right thro' me — like water — and at 12 o clock I went down to the Trattoria and eat Maccoroni — greasy Cutlets — roast Potatoes & Maccoroni Pudding — like a Fool. — In the evening at 6 I was seized with the halo before my eyes — which encreased — and I had 4 convulsive Fits — altogether it must have been 9 hours — when it all came off my Stomach. — I was sensible between whiles — D[r] Clark attended me with all my Friends. — when my Bowels were opend with a Glyster — I went calmly to sleep — Now they tell me — particularly D[r] C that this was occasiond by putting such an indigestible Mess into my Stomach weakened by Physic. — and that it is nothing constitutonal — this is the 3rd attack. — but all from the same cause — I had the halo alone once — but it went away after a few minutes — D[r] C— found my inside in a terrible state. — my liver full of Bile my evacuations were black and unnatural for 15 days — This is the 20th day and Clark only allows me to take a little broth with a bit of Toast — Seago or Arrow Root. — but little — he has now restored my stomach — my evacuations are the proper colour — but I am weak and reduced — and unable to study. — he said my Nerves were so shaken — that I must remain in bed for the 13 days. — Now my dear Brown. I look at all this as a Providential thing — for my eyes are opened to so many wrong things I am accustomed to do in eating &c — that I might have gone on and on until this would have become constitutional Now please God I will so alter my course that I hope it will never occur again. — I have ever had that vice of eating by quantity — and taking more than my Stomach will contain — Tell me my dear Brown your opinion of all this — give me your advice — for I hold a high respect for your judgment — I do assure you this time I have been miserably

[1] He had come back to Rome at the beginning of November.

frightened — and am now sadly depressed in my spirits. — My Friends have watched from the 1ˢᵗ moment with great tenderness — and Clark shows me most consoling attention

I had just given my directions about poor Keats Grave Stone. — your mention of your still existing wish for the Epitaph as it stood. — made me all consent [2] — I saw the superiorty of it — it is doing so —

I am all anxety to know about poor Miss Brawn pray tell me this — if you have more accounts — I shall be most ravenous by May to have a sight of you — what must regulate the time is the finishing my Alexander — after the "Greek Sheapheards" now going on — this with "Falstaff" and I hope Keats's Portrait will be in the Exibition next Summer in London — [3]

I have try'd — but not every way to my satisfaction in my Sketch of Arthur.[4] — the manner of it I like — but it wants consistency — but still I must fix on a subject for this kind of Picture — that is to paint in Italy — I have now another subject to ask your good advice on. — Do you remember the attempted assassination of Lorenzo di Medici — at the moment when the Host was raised in the Church. — I recollect it in Roscoes Life of him.[5] — This subject I long since cogitated. — Giulielmo [6] di Medeci has just fallen from the assassins blow — who is rushing up to Lorenzo — encircled by Friends — protecting him and receiving the blows on their Arms. — The Church is in [7] horror at the danger of the good Lorenzo. — I am so delighted with the character of Lorenzo for a picture. — he is [8] calm and prepared for this event — in the midst of his astonishd F[riend]ˢ — I would introduce the Portraits of all this Age — Raffaello — M. Angello — &c &c — even the Church still exists. — I can find Portraits and all the beatiful

---

[2] See numbers 35, 43.

[3] "Greek Hill-Shepherds Rescuing a Lamb from an Eagle," founded upon *Endymion*, I.266–267 (Sharp, p. 126), sent to the Royal Academy in January 1824 but apparently not exhibited there; and "Falstaff Passing by the Counter Gate," based on *The Merry Wives of Windsor*, III.iii.84–86 (Severn to his father, December 7, 1822, Keats House, Hampstead). For "Alexander" and the portrait of Keats see numbers 30, 37.

[4] See number 37.

[5] William Roscoe, *The Life of Lorenzo de' Medici*, 2 vols. (Liverpool, 1795).

[6] Severn should have written "Giuliano."

[7] *Written* in in.

[8] *Written* his.

Cos{tumes} in the Florence Museum's. — This subject would so
well {depict} this magnificent period. — then its materials would
make such a Venetian picture. — tell me how you like this — if I
like it as well when we meet in Florence — I will collect all my
Materials and [9] make a small finished Sketch there.[10] — I believe
I said that it is my most darling wish to go after to Venice. — this
is most important to me — I shall make many studies there — now
if I might hope to be favored with your fine company in this
journey I shall think myself not a little happy — I am engaged
to accompany M[r] Eastlake.[11] — but I fear may not go — he disappointed me last Summer and may this — Will you like this
journey my dear Brown [12] — And why tell me that Work of Lord
Byrons was published on the first of Oct[r] and not promise to send
me a Copy of it [13] — You have set me a longing dreadfully — Did
you ever have poor Keats papers? — Know you about the Life —
Taylor is going to publish after all — he has never written to me.
— is this kind? — I am proud to have you approve of my Sheapheards —

Poor Shelly's ashes have arrived — when I get out — I will
conduct them to the Grave [14] — with the respect due to the Friend
of Keats. — I have not yet heard from Hunt — or Lord Murray [15]
— Pray say nothing about my illness to England

believe your anxious Friend

18 Via di San Isidoro — 2[d] piano   Joseph Severn

Have you got a spare Copy of the Lamia or the Endymion — I
have been cheated out of mine and I am so vexed to be without —

[9] *Written* in.

[10] At Florence Severn made many studies and drawings for this 12' x 18' picture,
"Rescue of Lorenzo de' Medici from Assassination," which he planned to begin on
January 1. Shortly after that date, however, he gave up the project "for the present"
(Sharp, pp. 137–138, 140).

[11] (Sir) Charles Lock Eastlake (1793–1865), historical painter and art critic, later
president of the Royal Academy and director of the National Gallery.

[12] They went to Venice late in the following August (numbers 52, 53).

[13] The *Liberal*. Severn had still not seen it as late as May 10, 1823, when Hunt
wrote to him (in a letter now at Harvard), "I have sent you copies of the 1st & 2[d]
Liberal *through Brown. . . .* I thought you would be with him before the packet
could have got to Rome."

[14] They were buried in the Protestant Cemetery on January 21. "It is quite evi-
dent that Severn had much to do with making arrangements for the burial" (F. L.
Jones, *Letters of Mary Shelley*, I, 190n).

[15] Presumably Lord Charles Murray (see number 41).

My friend Mr Gott [16] — (the Sculptor who had a Gold Medal with me) — is doing something from Endymion — and I have a drawing going on from St Agnes Eve — pray think of us —

· 46 ·

TO THOMAS RICHARDS

Address: Inghilterra. / To / Thos Richards Esqr / Storekeeper's Office / Ordnance Department / Tower / London.

Postmarks: Pisa; FPO JA 27 1823

AL: Keats House, Hampstead. Printed in *Some Letters*, pp. 16–22.

Pisa. 11th January 1823.

Very ingenious indeed, my dear Richards! Let us hope it is true.[1] So, you keep accounts with the accuracy of a Banker's Clerk, mark your time like St Paul's minute hand, are equal to a guillotine in promptitude and decision, and as for the accusation of "infirmity of purpose",[2] lord! it was never your fault, but the fault of vile complimentary acquaintances. I'm glad I did not call you bald-headed, for I should have had such a story of a thick curly periwig, — not bought at a barber's, but quite natural, your own growth, and in fact, Brown, though my head may have appeared otherwise to you, my head never was like a tortoise's, but, on the contrary, like a little owl in a monstrous ivy-bush. I've done! I agree to the good character, in the plodding way, that you have given of yourself. And now mark how you are thralled. You are caught, trapped for ever. Negligence in any way will be infamy. You cannot offer an excuse. Unlike any other man, you must always continue regular in your motions as the spheres, or you are damned. You are a star; and if you fall, 'twill be like Lucifer.[3] Thank Heaven, my friend Richards is so wise a man. Why, you're a nonsuch, — and that's the reason that Eve your Wife

---

[16] Joseph Gott (1786–1860), who lived with Severn at this time.
[1] That is, Richards' excuse for lagging in correspondence.
[2] *Macbeth*, II.ii.52.
[3] *Henry VIII*, III.ii.371.

fell in love with so excellent an apple. But what a want of perspicacity on my part! I'm all amort. I can't help humming the tune of "O Ally Croaker!" [4] I'm a dog without a true scent. Lack a day! I am ever offering an opinion of another, and ever mistaken in that other's opinion. A very sorry dog, — not better than a snarling cur that is of no use but to make quiet honest gentlemen take care I don't tear their coat-tails. You have caught up your's under your elbows, and strut like a Trojan in spite of me. There he goes! He has frightened that barking Carlo from his heels! No hole in his coat, — O no, you so adroitly filched it from my fangs that I have not even hurt the nap. A clever fellow! O dear! I said I'd have done! Then let me, if possible, (and I'm writing before dinner,) talk soberly. Add this I must, — that, even now, while you talk of time, you seem to think that time will stay for *you*. On 2nd May my £50 will be ready. As this will be in good time, according to your letter, I won't strain a point to make it earlier. I shall write to Mancur to that effect.[5] By all means make your shop smart, — £5, — or 10, — or even £20 per ann: are well laid out on that point; tho' it may gain nothing with many, it will lose nothing with none, and fools and strangers are taken by smartness. How I long to buy a quire of paper & a stick of sealing wax in Richards' shop! [6] So far I will own, — the mere idea of such wisdom is wisdom itself. You will make me proud to see it carried on wisely. How uneasy I have [7] b{een, but the cause of sai}d uneasiness I will not mention, — and why should I? {. . . Fo}r the third time, I say *I have done.* Now about {Byron: . . . I have heard} a great deal about him, but not a word touching {. . . the charge

---

[4] "A song popularized by Mrs. Harriet Waylett (1798–1851), the words of which seem to me inapplicable to both Brown and Richards" (M. B. Forman, *Some Letters*, p. 16n).

[5] Mancur, Brown's financial and literary agent and a friend (perhaps a schoolfellow) of Dilke, is mentioned many times in these letters. Perhaps (as Rollins suggests, *Letters*, II, 27n) he was John Mancur, wholesale hosier, of 17 Lad Lane, Cheapside — the only Mancur listed in Pigot's *Commercial Directory* for 1823–1824. Richardson, *The Everlasting Spell*, p. 234, has a note on some other possibilities. In 1839 his address was 25 Great Winchester Street, London (number 134).

[6] Richards' stationery shop was apparently a sideline, since, according to Forman (*Some Letters*, p. xi), he held a clerical appointment in the Storekeeper's Office until his death.

[7] The lower inside corner of both leaves has been torn away, and several half-lines of text from each of the four pages are lost. The emendations here and below are purely conjectural.

of} blasphemy. I heard of it thro' Galignani's {. . .} Dilke.[8] An Italian told me it was for {. . . Byro}n's poem. Is this Saint's net {. . .} buzzed about (and Pisa is an {. . .}tions) I prophecy, unless {. . . Byr}on will go to England {. . .} and the letter sent to Murray, he told me he was actually preparing to go to England, — for it appears he had received news of Cain being legally held blasphemous.[9] I have not heard from Genoa [10] since I wrote to you last, — yes, one letter, but nothing about these subjects. Every one takes it for granted I know every thing about the Liberal, when the truth is I know less than any body who desires to know any thing respecting it. I wrote to John Hunt some time back,[11] but there's no answer yet. Hazlitt's "Lodging-house Romance" pleases me in idea extremely; I would rather read that than any of his other works.[12] What you say of Shelley's memory strikes me as written with an inexplicable feeling. Is he called a God? The story you mention against him, respecting his first wife, I have heard repeated oft and oft, and much in the same words. He was then, I believe, 18.[13] Now in such matters, when there is generally more passion than cold heartedness, we should be acquainted with all the circumstances, or pass no judgment. He may have behaved cruelly towards her, or she towards him, — who knows? Suppose, when you & I talked of such a thing, Abby had drowned herself. Would not the world have laid all the blame on me? Or put it thus, had I lived a heretic in Ireland at the time, what would the

[8] He probably wrote something like "thro' Galignani's magazine, which arrived containing some articles by Dilke." In a lost letter of 1822 (*Papers of a Critic*, I, 15) Brown noted that "Galignani has republished some of Dilke's articles in his *Parisian Literary Gazette*." Galignani published the *Paris Monthly Review of British and Continental Literature* from January 1822 to January 1823, and continued it for three more months as *Galignani's Magazine and Paris Monthly Review*.

[9] *Cain* was published with *Sardanapalus* and *The Two Foscari* on December 19, 1821, and immediately pirated. The publisher John Murray was at first refused an injunction against the sale of the pirated edition on the grounds that the work was blasphemous and therefore not subject to copyright. See Byron's *Poetry*, ed. E. H. Coleridge, V (London, 1901), 203–204, and, on the sensation created by *Cain*, S. C. Chew, *Byron in England* (London, 1924), pp. 76–104.

[10] The Hunts and Byron were living at Albaro, near Genoa.

[11] For copies of the *Liberal*. John Hunt was its publisher.

[12] *Liber Amoris; or The New Pygmalion* was not published until the first week of May (Howe, *Life of Hazlitt*, p. 326).

[13] Harriet Shelley (b. 1795) was discovered drowned on December 10, 1816. Many believed that Shelley had driven her to suicide, among them Landor, who refused to meet Shelley in Pisa because he "believed the disgraceful story" (Super, *Landor*, p. 150). For other details of Shelley's first marriage (at the age of nineteen) see number 68.

world of Catholics have said of me? I know none of the particulars
of Shelley's first wife's fate. This I know that his character among
the Pisans stands high. By every one he was regretted, — they speak
no evil of him. Then again, his second wife lived very happily
with him. And what a friend has he been to Hunt? And did he not
send that kind letter to Keats? [14] — and that same kind offer has
been repeated to Severn, just before he was drowned. It requires
much to overthrow these positive evidences of a good heart. And
even if he was bad at 18, does it follow he could not prove himself
good for many years before his death at 33? [15] Here is an Irish
Catholic, a bigotted one, his acquaintance, who speaks of his
moral conduct with praise, and even of his religion with respect;
lately in conversation he denied to me that Shelley was an
Atheist, — "say a *Theist*, Sir." [16] This Irishman is the only British
acquaintance I have, saving Carlino, and a young Englishman
whose mother is a Greek. The last has just paid me a visit. He
studies physic at our University, but studies shooting more. Now
this requires a licence (which however is gratis) and to obtain it,
the Grand Duke,[17] who lives here in the winter, must be *personally* petitioned. I tell this anecdote to let you know something of
our Grand Duke, who is an extraordinary man in the *good line*,
as every one witnesseth. Away posts this young Englishman, as
blunt as any, to the Palace, walks up stairs, and asks for the
Grand Duke. A solitary servant posted at a door says — "In this
chamber, Sir." He enters, makes his bow, and cries out "May it
please your Royal Highness, I want a licence for shooting, — not
in your preserves — I don't ask that — but particularly to shoot
the woodcocks in the fens on the side of it, — and I should {like
to have permission} to go into your preserves, promising on my
part {. . . not to take any} game, because it's the nearest way
home." After {the Grand Duke considered this in} a good hu-

---

[14] Of July 27, 1820 (*Letters*, II, 310–311; *Letters of Shelley*, ed. Jones, II, 220–221).
He wrote a second letter to Keats in February 1821 (Sharp, p. 63; *Letters of Shelley*,
II, 268).

[15] He was twenty-nine when he died.

[16] The Irishman was John Taaffe, Jr. (1787?–1862), poet and author of *A Comment on the Divine Comedy of Dante Alighieri* (1822), on whom see C. L. Cline,
Byron, Shelley and Their Pisan Circle (London, 1952), esp. pp. 16–21, 199–202. Of
Shelley, Taaffe wrote in his autobiography (Cline, p. 23): "Some call him an Atheist,
but it is not true; at least he was none when I knew him. He died none."

[17] Ferdinand III (1769–1824).

moured laughing mood, he said — "But do {. . .} as well as yourself?" "O yes, I know your {. . .} then, answer this question: if in passing {my preserves . . . a bird should} come in your way, do you think you {could refrain from shooting it?"} "Humph! that's a hard question {to answer." I} thought so, and therefore, you {. . .} I'll give you no licence {. . .} preserves excepted." Now {. . .} accessible to all, and {. . .} to me, on the part of the Police or such understrappers, I should go bolt to the Palace and state the case. Such conduct he likes, I understand, and I'm sure I like it. Such a cause however is not probable. Tuscany's is, to my thinking, the best Government in Europe, if by the best, we are to understand a Government which makes the most happy, — that is, with means to live, & without tyranny. Where so many are miserable, as in England, Ireland, & Scotland, you may talk of your *free-borns* as you will, I say that Government is the worst. Yet do not imagine but that I earnestly desire a Constitution for Tuscany, even though this man were immortal, — yet at present it wants it the least. Other parts of Italy are as distinct as the happy Cottagers in France are to the starved Irish, — no, not quite so, — for that is a distinction that cannot be parallel'd. As for the Tuscans themselves, as far as I am acquainted with them, I like them, all in all, better than the English, — you need not start, for I am more a Citizen of the World than an Englishman. Why the devil should a mountain or a river, or another language change my daily experience back again to a silly prejudice? Indeed I never was a downright Englishman, — God forbid! When I speak of the kindness of the people of the house where I live, perhaps you will imagine I judge of all others by them, but I am not singular in bestowing an amiable character on the Tuscans. In the week before Xmas Carlino was dangerously ill, inflamation in his bowels was actually beginning. I owe his preservation to my own doctoring, and had I waited for a Doctor either at the first attack, or on the third night, I think I should have lost him. On the third night at 10, I saw the horrid symptoms, and despatched the servant for several articles to the Apothecaries. All their shops were shut. I went down stairs to my Landlord; [18] where every one was at supper. I told them his situation, & wanted

[18] Gordini (see number 51, n. 12).

to know where an Apothecary *lived*, that I might knock him up. "O," said the Padrone, "you sit by his bed till you fancy all sorts of things, — come and sit down with us." "Ah, sit down with us," they all echoed. "Sit down!" (and I suppose my manner was exorbitant,) — "are you all crazy? — the child will die at half past twelve!" Never shall I forget the effect of these words. Like soldiers at the word of command every one bolted up from his chair. Among them was a Greek who had studied physic. He sent one into the Garden for mallows, the Padrona ran over the way to borrow other matters, all were in motion. Then they came into my sitting room, the Greek administer'd to my wish, — yet still they staid, and I sat hoping they'd wish me "felicissima notte", — but they would not off, trying to amuse me to their utmost. At last the clock struck *one*. The Padrona looked at the rest and laughed, and said, "Well now, thank God, the child can't die at half past twelve, — so we need not stay any longer." Ah! my eyes were opened. I saw the reason for so long a visit. And at day break, one by {one they appeared at} the door, asking how the "Bimbo" did, and creeping {away when they saw that a}t last he slept. "Honest John Bull" might, now and {then . . . show as} much feeling for a lodger and his child, but, {. . . he would at any ra}te stay to finish his supper; and then having {finished . . . would have} thought nothing of the father, — at least {. . . per-ha}ps on superstition, though *I* had {. . .} every thing I desired, yet that {. . .} a bad cough, but he is {. . .} early and most bit-terly {. . . I} have seen ice in the ditches, without the City, *two* inches thick. "O dolce Pisa!" Yet notwithstanding other Italian towns are colder than this, I would even now be off for Florence, but for two reasons, one is that Carlino suffers much from the cold as has been proved, and the other is that I am so comfortable with these people. So, I shall not see Florence till May-day. The air of Pisa, good for weak lungs, is to a hearty strong Englishman in-jurious. I am convinced of it. It is rare that I eat with appetite, beyond the two or three first mouth-fulls. Digestion here is diffi-cult, and a good stomach has bad bile. Not that I suffer from the last, because I am careful to prevent it. Exercise makes little difference with me. I walked to Leghorn a short time ago, but neither there, nor here on my return, had I an appetite. Still my health is excellent, bating a severe cold I caught in watching the child. That you teach my Godson [19] to imitate my Godsend has something very affectionate towards me and mine. Give my love to your Wife and the children, and to *Miss* Richards,[20] and remember me, as usual, to all friends. If I understand you righ{tly my article} [21] is advertised in the 2nd N⁰ of the Liberal, — this I {am . . . to} know. Hunt writes of every thing but what is {wanted . . .} for the N. M. Mag: two pages, & a little more, {. . .} — fables — which I think will please you {. . .} tho' they are as much so as Fairfax's [22] {. . .} in one, the measure of the original; {. . .} but which seemed to me to ex{. . .} 7 syllables. I have transl{ated . . .} my portfolio, waiting for {. . .} day was a jolly one, with r{. . .}

* 　 * 　 *

· 47 ·

TO JOSEPH SEVERN [1]

Pisa,

My dear Severn,　　　　　　　　　　　February 7th, 1823.

There is one subject in your letter [2] that has employed my consideration, and that to the best of my ability — I mean the erecting of a monument to Keats's memory in England. In one word, I cannot but disapprove of it. The fact is this: his fame is not sufficiently general; with the few and the best judges it stands high, but his name is unknown to the multitude. Therefore I think that prior to his name being somewhat more celebrated, a monument to his memory might even retard it, and it might provoke ill-nature, and (shall I say it?) ridicule. When I quitted

---

[19] Sidney Richards.

[20] Harriet Richards, the eldest child.

[21] "Les Charmettes and Rousseau."

[22] Presumably Edward Fairfax (d. 1635), whose translation of Tasso's *Gerusalemme liberata* first appeared in 1600.

[1] From Sharp, pp. 134–135.

[2] Of January 21 (Forman, 1883, IV, 370–371; Sharp, pp. 123–124). Severn asked Brown's opinion of "a little Monument to Keats . . . to be placed . . . in Hampstead Church," for which he would get "several gentlemen to subscribe 20 guineas."

England his works were still unsaleable. For that cruel word *ridicule* I must explain myself. There appeared, some time after his death, in one of the Government newspapers, an article scoffing at him and joking at his death.[3] I did not read it, I could not, but I heard of it, and it put me in a fortnight's irritation. In prudence we ought to wait awhile. First, let his merit be undoubted. Let it not be said that not only bad men have costly tombs with flattering inscriptions, but that nowadays bad poets have the like. This will be as unpleasant as irksome, as discordant for you to read as it is for me to write; but I must tell you the truth, his name is yet scarce anything in England; it becomes, and will become, more ennobled every day, while a monument might throw that happy time back. Ten years hence, to my mind, will be time enough. You, in your affection for him, think nothing can be done too much. Alas! I, knowing the wretched literary world, think otherwise. Yet still all this is but one man's opinion, and one as likely to err as yourself, and from the same motive, though our opinions are contrary. I regret that I am against the interest (in this instance) of your friend the sculptor,[4] whose *name* I cannot make out in your letter; but if you mention my reasons to that gentleman, he will surely understand me. I could say much more on this head, but why? — you with this already written can fill up the rest. I thank you for the particular account you give of the ceremony of depositing Shelley's ashes; that disturbing of other bones — though I am by no means scrupulous about such matters — made me start, for it might happen that some living friend of the skeleton should hear of it.[5]

*   *   *

[3] There were several in *Blackwood's* (see MacGillivray, *Keats*, pp. 75, 88–89). Perhaps Brown refers to the "Letter from a 'Gentleman of the Press,'" 12 (1822): 60, "lately, Johnny Keats was cut up in the Quarterly, for writing about Endymion what no mortal could understand . . . . I am sorry he is dead, for he often made me laugh at his rubbish of verse, when he was alive."
[4] Joseph Gott, who was to make a bas-relief for the monument from Severn's design.
[5] Attempting to disinter the body of Shelley's son William for reburial with Shelley's ashes, Severn and the others had found "a skeleton of 5½ feet" under the child's gravestone (Sharp, p. 123).

· 48 ·

Address: Al Signore / Il Signor Carlo Brown / Gentiluomo Inglese / Poste Restante / Pisa

Postmarks: ROMA; 16 APRILE

Endorsements: Joseph Severn.; Ans^d 10 May 23.

ALS: British Museum. Extracts are printed in the *Athenaeum*, August 30, 1879, p. 271, in Forman (1883), IV, 372, and (from the *Athenaeum*) by Sharp, pp. 135–136.

My dear Brown   Rome April 9th 1823

How I long to knaw a bone with you — in the Trattoria "della Vigna" — be it so. — but it cannot be the 1st May. — in desire. in love I'd set off tomorrow. — but Alexander the Great says no, — his unfinished face — and 10 feet of Canvas for him to sprawl in — are the reason's — therefore I'll knock of[f] these shackles and fly to Florence after. — But I *did* say (anticipating this Master Alexander) the 1st June.[1] — it seems a grevious length of time — but I shall paint it off — (except when I think of you) in a Presto movement —

There is a Mad Chap come here — whose name is Trelawny I do not know what to make of him further than his queer and I was near saying shabby behavior to me. — He comes as the friend of Shelly — great — glowing and rich in romance. — of course I show'd all my paint-pot politeness to him — to the very brim — assisted him to remove the Ashes of Shelly to a spot where he himself (when this world has done with his body) will lie — He wished me to think, myself, and consult my Friends about a Monument to Shelley. — The situation is beautiful and one and all thought a little Basso-reilevo would be the best suitd. — I was telling him the subject I had proposed for Keats — and he was struck with the propriety of it for Shelly. — and my Friend M^r

---

[1] Actually Severn did not come until the middle of June (Sharp, p. 137; *KC*, I, 271), at which time his painting ("Alexander the Great Reading Homer") was still several months away from completion.

Gott — (whom I mentioned to you) was to be the doer of it. — I made the Drawing which cost us some trouble — yet after expressing the greatest liking for it. — this pair of Mustachios has shirk'd off from it without giving us the Yes or No — without even the why or wherefore.[2] — I am sorry at this most on M[r] Gotts account — but I ought to have seen that this Lord Byrons Jackall was rather weak in all the points that I could judge — though strong enough in Stiletto's — we have not had any open rupture — nor [3] shall we — for I have no doubt that this "Cockney Corsair" fancies he has great[l]y obligied us by all this trouble we have had — But tell me who is this odd fish? They talk of him here as a camelion who went mad on reading L[d] Byrons Corsair — that he sailed as one — and has since made both ends meet — I told him this — and to my surprise — he laughd and said it was true.[4] — He told me that he knew you —

I have finished my Shephe[r]ds [5] after taking much pains with them — it make rather a nice picture it is certainly my best work — I am going on merrily with my 12 Tempest Compositions.[6] — O — I have got such a subject for a Tragedy — but when we meet — I have got into decent and gentlman[l]y hea[l]th thanks to you — and am able to proceed with my Studies manfully —

I had some rather unpleasant news from England about my youngest Sister Maria — she was going to be married to a Young Sculptor — a great friend of mine — altho a Methodist. — he wrote the most warm letters to me about the marriage — when he suddenly discovers we were not of his Religion — and makes his finale with breaking off the match. — I frightend him — and he defended himself so weakly — w[h]iningly — & miserably that I could find

[2] About this time Trelawny wrote to Mary Shelley (R. Glynn Grylls, *Trelawny*, London, 1950, p. 104), "I have consulted artists here but all the designs I have mentioned to them they cannot execute under £200 to £500 — and this is beyond me at present."

[3] *Written* not.

[4] Trelawny never forgave Byron for a similar remark: "Tre was an excellent fellow until he took to imitating my *Childe Harold* and *Don Juan*" (Harold Nicolson, *Byron: The Last Journey*, London, 1924, p. 97).

[5] See number 45, n. 3.

[6] Brown wrote in the *Examiner*, October 3, 1824, p. 627, "Mr. Severn has made many studies of composition from the 'Tempest;' and may he paint them all, for they are in the true feeling for Shakspeare." Perhaps two of them became "Ferdinand and Miranda" and "Ariel Aflight" (see number 59, n. 10, and numbers 104, 106).

it in my heart to make water on him — but let him go — and run his head into a lump of his own Clay — and make Wings to it — to delight himself with what a sweet Cherubim he will make in the next World [7] — it is wonderful how people can pray themselves out of their little wits — and make a kind of Gentleman's Carriage of their consciences —

Taylor sent me a kind letter — but it was dated June [?] it came in a Case. — Keats' Memoirs were not done — but Christmas was to compleat them

Mind — we go to Venice. — my mind is pampered up to it — if you say no I shall shed enough tears to wash round another City. — We will stay our Month in Florence — I anticipate that we shall meet Hunt [8] O how I long to see you[r] jolly face — with your Puns and your Rig's — you old Mother Brownrig [9] — but are you as fat as ever? I hope I shall pick up even a little fat in your Society — besides all the other good things — from Cookery up to Greek

Yes that was a high flyer — that last of yours [10] it came to me when I was very sad

So once more the 1st of June we'll meet we'll meet the 1st of June my sweet — my sweet — like R Burn's [11] — by Jupiter — good bye — Lord — we have never talked about Italian — I suppose you are a famous hand — as for me I never open my mouth without putting my foot in it. — what is — but Good bye

Sincer^{ly} yours Joseph Severn

[7] On March 23 Severn told his sister Sarah (ALS, Keats House, Hampstead), "I . . . cannot but be happy at the conclusion that she [Maria] has escaped such a canting selfish Husband. — I have just written my 2^d Letter to this Mr Peck — but something less severe than my 1st . . . . Maria deserves and will have a better husband . . . than this Peck of Methodism — with not half a Pint of true Religion in the whole Composition." Probably he was Henry William Peck, of 23 Gloucester Street, Hoxton, who exhibited at the Royal Academy in 1817, 1818, and 1820 — Algernon Graves, *The Royal Academy of Arts*, VI (London, 1906), 94.

[8] Brown later told Richards (number 56), "It was a joyful meeting for L H and Severn."

[9] Severn refers to Elizabeth Brownrigg, who was hanged at Tyburn on September 14, 1767, for the murder of an apprentice, Mary Clifford.

[10] Perhaps the preceding letter, of which only the extract printed by Sharp is known.

[11] "The Jolly Beggars," l. 272, "In raptures sweet this hour we meet."

· 49 ·

TO THOMAS RICHARDS

Address: Inghilterra. / To / Thomas Richards Esqʳ, / Store-keeper's Office, / Ordnance Department, / Tower, / London.

Postmarks: PISA; AUTRICHE PAR HUNINGUE; FPO MY 15 1823

ALS: Keats House, Hampstead. Printed in *Some Letters*, pp. 23–29.

My dear Richards,   Pisa. 30ᵗʰ April 1823.

Your letter came with three others. I choose to answer those three first, — you deserve no better. Then I made you wait two or three days more, till I had finished and despatched an Article on "Letter-writing",[1] where I took my revenge by throwing something back into your teeth, — I hope you will be truly sensible of the justice of it, — if you find me out. So, with a good conscience, I have made you wait the enormous space of eleven days. I am now, thank God! sitting in the garden, delightfully shaded. The weather is good Nankeen Jacket weather, and there is a little breeze, just enough to refresh me without blowing my papers off the table. Again I say, thank God! and my religious gratitude is surely as sincere as any Ultra-Catholic's, as he bows down his head before the Madonna. Talking of religion, two nights since I heard a great noise in a little Church, so in I went. There was a Coffin, appropriately furnished inside and out, the pall decorated with real skulls and cross-bones, and surrounded by half a dozen prodigious wax-candles, bigger than links. I found myself with one Priest, and one Acolyte, and a company of the "Misericordia".[2] They were chaunting the seven penitential psalms, and now and then treating us with singing-lectures of certain devout passages in scripture, greatly to the comfort and edification of the dead body. They behaved towards me with great politeness; one advanced to take my hat, which he put by with a due consideration

---

[1] It appeared in the fourth number of the *Liberal*, 2 (1823): 333–343, on July 30.

[2] A confraternity founded in Florence in 1244 to assist the injured, sick, and dying, and to arrange and attend funerals. Brown wrote an article on the Misericordia in 1826 (see number 85, n. 14).

for the nap; and another gave me a cumbersome book of the service; so I thought I could do no less than stay and see it out. All at once we lost our lolling attitudes, (for the benches were commodious enough,) and up we rose on our feet. Then what was my surprise to see a fellow bow to me, and present me with a wax-taper! As I happened to be at the corner of the front row, I was served first, which staggered me a trifle, till I found every one else was also served with a similar wax-taper. At the ringing of a tinkling bell, all the tapers were lighted, mine among the rest. Only imagine Signor Carlo, with one of his gravest faces,[3] standing bolt upright with a lighted wax-taper in his hand! It struck me we all looked very brilliant, till unluckily it popped into my head we bore some resemblance to the congregation in Hogarth's "Medley"; [4] and I was forced to call up my whole store of gravity, in order to refrain from a laugh, — happily I succeeded. Then a horrible suspicion darted across my mind that I was let in for a Procession through the streets! This worked upon me till I began to sweat, perplexing myself as to which course was best, — to expose myself, or throw down the taper and run away. With great emotion I saw the Priest arrive towards the conclusion of his blessings and fumigations. Now, thought I, we are going to pair off, two and two! Give me joy, you rogue! there was no such thing; we all of us took our departure "ad libitum"; and I got home relieved of a hundred weight of trepidations. This may be very uninteresting to you, but I can't help that. An advantage in living at a distance is that one's friends' illness, unless it appears of a frightful nature, does not prey upon my mind. I hear that M^r or M^rs So-and-so is ill. That is a bad affair indeed; but my comfort is that by the time the letter is in my hands, he or she must of course be perfectly recovered. This is just the state of my thoughts respecting your wife. By the by, I omitted to mention the aforesaid advantage in my essay on "Letterwriting". Give my love to your wife; and I have no objection to your giving her a kiss for my sake. Harriet, and Tom, and Sophy, and Sidney, are all nodding at me, in my imagination, and wondering I don't kiss them; — well, I do, — there, one, two, three, four, — now wipe your

---

[3] On Brown's "grave face, — my curse" see number 95.
[4] "Credulity, Superstition, and Fanaticism: A Medley" (see number 11, n. 5).

mouths and be happy. Respecting that business between you and Mancur, — I am content it should rest between you and him, — he has a word from me on the subject in my last dated some ten or twelve days since, — I can't exert myself to go into the house to look for the mem of the date. Bless me! it is growing very luxuriously warm, and the breeze has increased, — it got the better of this sheet of paper just now, — but Carlino saved me the trouble of picking it up. Apropos as to Carlino. I leave him behind when I go to Florence, — but that you have heard from Dilke. He (not Dilke) talks Italian very prettily, and with a careful articulation, running the vowels at the ends of words into the vowels at the beginings of words, as if he had been taught at half a guinea a lesson. What a curious thing it is to watch how a child gets into all the moods, and tenses, and genders of a language! The Monkey came to me not half an hour since with a bit of cake, and thus he went on: — (you have Italian enough to understand it,) — "Papa, questo è buono! Vuole Papa lo *mangiare*? No? Dunque, il Bimbo lo *mangia*. Ecco! tutto è *mangiato*!" The "lo" ought to come after that same infinitive mood, but that is no matter. Give my remembrances to Mrs Gooch, — and ditto to Mr Vincent; — but mind, I do not put them together, — Diana forbid it! It did not a little displease me to read in your letter the account of my conduct being canvassed in such a way, — especially by Rice. He has certainly, in his half jest and half earnest fashion, given many of my friends a very wrong idea of me. Whether he has done me an injury or not is another question; but it is no mistake on his part, as he knows me better; and I am inclined to think every thing that is untrue respecting the character of another, will, sooner or later, do him an injury. I never have been captious on such a point, and am not now, — glad enough that neither friends nor enemies can say worse of me; still I regret he should give a licence to his tongue, not in my favour, and while I am absent. The giving being to Carlino is a great fault, nay a heinous crime, in the eyes of many, — I am perfectly aware of that; but that fault, or that crime, is nothing compared to these words which Rice spoke to me soon after his birth, — "As for getting the woman with child, there was no harm in it; but there is harm in taking the child into your own house. I tell you what, Brown, — I can't bear that folks should pretend to more feeling than their neighbours." You may tell him that, bad as I am, I blushed for him, — or rather coloured with resentment at his inhumanity, and his insinuation at my *pretensions*. I cannot leave this subject without repeating my dissatisfaction at that old sin among litterary men, of sitting in company for the sole purpose of saying hard things against each other. There is no great credit in it, — the art is soon learnt by a bad hearted man; and men of kinder feelings, like yourself, should rather rest content with the knowledge that they either can or cannot retort. You will perceive some of this preaching is flying obliquely at you. Indeed, though I sincerely thank you for not sitting dumb when any thing was breathed in my disfavour, I cannot *read* your triumphant repartees without a feeling of regret, though, in all probability, had I *heard* them, no one would have enjoyed them more. Reading however brings them to the test. "Come," you will say, "if CB can't say a smart thing, he can, at any rate, write a severe one." So, Genoa is within my ear-shot; [5] why, it is a hundred miles off; what an ear I must have! Take this for Gospel; — I know no particulars of the Liberals, except what I have picked up from my friends in England. How should I? L. Hunt, when he writes, is too weary of the Articles, to say a word about them; and besides, it is not his humour. But it is not only of the Liberals that I wish to know. Dilke and Mancur, ever and anon, give me a snatch of litterary news, always with the idea it cannot possibly be news to me! You, I observe, have a taste for dwelling on it, and therefore I think it worth while to give this hint. So, you tell me, I am christened "Carlone"! I confess it is not so agreeable, nor so pretty a name, as "Carluccio," which was fixed on between me and L. Hunt as my "alias." [6] You see how ignorant I was, till you informed me of it, even of my own name. "Carlone" is worse, not only in English, but in Italian. It is better to be called "Charley" than "big Charles." I have written to Genoa that it would not surprise me if I should be nicknamed "Carlaccio," which has no politer meaning than "big ugly Charles"; — egad! perhaps L. Hunt, in one of his moods, may bestow it on me, as I have un-

[5] See number 46, n. 10.
[6] Brown's first article in the *Liberal* is signed "Carlone," his second "Carluccio." The third is unsigned.

luckily given him the mischief of it. I shall yet remain three or four days in Pisa, as that abominable Severn writes me word he cannot meet me at Florence till 1st *June*. You need not imagine I shall laugh at your writing Oratorio-criticisms.[7] It is better to write than be idle that way, and better still to write for money, — to which I see no just cause or impediment why you should not. While the Carnival lasted, we had a very good company for the Opera; and I think I never saw a more lovely looking creature than our Prima Donna in her three different dresses as "La Cenerentola,"[8] — but, woe is me! she was quite another sort of creature off the Stage! You must know I have fallen in love with Operas, — which is a lucky affair for a man in Italy. Then came a company of players, — a sad set, — they made my stomach ach[e]. Now we have another Opera company, but very unlike our Carnival one. I went once, and was so disgusted with the pot-bellied first tenor, and his attempts at singing, that I made a kind of vow never to see him again. The Pisans were as angry as myself, and so the Manager has sent for another in his place, — and we are to have *two* prima Donna's, — and they are getting up a new Opera for the occasion, — and it is promised every day, — and, hang them! they every day disappoint us. I see by the papers[9] that "La Cenerentola" has been a favourite lately at Paris, — has it found its way to London? By the by, talking of Paris, I see at two theatres, they have dramatic pieces under the title of "Trilby." These are of course taken from Nodier's Novel, who took it from me, though he impudently calls the story his own invention.[10] To give

---

[7] Richards had written some theatrical reviews for the *Examiner* in 1821 (see number 61, n. 8).

[8] In Rossini's *Cenerentola* [Cinderella], *ossia la bontà in trionfo*, first produced in Rome on January 25, 1817.

[9] Perhaps in *Galignani's Magazine*.

[10] Actually there were three "dramatic pieces" — *Trilby, ou le lutin d'Argail* (by A. E. Scribe and P. F. A. Carmouche), *Trilby, ou la batelière d'Argail* (by T. Marion Dumersan, F. de Courcy, and P. J. Rousseau), and *Trilby, ou le lutin du Foyer* (by M. E. G. M. Théaulon de Lambert, W. Lafontaine, and A. F. Jouslin de la Salle) — one-act comedies produced at different theaters on March 13, 20, 24, respectively, and published in Paris during the year. All were based on Charles Nodier's *Trilby, ou le lutin d'Argail* (Paris, 1822), the subject of which Nodier said he took "from a preface or note to one of Sir Walter Scott's novels, — I do not know which." Brown thought Nodier took the story from his own discussion of the Trilby legend in "On the Superstitions of Highlanders and Londoners," *New Monthly Magazine*, 2 (1821): 566–567.

rise to pieces on the Stage would, in the days of my minor vanity, have half turned my brain at my cleverness; now, alas! I can do nothing but laugh at it; a child enjoys his sop, but an alderman likes to wallow in a sea of turtle; — there's a sage reflection for you! I've a great mind to conclude my letter with it, — it is so very good, — especially as I'm too hot and lazy for filling up my usual back-spaces. Courage! I must not set a bad example! What a walk I'll have at sunset! The leaves are all young and beautifully green, — and I know who will be in a certain spot, — and it will be so comfortable, — so delightful! "I tell you what, Master Carlino, if you climb on the table, I'll daub your face with the ink." This was said in my best Italian, — though, be it known, not able to find a word for "daub", I was forced to say "paint". Yet as the boy has a care for his beauty, the threat had its due effect. "No, no, Papa, non lo voglio, — mi farebbe brutto! Subito vado giù!" There, — is it not provoking? — after toiling to fill up these back-spaces, I see, by your letter, you don't merit any thing of the sort. Fie upon you! Now I'm resolved not *quite* to fill them up, — I'll say no more than that I am, Your's sincerely,

Chas Brown.

· 50 ·

TO ROBERT FINCH [1]

Address: To / R. Finch Esqr

Endorsement: Brown.

ALS: Bodleian Library. Printed by Nitchie, *The Reverend Colonel Finch*, p. 88.

Dear Sir,   [1823 (?)]

My poor Keats will surely accompany me in all my ramblings, whether to Rome or to Mecca. As for a copy,[2] I'll be hanged if I

---

[1] On Finch (1783–1830), parson, traveler, antiquary, philanthropist, and pathological liar, whose letter to John Gisborne first informed Shelley of Keats's death, see Miss Nitchie's study.

[2] Presumably of the drawing made of Keats at Shanklin (see number 37, n. 6).

think I can make one, — but this may be attempted, — I did begin one for L. Hunt, but it still remains begun and no more.

Your's most truly,

Chas Brown.

Wednesday Morn^g

· 51 ·

TO THOMAS RICHARDS

Address: Inghilterra. / To / Thomas Richards Esqr, / Storekeeper's Office, / Ordnance Department, / Tower, / London.

Postmarks: FIRENZE; AT; AUTRICHE PAR HUNINGUE; FPO SE 6 1823

ALS: Keats House, Hampstead. Printed in *Some Letters*, pp. 30–37.

My dear Richards,   Florence. 22nd August 1823.

From all I know of you I should have said you would be the last to write to me on "visions and affairs of state"; yet you have turned out to be the first. Pray be careful. Since some late events every one is cat-watched. Banishment would be a nuisance, as I like the country. The being tongue tied on certain matters, as we are at present, is no nuisance to me, as my mind seldom wanders on those things which I can neither further nor retard. You not only gave the most imprudent news, but wrote it on the direction side of the letter, so that, by mere peeping in, it could be read. The consequence was, they supposing there must be more of the same stuff in it, your letter was detained from my hands for a week, and afterwards delivered to me cut with a knife in such a way that they could, without breaking the wafer, read every sentence. You will be ten times more displeased at this circumstance than I am, — so I shan't say another word about it. It is unpleasant to learn that you and your family have been in crazy health, — but you were tolerably recovered, and M^{rs} R better than she was a twelvemonth ago, and my godson walks about. Give my love to them, every man Jack and every woman Gill. I will write

to Davenport [1] as you request, very soon, for I have just received
a letter from him. Severn has read your straggling lines, which
don't hold so much as one is apt to imagine at first sight, — the
words look frightened at one another, — however you pen away
pretty well. He, (Severn,) and I have been together for these two
months. We are now on the wing for Venice. He desires to be
remembered, but I forget in what words, — and he is not at hand
to repeat them, being occupied in a sketch from Raphael in the
Grand Duke's palace. Every body, English and Italian, hold him
in high esteem, both as a man and an Artist. I am daily expecting
to see L. Hunt & family here.[2] The heat is so excessive, it is
probable their journey may be delayed beyond the time of my
departure, which is fixed for the day after to-morrow; however as
I shall return by Florence in my road to Rome, I shall then see
him assuredly. Severn wishes for a month at Venice, so it will be
for a month. Just as I had finished the last sentence, in came an
old gentleman to take formal leave of me, kissing me on both
cheeks, and wishing me all sorts of good. My progress in kissing
formed an appropriate subject for Mrs Dilke; — the first time a
young fellow ran up to me in the street and gave me a kiss I own
I was taken by storm and quite confounded, — now it is a matter
of course. Only imagine me, on my return to England, giving you
a kiss! — nay a couple, "to make his balance true!"[3] Give M^r
Vincent a shake of the hand for my sake, not wishing to trouble
you to play at slabber-chaps with him. I hope he will enjoy a
pleasant tour in the north, but the accounts I hear of your summer
are abominable, — it pleaseth me to be away. Many thanks for
your literary news. In return I'll give you an account of Milton's
Vallombrosa, together with the whole of a tour I have lately
made.[4] It shall be drawn from some notes I took during the time,
and the exactness of time and distances, with many other petty

[1] "Burridge Davenport, of Church Row, Hampstead, and merchant of 3 Dunster
Court, Mincing Lane" (M. B. Forman, *Some Letters*, p. 30n). Brown called on him
in February 1819, and introduced him to Hunt in April 1819 (*Letters*, II, 62, 83).

[2] They left Genoa for Florence on the day this letter was written (Blunden,
Leigh Hunt, p. 208).

[3] Cowper, "The Diverting History of John Gilpin," l. 72.

[4] See *Paradise Lost*, I.302–304. Brown described this tour in "Vallombrosa, Camaldoli, and La Verna," *New Monthly Magazine*, 14 (1825): 261–266, 346–352 (the
two-part article is reprinted in *Some Letters*, pp. 59–81).

matters shall all be included, as these things (as De Foe well knew) make trivial adventures of great moment. So, after mending my nib, here goes. On Monday 11th ins^t, at 2 o'Clock AM, we set off from Florence in a hired carriage. The *We* consisted of a M^r & M^{rs} F, a Miss T,[5] Severn, myself, and a man servant, — oh! I forgot the driver and the horses! Saw the dawn break upon some agreeable landscapes to the right and left. At 4 crossed the Arno to the south side, at the town of Ponte à Sieve; where, at this early hour, all was life and bustle, especially at the Market-place, as a "festa" was to be held there that day. You must spread out a map before you, or it will be impossible for you to understand me. After 14 miles arrived at Pelago, a village, whence we were compelled to leave the carriage, and proceed up the hill, by a winding bad road, as we could. The ladies hired horses; but as there were no such things as side-saddles, and as they would not consent to ride like "men of wax," [6] there were a thousand complaints and trepidations amidst a fund of merriment on all sides. On we went, the gemmen on foot, ready to catch a lady if she was inclined to make a slip. At last they gobbled on with more courage. I began a ballad on the occasion, then M^{rs} F: added a stanza, then Miss T another, all uncommonly witty at the time, but far from being capable of staring on paper, I question if they could bear repeating. This up-hill work lasted 6 miles, — the sun rather burning, tho' the road was sometimes shaded, — and at ½ past nine we arrived at the Convent; for Vallombrosa has been peopled by Monks ever since the 8th century only excepting the time of the revolution. The mountains on every side were finely wooded, tho' not so luxuriantly as in times past, — folks say the French cut down a great deal of timber here. I found fault with the fir-trees for giving too much formality to nature, — yet I and the whole group were delighted, and the pure elastic mountain air gave us new spirits and vigour. Ladies not being permitted to advance their feminalities beyond the chaste threshold of the convent, our party was shown into a building near at hand for the accommodation of such mixed visitors. At midday we were served with dinner, and, sooth to say, with not one of the best of all possible dinners,

---

[5] Mr. and Mrs. Robert Finch, and Mrs. Finch's sister Eliza Thomson.
[6] *Romeo and Juliet*, I.iii.76.

— yet the wine, both red & white, was excellent. Formerly the Monks used to treat all comers gratis; now their means, since their restoration a few years back, are more straightened, and they expect a handsome douceur at parting, which must yield them, from their many visitors, pretty pickings. The English, more frequently than others, go there; and are not only well received as good pay-masters, but as serving to colour the monotony of their lives, with news and compliments, — besides they give them opportunities of saying civil things in return, and of conversing with petticoat-wearers, — all very pleasant no doubt, — egad! one of the Monks looked and talked somewhat delightfully (to say no worse) with Miss T. We men, the contraband sex being left behind, explored the convent. Neither inside nor outside is their any beauty of architecture, nor has it the charm of antiquity. The Church, tho' small, was striking; but it could boast of no fine paintings, — so much the better, for those they have are injured by damp, as during the winter they live, as it were, in the clouds. The monks shave their chins, and wear black; their number is 20, — one half lay brothers. After dinner we toiled up to their Paradisino (little Paradise), a chapel on a high rock, commanding a most extensive view, but none of the best considering its heavenly name, — Florence looked beautiful in the map, for it was very like a map. At ½ past 2 we left Vallombrosa, the ladies horsed as before, and the rest on foot. We had another 5 or perhaps 6 miles of the worst kind of hilly roads, with little to repay us in the views. At last we got to the high road, at a place called Consuma, whither the carriage had been driven round to meet us. Then 12 miles more of easy riding brought us to the town of Prato Vecchio. Lack-a-day! I omitted to mention that Severn left us at Vallombrosa as he had seen the Convent of the Camaldoli in his way from Rome, and as he laudibly determined not to lose more than one day from his canvas, so back he went to Florence, where he arrived on foot at midnight. At Prato Vecchio, after some woful fears to the contrary, we got well housed in its only inn, and ate good beef-steaks for supper. On Tuesday at noon (for we all wanted a long sleep) away we went by another mountain track for the Camaldoli, the Ladies always horsed, except, now and then, when they left their nags in disdain and trudged with us on foot. This was for 6 miles

more of rough work, — yet the scenery repaid us amply for the
toil, and the sun, owing to a thin veil he wore, was not too fierce.
It was a woundy up-hill business for the greater part; then, on our
left, was a grand hollow, cut into a hundred deep ravines; on the
opposite side appeared Monte Falterone, an important Signor,
whence the Arno takes its source; then, presently, on our right,
was another deep, with a village near the bottom. Few of the inhabitants of this village remain during the winter, as the snow
keeps them prisoners, — they were all comfortably clothed and
well fed, as are all the Tuscan peasantry. We had to trot down to
the village, & then up again, and then down, gradually down for a
mile, to the convent. This last mile was like enchantment. I never
beheld any thing of the kind in my life. The Highlands beat it,
out and out, in wildness, romance, and terror, but I never, in my
most fanciful moods, could picture to myself such a scene of
beauty. What foliage! what richness of colouring! what never
ending, still beginning [7] woods, on gentle slopes and rocky steeps!
— how admirably were the trees contrasted! how they waved,
whole mountains of them, in the free air! Here the firs mixed with
the chesnut, the elm, the oak, and fifty others, as if nature's hand
had planted them, — and so perhaps it was. The convent itself has
little more to boast of, in appearance, than that at Vallombrosa.
The Monks wear white dresses and beards; they shave the head
and the upper lip. Their number is 40, one half lay-brothers;
before the revolution their family consisted of 90. Their best
books were taken by the French. An English party (whose invitation to their room was not accepted, as we could not, according
to our nation's silly caution, know who they might be) were before us; and so, in our pride, we dined in a carpenter's shop. [8]
Mercy on us! what a dinner! what delicate cookery! The very
sight, not to say the taste, of any one of the dishes, would make a
man an epicure for life. O, the jolly rogues! "And do you always
live so, my good Fathers?" quoth I. "God forbid!" replied one, "if
it were a fast day, we could not give you meat!" How fat the

[7] Dryden, "Alexander's Feast," l. 101.

[8] In his article (n. 4 above) Brown adds, "The fittest punishment for such artificial reserve fell upon all of us on our return to Florence; when it was discovered
that the other party, a gentleman and his two sisters, were . . . [Finch's] intimate
acquaintances, on their way from Naples, whose arrival he had long expected."

rogues were! — and how they smirked and smiled at the women! Soon as dinner was over we climbed a steep hill above the convent to see the Hermitage. It was two miles to the top, and the air there was very cold. Never was so lovely a walk. This Hermitage is now untenanted, so the Ladies were admitted. It is a wall-enclosure, containing a Church and I know not how many houses (seperate) for the hermits, — each house has a small oratory, a parlour, a study, a kitchen, and a garden, — no bad mode of living, putting solitude and the religion out of reckoning, — they are left in statu quo, just as when the establishment was suppressed, the walls decorated with trumpery prints of holy tales, but the gardens [9] are overrun with weeds. The descent to the convent made our knee pans ache. The Ladies were lodged for the night out of the holy pale. F: and I supped and slept in the Convent. While talking about eye-sight in the Refectory, I boasted I could write the Pater Noster on a bit of paper the size of my little finger-nail, — lord! what a posse of Monks I had about me, pretending incredulity, in order to provoke me to make them such a present. They promised the finest paper, — crow-quills, — every thing I could want; and I had scarcely risen from a good bed, when pop came one with all the apparatus. I wrote three for them, — and then I was to settle for which particular fathers they were made, or a sad feud I should have left behind me, — at least it appeared so to me. They were as fond of them as any children of their toys. The Wednesday morning was passed loungingly, enjoying the beauties of the Valley, and M[rs] F, the only busy one, took a pretty view of one of the prettiest spots. Again we partook of their excellent dinner-cheer, and could not quit the place till 5 o'Clock; when we returned to Prato Vecchio as we came, and then rode, the following day, (30 miles) to Florence. It was a happy jolly jaunt; and I have given you, deny it who dare, a full, true, and particular account; — indeed so long a one, that I cannot bear the thought of rewriting it, and therefore you will oblige me by letting Dilke read it; for I recollect his saying "Of course, Brown, you will make a point of visiting Vallombrosa", and that implied a demand for my opinion of the said visit. I know it will in some measure satisfy his curios-

[9] At this point, with a fainter pen, Brown has interlined a parenthetical "also" followed by a single letter or character now illegible.

ity; and, if you are a good fellow, you won't grumble at my request. On the second day after our return to this City of flowers, away went F:, Severn, & I to Pisa. The old Fresco paintings there, in the Campo Santo,[10] disappointed Severn, but I was by no means disappointed in the sight of my dear Carlino. He visited me in Florence on St John's day,[11] and staid a week. Whether this my farewell visit till next Spring made me regard him with more than usual partiality, or whether he really merits the opinion, I know not; — but, for the first time, I made up my mind he was a clever good tempered boy. It is strange he and I should talk Italian together! Next year, however, he will live at my knee, and then for our English. I taught him a little English in the three days I was with him, — a child picks up a language as fast as Pidgeons do peas. He grows tall, not thin but rather spare, keeps up his rosy cheeks in this hot weather, and calls for his ice after dinner quite as a matter of course. It will be a painful affair to take him away from my Pisan Padrona,[12] — when I said my next visit would be to place him in my own house, where I knew not, the old woman burst into tears. I never will ask you again to be a good correspondent.

Your's most sincerely, Chas Brown.

[10] "The Campo Santo or Burial Ground," wrote Hunt in the *Liberal*, 1 (1822): 105, 109, "a set of walled marble cloisters full of the oldest paintings in Italy. . . . The crowning glory of Pisa."

[11] June 24. During this visit Severn painted a miniature of Carlino (Joanna Richardson in *Keats-Shelley Memorial Bulletin*, no. 5, 1953, p. 49) that Richard Westmacott, Jr. (Sharp, p. 142), thought "very like him."

[12] Carlino lived with "a worthy Italian family of the name of Gordini" (*KC*, I, lviii) from September 1822 to May 1824.

· 52 ·

(WITH JOSEPH SEVERN) TO ROBERT FINCH

Address: Al Signore / Il Signor Roberto Finch, / Gentil'uomo Inglese, / Firenze, / Toscana.

Postmarks: Venezia; 6 [S]ETTEMBRE

Endorsements: Rec^d Sepr 6. 1823. Ans^d 11.; Brown.

ALS: Bodleian Library.

My dear Sir,   Venice. 3rd September 1823.

Alack-a-day! that the world should be guilty of such scandal! Why, nothing is more easy and pleasant than to travel to Venice.[1] There is not a jot more trouble with passports than in Tuscany; add to which, the Police has behaved to us very civilly, and use a becoming despatch gratis. Now in the Papal dominions it cost me and Severn together the monstrous sum of eleven pauls[2] for our passports, and I suppose it will cost the same to return, — twenty two pauls! — "think o' that, Master Brook!"[3] — while we have not yet paid a farthing to the Austrians. Then again, on the frontiers, — what politeness! Our words were taken for the contents of the portmanteaus, and after many compliments on both sides, (our's consisting of a couple of franks,) we proceded with as little molestation as any member of the Aulic Council. Etty[4] can tell you a different story about the searching of his trunks, — but let every man speak for himself. They say a good face is a letter of recommendation; proverbs have their exceptions, and therefore it may be that bad faces answer the purpose better on certain occasions; at any rate I feel the compliment paid to us as rather of a dubitable gender. Yesterday Severn began at Peter Martyr,[5] of which he intends to make somewhat more than a rough sketch.

---

[1] They had left Florence for Venice early on the morning of August 24 (number 51; Sharp, p. 137).

[2] About 5s. 6d. (see number 67, n. 2).

[3] *The Merry Wives of Windsor*, III.v.124.

[4] William Etty (1787–1849), painter of nudes.

[5] Titian's altarpiece for the church of San Giovanni e Paulo (destroyed by fire in 1867).

Your friend the President is not here,[6] but Severn's having the letter in his hand will be an introduction to those who remain in the Academy, — where he intends to work for the first half of every day, — the latter half will be employed in the Churches. We promise to go on swimmingly. We staid at Ferrara only for an hour; during that time I managed to visit Sig. Taveggi, who received your letter most handsomely. I am to call again on our return. He inquired a great deal, and kindly, after you, and about Mrs Finch's health. I thank you for giving me his acquaintance. Because I am at Venice, it does not follow I should give every body a description of it; and as for you, — you know it better than I do. We were very well satisfied with our Vetturino, and intend to travel with him and S. Antonio all the way to Rome,[7] if he should be disengaged at the time, and willing to accept of our terms. Make my respectful Compliments to Mrs Finch and Miss Thompson, — I expect to see that landscape brought out in fine harmony, and to hear wonders about the Camera Lucida. I wrote to West [8] yesterday, and when I have tagged my name to the bottom of this, I shall give L. Hunt a memento that I am his — no —

Your's most sincerely,
Chas Brown.

My dear Sir — Here I come in, on this bit of paper like Q in a corner — always behind, "just like Severn" — but I am content — to be behind in Venice is equal to before in every other place. — We have dropped down here, — to a City like the New Jerusalem — as it were by the aid of Fortunatus's Cup — without any opposition but the Air — We have come to a Paradise where Painting is abstracted into itself — to a perfection I could never dream off — Tintoretto's Miracle of the Slave [9] — is a Miracle in itself — it is — but I must not get into a rapture on this bit of paper. — present my painter-like Comp^ts to M^rs F & Miss Tomspon

& believe me very truly Yours Joseph Severn

[6] Leopoldo Cicognara (1767–1834), president of the Venetian Academy of Fine Arts.

[7] They remained at Venice until September 29, were back in Florence for a few days in the first week of October, and then went on to Rome, where Brown spent the winter and spring (numbers 54, 56).

[8] William Edward West (1788–1857), the American artist who painted portraits of Byron and Teresa Guiccioli in 1822.

[9] Also known as "The Miracle of St. Mark," painted for the Scuola di San Marco.

· 53 ·

(WITH JOSEPH SEVERN) TO LEIGH HUNT

Address: Al Signore / Il Signor Leigh Hunt, / Gentil'uomo Inglese, / Firenze, / Toscana.

Postmarks: Venezia; 6 SETTEMBRE

ALS: British Museum.

My dear Hunt,   Venice. 3rd September 1823.

This comes to assure you Severn and I are at Venice, and that we shall be at Florence about this day next month. Besides, I want to tell you I have taken the liberty to give two letters of introduction to you. Upon coming into a new City they would, I thought, be useful to yourself. You will find Mr Finch a kind hearted man,[1] and a very good scholar. Mr Marchettini (Signor I should have said) is a young Artist, who will, when you are inclined to visit the Galleries and Museums, be happy to accompany you. I saw Gianetti [2] lately in {Pis}a, and he desired to be remembered to you; {per}haps you have seen him in Florence. I am anxious to hear how Mrs Hunt and her family travelled through our hot weather. If you forget to satisfy me on this point, I hope West [3] will tip me a stave about it. Alas! Venice disappoints me! The canals, at this time of the year, stink abominably; and tho' we live far from the worst of them, I am not content. The Piazza di S. Marco, to be sure, is wonderful; and as for the Venetian paintings I could gaze at them from morning to night, day after

---

[1] Hunt wrote to his brother John on October 14 (Brewer, *Holograph Letters*, p. 158), "A gentleman here, whom Mr. Brown at his request introduced to me, and who is a man of fortune, has introduced me to his banker [Messrs. Orsi and Company], who is *this day* to advance me £50." According to Nitchie, *The Reverend Colonel Finch*, p. 17n, "Finch brought 'the first Doctor in Sienna' to see Marianne; he and his wife and sister-in-law all showed 'great anxiety' about her."

[2] "My young acquaintance, Luigi Gianetti" (Hunt, *Lord Byron*, I, 39), a student at the University of Pisa "who made a very kind and attentive master" to Hunt's children in the summer of 1822, "and promises to be an excellent instructor" — *Liberal*, 1 (1822): 98n. In 1824 he came to Florence to study law, and Hunt told Elizabeth Kent on June 2 (*Correspondence of Leigh Hunt*, I, 221) that he "is in the habit of being with me every morning at six to interchange languages."

[3] About this time West made a "Florentine picture" of Hunt (*Letters of Mary Shelley*, I, 347; Brewer, *Holograph Letters*, p. 137).

day. I fancy the cause of my dislike to this City is that we are so straightly enclosed by the sea, — it gives me a sensation, as if I had been a great man, and that I am now prisoner on a small island. Mr Taaffe wrote me an odd letter, rather rude, — all about you & his Article; [4] as I had previously resolved to cut him, I answered it, but in as odd a manner, and perhaps rather rude. Give my respects to Mrs Hunt, and love to the children. I leave a space for Severn.

Your's most sincerely,
Chas Brown.

Pray don't write to us after the 20th of this month.

My dear Hunt

O! that I could paint a letter — to have you enjoy with me this Paridise of Art — where Painting is abstracted into itself — and the Painters are like Giants — in mind & body. — I had no idea of this Perfection of Art. — Venice is covered by Painting like the sands of Sea. — all full of sp[l]endor and fresh nature which to me are a new element. — I long to have [you] write a description of Venice — nobody else can do it — We shall soon meet — ever yours

Josh Severn

4 Probably Hunt had rejected an article intended for the *Liberal*, though it is possible that Brown refers to the "long [article] . . . with an extract or two" that Hunt had promised but had not written in praise of Taaffe's *Comment on Dante* (Brewer, *Holograph Letters*, p. 145).

· 54 ·

TO ROBERT FINCH

Address: Toscana / Al Signore / Il Signor Robert Finch, / Gentil'uomo Inglese, / Firenze.

Postmarks: Venezia; 25 SETTEMBRE

Endorsements: Rec^d Octr 3° 1823; Brown.

ALS: Bodleian Library. Extracts are printed by Nitchie, *The Reverend Colonel Finch*, pp. 88–89.

My dear Sir,   Venice. 19th September 1823.

You are a grave gentleman and no jack-pudding. How then could you commit your gravity into such unholy keeping as our's? Never speak, far less write to make another laugh. Wot you not that he who setteth the world a grinning loseth the world's respect? Thou shouldst ever be serious as an Alderman before his turtle soup, or as an old man making love to a young woman, or as a young man scolded by a rich uncle, or as a donkey at work, or a pig asleep, lest thy character should not be held in respect. At thy approach men ought to be chop-fallen,[1] women should behold thee with a distant awe, and boys should look up in thy face demurely as at their schoolmaster's. As for your advertisement from the Florence gazette, here is a pretty parody on it from the Bologna one.

Found.

"In the Palace of the three Moorish Kings, stuffed between two mattrasses, a snuff-taker's flag of abomination, by no means appearing to have been lately washed, the silk much frayed, owing, it is conjectured, to the roughness of the owner's beard. In the corner are the initials *R F*, which probably may stand for "*Wrong-headed Philosopher.*" From its appearance, and accidental circumstances, it is supposed to belong to a tall, stout, careless gentleman, who was seen going out of the said Palace on the 27th of August last at an early hour, and who is a dealer in snuff. On producing a clean-shaven chin on the 3rd of October next, it will be restored

---

[1] See number 5, n. 2.

to the lawful owner for a proper acknowledgement; but no application will be attended to after that time, as the article will be sold to defray the expence of washing."

22ⁿᵈ Septʳ. Why this letter was not finished off hand, is more than my idleness can account for. But, be it known, I have much to do in these our Venetian lodgings. In the first place the Landlady's tongue is to be kept in order, — no trifling task. Then as she is a bad cook, I am obliged to be a good one. Severn is astonished at my right down English dinners. He, and Messʳˢ Etty & Evans,[2] dined yesterday with me on a boiled leg of mutton, caper sauce, and carrots. What d'ye think of that? And all admirably cooked I assure you. 'Twas I that scraped carrots & cut capers, and mine was all the praise.[3] Talk indeed of *my* supper-appetite! — why I nibble like a mouse in comparison with these canvas-gentry, who ate as if they had not been blessed with dinner or supper since they began to brush in Italy. On Sunday (29ᵗʰ) we shall set off, please the pig of S. Anthony, and glad shall I be to be out of this stinking, gnat-tormenting city. Severn & I send our Compᵗˢ to Mʳˢ Finch & Miss Thomson, and hope they had fine weather for their second jaunt to the Camalduli, — and I

call myself your's sincerely,
Chaˢ Brown.

· 55 ·

TO LEIGH HUNT

Address: Al Signore / Il Signor Leigh Hunt / Gentil'uomo Inglese / Firenze.

Postmarks: AREZZO; 9 OTTOBRE

ALS: British Museum.

My dear Hunt,   Arezzo. 8ᵗʰ Octʳ 1823.

This is to give notice that I could not find the key, which I promised to leave out for you at the Locanda, — but it is of little

---

[2] Richard Evans (1784–1871), portrait painter and copyist.
[3] Shakespeare, Sonnet 38, l. 14, "The pain be mine, but thine shall be the praise."

matter as I shall tell you. There are four packages, (one belonging to Trelawny) [1] and in the square deal box, formerly an English soap-box, is a bunch of keys to open every thing. This deal box is fastened by a padlock, and if you take the staple out, or break the lock, every thing will be at your service. So be it.

Had it not been for this key-affair, you would not have heard so quickly from me on our journey.[2] John seems resolved to be obedient, and *of course good*; — if he continues in this mind he will be an entertaining little fellow.[3] I wish to know what you will think a moderate charge for teaching him Latin. If you have any latin books to spare for his use, would it not be better to send them with his clothes, instead of buying others? He is very well and says he has "only to send his love" — yes, now he adds he shall send you a long letter from Rome. Severn & I abound in remembrances, which please deliver to the respectable parties in due and lawful proportions. The weather for our journey is delightful, but the mules are sorry ones.

Your's sincerely,
Chas Brown.

[1] Trelawny had visited Brown and Severn in Florence sometime during the summer (Trelawny to Hunt, October 25, 1823, British Museum).

[2] They had left Florence on the preceding day.

[3] John Leigh Hunt. In 1862 Thornton Hunt (*Correspondence of Leigh Hunt*, I, 273–274) told how Brown, "thinking that the father put too harsh a construction upon the lad's [John's] foibles . . . took him to join a select circle of friends at Rome. Here a very careful encouragement was given to all his better qualities, while the utmost vigilance was exerted to check his misconduct, everything being done in the kindest spirit. But, after some time . . . [Brown] was compelled to send him home to Florence, then barely eleven years old." For more details see the next two letters.

· 56 ·

TO THOMAS RICHARDS

Address: Inghilterra. / To / Thomas Richards Esqʳ / Store-keeper's Office / Ordnance Department / Tower / London.

Postmarks: ROMA; AUTRICHE PAR HUNINGUE; FPO NO 15 1823

ALS: Keats House, Hampstead. Printed in *Some Letters*, pp. 38–43.

My dear Richards,   Rome. 27ᵗʰ October 1823.

Your wife's illness gave me considerable uneasiness in the first part of your letter: however as I went on, the anxiety went off, and I am happy to be able to congratulate her and you on her recovery. We saw L Hunt at Florence, where, on our return from Venice, we staid no more than three days. He and the children are all well, and Mʳˢ Hunt is considerably better, thanks to the little Genovese she bears at her bosom.[1] It was a joyful meeting for L H and Severn, and we all chatted of and concerning our old friends in England as prodigiously as you can imagine. One day I offered, half joke and half earnest, to take his son John (my favourite) to Rome, and the offer was accepted, so here I have him. L H however first insisted on telling me all his bad qualities, leaving me at liberty to refuse to take him. The list was a very long one; enough to startle one;[2] yet I had formed so good an opinion of the boy's heart, that I did not allow his faults to sway me in the least. He was plainly too much both for father and mother to manage, distressed them daily, hourly, by his conduct, and as he had lost all pretence to a good character at home, there was no hope for him. His father said that to be relieved of him for half a year would make the family happy, though, at the same time, he could not endure that another should be tormented, and

---

[1] Vincent Leigh Hunt, born at Albaro on June 9.

[2] According to Thornton Hunt (*Correspondence of Leigh Hunt*, I, 274), John was "devoid of any faculty of self-restraint . . . . On several occasions he attacked his brothers with knives; on one, actually stabbing his third brother . . . . It was after this, that, in order to extort some indulgence from his mother . . . he held the carving-knife over the soft part of the head of an infant brother."

therefore he said his worst of him, — "and now, Mr Brown, do as you please, — take him or leave him." John has now been with us, including the journey, exactly three weeks, and his worst qualities are either destroyed or concealed.[3] He is most anxious to earn a good name. We have had one dire struggle, when, finding he *must* yield, he did so with so pleasant a grace that I could scarce forbear laughing; and since that time he has never once attempted to contend. He is only 11 years old, and, if I mistake not, his talents are considerable. L.H. has, I believe, taken a house two miles from Florence; in the spring I shall take another in his neighbourhood,[4] and sit down to teach my Carlino English. I had a letter four days since from Pisa, giving, as usual, the best account of his little worship. Severn sends his friendship to you and your's; we keep house together, and I am head-cook; you cannot imagine how well I succeed in rump-steaks, soups, stews, hashes, vegetables, boils and roasts. I have just now a soup cooking at the fire, and though I say it that ought not, it will be most extraordinarily excellent. We get up at about ½ past 6, dine at 1, sup at 8, and go to bed at 10; — is not this in the right vein? The "curious fact" of my committing six blunders in spelling in one letter does not in the least surprise me. On that point I know myself tolerably well; and I'll not be at the pains to turn to a Dictionary for your sake, till you turn Editor, and pay me handsomely for my articles. But why were you so touchy about my translating "paradisino"?[5] Wot you not the letter was to be read by Dilke, who cannot afford to be puzzled with outlandish jargon?[6] As for yourself, an admirable Italian scholar no doubt, I never shall think of translating for you, — Anzi, caro lei; mi piace a lasciar i matti in loro bujo. Severn, who has a vile trick of mingling the two languages, when he pretends to speak English, goes on in a style that *you* may understand, but it would puzzle many a one. "Now, *Signor* Brown, *guardi un*

---

[3] Richard Westmacott, Jr., however, who saw him in Rome, describes him (Sharp, p. 142) as "our old plague, Johnny Hunt." Brown kept the boy only three and a half months (see the next letter).

[4] See number 58.

[5] In number 51.

[6] In his fictional portrait of Dilke in "Walter Hazlebourn" Brown later wrote, "he laudably endeavoured to teach himself Latin and French; but it was too late, or he was incapable of so persevering an effort. Consequently he railed against all languages but his own" (Richardson, *The Everlasting Spell*, p. 91).

po' at my Alexander's *scudo*. *Diavolo mi prende* if I make it a *scudaccio!* — but I can't please myself about the *figure*. *Viene qui,* let's have a look at the *costumi d'Esperanza*," (Hope's costumes); [7] "*ecco!* what think you of *questo? Come pare? Pare a me bravo assai,* but how do you *piace* it? Who's knocking at the *porta?* O, the *fornajo* with *paniotti,* — Brown, you must come out with your *baiocchi*." — Severn, Severn, when will you learn to speak English, — duly and truly? — "*Ah! che cosa! Scusi, Signor Carlo,* I will, indeed I will, correct my *lingua,* — I have certainly got into a very bad *abitudine*." You must know that, bating this fault in Severn, I think him quite a perfect fellow. He has a generous way of thinking on all occasions and an independence of spirit that I seldom saw equalled. He looks very well, — I think younger than he did in England. As for his painting, I may be too partial to speak of it properly, — let it (and I fear not the trial) speak for itself. He has a twelvemonth to come of pensioneering from the Academy; and has no idea of leaving Italy at the end of the term. I have to pass, continually, the house, nay, under the very window, where Keats died.[8] This to me is a stronger memorial of his death than his grave. You ask me for my feelings and observations at his grave; — I saw it, rather from a distance, as the keeper of the ground was absent, with no feeling whatever. A grave never affects me; the living man was a stranger to it, and it only contains a clod like itself. One single circumstance of his life, brought to my mind by a trifle that he loved or hated, affects me always, — but not mournfully, — quite the contrary. I have taught myself to think with pleasure of his having been alive and been my friend, — not with sorrow at his death. This I dare own. It is that state of mind which I am convinced every man can acquire, and if he loves happiness, let him do it as quickly as possible. If your eternal sorrowers think it very odd in me, — why, — I'm an odd fellow, you know, — and so let the argument end. I am glad to hear that Dilke has articulated in the New Monthly; now he has put his foot in it I have some hopes. You will laugh to hear that L. Hunt, when he passed thro' Pescia from Genoa, wanted to find out the

[7] Thomas Hope, *Costume of the Ancients*, 2 vols. (1809). Severn was still working on "Alexander the Great Reading Homer."
[8] No. 26, Piazza di Spagna.

shop where my "bella Tabaccaia" lives.[9] He believed in every item of the story. How I chuckled to find I had taken in the knowing one! When I told him that it was entirely a fiction from the first line to the last, — "Indeed!" quoth he, "then you permit yourself to be called a Gentleman that tells — that is — that is not deserving of credit." It deceived Severn, when I read it to him, but at that I was not surprised, — and Severn was very *angry* it was not true. But how curiously circumstances sometimes hit together: when at Florence I had just concluded that part about a Pisan student holding a knife to a woman's throat, an Italian gentleman entered my room, and presently came out with — "Shocking news from Pisa, Sir, — a young student there has murdered a woman in her bed for her money!" Now I had mentioned at Pisa my story to my young friend Gianetti, a Pisan student, and he gravely told me I had no right to *suppose* any one of his fellows could be guilty of so cowardly & atrocious an act, — was not the coincidence a strange one? Some may imagine my story had got wind in the University, and put the murder in the young villain's head! While in Rome I shall buy all the good engravings I can lay my hands on for my modicum of money. They are to be picked up here and there. When weary of them, or in want of cash, I must sell them again, — and really good engravings are always saleable, especially in England, and the enormous duty is now taken off. I have just purchased a book containing 191 large and small of Wierotter's engravings for £3. 15/–.[10] How is Wierotter estimated in England? Severn says he thinks such a work, with good impressions, such as mine are, would be a ten-guinea-affair without any trouble. They are the most beautiful landscapes, and bits of landscapes, you can conceive, and they do not average so much as 5d each. Are Piranesi's works still much sought after? [11] I must buy some, — they are glorious prints, full of poetry and lies. The modern style of engraving in Italy is as hard as the copper; the artists might copy Ben West tolerably, but their copies of Raphael &c are intolerable,

---

[9] Brown's "La Bella Tabaccaia" (reprinted in *PDWJ*, December 12, 1839, and in *Some Letters*, pp. 94–108) first appeared in Hunt's *Literary Examiner*, September 20, 1823, pp. 177–185.

[10] Franz Edmund Weirotter (1730–1771) began publishing engravings in 1760. For Brown's reselling of a collection of Rossini's engravings see number 87.

[11] Giambattista Piranesi (1720–1778), engraver and architect.

— they have no idea of an indefinite line, and, vain fools! they insist on making some cursed alterations in light or shade, or something they cannot understand. You will be surprised to hear that Italian painters make no use of their fine old masters; they boast of them, and expatiate on their excellence by rote, — they never profit from them. They are fully persuaded the modern school is the best, in imitation of the French, whose school they follow with obedient heads. In professed copies from Titian or Raphael they lay on their positive blues & reds, while the originals are entirely painted in mixed colours, and tell you the originals are *faded*, — this is incomprehensible. It is needless to say they have a poor opinion of English art, which certainly emulates the old masters. — I see this letter is determined to be a chit chat one, so I can't help it. — I despatched a long letter to Dilke from Florence, and one to Mancur from Venice.[12] Rely upon it Lord Byron behaved most shamelessly to L. Hunt. I would not say so, were I not assured of it. Nor has his Lordship confined his ill conduct to H: alone, but he has shown himself unfeeling and unjust to others.[13] I have, thank Heaven! nothing to do with him, for you may truly parody Butler,[14] with

> "Ah, me! what perils do environ
> The man that meddles with Lord Byron."

I could excuse his frivolity and wilfulness, but his bad heart, which I never believed in, I neither can nor will excuse. Soon, I prophecy, you will hear of his being sorely sick of the Greeks, and perhaps of behaving shabbily about his own subscription,[15] — in fact, I have something whereon to hang my prophecy. You may drink as much ale, grog, and port as you please, only allow me not to touch one of them, but to swallow wine by tumblers-full at 3ᵈ to 4ᵈ per bottle. When I return to England the loss of

---

[12] Neither letter is known.

[13] See numbers 59, 61. Actually Byron had advanced Hunt £250, paid another £50 for furniture, provided him with an apartment and given him £70 at Pisa, and paid the costs of his moves from Pisa to Genoa and from Genoa to Florence (Cline, *Byron, Shelley and Their Pisan Circle*, p. 242). Marshall, *Byron, Shelley, Hunt, and "The Liberal*," pp. 194–196, thinks that "unfeeling and unjust to others" refers to Byron's recent behavior toward Mary Shelley.

[14] *Hudibras*, Part I, Canto III, ll. 1–2, echoed by Byron in *Don Juan*, III.xxxvi.

[15] Byron (who had sailed for Greece in July) about this time lent the Greeks £4000 "to set their Squadron in motion" while they negotiated for a larger sum from England — Byron's *Letters and Journals*, VI (1901), 284.

these delicious small wines will be a sad misfortune. When does Taylor intend to publish a life of Keats? Is it known? I have just despatched an Article to L. H. but don't know when or where it may be printed; for perhaps the Indicator [16] may not last. If Colburn [17] would behave with decency, he would always be a dernier resort, — yet, if possible, I will still write in company with L. H., as he knows me and I know him, which makes the labour a less labour, with no misgivings. I've an admirable plot for a Novel, or a Romance,[18] — what you will, — the scene in Italy. I flatter myself I am waiting for some histories, to serve as pegs for my story. It is an awful thing to write the first paragraph of three or four volumes. Nor am I fixed on the particular style, — yes, the *style* will be in my matter-of-fact method of telling lies for truths, — but the *manner* of it, the mode of telling and conducting it is the puzzle, and I wish to strike out something original in this way. Give my love to your Wife, & Tom, & Sophy, & kiss Sidney for his godfather's sake, & make a bow to Miss Harriet Richards, at full length, just as if it came from me. Why could you not fill up this part of your letter? [19] And what did you mean by "really I cannot find any thing more to say, and so &c"? Now to punish you, I won't say a word more, except that I am,

ever your's sincerely,
Chas Brown.
30th Octr 1823.

[16] That is, the *Literary Examiner: Consisting of the Indicator, a Review of Books, and Miscellaneous Pieces*, which ran from July 5 to December 27, 1823.

[17] Henry Colburn (d. 1855), publisher of the *New Monthly Magazine*.

[18] About Bianca Capello (1548–1587), mistress and then wife of Francesco de' Medici (1541–1587), grand duke of Tuscany. The novel is mentioned again in numbers 68, 82, 86, 94.

[19] Brown is here writing on the fourth page, below the address.

· 57 ·

TO LEIGH HUNT

ALS: British Museum. Extracts are printed by Richardson, *The Everlasting Spell*, p. 58.

My dear Hunt,   Rome. 21ˢᵗ Janʸ 1824.

John set off with Mʳ Ward yesterday morning.[1] Our taking leave was a little painful. He made use of some words, wonderful for a child, — "I am very sorry, Mʳ Brown, that I do not feel I love you so much as I know I ought." This proved to me he loved me more than he was aware of, — but me and restraint on his actions he could not love together. I omitted to mention I had given to Mʳ Ward a sum sufficient for all his expences on the road; and lest you should receive John before this letter, I told him to inform you of it, in order to prevent any unpleasant hesitation on your part with Mʳ Ward, — it never entered my mind when I wrote on Sunday and Monday to mention it.[2] I wrote about John's offer to betray private conversation, and you may tell him, if you think proper, of the consequence; for though it neither makes his fault greater or less, yet the knowledge of the mischief he has committed may teach him never to be guilty of the like again, — and therefore I relate it. It is true Mʳ Ewing[3] stopped him before he was allowed to say what it was that Severn had spoken against him; but John's reply of "Yes, it would certainly be wrong for me to tell you, because, Mʳ Ewing, you would not like me to tell Mʳ x x x that you called him a manner'd man." From this Mʳ Ewing perceived, so it now appears, that Severn's observation was against his own address and manner, as it really was; and Mʳ E: is extremely sensitive on this point as he prides himself much on his gentlemanly address, without having his notion flattered by any one. Now — (and John will, I fully believe, be shocked to hear it) — as soon as John had left us, Mʳ E made allusions to the subject with Mʳ Severn, and acted towards him so as to leave little doubt

---

[1] See the two preceding letters.
[2] Brown's letter has not survived.
[3] Ewing had been staying with Brown and Severn in Rome.

of all the cordiality of their friendship being destroyed. Thus, by those few foolish words, he has tainted the kind feelings between them, which had their origin in the best source, — in actions of good will towards each other. This I have mentioned for his ear, if you think fit, but I am sorry you should be acquainted with it. The great struggle I had in making up my mind to part with him was on your account. You had earnestly hoped, as I had confidently expected, to receive him, at the end of six months, from my own hand, a good affectionate boy, and I cannot bear to think of your disappointment. Yet, as I have told you before, — he is better in respect to truth, honesty, and cleanliness, and for that amendment he merits your praise. We all send our remembrances, and to all; Mr Kirkup hopes you will come to Rome, but I think he will pass next summer in Florence.[4]

> Your's most sincerely,
> Chas Brown.

Pray tell Mrs Hunt I had no time to get John's linen washed. One or two towels of his are at my washer-woman's, — one I think, — and I will carry it with me to Florence.

· 58 ·

TO JOSEPH SEVERN [1]

> Maiano (Florence),
My dear Severn,   May 20th, 1824.

   Do not think me unkind for not having until this time made you acquainted with a matter of the utmost moment concerning myself. Indeed, it would have been useless in me to ask your advice on such a point, as no opinion of yours could have changed my resolution. You, who know me well, must be aware that though I have heedlessly, perhaps too heedlessly, gained among my friends and associates a character at times approaching to folly and buffoonery (for which I am now as repentant as I ought to be), yet

---

[4] The artist Seymour Stocker Kirkup (1788–1880), hereafter mentioned many times in these letters, visited Florence sometime before September 7 (see number 64).

[1] From Sharp, pp. 143–144.

that I have always, beneath that trivial behaviour, entertained the most serious reflections; you, I say, know this well, and ought not to be surprised at the step I have taken. My future happiness has been the constant idea in my mind ever since I left you; and hating as I do the vain and gaudy glitter of this world, and feeling that nothing but a religious retirement can give ease to my soul, I have determined to enter a convent. I am now bound by law to remain there for five months, and at the end of that period I cannot believe I shall once desire to bid adieu to so blissful a habitation. Before this reaches you I shall have entered within its holy walls. Hunt speaks very kindly to me under the circumstances — I know he means kindly — but nothing he can say shall make me waver; indeed, it is now too late. My Italian friends, Gianetti and Magini, when I first acquainted them with this change in my situation, not only refused to believe me, but when I assured them of the fact, they began — would you credit it? — to jeer me; yet, what was their astonishment when I let them into the secret that I was going to live in a Convent of Nuns! Tol-de-rol-lol! Fal-lal-lal-la! Yes! you rogue, I have taken half a suppressed Nunnery for a villa, with four rooms and a pantry and a kitchen on the first. I am buying furniture at a swinging rate. By-the-by, I occupy the Abbess's apartments.[2] Charlie and I intend to be as merry as grigs here. Leigh Hunt talks of taking the other half of the Nunnery next October. I pay only 31 ½ crowns per annum.[3] I forgot to tell you I've a glorious romping place, as big as a ball-room, at the top of the house. Did I take you in as you read the former page? Yes, Severn, thoughts of my future happiness make me retire to this convent.

*   *   *

[2] Brown occupied the convent of St. Baldassare, near Maiano, until the beginning of November, when he moved into Florence.
[3] That is, about £7½.

· 59 ·

TO THOMAS RICHARDS

Address: Inghilterra. / To / Tho⁵ Richards Esqʳ, / Storekeeper's
Office, / Ordnance Department, / Tower, / London.

Postmarks: FIRENZE; AT; AUTRICHE PAR HUNINGUE;
FPO AU 14 1824

Endorsement: Aug/24

ALS: Keats House, Hampstead. Printed in *Some Letters*, pp. 44–50.

My dear Richards, Villa near Florence. 26ᵗʰ July 1824.
  Many thanks for your kind letter of 20ᵗʰ Novʳ 1823, for I am
convinced that is its true date, tho', oddly enough, it pretends to
another. What a time it has been on the road! The good news in
it set me in high spirits, yet I cannot but be anxious to learn how
you have been getting on since that time. Are you all well and
happy still? Do you continue in your house in Westminster near
Storey's gate? I know I shall hear from you again quickly, for I
read an oath to that effect at the tail of your letter. Let us hope it
will arrive in due course, without any delay whatever. I'm sorry
I've no smaller writing paper at hand, and I forgot to cut it before
I began; however I trust you will forgive the length of these
lines, and the unconscionable number of them on each page. Of
Harriet you write nothing except that she sends her "so and so";
why, she must be a great tall woman, apt at all household affairs
and poetry, puddings and Italian, — the last I suppose she speaks
like a Roman and like a Tuscan writes. So Tom scours across the
Park to his other father,¹ and is an excellent boy. And Sophia goes
on trimly, but always away from home. And Sidney is going on for
three years old. And Mʳˢ Richards remembers me. God bless 'em
all, and give my love to every one of them. Your exertions for
young Thornton ² deserve my thanks as well as his and his father's;

---

¹ His godfather, Charles Cowden Clarke (*Some Letters*, pp. 139, 141).
² "Perhaps the 'young, long, raw, lean Scotchman' mentioned by Keats in his
journal letter, 17 January 1820 [*Letters*, II, 245]. Brown may have met him again
in Dundee when he was on his second Scotch tour; apparently his Christian name
was James" (M. B. Forman, *Some Letters*, p. 44n).

I'm afraid I left a troublesome job for you; as I've no idea of him but as I saw him last in Dundee, please to remember me to "little Jamie." My Charley is with me and about me at every turn, in all the glory of high health and spirits, but at this moment somewhat interruptive. He is a dull rogue at his alphabet, and tells me he thinks it of no importance in order that he may read, which is duller still. As for his English, he appears to me equally dull there; tho' now I begin to talk to him in it, and he understands me on common matters; and sometimes he favours me with a few words of his own. I am very impatient in this affair, by no means liking to talk to my own boy in Italian. We have now been nearly three months together, and I grow angry at his obstinate southern tongue. In all other things he is sharp enough, and promises to be clever; but his talent for music is not quite to my taste, at least I shall not prefer that as the predominant one. His affectionate heart remains the same as ever; and, as we used to remark together, he requires a watchful eye and good government to keep him in the right path. The folks in Pisa [3] took great care of him, and managed his disposition tolerably well, — which is a rare thing in Italy, as a child, out of their great love, is apt to be spoiled. Never was a people so fond of children as Italians. I observed it immediately I passed the Alps, and it strikes every one in the same manner. This is the children's Paradise. But surely I am wrong in saying they are apt to be spoiled. I have written a slander; for here it is rare to hear them cry, and go where you will, tho' they expect to be noticed and delight in it, they are never forward and troublesome. One thing is, they are fed badly, — I don't mean poorly but the contrary, — and their stuffed stomachs make them more dull and heavy than English children, and so they are quieter. Carlino is too much alive not to be easily spoiled. I think it was at Suza, where going up the stairs of the inn with Carlino in my hand, I saw three military gentlemen in grand uniforms talking on the landing place, and they no sooner saw the child, than breaking off their conversation they called out — "Here's a little one, — a pretty little child!" — and making a sort of bow to me, they seized upon him, dandling him about, kissing him first one and then the other, and setting him to play with their sword-hilts

[3] The Gordini family.

and epaulets, — all to my great astonishment, for I never before beheld a gentleman-soldier so lose his dignity for the sake of a live-doll. But I soon discovered it is far from being thought un-manly to play the nurse in Italy. This puts me in mind, talking of my journey, of Mrs Edwards.[4] She promised to write to me from Trieste, to give me her address, and so on; and I've never heard of or from her; can you tell me how she is, and where she is? —— (27th) I've just had my usual breakfast of salted tongue and fruit, — and having also settled accounts with my servant Francesco, I'll give you our fruit prices, viz: Apricotts 1^d per lb, Melons ¾ each, Plums ½ per lb, Greengages 1 ½ per lb, Figs 2 for ¼. As this sum-mer is much behind-hand, the fruit season is not yet at its height, so these are high prices; and fruit, like every thing else, is cheaper in the city than here in the country where there is no competition. The weather's very warm and very pleasant, thermometre at eighty six; I wonder what it may be in England just at present, — perhaps it stands at forty three or under;[5] there's a fresh stirring breeze, and yet a peasant wisely proclaimed he thought we should have thunder; the sun is wide awake, the waters dreaming, the birds in covert, the cicala screaming. I wish that same cicala would be quiet, he worries out a country life in Italy with his con-tinued, teazing, one-note riot; and yet the country here looks very prettily, with corn, wine, oil, and every thing for diet; and on that hill (I think) I think more wittily, when strolling near the villa of Boccaccio,[6] with my Carlino, — sometimes my Carlaccio. Leigh Hunt lives ten minutes walk from this, far up a hill, for that air has been recommended for his wife; he has been there since last October, and will leave it the next, but for what other villa is not yet determined; — possibly he may come into Florence for the winter, whither I shall certainly flit as soon as I can meet with a

---

[4] See number 41, n. 2.

[5] According to the *Gentleman's Magazine*, vol. XCIV, pt. 2 (1824), p. 192, the temperature in London on July 27, a "cloudy" day, ranged from fifty-five to sixty-six degrees.

[6] "Boccaccio's father had a house at Maiano, supposed to have been situate at the Fiesolan extremity of the hamlet. . . . [Boccaccio] was so fond of the place, that he has not only laid the two scenes of the Decameron on each side of it, with the valley his company resorted to in the middle, but has made the two little streams that embrace Maiano, the Affrico and the Mensola, the hero and heroine of his Nimphale Fiesolano" (Hunt, *Lord Byron*, II, 372).

good lodging there. The inconveniences of the Country here, and
also the torments, are too much; I am convinced the Italian gentry
are right in quitting the "paese" in mid-summer and mid-winter,
— *their* months for ruralising are May and October. L. Hunt talks
of writing to you, acknowledging himself your debtor, but he has
weak health (without being ill) and makes his excuses justly; his
wife is tolerably well, and the children very well, — tho' the girl [7]
has lately had a sort of intermittent fever. How do you *like* the
"Wishing Cap?" [8] (28th) I intend to creep on from day to day
to the end of this letter, or, if the wind sits fair, I may finish it in
half an hour; tho' there is no use in that, as it will not take its
leave per post for three days to come. Severn I left in Rome, which
he has now left for a healthier air during the hot months in Albano. Never has he enjoyed such good health, which he ascribes
to Dr Clarke and myself, — and I don't know but he places me
before the Doctor, and I don't know but I deserve it. He is now
rather fortunate in his profession, and that gives him the highest
spirits; and he is or fancies himself to be in love, — but whether
(as the women say) it will ever come to any thing is more than a
body may say, — perhaps *two* bodies know more about it. — (I
wish you'd speak to Charley, and not let him annoy me so just
now.) — Give my remembrances to Mr T. H. Severn [9] when you
see him, and say it is quite a toss-up — heads or tails — whether
or no he is to be blessed with a sister-in-law; [10] however she is a
good and delightful creature, he may rest assured of that; and I

---

[7] Mary Florimel Hunt.

[8] An irregular series of twenty-seven essays by Hunt in the *Examiner*, March
28, 1824–October 17, 1825. Brown provided all but a few sentences of the sixteenth
and eighteenth essays (October 3, 24, 1824, pp. 626–628, 674–676).

[9] Severn's brother, Thomas Henry Severn (1801–1881), conductor and composer.

[10] Severn had fallen in love with a niece of Thomas Bruce, seventh Earl of
Elgin (1766–1841) — Maria, "twenty-three years old, very gentle and pretty," who
lived in Rome with her sister and widowed mother, a Mrs. Erskine. He visited
Naples with the ladies in 1822, squired them about Rome in 1823, painted Maria's
portrait in "Ferdinand and Miranda Playing at Chess" ("Never was love delineated
with more grace and sentiment," said Brown in the *Examiner*, October 3, 1824, p.
627), and just now was with them at Ariccia, near Albano. The affair ended when,
upon the mother's sudden death at Ariccia on August 22, 1824, Maria and her
sister returned to Rome and thence to England (Birkenhead, *Against Oblivion*,
pp. 124, 126; Severn to Finch, October 4, 1824, Bodleian Library). Possibly Maria
was Mrs. Erskine's daughter by an earlier marriage; in a letter of January 14, 1828
(Keats House, Hampstead), Severn asks his sister "if my old sweetheart Miss Hough-
ton is married or no."

had well nigh fallen desperately in love with her myself. You are
sadly in error imagining that L. Hunt should feel himself so
unfortunate in the death of Lord Byron.[11] Why should he? He had
been ill used enough by his Lordship to destroy all feeling of
sorrow at his loss, and threaten'd with worse, had not fear of
retaliation withheld that worse. Talk of Lord Byron as a poet
ad libitum, but as a man you had better be silent. There is more
truth in those unfeeling sentiments of his "Don Juan" than the
world believes, — all the heartlessness, the faith in the badness of
mankind, and the anger shown towards goodness, were parts and
parcels of the author's self; — never was any thing written more
"con amore" than the address to *gold* at the beginning of the 12th
Canto,[12] — but he could not only be miserly, but despicably mean
in saving his cash, and not only ungenerously so but wrongfully.
The other day I read his "Childe Harold" for the *first time*; I had
often peeped into it, but never finding a good stanza, I used to
shut it up again. Why I at last read it is more than I can well
explain, — and indeed I could not help skipping now and then,
especially when he talks of his "unhappy mind", his "blighted
hopes", his "heart forlorn".[13] Never was there a more gross piece
of quackery. There was a time when I believed in all this, and
only thought the man should keep his sorrows more to himself.
To my mind there is very little poetry, and no music of verse in
the "Childe", — his "Don Juan" is his best work, with all its inhu-
manities. How delighted I have been with Anastasius! [14] I am not
generally partial to such misbegotten half villains, but he is king
of them all. The style is too laboured, — you see the author thro' it;
which is a pity, as it has much profoundness and wit; the last part,

---

[11] At Missolonghi, on April 19. See number 56, n. 13.

[12] XII.iii–xiv. See Byron's *Letters and Journals*, VI (1901), 11, 163, and *Correspondence*, ed. John Murray (London, 1922), II, 97, 101–105, 214, 217. Of the final
couplet of *Don Juan*, I.ccxvi ("So for a good old-gentlemanly vice, / I think I must
take up with avarice"), Hunt says (*Lord Byron*, I, 130), "it was very true. He had
already taken up with the vice, as his friends were too well aware." Elsewhere
(*ibid.*, I, 85, 137) Hunt mentions Byron's love of money, and Mary Shelley (*Letters
of Mary Shelley*, I, 231) speaks of his "unconquerable avarice."

[13] Brown invented these quotations. Compare "Unhappy Thing" (*Childe Harold*,
II.iv), "loveless heart" (II.xxx), "his own dark mind" (III.iii), "nought of Hope
left" (III.xvi), "blighted their life's bloom" (III.xciv), "hasty growth and blight"
(IV.ix), "the broken heart" (IV.cxxi), "heart riven, / Hopes sapped, name blighted"
(IV.cxxxv).

[14] Thomas Hope, *Anastasius: or, Memoirs of a Greek*, 3 vols. (1819).

where he is travelling in Italy, with his little son, and where he loses him, cut *me* to the heart, and I could scarcely read all that anatomising of his grief afterwards, and yet I could not leave off for a moment, — I had Carlino in the agonies of death, then a corpse in my arms, then in his coffin, and then I put him in his grave, over and over again at every sentence, — pretty novel reading this! You are fond of odd things, — I'll tell you one. Did the last stanza of "Adonais" never strike you as a curious coincidence with the death of Shelley? Severn first remarked it to me, and looked very serious. Lately I mentioned it to L. Hunt, who let me know there was something still more curious connected with it; for Capt[n] Williams (who was drowned with Shelley) had been always much struck with that concluding stanza, and, being an amateur draughtsman, absolutely made a sketch of the "bark driven far from the shore and to the tempest given" — while the soul of Adonais "like a star", "beacons from the abode where the Eternal are"; — and this, almost immediately before that storm in which they were both drowned! [15] Come, I think this story beats your's hollow of the fatal mouse, — though it may only tend to make your own the more absolute. For my part I am willing to believe in both, and a thousand others, but cannot; — but pray don't burn me alive for this, or even cause me to be fined and imprisoned. By the by, it would be just as reasonable as to put Carlisle's men in limbo; [16] for I have hereby published my disbelief in what your Worship *may* call Religion. To return to N⁰ 1. I have a smart clever servant, yclep'd Francesco, a man of all work, a factotum; he makes beds, keeps the house clean, is an excellent cook, goes market*ting* (for we have no market here), dresses and undresses Carlino, mends his clothes or puts a button on, runs on messages, and in fact can do every thing but read and write. I, in my charity, sounded him on the shame of this deficiency, when he twiddled his features about, and blushing up to his forehead, said

[15] Severn also noted the coincidence in his manuscript commentary (1873) on *Adonais* (Sharp, p. 122), which is now at Harvard. A sketch by Williams of the *Don Juan*, the boat in which he and Shelley were drowned, is reproduced in *Maria Gisborne & Edward E. Williams, Their Journals and Letters*, ed. F. L. Jones (Norman, Okla., 1951), facing p. 126.

[16] Richard Carlile (1790–1843), freethinker and publisher, his sister, and several of his shopmen were imprisoned at various times during 1818–1825 for publishing obnoxious literature.

— "he had once begun to read, but the Doctor said it was bad for his eyes." — "But your eyes are good enough now", said I, "and I will teach you, if you choose." — "They are certainly good enough", he answered, "and so are you, Sir, but — but I'll think of it!" At present I give him no more than £16. 10/– per ann:, without board, — too little, I must (and he hints as much,) increase his means. He has a wife, a she-tailor in Florence with two infant children. "I thought it better," he told me, "to marry a woman with *talents*, than with a *portion*; and my wife works on, supporting her children, and allowing *me* two pauls a day." Surely, thought I, (vide Franklin), she "pays too much for her whistle." [17] But, according to our Italian fashion, I suppose it is not only one whistle she has bought, — tho' mind, I don't speak this with certainty, — Crimcon [18] forbid it! — besides, tho' a good trim pretty figure and not bad features, she is pitted with the small-pox, and that I never can abide, unless in a woman who has wit enough to be the life and soul of one's being, and with her, tho' a Duessa unmasked,[19] I could live, and live on for ever, and think I could never die. But more of this anon when I write amorously, for at present I am only

Your loving friend, Chas Brown.

[17] "The Whistle: A True Story. Written to His Nephew," included in nearly all editions of Benjamin Franklin's *Works* beginning in 1793.

[18] "Criminal conversation," adultery.

[19] *The Faerie Queene*, I.viii.46–49.

· 60 ·

FROM C. W. DILKE

Address: Florence Italy / Al Signore / Il Sign[r] Carlo Brown, / Gentiluomo Inglese, / Firenze, / Italia

Postmarks: F 24 42; CHAMBERY; CORRISP[za] ESTERA DA GENOVA; 19 AGOSTO

Endorsements: Ans[d] 6 Sept[r] 1824; Cha[s] W. Dilke.

ALS: Keats House, Hampstead. Printed in part by Richardson, *The Everlasting Spell*, pp. 191–194.

31 July 1824

Upon my conscience, Brown, I believe I am one of the most kind, considerate, affectionate, pleasant, sociable, unsociable fellows that "lard the lean earth." [1] — I have not had your letter [2] six hours, but, though perplexed with more than my usual no-occupation, here I am having a chat with you. — I believe there is something in good spirits, & warmheartedness, more infectious than plague, pestilence, methodism, or hunting, & your letters have the spot upon them, so that one half of my amiability is to be set off to your account. — I know not that you are a "good letter writer," or any other thing that is *good*; but somehow you contrive to put one in a good humour, & the first feeling after the second reading is to do one's best to thank you. — However I must not this month or two run on after my old, idle, desultory *self* talk — Fortune, Brown, & Circumstance, have thrust honors upon me in the way of business, & I must be as dull as becomes one upon such occasions. — First then, respecting M[r] West's picture you will know all I know long since. — I am sorry my report could not be more favorable. About Severn's magnificent copy from the Frescoes of Raphael [3] I promised some information more valuable as a groundwork for his judgement, than my opinion, & I have at length procured it.

---

[1] *1 Henry IV*, II.ii.116.
[2] It is now unknown.
[3] Specifically the "School of Athens." Brown copied this and the next four sentences into his letter to Severn of September 8 (number 64).

— I mentioned to you that Harlowe, a very clever artist, & somewhat known, had made a similar copy of the Transfiguration, I think. — Harlowe threw a right interest about the exhibition to catch the English, by dying at the critical moment; notwithstanding which I have the best authority for saying that *the exhibition did not pay the expences*, that the picture was eventually sold for that purpose, if not legally seized, & only brought £149.[4] — In a *direct pecuniary* view such a work, I think, could not *therefore* be expected to succeed. How far Harlowe had he lived, or Severn, who I hope will live, might have benefited by the reputation of having done it, & the aldermen's jowls he would paint in consequence, he is a much better judge than I can be, & I offer no opinion. — Having thus made a clearance of the old account, I think I should, to be in character, say, struck the Balance, I am about to open a new one; & as I reduced your odd hundred thousand specious truths, *one*, on a former occasion, I now have to score up another, that may stand as a cypher at the *right* end of the Balance. — What will you say, or how open your eyes & fix your attention, when I tell you that I have had a letter from Geo Keats.[5] — Aye and just *such* a letter, mind I have nibbed my pen, as in "my strange obstinacy"[6] I always maintained he would write, when he wrote at all. — It is three sides of foolscap, & from one end to the other, with the exception of some half dozen lines of common decent civility, an explanation of *all* transactions between himself & his Brother. — I have not the letter to refer to, having sent [it] to his Sister at her request; but the main facts I can give you; & I feel bound to do so in justice to a man, who certainly treated me negligently & slightingly, & therefore whom I feel bound *Not* to neglect, as a *self* satisfaction & assurance that I did not deserve it; whose character we should be all willing to uphold in respect to his Brother's memory, & to that just pride &

---

[4] George Henry Harlow (b. 1787) won fame in 1818 by copying Raphael's "Transfiguration" in eighteen days. He died on February 4, 1819, and his works, after being exhibited in Pall Mall, were sold by auction on June 21.

[5] Of April 10 (*KC*, I, 276–281). George Keats's conduct in financial dealings with John — the subject also of numbers 63, 97, 101, 103, 108, and parts of several other letters — is discussed in section VI of the Introduction.

[6] Probably a quotation from one of Brown's letters now lost. On Dilke's "enigmatical positiveness" see numbers 103, 106, and Keats's comment in *Letters*, II, 213.

independance which having led him into the wilds of America, has put it out of his power to protect it himself. — In the first place, for I must begin with the beginning,[7] he acknowledges to have received letters from yourself & Mr Haslam, & excuses his not having answered them from the insurmountable aversion he felt to offer exculpation or explanation when he had been so cruelly prejudged, & to men who domineered & dictated, after that fashion, when they had no right to do either [8] — He more than once attempted it but found it impossible — As I am giving *his* defence, you will have the goodness *so* to understand it. — He finds it still impossible to sit down without reply; and as certain specific charges have reached him through a relation of Mr Taylor's at Cincinnati,[9] he has at length thrown his defence into my hands & request[ed] me to give all possible publicity to it; have the goodness therefore to convey the spirit of what follows to Mr Hunt [10] & any other likely to have heard of the charge, which, as he understands it assumes its most tangible shape in form "that he on his second return to America took with him £700 of his Brother's money". — Now he is not content with denying this, but he enters into most *minute particulars,* quite conclusive in my judgement & of others that have read them, to *prove* that it was impossible. — John's whole property, at *the first,* was *£1500.* — He then proves, by sums & dates &c & all of which I really cannot give, that *more* than £1000 was expended by & for John before he was of age. — That it was nearly one year & ten months, or two years, after [11] before Geo *first* went to America — That as John was not more than ordinarily *near* at *that time,* it is not overrating his expences to say, every thing included, his expences

---

[7] Perhaps Dilke has in mind *Don Juan,* I.vii, "My way is to begin with the beginning."

[8] George merely wrote (*KC,* I, 279 — near the end of his "defence"), "Haslam or Brown should have had it [an explanation] long ago if I could have submitted to offer palliatives to men who domineered as they did." But see his letter to Brown of March 3, 1821 (quoted in number 108), and his later remark to Dilke about "the goading letters of Haslam and Brown" (*KC,* I, 329).

[9] James Tallant, in whose favor Taylor and Hessey had drawn on George for £150 in 1821 (*KC,* I, 216). Mrs. Tallant, née Mary Drury, was Taylor's cousin (Robert Gittings, *The Mask of Keats,* London, 1956, pp. 108–114).

[10] Brown did so before September 6 (see the end of number 63).

[11] That is, afterward. Keats became of age on October 31, 1816, less than a year and eight months before George sailed for America in June 1818.

could not be less than £200 per ann. That in conversation with
his Brother, he at that time informed him that he had lent about
£170. — & therefore without going into minute details, it is clear
that when Geo first went to America John had not *one shilling*,
nay he was already indebted to Geo; and notwithstanding this
Geo left him *£300 in hand*. — How Geo was enabled to do this,
he explains thus — John['s] Premium, hospital expences, &c &c
& his living for four years nearly before he was of age, owing to
his quarrel with the Surgeon [12] & leaving him he shews cost John
this amount; whereas Geo was taken into Mr Abby's without expence, lived with him, & at the end of the time had expended
a mere trifle more than the interest of his money, & Mr Abby made
him a present for his services of nearly £100 — That the funds
having risen his money sold for more than 1600, & though within
three months of being of age he left England, he did not in consequence of his advances to & for John carry with him £1100. — Up
then to this time his Brother is very considerably his debtor. —
But from the charge specifying £700 he presumes it has relation to
his second visit, this being the exact amount he carried back with
him. — Whatever monies John had after he left arose from Tom's
estate, & with very trifling exceptions, *could* arise from no other.
— Now Tom's estate, after paying his debts, funeral expences &c
&c amounted in a gross sum to £1100. — On this his Sister had a
previous & seperate claim for £100. — On Geo's arrival he found
John *had* received £100 & had remitted £100 to him in America.
— Then, after the Sister's portion was abstra[c]ted their remained
£540, he thinks exactly to divide. — From this they each took £100
more, & the half of the remainder [13] being £170 he borrowed of
John — being all he ever did or ever COULD HAVE BORROWED, if it
is to be called borrowing when his Brother was indebted to him
more than £400 at that very time. — How he came to take this he
explains by those necessities & engagements to complete which he
was obliged at a great expence & all hazards to return to England; [14] & then to borrow & scrape money in every direction. —

[12] Thomas Hammond, of Church Street, Edmonton.

[13] Dilke first wrote "the remaining half," then altered it in such a way as to leave
"the half of the remainingder."

[14] In January 1820.

That he does not offer this as an apology for not having remitted money to his Brother — that would be conduct without excuse or impossible to be excused by any balancing of accounts, had it been in his power — but that it was as absolutely out of his p{ower} as, to use his own forcible words, if he had suffered ship wreck on his return. — That the charge can have originated directly from any thing said by his Brother he cannot believe — for his Brother knew little or nothing of his own affairs — & was so depressed, that Geo felt it to be impossible to tell him the facts, & that he had but £170 in the world beyond what he had in his pocket, some 60 or 70 when he left him, & this £170 not his own. — That though his Brother never could have believed that the whole £700 was his own peculiar, he might, & Geo thinks he led him to believe that it was the proceeds of Tom's estate, although it can be proved that they had but £540 *to divide* when Geo landed in England. — That if it has arisen from any thing vaguely & indirectly said by his Brother, it has originated in those vague & general terms, which, with the kindest possible intention he had himself always used when speaking to his Brother; for such was the dreadful depression of his spirits at times, when speaking alone to his Brother, that he always feared the most dreadful consequences should he ever ascertain the exact situation of his affairs. He therefore always purposely left his Brother in uncertainty, intending & hoping, under pretence, for a time, of balancing Accts, to remit sufficient for his maintainance, & he has only to hope that having shewn the positive fallacy of the cruel charge against him, those whom it may satisfy, will do him the justice to believe that he would have remitted the first & very first moment it was in his power — and he now intends, whenever circumstances will permit to discharge all debts due by his Brother, & in furtherance of this object has given Bills to Taylor.[15] — — I have very great pleasure in concluding this long explanation, which if it be not perfectly satisfactory must arise from my imperfect telling, but if I had the letter I really could not go more

---

[15] Through Tallant, who did not forward them. On March 18, 1825, George asked Richard Abbey to settle the account (*More Letters and Poems of the Keats Circle*, ed. H. E. Rollins, Cambridge, Mass., 1955, pp. 27–28), but Abbey did not pay it until 1828 (*KC*, I, 317).

into detail. — Thus I take leave of business, but it is too late in the sheet to add anything, but that we are all reasonably well. John Snook about whom you inquire was attacked in Jany or Feby last, suddenly, indeed momentarily, while biting a biscuit with a stiffness of the jaw. — He has since been a good deal better, but was partially affected a short time since, after bathing — He is now with us, & under Astly Cooper,[16] who says it was a spasm. He is otherwise perfectly well. — We have been expecting a visit from my Father, but the very last day, he was obliged to write & acknowledge he did not feel himself equal to the journey. — But we leave town in ten days or a fortnight for Chichester, & shall then I hope find him reasonably well. — My Mother I believe is better than usual. — Will is with them. — Richards called on me a few days since after an absence of months, & Mancur was with me last night. — All well. — The latter is got into *a*, not *his*, the phrase makes a difference, second childhood. — He is a great cricketer, & tomorrow morning at 7 is to run a race for a sovereign. — Here's Success to him

Yours truly CWDilke

. 61 .

TO LEIGH HUNT [1]

ALS: The Brotherton Collection, University of Leeds.

My dear Hunt,   Florence. 20th August 1824.
    The opinion you ask of me on the state of your affairs,[2] especially as they are affected by the last letter from your brother M^r

---

[16] Sir Astley Paston Cooper (1768–1841), surgeon, whose lectures at Guy's Hospital Keats had attended in 1815–1816.

[1] This letter was actually written for Vincent Novello (to whom Hunt forwarded it with number 62) and John Hunt. Like number 91 it is a formal statement on the dispute between John and Leigh Hunt over "a question of Partnership in the Examiner." See also numbers 65, 66, 69, 70, 73–75, 78, 83, and section IV of the Introduction.

[2] According to number 65, Brown had learned the details of Hunt's affairs only on the preceding day, August 19.

John Hunt, dated 20th July,[3] I will give to the best of my ability. But on examining into the several letters and papers you have placed in my hands, I find the chief question you propose is a matter of minor importance to others which I will endeavour to discuss. Yet as that question is of the most moment for the present support of your family, I will begin upon it first. It relates simply to an agreement entered into between your brother and yourself, the terms of which are gathered from the following passage in his letter of 8th Feby last:

> "My proposal was, and I repeat it, that you should be paid £100 a year from the Examiner, an annuity to be charged upon the Paper, to be paid to you and your heirs as long as the property exists. And further, that you should be paid 2 Gn^s for every article you supply, which is printed in the Paper: and if, in the opinions of joint friends, such contributions aid in increasing the sale, your annuity shall be increased in proportion — such increase of annuity also to be paid to your heirs. I dare say you would not often write Articles which would be deemed inexpedient to insert — still, I think the power of omission, under all the circumstances, should be left with those who conduct such a concern on the spot."

In the above it is not expressly stipualated that one of your articles should appear in every succeeding Examiner; but that stipulation is implied, as how else could your exertions have a fair chance in aiding in the increase of the sale? — and the only bar mentioned against the insertion of any one is its being deemed inexpedient. The power of omission therefore is confined to objectionable articles, and by no means applies to their being published irregularly. However, if this is doubtful, which in my opinion is not, the fact of your having written to your brother that you understood the engagement in that light, and his not having replied in the negative, should, I think, settle the interpretation. Now, on the faith of this, you have constantly sent an article for every week, relying on a present positive income, and looking forward to a time when by your exertions you may so far have increased the

[3] This letter, like several of the others mentioned in the dispute, is now in the British Museum.

sale of the Examiner as to obtain a larger annuity for the benefit of yourself and heirs. In the midst of this reliance on your brother, you receive a letter from him, dated 20ᵗʰ July, by which it appears that only 8 "Wishing Caps" were inserted during 12 weeks, and he informs you, without any previous notice, that your income arising from the annuity and the 2 Gnˢ per week for those articles, making together £209. 4/–, is reduced to £168, or £14 per month. His own words, to my mind, bear evidence against his right to inflict such a hardship. By those you were entitled to the insertion of an Article every week in the Examiner, and to £109. 4/– per annum, that sum being their value at 2 Gnˢ per week, and also to an increase of your annuity of £100 to yourself and heirs proportionable to the increase of sale arising from your contributions, according to the opinions of joint friends, and which you can never hope for unless they are inserted regularly. If your brother, upon further consideration, conceived he had entered into an improvident agreement, or one that was inconvenient on account of the press of temporary matter at certain times in the Paper, and therefore wished to break it, the least that is done in such cases is to give a timely and sufficient warning. As it is you are suddenly thrown, or soon will be so, into a state of want, and recommended to write for a Magazine.[4] But it will require time before you can realise any thing from the proprietor of a Magazine; and during that time, as Italy is not a land of credit, the question is how you and your family can exist. To avoid being thrown into a state of want, you say it is necessary you should continue to send articles for the Examiner up to next month (inclusive); and I have no doubt your brother will perceive the justice of accepting and paying for them, to be inserted with those already on hand at his pleasure, and thus grant you some little time for following his advice to write for a Magazine in order to procure the means of support. That you may make this as convenient as possible to him, endeavour, and I think you can do it, to draw at 3 months. Then, for the future, till something definitive is settled, you must draw for no more than at the rate of £100 per annum. Your brother in his letter of 6ᵗʰ July (dated by mistake 6ᵗʰ June) states you had, up to 3ʳᵈ July, overdrawn your account this year

[4] Colburn's *New Monthly Magazine* (see number 62).

£58. 4/–. In his sense of the word you have overdrawn to that amount, as he does not credit you for the articles till after they appear; but you, on the other hand, always drew for the amount when you forwarded the articles, imagining yourself at liberty to do so, nor was it objected to on his part. It should rather be said you have foredrawn than that you have overdrawn, because he will find he has received value for all your drafts excluding the first £30, on another account, this year up to 3rd July.

Whether it is found inconvenient or impossible to insert your Articles regularly, or whether being purely literary they are not adapted for the Examiner in its present character, or from whatever other cause, it is of immediate importance that the question between you and your brother should be reconsidered. I think Mr Novello, upon reading this letter,[5] will be of the same opinion, as well as your brother himself, especially when some matters are explained which he appears to have misunderstood in your disfavour. His offer was very fair that your claim should be arbitrated by competent and disinterested persons; and, unless it can be settled between yourselves, nothing can be wiser than that it should now be referred in that manner. I recommend that each of you should appoint an arbitrator; and that the two elected persons should be empowered, in case they cannot agree in their award, to choose a third. According to the usual method both you and your brother ought previously to sign an Arbitration-bond, binding you severally to the award, though this does not seem necessary; but surely it is indispensible that their award should be secured to you out of the profits of the Paper in a legal manner, — in such a way that in case, (putting other risks out of the question, and which cannot be entertained,) from the hazards of trade your brother as bookseller and publisher should become bankrupt, your claim will remain a legal and indisputable one. This is particularly essential to you, the father of so young and so large a family. Your arbitrators will have to settle whether you

---

[5] See n. 1 above. Vincent Novello (1781–1861) — organist of the Portuguese Embassy chapel in South Street, Grosvenor Square, conductor, composer, editor, publisher of music, and a close friend of the Hunts — was asked in the early days of the dispute to be an arbitrator between the brothers. It was he who recommended the terms of settlement offered by John Hunt in the letter of February 8 (quoted in the first paragraph of the present letter).

are or are not a joint and equal partner in the Examiner; and if not, then what is the fair and just consideration due to you, under all the circumstances; and in addition to this they should be empowered to examine into, and (if needful) to correct the Accounts.

Your legal right as equal partner with your brother has not been disputed; and as far as I can judge from my knowledge in the law of partnerships it cannot be disputed. You once were a public and joint proprietor in the Examiner, and you signed a paper giving up all interest in it, merely that you should no longer be a public proprietor,[6] upon the promise that a Deed or some legal instrument should be executed securing to you and to your heirs your former share in the profits. This Deed never was executed; but your brother (8th Decr 1823) writes very honourably on this point: — "Be assured that the paper you allude to, in which you renounced your proprietorship, if it exist at all, will never be brought forward in resistance of your claim. It was designed for a particular object, which it answered." Valuable as your partnership was at that time, (when you signed the paper,) it stands to reason you were either to recommence as equal sharer in the profits, or that you should receive a due consideration in their stead. The former was acted upon, and year after year you continued to be credited for a share in the profits equal to your brother's. This constituted you a partner, and to that extent; and I never heard of a partnership being dissolved unless by mutual consent, or by the expiration of the term of years originally agreed on. I have an Account before me, delivered to you, called "Examiner 1821," in which the balance of profit in that year is stated at £551. 5. 9½; and at the foot of — "An Account of the sums of money paid to and for Mr L. Hunt by Mr John Hunt, on acc^t of the Examiner, in the year 1821" — I read the following "Memorandum — Due from the Examiner to Mr L.H, for 1821 — £275. 12. 10¾". This memorandum alone, allowing one half of the profits to you, I believe, legally speaking, settles your right.

But the question of your claim is argued more as a matter of justice than as a dry point of law. In this view your brother objects

---

[6] "In order," as Hunt told Shelley on March 1, 1821 (*Correspondence of Leigh Hunt*, I, 162), "that Government might not be able to imprison both of us at once," as it had in 1813–1815.

to your continuance as partner on the following grounds. 1st The entire responsibility rests on him. 2nd His labour and exertion are and always have been greater than your's. 3rd The new plan of the Paper will not allow of regular literary Articles. 4th It would be most impolitic to think of another alteration. 5th He gave up good and certain prospects at its commencement for which the Examiner has not afforded an equivalent. 6th It is doubtful if you ever can be a regular contributor. 7th You did not fulfil your engagements up to the period you left England. And 8th You at last abandoned the interests of the Examiner. In his letters of 21st Octr and 8th Decr 1823, after carefully perusing them, I cannot perceive any other reasons against your claim as partner.

1st The entire responsibility rests on him. In pecuniary matters you as a partner are equally responsible with himself for all losses in the concern. As to personal responsibility, it was entirely at his suggestion, and at his earnest request, that you ceased to be a public proprietor. Afterwards, on account of the promised Deed not forthcoming, you expressed a desire to have your name again placed in the Stamp Office as proprietor, and the offer was declined.

2nd His labour and exertion are and always have been greater than your's. This is so difficult a point to settle, previously to your falling into ill health, that it is almost needless to attempt it. The words signify judgment and application on his side, and literary ability on your's. He contends he "devoted more hours weekly to the Paper, than you did monthly for all you did to it." But who can decide how many hours it requires in reading and reflection for a purely literary or Political Article, even before the pen is taken in hand to write it? It is acknowledged that you wrote up the Examiner; then without your abilities there would not have been such a Paper; though it is certain its existence depended on his judgment and application. But why should one claim more than the other on either account? Latterly your labour and exertion in part ceased, owing to severe illness; and afterwards they entirely ceased for a time, owing to another cause which I will explain in its place, as well as to a continued weak state of health.

3rd The new plan of the Paper will not allow of regular literary Articles. This new plan was carried into effect without your consent, and even without consulting you. Whether the change was judicious or not is a question by itself; but I cannot think it right that, after you had written up and established the Paper, your partner should of his own accord, and without any warning, change its character, and then make that change a plea for thrusting you out.

4th It would be most impolitic to think of another alteration. Perhaps so, but that is not your fault. However your brother himself must have altered his opinion on this point, when he afterwards accepted an offer from you to write in the Paper.

5th He gave up good and certain prospects at its commencement, for which the Examiner has not afforded an equivalent. Surely this notice of an injury done to himself ought to have been omitted, unless at the same time it was acknowledged (which none can deny) that your connection with the Paper as a political character did most serious injury to you in your success as a poet and man of letters. But neither the one nor the other is in the slightest degree to the purpose.

6th It is doubtful if you ever can be a regular contributor. If this doubt ought to be admitted against your claim, at any rate it has lost much of its force when the regularity of your contributions during this year is considered.

7th You did not fulfil your engagements up to the period you left England. It is certain you did not fulfil them, because you could not, owing to ill health both of body and mind; and the penalty for this unavoidable neglect is fixed in one of the Accounts at the sum paid during the year to Mr Gorton [7] for Political and Theatrical Articles. Your brother however accuses you of deficiencies (and I trust he will pardon me for saying so) too hastily and without examination. He says, "You know that for the year previous to your leaving England, you did not contribute much above a dozen Articles for the Paper"; when on reference to a file of Examiners for that year (1821) I find that from Jany to the end of Octr, 43 weeks, you contributed 48 Articles, viz: 25

---

[7] John Gorton (d. 1835), a translator of Voltaire (1824) and the compiler of a *General Biographical Dictionary* (1828) and a *Topographical Dictionary of Great Britain* (1831–1833).

with the usual mark of your *hand*; 1 signed Leigh Hunt; 5 signed
Harry Brown; and 17 Theatricals by Mr Richards and myself,[8]
who wrote at your request and for your advantage, and therefore
they should be included in your contributions, at least in one
sense of the word; but excluding them, the Articles written by
yourself during that period amount to 31. Again, you promised
to supply 15 or 16 Articles in hand before sailing from England,
and he says, "You were detained several months on the coast,[9] but
during that entire time you did not supply a single Article for
the Paper, — although you had not kept your engagement respecting the Articles to be placed in hand." The sole cause of
your not having supplied these 15 or 16 Articles was ill health,
utter inability to furnish them according to your promise; but
you did send from Plymouth Fables and Criticisms,[10] which he
forgot, and of which fact you reminded him on 7th Novr last.
He mentions, 8th Decr 1823, that "besides the superintendance of
the printing, publishing &c, all the editorial drudgery of the
Paper you left to me, — and though I pretend to nothing in the
execution of it, and never complained of its being so left, yet the
fact should not be lost sight of" &c. Now to my mind, after the
concessions made in this very sentence, the fact should be lost
sight of altogether, except as a matter of feeling between brother
and brother. But here more may be observed. You tell me you
recollect having written to him, or sent to him by message, from
Horsemonger Jail,[11] to say that you would take that part of the
work out of his hands, and that you actually did proceed with it.
Some time after, on account of illness, you requested him again
to fulfil the duties of Editor or Compiler, when he acceded to it,
expressing himself mortified that ever those duties had been
taken away from him. Besides he does not mention, and you
cannot inform me, whether the duty of compilation was not

[8] Brown's (signed with an inverted "C") appeared on May 13, 20, 27, June 10,
July 8, 15, 29, August 12, September 2, 16. Richards' were very likely those signed
"X" — six reviews of "Italian Opera" plus a short article, "The King's Visit to the
Italian Opera" — published in the issues of May 6, 20, 27, June 17, July 1, 15, 29.

[9] In the winter and spring of 1822.

[10] A series of ten "Fables for Grown Children" and six "Letters to the Readers
of the Examiner," published in the *Examiner* in 1822.

[11] Horsemonger Lane Jail, in Surrey, where Hunt was confined for two years in
1813–1815 for libeling the Prince Regent.

your brother's work, according to the original agreement. If it were not, and he was merely printer, publisher &c, have not Mr Gow [12] and Mr Appleyard [13] been employed to perform part of your brother's duty as printer and publisher, according to the original contract? And if so, have not the salaries paid to Mr Gow and Mr Appleyard been charged year after year to the general concern of the Examiner? These two last points I notice merely as queries, because I cannot learn any thing, one way or the other, in a positive shape from your own knowledge or from his letters.

8th and last. You at last abandoned the interests of the Examiner. Be it understood you are accused of abandoning the Paper only from the time you arrived in Italy [14] to Octr last year. And how and wherefore did this abandonment take place? I will state the facts as they were. You came to Italy in order to establish, with Lord Byron and Mr Shelley, a periodical work. Mr Shelley was unfortunately drowned soon after your arrival; but still the work was preparing to be set forth, and with the highest hopes, under the name of the "Liberal." That these hopes were not sanguine merely on your part, the circumstance of your brother believing it proper to strike off 7,000 copies of the first number is a proof of what he thought would be its success.[15] Your health was then far from being good, and without the assistance of Mr Shelley, you found you could not write both for the Liberal and the Examiner. Under these circumstances, and for some kindly reasons, you forbore to write in the latter, that not only yourself but your brother might receive a greater benefit. Here I am a witness. When at Pisa, Septr 1822, I recollect your talking of the Liberal as the means of great enrichment, and saying that now you would benefit your brother equally with yourself, in return for all his kindnesses and anxieties on your account, as well as for your necessary cessation from the Examiner at that

---

[12] Perhaps John Gow, who in 1823 was in business with his son selling music and musical instruments at 162 Regent Street.

[13] Joseph Appleyard, of 19 Catherine Street, Strand, publisher of Hunt's *Indicator* in 1820–1821.

[14] In July 1822.

[15] The first number of the *Liberal* netted £377 16s., but the second lost £41 14s., and the third and fourth made only slight profits of £2 11s. 6d. and £14 6s. 4d. (Marshall, *Byron, Shelley, Hunt, and "The Liberal,"* pp. 160–161, 178).

time. Lord Byron, Mrs Shelley, and Mr Trelawney (you tell me) contended against your yielding up an equal share with yourself in the profits of the Liberal as by far too much; and you, from an impulse of justice and brotherhood, insisted on acting in that manner. You say you informed your brother [16] of the impossibility on your part to attend to both the publications, and that therefore you made choice of the Liberal, as more conducive to both your interests, as he was to share with you in the profits, — or words to that effect. What follows? He never once answers you objecting to this arrangement, until the Liberal, contrary to every one's anticipation, becomes unprofitable and is dropped; and then, when Lord Byron had left you here destitute of every thing but your share in the Examiner,[17] your brother on a sudden asks what is your claim upon it, and declines, as he terms it, a reunion, principally on account of this temporary secession from it, acted on for his advantage as well as your own, thus turning the good you intended towards him into evil against yourself; and afterwards, when reminded of the fact, he calls it — "offering me indeed something by way of an equivalent, but which I deem nothing like an adequate one, and therefore cannot accept." Why did he not object to this proposition at the first, when it was thought to be more than adequate in his favour, and not wait till it was proved inadequate? Why did he not object to that temporary secession from the Examiner at the first, and inform you of the consequences as he interpreted them? And why is there nothing acknowledging your wish and intention to do him this service? All this is so utterly unlike your brother, that I dare pronounce it was occasioned by some mistake. Either you did not (though you believe you did) write to him at that early period that you considered him as equal partner with yourself in the Liberal; or he forgot your having written so; or your expressions were indistinct and therefore misunderstood or the letter never reached him. Thus he possibly conceived (if indeed he could possibly conceive such a thing), when you (7th Novr last) reminded him of this,

---

[16] On October 10, 1822 (Luther A. Brewer, *My Leigh Hunt Library Collected and Described: The First Editions*, Cedar Rapids, Iowa, 1932, pp. 119–120 — hereafter cited as Brewer, *First Editions*).

[17] See number 56, n. 13.

that you then, for the first time, were offering him an equivalent, known to yourself to be none. This explanation I take great pleasure in, as I am convinced your brother, when he hears of it, will regard the whole affair between you in another light, and feel more happy thoughts towards yourself. That nothing may be wanting to this explanation, let Mrs Shelley be appealed to; and in addition to my testimony as above, I assert that, up to a very few days past, you believed you were credited for only one half of the profits of the Liberal, till I, with my finger on the Accounts, convinced you to the contrary, so strongly were you self-persuaded that your offer was well understood from the first.

Thus I have endeavoured to answer every objection urged against your continuance as Partner. If I am right, it will only remain to fix the sum to be carried to your debit for that part of your duty which illness prevented you from performing, and which has been paid to another for performing it in your stead. It will be a question, under the circumstances above stated, whether you ought or ought not to be charged separately with any sums paid for doing your part of the duty, during what is called your secession from the Paper. I have not throughout imagined that your brother will argue that sickness, and sickness alone, disabling you for a time, for ever deprives you of your rights as Partner. If he should, much may be said, but for the present I shall merely ask the following questions. Are you not in the same situation now, virtually if not actually, as before you signed that paper renouncing your proprietorship? Then are not the conditions of the partnership bond, to which Mr Whiting [18] was a party, still in effect? Did not those conditions secure to you and to your heirs an equal share with your brother in the Examiner? Now supposing, even the day after that bond was signed, you had been struck with idiotism, would not you and your family have been entitled to a continued equal share in the property as long as it lasted? Nay, had you died, would not your heirs have enjoyed that equal share in the same manner?

[18] James Whiting, who at "Finsbury Place" printed four editions of Hunt's *Juvenilia* in 1801–1803. Pigot's *Commercial Directory* for 1823–1824 gives his address as 3 Lombard Street. According to number 91, he bought a third share in the *Examiner* for £800 in 1809, and exchanged it for a £200 life annuity in 1819.

I will now speak of the Accounts, as delivered to you, from 1st Jany 1821 to 31st Decr 1823, now lying before me. It appears from a warm expostulation on the part of your brother, that you had expressed an opinion of their incorrectness. After what he wrote in reply, I am sorry to assert they are incorrect, not only in minor points, but in matters of great importance. I will first notice the minor points. You wrote two Articles for the Examiner in 1823, for which you are allowed in one Account £6. 6/–, and eventually this sum is carried to your credit as £4. 4/–. In one Account is "paid Mr Hunter for books" £5. 5/–, and "to Sir R Phillips [19] for ditto" £2. 1/–; and in another Account (which ought to be a duplicate) these sums are stated to be £4. 0. 6 and £1. 11. 9. You are charged, 27th Septr 1821, for "Mr S. Brown's second bill and expences" £26. 2. 6, instead of £25; [20] the expences being £1. 2. 6 and occasioned by Mr Henry L. Hunt's [21] forgetting the day of payment, and going out of town at the time, as he himself informed me. In May 1822 there is "Rec^d from Mr L.H. at Plymouth" £50, when the sum was £250; in the correspondence I see it mentioned that the remaining £200 was expended on your account, but the items have not been brought forward, and you cannot recollect all of them; — this last may be easily explained. Now I will point out errors of greater importance. It must be granted I am to regard these Accounts in one of these two points of view: firstly, supposing you a partner in the profits and losses of the Examiner; or, secondly, supposing you to have no interest as proprietor in the concern. In both cases I engage to prove them erroneous. If, during this time, you were a partner, then there are three errors. 1st You are not credited for the half nett profits on the Examiner for either of these three years. 2nd You are not entitled to the return of sums paid from 1819 to 1823 (5 years) to

[19] Rowland Hunter, for whom see number 77, n. 1, and Sir Richard Phillips (1767–1840), author, bookseller, publisher. In these sentences Brown is citing accounts sent by John Hunt in letters of September 19, 1823, and July (misdated June) 6, 1824, both now in the British Museum.

[20] Apparently Hunt owed S. Brown £200, which he repaid in quarterly installments from June 1821 through March 1823.

[21] John Hunt's son, whom he employed and in 1824 took as partner in his publishing house at 38 Tavistock Street, Covent Garden. When John Hunt retired from the business in the spring of 1825, Charles Cowden Clarke joined Henry in his place until the firm failed in 1829 (R. D. Altick, *The Cowden Clarkes*, London, 1948, p. 51).

Mess[rs] Magnay & C[o] [22] amounting to £534, as placed to your credit. And 3rd you are not entitled to the £6. 6/– or £4. 4/– for two Articles written for Examiner 1823. If, on the contrary, you had no interest as proprietor in the concern, then there are two if not three errors. 1st The sum of £105 "paid M[r] Gorton for Political and Theatrical Articles" ought not to be placed to your debit as it now stands, any more than it ought to be placed to mine, or to any other indifferent person's. 2nd You ought to be paid, which you are not, for 48 Articles contributed by you in 1821, and for those you forwarded from Plymouth in 1822, upon the same principle that you were paid for those two in 1823. And 3rd it appears to me you should be credited £300 for your annuity for these three years; because both in your brother's letters and in that from M[r] Novello [23] the annuity is implied to be granted in lieu of your share as partner, and then of course it should commence at the moment you cease to be partner. This last I do not notice positively as an error, though it appears to be one to me. I say nothing positively except where the Accounts are in themselves contradictory. It was for this reason that I urged the propriety of laying before the Arbitrators not only the question of your partnership or claim on the Examiner, but also the Accounts for their adjustment and correction. Nor is it too much to suggest, seeing these errors, that it is possible that similar ones may have crept into the Accounts prior to 1821, of which I cannot judge as you have left them in England. Yet there is a strong presumption that in the Accounts of 1819 & 1820 you have not been credited as a partner, else why is the return of sums paid to Mess[rs] Magnay & C[o] carried back so far as the commencement of 1819? What you would be entitled to in those two years I cannot decide, supposing you credited as a partner. But if not as a partner, then ought not your Account to be credited as an Annuitant? If so, £500 are due to you for those five years; and £105 paid to M[r] Gorton and charged to you by mistake; and possibly £300 more, the value of all the Articles from 1819 to 1822 (four years) contributed by you to the Examiner. These several credits would

---

[22] Christopher Magnay and Sons, wholesale stationers, of College Hill, Upper Thames Street.
[23] Of December 15, 1823 (Blunden, *Leigh Hunt*, pp. 204–205).

reduce the balance against you of £1,790. 19. 10 to less than one half. This must, with every thing else, be considered by your mutual friends, in case they should settle that you were no longer a partner from 1st Jany 1819. As it is, it seems that for the five preceding years, you have neither been allowed a share, nor an annuity, nor payment for the work you have performed, and moreover been charged with part of the expences of the concern. No wonder the balance against you amounts to £1,790. 19. 10

If Mr Novello was not acquainted with all the essential facts stated in this letter, or if he misunderstood them, he will, I think, feel that he had given his advice under a wrong impression, and recommend that the whole question should be reconsidered. If Mr Novello still feels otherwise, then your brother having broken his agreement this year according to our interpretation of it, and according to his own, as far as a silent acquiescence in your interpretation goes, then you are at liberty to refer the whole affair again, either to Mr Novello alone, or to another, or to others, as may be agreed on; and to this, I repeat, I believe your brother will willingly agree. In the mean time, till an award shall be given, every one will recommend, nor can he be averse to it, that you should have liberty to draw on him at the rate of £100 per ann. beginning from 1st Jany last, as already allowed you, and without which you and your family would be in want.

The Arbitrators will doubtless take into consideration that the profits on the Examiner, though at present small in comparison to what they once were, are by no means inconsiderable, though encumbered with a debt to Messrs Magnay & Co of 4 Gn^s per week, and a life annuity to Mr Whiting of £200; that the former will cease at the close of 1829, and that the latter may cease tomorrow; besides which it appears the property is yearly increasing in value. It perhaps would be adviseable for you living here abroad, and more advantageous to the future interests of your brother, and more especially to those of his son, that you accept an annuity in lieu of continuing a partner; but the heavy debt hanging over your head renders this impracticable. As it is, you have no alternative but to exert yourself in again raising the Paper to its former prosperity, as a partner; that being the sole hope you can entertain of repaying this debt to your brother.

You are willing to do this, and the evidence of this year proves you capable of constant exertion. If you accept an Annuity, this debt may at any time crush it; for should your brother unfortunately fail in business, his creditors (without imagining he could act so) would place your debt against your claim as Annuitant. I would ask, when your brother offers to you and to your heirs an annuity of £100, why does this show of debt continue? — for he must know it is only a show, as with that income, and with whatever you may earn besides, (as experience has shown of your gains as an author out of the Examiner,) how can you with a wife and seven very young children ever be able to repay £100 of it? On the contrary, as a partner, you may not only hope to pay it off, but in the end to realise something for your family. It is on this account that I advise you to insist on your right as Partner, nor do I think, either in law, in justice, or in feeling, it can be denied you. This debt of £1,790. 19. 10, according to the errors in the Accounts for the three or five last years, must in any view be greatly reduced; and in one view it would be reduced to less than a half. But whatever the amount may be, before he makes you an Annuitant, can he do otherwise than consider you bankrupt, and receive your nothing in the pound? Then were he to grant you £100 per annum, and that grant to be increased to £200 in 1830, when the present {en}cumbrance of £218. 8/– per annum to Messrs Magnay & C° will be paid off, it would n{e}ither put him to present nor future inconvenience, nor would he forego any other reasonable hopes. I cannot say whether this conduct would be fair and just, or noble and generous, but I believe the latter. When you accepted Mr Novello's proposal, you hoped to increase your annuity eventually to £200, and still to receive your payments of 2 Gn^s per week, and in that hope you accepted it. Still whatever may be definitively fixed upon, let me entreat you, for the sake of every individual in your family, to insist on the agreement being a legal one; so that not a doubt may exist injurious to the interests of even your last infant in arms, though the injury may never fall on him till after the deaths of yourself, your brother, and your nephew. If legal instruments are requisite for the security of property among strangers, and always considered so by both parties, how much more necessary is it that a brother's property should be so secured, especially when he is surrounded by so many children.

Much as I have written, though unconscious of having omitted any thing in favour of your brother according to his letters, I perceive I have omitted some points in your favour, and that I have too slightly touched on certain facts that ought to be further argued on. These are of importance, but I have already said enough for the present, and they can be reserved for the consideration of your Arbitrators, when you furnish them with your statement.

And now, my dear Hunt, I have given you my opinion, after mu{ch} reflection, and to the best of my judgment. Though I began this letter on 20th Aug^t, in {hopes} I could finish it for the morrow's post, it is now the 1st Sept^r; nor could I prepare {it} more speedily, so much more time, labour, and consideration did the subject require than I had calculated on at first. I may say I have been perfectly unbiassed on {each} side, as if both parties were {s}trangers, for I sat down to my {ta}sk with an equa{l} respect, an equal friendship towards your brother and yourself. Nor can I ever thin{k} without pain on my having given an opinion so entirely against him.

Your's most sincerely,
Chas Brown.

To Leigh Hunt Esqr,
     near Florence.

. 62 .

LEIGH HUNT TO VINCENT NOVELLO [1]

Address: Angleterre. / Mr Novello, / Shacklewell Green, / near Kingsland, / near London, / England. / Inghilterra. / Via Francia.

Postmarks: FIRENZE; AT.; AUTRICHE PAR HUNINGUE; [F]PO [S]E 21 1824; 4 EVEN 4 SP 21 1824

ALS: The Brotherton Collection, University of Leeds.

Dear Novello,   [September 6, 1824]

It is a monstrous thing to be obliged to send you a long letter of business, instead of a long one of chat. But what can I do? Fate will have it so: and as to making you pay the post for a letter extra, it is not to be thought of, especially as at this moment I am quite exhausted with writing of all sorts. Thank the Wilful [2] for her last letter, & yourself for the sequel to it, & Charles Clarke for his post-[s]cript; & beg them to forgive a sleepy-headed fellow for not being as vivacious as he would be, if he were in their company. I have been a good correspondent upon the whole, so I must repose a little on my past virtues. Tell Mrs Gliddon also, and Mr G. Gliddon [3] that I have been going to write them an enormous letter every day, & that I am very much ashamed for not having put said enormity into effect; but the delay is owing to any thing but an insensibility to their kindness; otherwise I should long ago have contented myself with a short one. I shall never be content till I *have* written. I cannot tell how long I should have continued to say nothing to yourself, if this matter of business had not forced me. It vexes me to bring you into it again, especially as I recollect what you said about your not being a man of business, & the prophetic horror with which you seemed

---

[1] Written on the eighth page of the preceding letter.

[2] "Wilful Woman," Hunt's "affectionate nickname" for Mrs. Novello (1787?–1854) "in recognition of her having a decided 'will' in matters right and good" (Clarke, *Recollections of Writers*, p. 205).

[3] Alistatia Gliddon (see n. 6 below) and her son George Robins Gliddon (1809–1857), later a famous Egyptologist. The latter had visited the Hunts at Genoa in August 1823.

to regard it; [4] but I hope, & I believe, that this is the last time. I thought never more to have been obliged to write to others about money, unless it was to return it; & indeed as to that matter, I hope it still, someway or other. I have been invited to write for the N. Monthly Magazine, where they pay well, & there I hope to see you about the 1st of November next.[5] What do you mean by stopping in doors so much, — eh, you ungrateful native? Why haven't you got English meadows, and pic-nic possibilities, & Wilful who wants you to "get out," and a head-ache, and "dear Mr Arthur," and dearer (at least to us of the brown sex) Alistatia? [6] How can you always keep at home? I have got none of all these, except the head-ache; & yet I go out. Come, I will put you upon your generosities, — if you have not survived those, as well as the meadows. Return good for evil, that is to say, a long letter instead of a short one, or let Wilful do it for you after the fashion of the delightful one she wrote me on my birth-night; [7] & let your subject be, one of the old pic-nics at Hampstead the first fine day. — I will drink all your healths before hand, & you shall drink mine on that day in *return*. — [8]

Your affectionate friend Leigh Hunt.

[4] Mary Shelley told Hunt on October 5, 1823 (*Letters of Mary Shelley*, I, 271), "I mentioned to him [Novello] your brother's proposition of referring the question of the E[xaminer] to him . . . . [He] objected to being a party on the sole score of not understanding the business & feeling himself incapable in consequence of doing justice to either."

[5] By September 1 Hunt had received through his brother "a fourth offer from Colburn" (*Correspondence of Leigh Hunt*, I, 232), and on November 4 he wrote to Elizabeth Kent (Brewer, *Holograph Letters*, p. 135), "Colburn after [having] repeatedly invited me to write in his Magazine, has agreed with me that I shall do so for a year certain and for £150 the first year, at the rate of 16 guineas a sheet; which he says is the largest pay given." He received £200 from Colburn on August 30, 1825 (*ibid.*, p. 143), by which he was enabled to take his family to England two weeks later. His "Epistle to B—— F——, Esq." appeared in the October issue of the *New Monthly Magazine*.

[6] Arthur Gliddon and his wife Alistatia (d. 1851), close friends of the Hunts and the Novellos. Gliddon was a tobacco and snuff manufacturer at 42 King Street, Covent Garden, and in 1820–1821 had been an agent for the publication of Hunt's *Indicator*. Two of his children, Kate and John, later married Thornton and Mary Florimel Hunt respectively.

[7] On October 19, 1823 (the letter is printed in *Correspondence of Leigh Hunt*, I, 208–210). Mary Shelley described the celebration to Hunt a day later (*Letters of Mary Shelley*, I, 274–275).

[8] Hunt had written to the Novellos on September 9, 1822 (Clarke, *Recollections of Writers*, p. 218), "We drank Novello's health on his birthday. Be sure that we always drink healths on birthdays."

Sept. 6. 3 o'clock. Novello's birth-day —
We have just dr{unk} his health.

P.S. See what pains Mr Brown has taken to look into my affairs for
me. Having him fortunately at hand here, I was resolved once for
all to ask a man of business to take this trouble. After having
read his letter, I wish you to forward it to my brother, mentioning
to him, at the same time, whether you believe you gave your advice under a wrong or a right impression; & whether your advice
has been acted upon, on his part, as you intended. — Mr Brown
desires me to present his remembrances to you. — L.H.

P.P.S. You will be good to keep Mr Brown's letter, after my
brother has read it, for the future consideration, if necessary, of
Arbitrators.

· 63 ·

TO C. W. DILKE

AL: Keats House, Hampstead. Printed by Richardson, *The Everlasting Spell*, pp. 194–197.

My dear Dilke,   Near Florence. 6th Septr 1824.
    Much as I desired to answer the letter I received from you on
19th August,[1] and that immediately, I was compelled to defer it
till to-day. I had undertaken a task, which as it was of great importance to the party for whom I undertook it,[2] I mentally swore
I would neither read nor write any thing else till it was fairly
finished, and it turned out to be far more tedious and laborious
than I had expected; and yesterday I washed my hands of it. This,
I believe, is the first excuse of the kind I have had occasion to
make; I have now lost you for 17 days, but had I done otherwise,
I should have neglected a more serious duty. What you have written about Geo. Keats has in some measure given me pleasure, as
I hope that what appears still doubtful may be cleared up. No one

[1] Number 60.
[2] Leigh Hunt.

would rejoice more than myself to find him guiltless of the charge against him; and when I can rejoice on that score, I will make him all the amends in my power. At present every thing rests on his own assertion, not only in opposition to his brother's, but to Mr Abbey's. Nor can I see, even if his assertion is correct, that he has any reason to complain of a charge being made against him, which by his own account he had taken every pains to establish. He purposely caused his brother to believ{e} it, and through him his friends, as J K's consequent destitution compell{ed} him to divulge the cause. His reason for this deception is so strange and uncommon, that it is barely credible; at least upon his last leaving England, when the reason could not, on the same grounds, have existed; still it is possible, from sheer want of common sense and common forethought. Now I will proceed downwards with your letter, not allowing a single fact you have stated unreplied to. He says I wrote to him like one who domineered and dictated; I deny it; my letter was very short, dry, and cold, not even accusing him, unless by implication; — what Mr Haslam wrote I know not.[3] It was always my belief, till I spoke with Mr Abbey, that he took with him £640, or thereabouts, from his brother John. During the autumn previous to G's return from America, J: went frequently to his guardian endeavouring to procure £500 of his own money to lend to Mr Haydon; he then told me that after that loan he should have about £200 remaining. This could not be effected on account of a trustee being in Holland at the time, and the idea of the loan was relinquished, from that and other causes.[4] So persuaded was J: that he had £700, that he used to enter with me on the calculations respecting laying that sum out in ground rents, and I could not believe otherwise. Afterwards he had, at his brother's request, George reminding him of an offer he had made to lend him money, lent all he had except £60 to him; so he told me expressly, thinking his "brother did not act rightly in leaving him so", — these were his words. He spoke in the same manner to

[3] In number 21 (in which he mentions his own letter to George) Brown asks Haslam to give George "such a sting as he has had from me," but no letter from Haslam to George has survived.

[4] Keats did lend Haydon a smaller sum, £30, in April 1819 (*Letters*, II, 54–55, 206). The only known trustee besides Abbey, John Nowland Sandell, had died in 1816 (Norman Kilgour in *Keats-Shelley Memorial Bulletin*, no. 13, 1962, pp. 24–27).

another person [5] (whose name I need not mention), and who
{in}formed me the sum was near £700, according to John's words.
Some {shor}t time after I went, at his desire, to Taylor & Hessey,
to ask for {a loa}n till Geo should remit back some of his money,
he authorising m{e} to tell T & H of his brother having borrowed
all his money; [6] they declined advancing money, and therefore I
borrowed some from Skynner for his purposes.[7] Under these circumstances, I say, I could not have believed otherwise than I did.
The charge therefore, contrary to G's supposition, did "originate
directly from his brother", not from any thing "vaguely & indis-
tinctly" said, but frequently, and positively and with complaints
against him, and for this there is other testimony than my own. In
the spring of 1822 I called on M[r] Abbey in Pancras Lane, when I
asked him the am[t] lent by John to George, upon the latter's
second voyage to America; he answered "about £350 to £400, —
he could not tell precisely without reference to his books, — something like that amount". When I said I understood it was about
£640, he said "that was a mistake, — it could not be so much." On
my regretting it was ever lent to him, his reply was — "And so do
I regret it; I told John at the time not to lend it, and said all I
could to prevent his doing so." [8] Thus it appeared John had
overrated his funds, likely enough in one so unused to any thing
like money affairs; [9] but it took nothing from the charge against
George, in a moral point of view, whether it was £640 or £350.
George says his brother expended £1,000 by the time he left the
profession of surgery; while {M}[r] Abbey expatiated to me on the
folly of his having left it, after he {h}ad spent £700 on it. You
can inquire of M[r] Abbey on both these points, {s}o contradictory
to George's statements; and though it is certain M[r] Abbey spoke
so to me, it is possible he spoke in both cases under an error, for

[5] Fanny Brawne, who on May 21, 1821, told Fanny Keats (*Letters of Fanny Brawne*, pp. 33–34) that George left John "*60* pounds when he owed *80*," and that the latter remarked, "George ought not to have done this."

[6] Taylor wrote to his brother James, August 10, 1820, "George has borrowed all his [Keats's] remaining Money, and taken it to America," and he asked George in February 1821 for "some of that money which John lent him" — Olive M. Taylor in *London Mercury*, 12 (1925): 259; Sharp, p. 99; *KC*, I, 214–215.

[7] On May 6, 1820 (number 84). Robert Skynner, whose address in 1839 was 42 Mortimer Street, Cavendish Square, London (number 123), was Brown's lawyer.

[8] See Abbey's letter to Keats of August 23, 1820 (quoted in number 108).

[9] Compare Brown's remarks on this point in numbers 64, 101.

George might have allowed him to believe that he was borrowing £350, which may be disproved by the Accounts; or Mr Abbey might have spoken in forgetfulness of a fact; and it is very possible he talked of £700 when he ought to have said £1000. George says he owed nothing to John for expences previously to the former's coming of age; this may have been the case, but John understood otherwise, for when walking in the Highlands, he told me George did owe him money on that account, and had repaid him, he knew not how much, as George in settling every thing before he left London, gave him no written account, and asked me if I thought he ought not to have given one. I am aware that John had debts owing to him of about £170, and he told me part of them were loans made by George, — but that he agreed to take them on his own shoulders, that George might have more to carry to America, and at George's request. This seems opposite to George's assertion of having left John £300 at that time; but John was likely to be in error, and it appears from George's account, it was his intention to deceive him on this point, not wishing it known he gave £300 of his own money. I cannot (I find) enter into the account of Tom's estate, as, through some slip of the pen which confuses it, you deduct £300 from £1100 and make £540 only remaining.[10] Nor is it necessary; I have mentioned enough to show I could not have believed and said otherwise; and that if George is guiltless, he I contend took the best means to show himself guilty. I cannot say, nor can Hunt, from your letter, that George at present is exculpated; it is far from satisfactory, and Hunt thought so, without being acquainted with the circumstances I have related from my own and other's knowledge. Mr Abbey may settle it quickly, and {I} shall be most happy to hear I have been in the wrong, though I {shall} never reproach myself for speaking on the strong grounds I went {upon.}[11]

*   *   *

[10] In number 60 Dilke does not make clear that George (*KC*, I, 278), after subtracting £300 from £1100 to get £800, had taken two thirds of the remainder to arrive at his and John's share, approximately £540.

[11] The present letter consists of a single sheet written on both sides. The remainder is lost.

· 64 ·

TO JOSEPH SEVERN

Address: Al Signore / Il Signor Giuseppe Severn, / Pittore Inglese, / Posta restante, / Roma.
Postmarks: FIRENZE; 11 SETTEMB[RE]
ALS: Harvard. One paragraph is printed by Sharp, p. 147.

My dear Severn,   Florence. 8th Sept[r] 1824.
    I have heard of the loss you have sustained, and can well imagine into what trouble you were thrown. Make my respects to the two ladies, and say how sincerely I condole with them.[1] We are all anxious to know how you and they are. It is to be feared that I also will have to endure a loss, which though not of one immediately connected wi{th} me, yet the fear of it goes to my heart. Have I written {to} you of poor Daniells? I think not; but it is enough {to} tell you he has a short time since sailed for Malta, {a} sea-voyage affording the only hope of saving his life; and if I may judge from the several letters he sent me from Pisa, I must say there is little hope indeed. When I saw him in May,[2] he was in high spirits and florid health; and within a month after, just as he heard of his aunt's dying and leaving his fortune to the family, he was struck with inflamation on the lungs, — then he had a second attack, and ever since he appears to have been wasting and fevering in an irretrievable consumption. But let me leave melancholy subjects.
    A letter from Dilke[3] gives you the following information:
    "About Severn's magnificent copy of Raphael's fresco I promised some information more valuable as a ground work for his judgment, than my opinion, and I have at length procured it. I mentioned to you that Harlowe, a very clever artist, and somewhat known, had made a similar copy of the Transfiguration. Harlowe threw a right interest about the Exhibition to

---

[1] See number 59, n. 10.
[2] Brown had stopped at Pisa on his return from Rome to bring Carlino to Florence.
[3] Number 60.

catch the English, by dying at the critical moment; notwithstanding which I have the best authority for saying that *the
exhibition did not pay the expences,* that the picture was eventually sold for that purpose, if not legally seized, and only
brought £149. In a *direct pecuniary* view such a work, I think,
could not *therefore* be expected to succeed. How far Harlowe,
had he lived, or Severn, who I hope will live, might have benefited by the reputation of having done it, and the Aldermen's
jowls he would paint in consequence, he is a much better judge
than I can be, and I offer no opinion."

I wish you to pay much attention to the above extract, as well as
to the other I lately forwarded.[4] It appears tolerably certain that
by exhibiting your copy, you will lose your money; and there {is}
no hope of selling so large a picture. These two points are
{mour}nful ones. As for the copying it being of service to you as
{a c}olourist, I put no faith in that, nor does Kirkup, nor any
{one} with whom I have talked,[5] capable of giving an {op}inion.
The only reason for executing it therefore is out of sheer love of
Raphael and the Art; and you, I contend, cannot afford either the
time or the expence for such a purpose. It will occupy twice as
much time as you reckon on at the least. Suppose, when finished,
you were to offer it as a present, either to the Royal Academy or
to any other body, I really doubt (purely on account of its size)
if it would not remain rolled up like Harlowe's Trans^n. {T}here
is more talk than love of Raphael in England; there colour is the
attraction, chiefly in the Dutch and Venetian schools. I am aware
you have purchased the canvas, but will it not be better to use it
for other purposes?

Geo. Keats has written a very long letter to Dilke, to excul-
pate himself from the charge against him, and expressing himself
very angry that ever it was made.[6] Dilke thinks his letter conclusive in his favour, and sends me the heads of it. I am sorry I cannot
agree with him, as his George's[7] assertions are directly in opposition not only to what John Keats said (who might on money affairs

[4] Perhaps in number 58, of which only the portion printed by Sharp is known.
[5] *Written* with whom I have talked with.
[6] See numbers 60, 63.
[7] "George's" is inserted above the line.

be easily in error) [8] but to what Mr Abbey told me. Therefore I have asked Dilke, in order to clear up all doubt, to call on Mr Abbey, and procure his further explanation. Should it appear that George is guiltless, I will not only inform you, but endeavour to do him justice with every one in my power. He owns, for the sake of John's feelings, that he voluntarily deceived him, making him believe he was at all times richer than he was, and also that he was borrowing money from him; John's consequent destitution of course made others acquainted with this, and therefore how can Georg{e,} however innocent, be surprised at the charge having be{en} made against him, grounded as it was on his own word{s} and deeds? This I think so strange that it is only possible. Indeed he makes out that when he first went to America, John had not a penny, and that he (George) under pretence of adjusting accounts gave him £300, without John knowing any thing of such a gift. When he went for the second time to America, he says he took from him only £170, — so that, by his account, John had been the better for his brotherhood to the amount of £130. Mr Abbey's story to me differed in *sums* and *facts* from George's. What think you of this?

If you still purpose to paint the School of Athens, surely you may ask Mr Craufurd for £50, — but not otherwise.[9] And whenever you want money you may ask Mr Erskine [10] for some, as he offered; — there can be no doubt on these points. There were no letters at the post for M^rs & Miss Clark.[11] You, and Westmacott, and the black butterfly ought all to be shut up in a glass case together as curiosities.[12] My Carlino is a healthy lively rogue, —

[8] Compare the preceding letter and number 101.

[9] Crauford, who repeatedly invited Severn to dine with him in Rome in May 1821 (*KC*, I, 241) and commissioned him to make a replica of Raphael's "Madonna della Sedia" in the Pitti Palace, Florence, in May 1823 (Sharp, p. 137), had recently offered him £200 to copy Raphael's "School of Athens" in the Vatican (Severn to his father, June 30, 1824, Keats House, Hampstead). From Severn's letter to Brown of September 27 (Forman, 1883, IV, 373) it appears that about this time Crauford called on Brown and read *Otho* with disapproval.

[10] Thomas Erskine (1788–1870), Scottish advocate and author, who spent the winter of 1823–1824 in Rome (*Letters of Thomas Erskine of Linlathen*, ed. William Hanna, New York, 1877, p. 39). He had recently commissioned "Cordelia Watching by the Bed of Lear," which Severn began toward the end of 1825 and exhibited at the Royal Academy in 1828.

[11] Perhaps the wife and sister of Severn's physician, James Clark.

[12] "One day Richard Westmacott, Leigh Hunt and others were taking the air

but just now there is a struggle for power between us, and as I insist on being King, I have bought a rod for my sceptre; — he has been not a little spoiled at Pisa, and as he grows more & more strong, he shows his wilfulness. The last time we quarrelled, he gently inquired what right I had to go to Pisa and steal him (rubarmi!) out of his *mother's* house! — arguing that I was bound, as a good *father*, to carry him back again, where he could do what he liked! Kirkup is so taken with Florence, that he will not, I believe, be in Rome so much as formerly, and perhaps he will settle here. He & Madama [13] dined with me in my Nunnery yesterday, with Hunt & two of his children; — and last Sunday West & a Mr Giles [14] (a clever artist) with Hunt and one child; — so, you see, I'm growing gay as I grow gray; — we all talked a great deal about you, and every one of course sends his remembrances. I have written an account of our Anglo Roman Artists, and of their work {i}n as good natured a way as I could, and others think it {re}ally so; it is for the Examiner; but I have kept my word in attacking your illiberal Academy, which possibly may displease some, but that is nothing to the purpose if they are wrong, — and I have stated nothing but facts, as Kirkup can vouch for, to whom I read my said attack upon you. I could not help having a fling at your lord and lady Amateurs, when speaking of the Art, — their's being the histrionick one; giving it as my opinion they did much harm to painters & sculptors, their rival artists, last winter in Rome. I suppose you will think me wrong on every point, — 1st I had no right to play the critic on you and your fellows; 2nd it is monstrous to attack your excellent Academy; and 3rd — what have I [to] do with Lords & Ladies? [15] Mind your daubing, Sirrah! and leave me alone with my blotting.

Your's sincerely,
Chas Brown.

---

and conversing. A black butterfly of remarkable size and beauty settled near them. They watched it with fascination. Hunt commented on the Psyche of the Greeks. The butterfly remained for an unusual length of time. The day was April 19th, 1824, — the day of Byron's death at Missolonghi" (Blunden, *Leigh Hunt*, p. 217). Brown had met the sculptor Richard Westmacott, Jr. (1799–1872), in Rome (Sharp, pp. 142–143).

[13] Presumably Kirkup's current mistress.

[14] James Giles (1801–1870), landscape painter.

[15] In "Actors and Artists at Rome," which appeared as the sixteenth "Wishing-

· 65 ·

TO H. L. HUNT [1]

ALS: British Museum.

To Henry Leigh Hunt Esqr   Florence. 17th Novr 1824.
My dear Sir,

My letter to your Uncle of 20th Aug^t [2] was chiefly intended as a document for the service of mutual friends to all parties in London, drawn from the correspondence and accounts laid before me here; as it appeared to be the anxious wish of your father that an arbitration should take place, and as the question between them would doubtless by such means be fairly adjusted. For the same purpose, should an arbitration be still approved of by both parties and in answer to your appeal to myself, I beg leave to reply to yours of 6th Oct^r.

The explanations you have entered into respecting the Accounts, have made them appear in a clearer light. My error in imagining that the debt due to Magnay & Co was chargeable on the Examiner arose from the following words in your father's letter of 8th Feby last, where (after stating the two last year's profits on the paper) he says — "but out of these profits there are to be paid the annuity to Mr Whiting, and the payments to Magnay & Co". It now however appears by your letter that the property of the Examiner is worth £218. 8/– per annum more than it appeared to be in your father's letter, which may make a considerable difference in favour of your uncle. I had no assistance, as you imagine, either from M^r or M^{rs} L Hunt in my

Cap" in the *Examiner*, October 3, 1824, pp. 626–628, Brown censures the English Academy at Rome for admitting only professional artists and for recognizing financial need rather than merit. He also tells that he was not invited to the private theater: "The company was always too select . . . and I am a plebeian. . . . In my opinion, Rome is not the proper place [for such a theater]." Severn's recollection in 1834 (see number 109) — "how much some years since you would have liked to have had the Tragedy acted in Rome when there were private Theatricals" — suggests that Brown had tried without success to get *Otho* produced there.

[1] A draft of the letter actually sent by Brown.
[2] Number 61.

examination of the Accounts. Nor do I think you need excuse[3] any person declaring them irregular & incorrect. They were the most perplexing papers ever laid before me: there were Accounts which ought to be duplicates, not only differing in sums but in *dates*, & in many instances without a word of explanation in the correspondence; the D^{rs} & C^{rs}, in different accounts, *changed sides*; there was a yearly account with a wrong year's date; nor was there any system that I could discover; add to which the errors you have acknowledged, and surely no one can be blamed for objecting to the Accounts. Your uncle told me, more than once, of Mr Robertson's[4] approval of the manner in which the books at home are kept; but of those I could have nothing to say; I spoke solely of what lay before me.

The argument you have used to prove that your uncle is no longer a partner in the Ex^r is this, — in your own words: — "The original contract was that my father should undertake the printing, the publishing, and in a word the whole *business* of the concern, (including the finding money for its establishment), and that my uncle should edit the Paper; for which respective contributions of labour each was to receive a half of the produce of the property, after paying the bare expences out of pocket." You then add that your father stood, as it were, as the capitalist in the concern, engaging to find money either from his own funds or from loans from others, "the employment of which ceased of course with its *prosperity*"; and that he employed your Uncle as Editor, engaging to give him one half of the gross profits, and that therefore when your uncle quitted England he ceased to possess any claim on the concern. Now it afterwards unfortunately appeared that your father could not keep to his contract as a capitalist; he could in part establish the paper, but he could not form its *prosperity*; accordingly Mr Whiting was applied to, who agreed to perform your father's duty, as capitalist, upon condition of receiving one third of the gross profits. It follows then, that every penny deducted from your uncle's stipulated half of the gross profits during his Editorship, from the time that M^r

---

[3] *Written* need not excuse.

[4] Henry Robertson, "a Treasury Office clerk, and the appointed accountant of Covent Garden Theatre" (Clarke, *Recollections of Writers*, p. 18).

Whiting became a partner, must be returned to him. I therefore cannot but conclude that either you are mistaken in stating the above to be the original contract, or that it was afterwards annulled when Mʳ Whiting became a partner. If your uncle exchanged his claim of one half to one third of the gross profits, surely it was for some further good in prospect, such as, for instance, a direct partnership for the benefit of himself and his heirs. When Mʳ Whiting became a partner, was there not some written agreement, some express deed of partnership between the three, the terms of which might settle this question immediately? If not, and if every one relied on each other's honour, then the original contract, as you state it, would have taken Mʳ Whiting's third entirely out of your father's half share, leaving your Uncle's half untouched, according to your father's engagement to him, as long as he continued Editor. Your argument cuts both ways, and worse against your father; and I am sorry it has been used, and made the ground-work of the whole of your letter. Your father earnestly desired the question should be referred to mutual and unbiassed friends; if he will appoint one in England, your uncle will appoint another; Without such an arbitration, I see it may never be settled, or it may be settled by that party possessing the more power in his hands; for it must be well known that your uncle's affection for his brother would prevent him from entering into any thing like a legal struggle. That your father believes himself in the right I cannot doubt; but his belief, in a matter of such importance to his brother and family, is not (permit me to say) enough; especially when others, unbiassed in the question, view it in an opposite light.

You are mistaken when you say — "My uncle has informed you, it appears, that he offered my father a half share in the Liberal, on condition of his being allowed to retain a half share in the Examiner." I never was so informed, and never wrote to that effect. By this mistake you have thrown all I said upon that offer into a cold shade. Upon this mistake you have also grounded an implication that your uncle was aware of his not possessing any share after he had quitted England. But this is not the case, as your father knows, for he received a letter from him, when at Pisa or at Genoa, asking for the Accounts of the Examiner, and your father in reply did not even then inform him that he considered all partnership dissolved. The time for such information, if such a forfeiture could take place, was before your uncle left him in London, but it never was hinted at until two years after. This, strange as it seems to me and others, was certainly the fact; and your uncle could not have the most distant idea of such a letter as that of your father's, dated 19 Septr 1823, where he desires to know what your uncle's opinion might be as to the extent of claim &c, adding that he *"should not think himself a proper judge on a question of this nature."*

There are several other errors in your letter, which I am compelled to set aright, as all of them, more or less, in your argument, tend against your uncle, and as I am completely enabled to do so with the whole of the correspondence at my elbow. 1st It was your father, and not your uncle, that first proposed an arbitration; the latter was too startled to yield to it, and wrote hoping it could be arranged between themselves; upon which your father answered as follows — "If my view of your claim upon the Examiner is so unreasonable and unjust, how is it that you decline referring the differences between us to the arbitration of mutual friends? Does not this imply a doubt in your own mind of the soundness of your demand?" Not exactly, I think; but such is your father's doctrine. 2nd Your father, several times, has possitively admitted a just claim on the property, not one of "sympathy and humanity" though always short of an absolute partnership. 3rd The Articles sent from Plymouth were rec^d as part of the number, (which your uncle from ill health could not complete,) for his work as partner in the Examiner as implied & indeed apparent in your father's letters, and not otherwise. 4th Those Articles were, at the time, highly approved of by your father, and not, as you suppose, merely permitted to be printed in favour of your Uncle's friends. 5th Your father must have committed a great error, (for his words are positive,) or the nett profits of the Examiner for 1822 & 1823, after paying Mr Whiting his two annuities of £200 each, amounted to £1,000. 6th Your uncle never (to me or to my knowledge) imputed a gross error in regard to a sum which he remitted from Plymouth; he requested to know how the remittance was applied, as he could not recollect the items, — so he told me, and so I stated it in my letter of 20th Aug[t]. 7th You are mistaken in thinking that your uncle endeavoured to press any thing (far from "every thing") into the service against your father, or to make any "insinuations" proper or improper, as far as my experience goes; — he was open and single-minded to me throughout, told me what he knew in answer to my questions, and always reminded me that, whatever my view might be, I was to put entire faith in his brother's wish & purpose to act rightly, however he might at present be in error. 8th Your uncle was guilty of no "contrivance", no "ex-post facto demand," in the affair of drawing for £30 on 1st Jan[y] last. I request you will look into his letter at the time, & see if there are not some words to this effect, — "I am unwilling to draw on you at present without giving you what I can in hand, therefore I send you this poem." [5] So I recollect his telling me. He was at that time thrown into unexpected destitution by your father's having, on 19th Sept[r] 1823, and by following letters, acquainted him that they were no longer partners. I am grieved to see that his necessities, arising from your father's will or right, and his silence for two years as to that will or right should afford a subject (pardon me when I say it) of threat and ridicule. 9th You say "my father is still willing to adhere to the grant of annuity which my uncle's friend M[r] Novello thought liberal, and which my uncle himself thankfully accepted." Can you mean no more than the bare £100 per annum, without any hope of future increase? This is entirely contrary to your father's promise, contained in two seperate letters; entirely contrary to what M[r] Novello thought liberal, according to his letter written at the time; and it is certain that your uncle did not accept the bare annuity. Your father, in plain terms, promised a future contingent advantage, and your uncle entertained great hopes of reaping it. 10th I perceive you have presupposed that your uncle would continue monthly to draw for £14 to the end of this year. I thought that both he & I had explained in our letters that he could not avail himself of those drafts. I mean that he could not honestly do so, & therefore he refrained, notwithstanding his urgent need of funds for his support. I have before said, that your father's tacit acquiescence in the interpretation of his engagement was, to my

[5] *Bacchus in Tuscany* (see the last extant paragraph of number 83).

mind, an agreement. He it seems thinks otherwise; though you mention he acknowledges he did not act explicitly enough, and wishes he had acted otherwise. granting that the annuity was accepted under certain conditions to which he did not object. At all events No one can deny that your uncle's present distressing situation is owing to that conduct of your father; he having first led him to believe his income would amount to a certain sum, and afterwards having suddenly let him know it by no means amounted to that sum. I am bound to say thus much, witnessing his situation and I trust your father will at least in this one instance think with me. When your uncle first understood an Examiner was published without one of his Wishing Caps, he & I both supposed that in a following paper *two* would be published; for we believed (until I heard to the contrary at the beginning of *last Aug^t*) that the Examiner still continued in its increased size of 24 pages; and he could not possibly entertain a doubt of your father's omitting them at his pleasure, and thereby reducing his income. So completely did your uncle rely on the promise in Mr Novello's and your father's letters, never conjecturing that there could be want of *space* in the paper, and wondering on what account there was even one omission, unless, as I feared, a packet had miscarried.

As I observe that my letter of 20th Augt is regarded as a "fresh embroilment of the matter," and as the blame is attached to your uncle, I cannot refrain from stating exactly the case. It was owing to his ill health, and continued low spirits, that I conjectured he was in pecuniary difficulties; upon which I hinted to him, being his only friend here on whom he could rely in such an affair, that I was ready and willing to assist him with my opinion. At first he declined such offers, partly from a reluctance to display the correspondence, and partly as he did not like to trouble me (as he afterwards said) with his concerns. It was not till 19th Augt that I was made acquainted with them. In doing what I had undertaken, and what I therefore conceived my duty, God forbid I should have embroiled any thing. While writing on business affairs, of right and wrong, in another's cause, and that a friend's, it was not possible (and I have felt the same in writing this letter,) to do otherwise than put my meaning in as strong and as plain a

light as I could. That he, in any way whatever, directly or indirectly, endeavoured to make it an embroilment, I can assert
was not the case. On the contrary he did the best sort of justice
to every one, and spoke of every circumstance on which I ques-
tioned him, (and that was seldom as I needed little more than the
papers before me,) with a delicacy nearly amounting to reserve &
as I thought against his own interest. He seemed to regard it as
a matter of painful necessity, and so indeed it appeared to myself.

Personally to yourself, as far as I am concerned, I must add a
few words. I have to thank you for your expressions of regard
towards me, and for the justice you have done me on this particular occasion. But I regret, exceedingly regret that you are
ignorant of your uncle. I know him thoroughly, and never have
seen any thing but what enhanced my esteem; and never heard
any thing against his moral character except from his political
enemies Mr Haydon ⁶ and yourself. The words you have addressed
to me, written in violence against one of my friends, I should blush
not to notice; but I now refrain from noticing them in a more
particular manner, as I had intended, on account of the subject
being so foreign to that of this letter.

I trust that your father, however widely we differ in our
opinions on this point, will ever continue to be assured of my
kindest and best feelings.

I remain, my dear Sir,
Your's very truly,
C Brown

P. S.⁷ Since writing the above Mr Leigh Hunt came into town &
called on me; when I asked if he recollected having, together with

⁶ Haydon's quarrels with Hunt (they became "jealous Neighbours" at 22 and
13 Lisson Grove North, Paddington, in 1817) over Keats's poetry, borrowed silver,
and especially religion led to a "parting for ever" in January 1818 (*Letters*, I, 168–
169, 205, 210; Blunden, *Leigh Hunt*, pp. 116–117). Of Keats's remark on December
17, 1818 (*Letters*, II, 11), that Hunt was "disgusting . . . in morals," Amy Lowell
(*John Keats*, Boston and New York, 1925, II, 124) says: "Haydon had been one of
the many people whom Keats had been seeing, for Haydon applied the word
'morals' to religious opinions, a subject on which he and Hunt were forever at
odds." Haydon renewed friendship with Hunt in a letter of 1832, and they met on
good terms in 1840 (Blunden, pp. 245, 280).

⁷ Perhaps written on Saturday, November 20. Three weeks after this date Hunt
told Elizabeth Kent (Brewer, *Holograph Letters*, p. 138), "On Saturdays I generally
go and take a chop with Mr. Brown in Florence."

Mr John Hunt and Mr Whiting, signed a deed of partnership, — he immediately replied in the affirmative. The terms of that deed, with which you appear to be unacquainted, may answer every purpose for both parties; and Mr John Hunt of course is aware in whose custody it is lodged.

CB

. 66 .

TO H. L. HUNT [1]

ALS: British Museum.

My dear Sir,   Florence. 30 Decr 1824.

Your letter of 7th instant arrived a few days since. I by no means thought of interpreting the word "Capitalist" in the sense you imagine I did, — never supposed that your father was to sink any money of his own in the concern. What I wrote therefore upon that point on 17 Nov^r [2] remains, to my mind, unaltered.

In reply to what you say respecting my omitting all notice of two out of the three reasons you had urged against your uncle's claim, I beg to refer you to my letter of 20th Aug^t,[3] where I endeavoured to discuss two of those points, & I did not think it necessary to repeat what I had there said. The third I did not notice, — perhaps I neglected it improperly, — and I now confess my unwillingness to enter upon it. This is a subject which places me in a very delicate situation. While I feel the warmest sentiments towards your father, and know the self-sacrifices he has undergone in his kindness towards his brother, — which I have every where acknowledged, — you compel me to repeat what I never said before except to your father himself. He will recollect my telling him [4] how wrongly, in my opinion, he had acted in having assisted his brother when his income was more than sufficient; that such assistance had fostered his imprudence; and that

---

[1] A draft of the letter actually sent by Brown.
[2] In the preceding letter.
[3] Number 61.
[4] In 1821 or 1822 (see the opening paragraph of number 69).

once having commenced on such a system, it was expected to be continued, thus blinding his brother's eyes to the necessity of care & economy. I am aware how bitter a thing it is, to hear that what we conceived to be our best actions have been real injuries; — but let you & your father consider these words as coming from a calm looker-on, — from one who may not even find another to agree in its fullest extent to so severe a doctrine, certainly not in any degree by your uncle, were I to read a copy of this letter to him, — for I own its severity, though I believe it cannot (strictly examining it) be denied. It would have been better had your uncle endured an ounce of suffering at the first, than thus be crushed with a tun at last, and when he has seven children to feed and clothe, and (if possible) to educate. I know not, to speak openly, which has been the more imprudent, the borrower or the lender. For the rest, I am well aware of the power a creditor possesses over his debtor, under whatever circumstances the debt may have arisen; but you seem to stretch that power beyond its possible limits. Besides, you yourself, upon reflection, would not advise your father to convert his former kindnesses into the means of depriving your uncle of what otherwise would be his just claim. The Deed of Partnership, from the quotation you have given, amply proves (as far as my knowledge allows me, I say so) that your uncle is still a partner; his ceasing to perform his contract as Editor cannot annul the partnership, unless a clause exists to that effect; he cannot be otherwise mulcted than with the amount of salary paid to another Editor in his place; and if necessary, he will return to his duties in England.[5] It strikes me as just that the question should first be settled, without reference to the debt; and that then the best means of liquidating it should be resorted to, as far as, with the utmost economy, your uncle can accomplish.

At present, according to your letters, the case stands thus: 1st your father claims the right which no *one* partner can possess of utterly dissolving the partnership; 2nd he will not consent to allow his brother more than £100 per annum, and that entirely at his will & pleasure, and, consequently, it may hereafter be at the will & pleasure of others; and 3rd he holds the debt for ever hanging

[5] Hunt had expressed his willingness to do so in letters to his brother dated October 3, 14, 1823 (Brewer, *Holograph Letters*, pp. 158–159).

over his brother's head, after depriving him of all hope of repaying it. This I cannot help thinking wrong; and as the propriety of demanding an arbitration is left with me by your uncle, I must demand it; and I do this, in his name, after the best consideration in my power.

Let it be remarked that your father has written differently from the above. It seems that you view the question in another light from what he has done. It was but very lately, (14 Oct^r) that he wrote that he could say nothing about cancelling the debt till an arrangement was completed; — (yet *that* I observe would necessarily form part of the arrangement) — except that he would be glad to do any thing that might relieve your uncle from the liability to any unpleasant consequences that might follow from want of — (*something*, for I cannot decypher that word) [6] — on his part. Now this is quite in opposition to your letters of 6 Oct & 7 Dec. Again I cannot forbear to mention that our correspondence on this subject is carried on to the disadvantage of us both; I am writing to an interested party, yet not to the principal; and you are writing to a disinterested party, who, it appears to me, you cannot but regard so widely do we differ as one more like an advocate than willing to speak of every thing in all its equal bearings, — if I have been so biassed, I am unconscious of it; and were it possible for me to have a half-hour's conversation with your father & yourself, I am convinced there would be no difficulty in coming to an arrangement, — such as, in the end, both brothers would be pleased with. I present my respects to your father, and am, dear Sir,

Your's very truly,
CB

[6] John Hunt had written "want of perspicuity" (ALS, British Museum).

· 67 ·

TO MARIANNE HUNT

Address: To / Mʳˢ Hunt.

ALS: University of Iowa. Printed by Brewer, *Holograph Letters*, p. 146.

My dear Mʳˢ Hunt,   [January 7, 1825] [1]
    I have settled with Nesti, without the several accounts. He says he received (he thinks) only 12 pauls for the inclosed Account; if he received the other half paul, he must return it.

    Nesti has Sugar, (but little worse than your's at 10 crazie,) for one paul [2] a pound. I use it, and advise you to try it. Never pay more than 6 crazie a pound for moist sugar, of the same quality as your's. A decrease like this in your Sugar-bills, I see, will be sensibly felt in your expences.

Your's most truly,
Chaˢ Brown.
Friday. 7ᵗʰ Janʸ.

· 68 ·

TO THOMAS RICHARDS

Address: Inghilterra. / To / Thomas Richards Esqʳ / Storekeeper's Office, / Ordnance Department, / Tower, / London.

Postmarks: FIRENZE; AT; AUTRICHE PAR HUNINGUE; FPO JA 25 1825

ALS: Keats House, Hampstead. Printed in *Some Letters*, pp. 51–56.

Florence. 10ᵗʰ Janʸ 1825.

    Many thanks, my dear Richards, for the kind offer you have made to remit me half of the £50 nearly three months before I re-

---

[1] While the Hunts were in Italy, January 7 fell on a Friday only in 1825.

[2] A paul was worth about sixpence. The values of Tuscan money (8 crazie = 1 paul; 10 pauls = 1 crown; from 420 to 428 crowns = £100) can be worked out from numbers 77, 85 (see also Sharp, p. 290).

quested any part of it. This I know how to value, albeit such a course would be of some disservice to me. Either you did not thoroughly read my letter,[1] or I have written it unintelligibly. There I meant to ask if Mr Chas Richards[2] will consent to my drawing upon him a bill of £50 due on 1st July next; and this is now the essential point to be answered. By such means I shall be in possession of the money here on 29th March, as the bill will be at three months date. Whereas, by your plan, I cannot touch the first £25 till 21st April; and I have engaged to repay, before the end of March, more than that sum, which I have borrowed from a friend, as I was much in want of present means. You will perceive I had arranged every thing, so as not to take any money from you till 1st July, when the two years will be expired.[3] Should your brother object to my drawing upon him, I must forbear; but I earnestly intreat you will as soon as possible give me notice of such an objection, that we may enter into an agreement for some other plan, tho' it will be rather difficult. As he is a man in business (known as such) there will be no difficulty here with the Banker,[4] — as I recollect mentioning before, — yet, strangely enough, this — the grand point for me to be acquainted with — is left by you utterly unnoticed. Again, I wanted to hear, if possible, some news of Mrs Edwards,[5] — not a word in answer, whether you know any thing or nothing. How very odd this seems to me! Yet you are not a jot worse than others. I had to write *five* times to Mancur, asking one of the simplest questions in the world, yet of importance to me and to another, before he would answer, — so that the best part of a twelvemonth was wasted, and when the news did at last come, it was too late! Again, he wrote me word he had sent my Article on "Love's labour lost" to the New Monthly; I told him how anxious I was to write in a Magazine, and begged him to give me intelligence when it might be inserted, as that would invite me again to write there; now I am here in Florence told an Article

---

[1] The letter is not known.

[2] Thomas' brother, of 100 St. Martin's Lane, printer of Keats's *Poems* in 1817 and Brown's *Shakespeare's Autobiographical Poems* in 1838.

[3] Apparently Brown repaid Richards a loan of £50 in May 1823 (see number 46), and then lent him £50 two months later.

[4] He was W. G. Johnstone, of Casa Ugolini, Via dell' Anguillara.

[5] Here Brown refers to his letter of July 26–28, 1824 (number 59).

with that *title* appeared on 1ˢᵗ Decʳ, — but whether mine or not, I cannot tell,[6] — so I am left waiting here *with Articles ready to forward,* and unable to do so from the lack of this little bit of information, thus throwing me for one or for two months out of receipt of money. O, the blessings of precision! He may never tell me, — for his head is full of love and marriage, — so pray let me not lose more than *one* month more, but see if my Article has been printed or not, & let me know; the signature I gave was H. M. and it began with "Why this should be Shakespear's labour lost is more than our love for the Poet can answer." I'm left in a considerable predicament about this, as the Editor [7] and I (or at least I with him) have had a quarrel. L. Hunt, with many kind expressions towards yourself, and thanks for your compliment, says he has twice before declined being Godfather, tho' both parties were particular friends of his, and that he cannot consistently be one. He talked of writing to you, but he is greatly harrassed just now with all sorts of writing. As for names his favourite for a boy is Alfred, — so it is mine, — for a Girl I like Emma, Emily, or Marian. Remember me kindly to Mrs Richards, and say I hope she will be far "better than expected" before you receive this. You may rely on this, — I never wrote an Article in the London,[8] — never wrote any but what Mancur has been duly informed of. (I'm now proceeding to answer every thing in your letter.) Severn will not certainly be married, — at least to the lady he once had some thoughts about; and I hear of his being quite "fancy-free".[9] I can't comprehend what you mean in your question about the "Racemation [10] in my neighbourhood"; — when you explain it I'll do my best to answer. Carlino goes to an English Day-school,[11] where he learns his native language very fast, — ditto his alphabet;

---

[6] It was Brown's, in *New Monthly Magazine,* 11 (1824): 516–521.

[7] Thomas Campbell.

[8] See numbers 20, 34.

[9] *A Midsummer-Night's Dream,* II.i.164. On Severn's love affair see number 59, n. 10.

[10] "The gleaning or gathering of grapes" (*New English Dictionary,* citing examples from 1623 to 1685).

[11] Run by a Miss Smith (see number 94), described by Landor (Super, *Landor,* p. 172) as "an excellent schoolmistress, who takes ten or twelve young scholars, none above eight years old. Here [at the school] they learn English, Italian, French and dancing, as well as drawing and accounts." Carlino continued at the school for four years.

he is remarkably well. I'm glad to hear so good an account considering the winter season of your little ones. I'll tell you in few words the story of Shelley and Lucy Westbrook, as I've heard it from L. Hunt and another of Shelley's friends,[12] — both accounts precisely alike. She was a girl of little or no education, and he, at 18, married her, hoping to mould her mind his own way. She however turned all his visionary schemes to air. After a time, her conduct was such, that her infidelities were scarcely the worst part, so that he could not live with her. They seperated, when he allowed her exactly *one half* of his income. This was not enough for *her*, tho' it was for *him*, and he borrowed more & more money for *her*, till he could not longer feed her folly and imprudence. One evening she went to her own relation's house in London, where, on account of her bad conduct, the door was shut in her face, and her wants unrelieved, — on which she turned from that very door, and went and drowned herself. If Shelley was to blame, why so are you and I. No one was to blame but herself, and her unreclaimable disposition and wanton extravagance.[13] There is a reading room here,[14] where three English daily papers, and some Reviews are taken in; I do not subscribe, as the terms are high, but sometimes I buy a day's reading for two pauls; besides they have a tolerable library; if I can afford such a matter I will subscribe. I am not, and perhaps never shall be invited to Lord Burghersh's, [15] — unless I'm at the trouble to procure a letter to him, — so I can give you no critique on his Opera; I know no more than that it is greatly commended. Should I meet with Mr Whitehead, I'll pay him all the attention in my power; tell Mr Vincent, with my compliments, he might have given him a letter

---

[12] Probably John Taaffe, Jr.

[13] On Shelley's marriage with Harriet (not "Lucy") Westbrook see number 46. Mary Shelley (*Letters of Mary Shelley*, I, 317) says that "Shelley did not allow Harriet half his income — she received £200 a year." The "relation" was her sister, Eliza Westbrook, who, according to Shelley in a letter to Byron, January 17, 1817, "may be truly said (though not in law, yet in fact) to have murdered her [Harriet] for the sake of her father's money" (*Letters of Shelley*, ed. Jones, I, 529–530 — see also I, 521, 523). N. I. White, *Shelley* (New York, 1940), I, 480, comments: "There is no evidence other than Shelley's word that she [Harriet] was driven forth by the greed and jealousy of her sister."

[14] Vieusseux's Library, Palazzo Ferroni, Via Tornabuoni.

[15] John Fane, later the eleventh Earl of Westmorland (1784–1859), British minister plenipotentiary in Florence. The *Dictionary of National Biography* gives the titles of seven operas by him.

to me; on another occasion, please to bear in mind that Mancur
has my exact address. The stanza I alluded to in Adonais (the very
last)[16] is that beginning with "The breath whose might &c." I
am glad you are succeeding so well in Music; one thing to excel
in is enough for any one man; though I regret you are, on another
score, so "incapable of your own *capacity*." [17] My reading, for
some time past, has been in old Italian, — the old Novelists; and
I have cooked up for the English taste some of the Tales, altering
them at my will, and often entirely remoulding them, — being any
thing but translations. These are my Articles ready to forward.
I would, if the Editor chooses, publish two a month. L. Hunt
thinks I have done them well. My first "An honest face" will
(mind, I prophecy it) be the subject of at least one Melo Drama;
it is certainly very interesting, — and, would you think it? some
of the scenes, at the latter part, affected me to pain, tho' all that
part is *my own* invention; besides, the story is quite novel. I've no
wish to plague myself again with Actors and Managers; [18] let
others browze on my fields (silly sheep!) and welcome. Then I've a
shorter story, which ought to have a poet's telling. Then there is
one of "Philolauro and Fiordespina", which must please all affectionate wives, as well as those who would fain be thought so.
My last, (tho' it was the first I wrote,) is called "Damages not at
law", — a comic affair, a cuckoldy business, but perfectly un-
objectionable to the honest reader, — indeed it must be thought
very moral and exemplifying.[19] I had great fun in scribbling it.
All these, and many more that I have pitched upon in these great
store-houses of invention, have never been, to my knowledge,
either in an English or a French dress. Tell me how you like "The
family Journal" in the New Monthly; [20] I believe it began with
the year. Nobody here can be called idle; every body that I know
works at something. By the by, I've gone on with a fairy tale, already reaching to fifty or more common romance pages, that

[16] In number 59 Brown says quite plainly "the last stanza" and "that concluding stanza."

[17] Perhaps based on *Hamlet*, IV.vii.179, "As one incapable of her own distress."

[18] As he did in the production of *Narensky* in 1814. On "let others browze"
see number 49, n. 10.

[19] None of these articles is known.

[20] January–December 1825, a series of essays by "Harry Honeycomb" (Leigh
Hunt).

pleases my friends,[21] — but I've quitted it for something of more immediate advantage, if I can get it. Do you think a fairy tale would be a purchaseable commodity? As for my intended Novel,[22] L. Hunt persuaded me not to pursue the idea; though I had worked up every thing ready to set down. He wishes me to write a Novel, where all the events are founded on my own experience,[23] not thrust into times past, and linked with history. I cannot see the difficulty, as you do, of connecting a few volumes as Novels go of Novel-writing together, — the only question with me is, how will my commodities sell? — I care for nothing else. If any bookseller would enter into a bargain with me for a Novel, a fairy tale, or a collection of old Italian Tales remodelled, I'm his man; and I say this without a particle of vanity, — my fullest or *foolest* extent is known in Articles I have printed, — they must be my warrant, bad or tolerable. But when I read such flat stuff as has come under my knowledge here, — Hadje Baba for instance or Lady Morgan's Salvator Rosa,[24] — and hear they are popular, I cannot forbear saying "I too might be an Author!" If my prattle runs on about myself, let my excuse be that I want to turn my inventions to account. Should I again be able to assist you in any undertaking, after this house-furnishing, by some profits on writing, you no doubt are aware how happy I shall be; — I shall be all readiness whenever it is in my power, — but that you know as well as I do. I shall expect a letter from you before the middle of next month, — glad enough that matters of business enforce you to be my correspondent. Give my love to your children, — and send it to Sophy,

Your's truly

Chas Brown.

[21] On September 1, 1824, Hunt informed Elizabeth Kent (*Correspondence of Leigh Hunt*, I, 232) that Brown was "writing a long fairy-tale." Perhaps this is his unfinished "The Fairies' Triumph," which occupies sixty-nine pages of a notebook now at Keats House, Hampstead. If so, the tale was begun some years earlier, for it contains a version of Keats's "Fairy's Song" ("Shed no tear"), which, according to Brown's endorsement on the holograph at Harvard, was "written for a particular purpose at the request of CB." See *The Times*, June 3, 1953, p. 21, and *Keats-Shelley Journal*, 10 (1961): 6–8.

[22] See the end of number 56.

[23] Brown began such a novel in 1838 or 1839 (see number 123).

[24] James Justinian Morier, *The Adventures of Hajji Baba, of Ispahan*, 3 vols. (1824); Sydney Owenson, Lady Morgan, *The Life and Times of Salvator Rosa*, 2 vols. (1824).

· 69 ·

TO JOHN HUNT [1]

Address: Inghilterra. / To / John Hunt Esqr, / Examiner Office, / Tavistock Street, / Covent Garden, / London.

ALS: British Museum.

Dear Sir,　　　　　　　　　　　Florence. 8th Feby 1825.

No one can be more sensible than myself of the assistance and kindness you have formerly shown towards your brother. I thought my letters had continually expressed as much; and, if I may be permitted to say it, I have ever among my friends in England mentioned yourself, and only two more, as far as my experience went, as exceptions to the general rule I had formed, that brothers are not friends, and often the worst of enemies.[2] Again, when Mr Leigh Hunt first accepted of my interference, I felt persuaded, — and I told him as much, — that the event would be in my declaring myself on your side, so greatly did I rely on you in every way. I repeat this that you may be convinced of my feeling on the matter. What I say is, and you must recollect I said as much in Cold bath fields prison,[3] that I think your kindness was misdirected and therefore injurious. The circumstances under which several of the loans were made, together with your many self-sacrifices, I had learnt from your own mouth at that very time; yet though they enhanced my delight in witnessing such friendship, my regret remained the same. I must either forego my experience, or acknowledge that money lent to a man possessing a sufficient income, in order to extricate him from difficulties arising

---

[1] Brown did not send this letter, but instead (probably on receiving new information via John Hunt's son Marriott, who arrived to begin a long stay with the Hunts around February 9) incorporated parts of it into number 70, written four days later. It is included here because it was originally a finished letter, addressed and ready to be mailed, and because it differs considerably from the new letter based upon it. In revising, Brown struck through "8" in the date and wrote "12th" beneath it, and canceled the paragraphs he did not retain with a vertical line.

[2] Brown is thinking not only of George Keats but also of his own brothers. The "exceptions" were probably the brothers of Richards and Severn.

[3] Where John Hunt was imprisoned in May 1821–May 1822 for printing a libel on the House of Commons.

from want of care, will in nine cases out of ten render him more careless, and plunge him into greater difficulties in the end. This is an ungracious office, but Mr Henry L. Hunt compelled me to it. He urged the debt against his uncle's claim, with the threat of one man's selling another's property, — which is impossible, and also with the threat of charging interest, — which is not impossible. But as he seemed to forget that acts of kindness cannot, without changing their name to one of the very worst description, be turned into acts of destruction, I omitted to answer that point in his letter. When however he insisted on no such omission, though he remained silent on no less than ten errors I had brought against him, six of which were in direct opposition to your own words, and of the most essential nature, I had no resource but to speak as I felt.

There can be no other fair way of adjustment than by first settling what your brother's claim is; and then let it be considered how he is to pay off his debt, to the utmost extent that his means will allow.

You say he had renounced all claim. This I was not aware of. I know he offered to accept, at Mr Novello's suggestion, £100 per ann: in lieu of continuing a partner, upon condition that an Article of his should every week be published in the Examiner, at 2 Gn^s each, together with a stipulation for a contingent future increase of annuity. The condition you either would not or could not abide by, and therefore he did not renounce his claim as partner, because the terms were not accepted. Besides, Mr Novello, as appears in his letters, gave his opinion in ignorance of several facts; and if no other, of the Deed of Partnership.

Except generally, I am unacquainted with the terms of that Deed. I have been forced into some knowledge of partnerships, and believe there are few things more tenacious. Unless, so it appears to me, there are certain clauses in that Deed to the contrary, and with penalties attached to them, your brother is still entitled to his due share of the nett profits, without any deduction even for the payment of another Editor in his place, and that as long as the Examiner exists, — notwithstanding the Deed itself sets out with stating that he should be Editor.

This possibly, if you think it worth while to make the inquiry, may be the strict law. But that is not what either your brother or myself am urging; and I chiefly mention it in order that you may prevent any future question (for I believe the Deed extends from Leigh Hunt to his heirs) by dissolving it by mutual consent, and nothing else can dissolve it. If I am mistaken, the fact of his claim remains the same as you have acknowledged it at the least; and much more as far as my opinion went, before I was aware of that Deed.

I cannot conceive in justice why your brother's claim should be less than Mr Whiting's, a life annuity of £200. I will not argue upon this point, but leave you to consider of it; and in the mean while, presuming that your brother is entitled to that annuity, I proceed to show how he may, in part if not entirely, pay off his debt.

His life, according to Morgan's tables,[4] is worth 19 20 or 21 years purchase. Let us say 20, which I believe is about the mark. Now if you pay him £100 per ann, as you have done for the last year, and which annuity you express yourself able and willing to continue, let the other £100 per ann go, during the 20 years, for the defraying of his debt to you. The debt is nearly £1,900; from which nothing has been deducted either in the way of annuity or as partner, for the years 1822 and 1823; an omission that I think no disinterested person can agree to, and with which, let it be noticed, Mr Novello was not acquainted. According to my calculation the present value of £100 per ann for 20 years, taking compound int^t in your favour, will be paying you exactly 18 shillings in the pound. I do not propose this to you as to a stranger, because it would not repay him; for a stranger would require every atom of his compound interest; though, without reckoning any interest, you will of course be repaid £2,000. I propose it to you under all the circumstances. If you accept this payment, supposing you acknowledge his claim to be equal to Mr Whiting's, then all that will be asked is that the annuity of £100 should be legally settled on your brother, and that he should, by the same instrument, be released from his entire debt to you, and further that he should annul the Deed of partnership. His life, I have said, is, by

[4] William Morgan (1750–1833), chief actuary of the Society for Equitable Assurances on Lives and Survivorships.

the doctrine of chances, worth 20 years purchase; but when you consider the destitute state his family would be brought to, in the event of his death before the expiration of that period, I hope you will make the term positive for 20 years, instead of making the existence of his family dependent on the life of any one human being.

Without entering into particulars, I cannot perceive any thing grossly in your disfavour by this proposition. I have taken a week to consider of it, and possibly your own inclination to such an arrangement, as appears in one of your late letters, has tended to bring me to this conclusion, as one not displeasing to yourself.

If however you should be averse to it, I must not, in my duty to your brother, who entirely confides in me, refrain from demanding that you should appoint your own arbitrator, when as speedily as possible his shall also be appointed; for I cannot imagine that any award would be more to his disadvantage than what I have proposed, especially as your brother is willing to set off for London, and there renew his duties as Editor, both political and theatrical.

We differ widely, Sir, in our opinions, or we seem, owing to the distance and the inefficiency of letter-writing, to differ.

I ought to acknowledge that I have been the means of withholding a letter from your brother to yourself. It was all heart; but I, confiding in your assurance of his brotherly love, and not wishing that his and my correspondence should be mixed, requested him not to send it for the present.

When I first stepped forward in this question my opinion was given indirectly to M[r] Novello.[5] However I have been drawn further into it than I foresaw; and I now perceive I speak directly to yourself. Matters of business, even when joined with matters of feeling, will rarely admit of a circuitous mode; and if my zeal, as it is called, has appeared obtrusive, let my apology be that I never had an idea of it.

I remain, Dear Sir,
Your's very truly,
Cha[s] Brown.

[5] In number 61.

· 70 ·

TO JOHN HUNT [1]

AL: British Museum. Brief extracts are given by Richardson, *The Everlasting Spell*, pp. 60–61.

Dear Sir,   Florence. 12th Feby 1825.

No one can be more sensible than myself of the assistance and kindness you have formerly shown towards your brother. I thought my letters had constantly expressed as much; and, if I may be permitted to say it, I have ever among &c[2] — means will allow.

These loans were made, I apprehend, upon condition they should be returned when ever it was in his power as is for the most part the condition among friends. Then how can they be urged against him, and in the heap, when he is driven to the utmost edge of poverty? Such a course would bear but one construction. It would even startle me into an idea that your intention, for years back, had been to enjoy the entire profits of the Examiner. But I make no such construction, and entertain no such idea.

In my letter of 20th Augt last,[3] addressed to Mr Leigh Hunt, and forwarded to Mr Novello, I spoke of this debt; and as my opinion remains unchanged, I take the liberty of sending the following copy of that part of it.

---

[1] A draft of the letter actually sent, based on the preceding letter. On the same day, Hunt wrote to Elizabeth Kent (ALS, British Museum): "To day a letter goes from Mr Brown to my brother, containing a proposal on my part to come over to England & resume all my duties in the Exam^r, political & theatrical. — Do not hope too much; but certainly the proposal ought to be accepted, & it appears to me that arbitrators would as certainly think so. Unluckily, I feel pretty much as convinced, that on Henry's account, every thing will be done to withstand it. I have had some strange & most painful changes of feeling, or *possibilities* of change, on some points with regard to my brother, owing, I doubt not, for the main part, to the influence which master H[enry]. has over him, & the inferior portion of sympathy which the latter feels towards his father's relations. But my brother & I are still affectionate in our correspondence, & I believe in our hearts. I hope the best, & yet am prepared for dissappointment."
[2] See the first two paragraphs of number 69.
[3] Number 61. Brown quotes parts of the third paragraph from the end.

"It perhaps would be advisable &c — be denied you." x x x x x
"Whatever the amount &c — so many children."

I wrote the above not knowing that a regular Deed of Partnership had been executed. If therefore you are inclined to annul the debt, to grant £100 per ann until 1830, and afterwards £200 per ann to him & his heirs, it will be necessary that he should, by the same instrument, agree to the dissolution of partnership; and that in order to prevent any future question, as I believe the terms of the Deed extend to Leigh Hunt & to his heirs.

Except generally &c⁴ —— be Editor.

At any rate he is willing to return to London, and there perform his part as Editor, both political and theatrical; and he bids me say this is what he proposes in answer to your demand of a proposal.

We differ &c⁵ — to differ. On one point however we agree, — on this: — that no man ought to judge of his own cause; and that he who shrinks from an arbitration, gives some evidence of distrust in it. Your brother does not shrink from it; nor do you, according to your own words, & those of Mʳ Henry L. Hunt — and it appears to me, I must not, in my duty to your brother, who confides entirely in me, refrain from demanding that you appoint your arbitrator, when as speedily as possible his also shall be appointed. As I have engaged to draw up a statement on his side for the arbitration, and as, for that purpose, it is necessary I should be acquainted with the Deed of partnership, you will much oblige me by sending me a copy of it, verbatim.

One passage in your letter gave me some disquiet, where you say that should his claim be admitted, it must be succeeded by your ruin. The ruin however on his part is nearly completed, — if he were again cursed with ill health for a month or two, it would be despairing. He lives here, with a wife and seven children, in a foreign country, without a friend but myself, and I have not the means of assisting him in a pecuniary point of view; his house is bare and comfortless; the furniture of the sparest and the shabbiest; there is but one servant, an unskilful drudge, as such a one consents to serve for a pittance; (the wife is in fact the

---

⁴ See the fourth paragraph of number 69.
⁵ See the tenth paragraph of number 69.

servant, struggling against disease and the children help to perform the duties of the house;) ⁶ the dinner of the family is one dish
of the cheapest kind; luxuries, though so cheap in Italy, are there
forbidden; they sit over a shivering fire during the bitter cold of
an Italian winter, and the cold, at least in Florence, is more wearing than in England; Thornton, whose abilities promised so
much, cannot be sent to school, owing to the expence of three
crowns a month, and thus his hopes seem to be blasted, — his
schooling stopped on receipt of your letter, dated in July last;
your brother is fearful of a visitor, — for all are fearful of exposing
a poverty-struck dwelling; no one is admitted, & from this cause,
but myself, — and your son Mʳ Marriott Hunt. These are undeniable facts. With all this misery, I know they cannot do better;
I am intimately acquainted with their house-keeping in every
way, and every paul that is spent is out of sheer necessity, — and
they have but few pauls to spend, considering the number of
mouths to be fed and backs to be clothed, however economical
may be the management.

· 71 ·

TO JOSEPH SEVERN [1]

[March (?) 1825]

*   *   *

I must tell you Hazlitt is here,[2] and will shortly, so he says,
proceed to Rome, where he is to study your favourite Raphael and

---

⁶ This parenthetical comment is written a few lines below (between "England;"
and "Thornton") and marked for insertion here by means of asterisks.

¹ From Sharp, pp. 149–150.

² Hazlitt and his second wife arrived in Florence during the second week of
February ("a few days" before February 12, according to Hunt's letter to Elizabeth
Kent of that date, British Museum). They went on to Rome in March, perhaps
shortly before the next letter was written, and then returned to Florence on
their way home in April (Howe, *Life of Hazlitt*, pp. 343–344). At Florence, Brown
consulted him about Hunt's affairs (see numbers 73, 75), offered to introduce him
to Landor (Forster, *Landor*, II, 201; Carlino in *KC*, I, lviii, gives a different account), heard him describe his recent divorce (Forster, II, 207–208), and kept some
books for him (see the next letter). Five years afterward he discussed Hazlitt with
Henry Crabb Robinson, who noted in his diary on October 6, 7, 1830, "Mr. Brown

Michael, and write a book on them. He will be accompanied by his wife. It is his wish to have a letter to you, which he certainly shall have. Don't let this news cause trepidation among the artists, though, it must be confessed, an Edinburgh reviewer is a formidable sort of person, and his pen is not one of the finest nibbed. I think you will like him extremely, and, between ourselves, he may be of the utmost service to you in your profession, as far as its patronage is concerned; and already he has a high opinion of your talents.[3]

What you ask about your painting, I think is easily answered. Painting is as poetry, where the art is to concentrate ideas, and to embellish common events through the medium of the imagination. Your naked boys treading the ripe grapes [4] form a beautiful subject, sufficiently natural, because it is not too far removed from possibility. A man *soiling* the grapes, as I should call it, is an unworthy object for painting, purely because it is unpleasant, however undoubtedly in nature. In poetry and painting, things are not to be represented as they positively exist, for there is not an entire pleasure in them in that view; but they should be embellished to the utmost, always however in taste, and in the feeling of the subject. Those who object to your boys, should, on the same principle, object to so many beautiful women assembled at the same moment in the same vintage — both are improbable, only the boys are less so. God has given us a real world and an imaginary one — both lovely and both perfect; and He has also given us the power to relieve our minds by flying from one to the other, and by mingling them at our will for our delight. The last belongs especially to the poet and the painter; when they fail to take advantage of it, they become matter-of-fact gentlemen, who use their fine words and their fine colours to no purpose. Your

---

. . . knew Hazlitt, of whom he speaks as *all* do. Congeniality of opinion made them intimate. . . . [He] spoke highly of Hazlitt's wife as a gentlewoman . . . [but] related anecdotes of Hazlitt's personal cowardice, as well as of his slovenliness." On the basis of other entries made at the same time Robinson later wrote, "Brown admired the writings of Hazlitt, but declared him to be the worst-tempered man . . . he ever knew" (*Henry Crabb Robinson on Books and Their Writers,* ed. Morley, I, 387).

[3] Robinson (*ibid.,* p. 378) noted on June 1, 1830, "Severn knows Hazlitt, by whom, as might be expected, he was ill-treated."

[4] Probably in "Italian Vintage," which Severn painted at Ariccia in 1824 (Sharp, pp. 144–145).

man is a matter-of-fact; your boys a touch of poetry. The former a disagreeable reality, the latter a brilliant probability, a threading of the imagination through the dull course of common events. Your own natural feeling led you to the beautiful, the poetic, and your fear of infringing on the *usual* mode, the *common one*, has startled you. Have I satisfied you?

*　*　*

· 72 ·

FROM WILLIAM HAZLITT

Endorsements: William Hazlitt / 28 March 1825.; Ans^d 5 Ap^l 25.[1]

ALS: Historical Society of Pennsylvania. Extracts are quoted by Payson G. Gates in *South Atlantic Quarterly*, 46 (1947): 248.

Dear Sir,   [March 22, 1825][2]

I beseech you send me word (by return of post) if the copy of Table-talk you have received is perfect, with Regal Character & Advice to a School boy at the end; also if the Spirit of the Age is a bookseller's copy, or the one I left at Paris, & forwarded to you for me?[3] Yesterday the first fine day. Remember me to all friends, & believe me yours truly

Wm Hazlitt

33 Via Gregoriana.[4]
Tuesday.
　　Severn is well.

[1] Brown's reply is lost.

[2] That is, the "Tuesday" before March 28 (see the endorsements), which presumably was the day (a Monday) on which Brown received this undated letter. Hazlitt had arrived at Rome "in the middle of March" after a six-day journey from Florence; see the second note to the preceding letter, and Hazlitt's *Complete Works*, ed. Howe, X (1932), 227.

[3] Paris editions of Hazlitt's *Table-Talk*, 2 vols. (1825), and *The Spirit of the Age* (1825). According to an entry in Robinson's diary (*Henry Crabb Robinson on Books and Their Writers*, ed. Morley, I, 387), "Hazlitt left his books with Brown" — apparently a trunk of books that had been seized by the Sardinian government and then forwarded to Hazlitt at Florence (see Hazlitt's *Complete Works*, X, 186–187). Brown still had them in 1830, and Hazlitt never recovered them (see number 106).

[4] The house of Salvator Rosa (Hazlitt's *Complete Works*, X, 231–232).

· 73 ·

TO JOHN HUNT [1]

ALS: British Museum.

Dear Sir,   Florence. 2nd April 1825.

Some delay has unavoidably taken place in replying to your letter of 27th Feb[y], owing to the nature of the subject.

The difficulty your brother feels in coming to any decision arises from the want of data to proceed upon. Nor can I offer advice, with his interests at stake, as well as your's, and your son's, while in the dark on the most essential points. You refer to the present sale of the Examiner, while we have no clue to the knowledge of what it is, except that the Paper is in a flourishing state compared to the years 1822 & 1823 when it was pronounced scarcely worth carrying on and yielded no more than £500 Nett profits per annum. I think you will see the propriety of his being made acquainted with the nett profits of last year, including or excluding (as you please) the duties of Editor, together with a note of the sum carried to debit for Wishing Caps during last year, and such is his request. He also requests you will send a copy of the Deed of Partnership.

The passage you allude to in my last [2] was objected to by your brother when I read it to him; and, had I conceived you would be offended at it, the letter would have been rewritten. I allowed it to go. I did not intend any such construction on my part, (and that I thought I explained,) but as what others, unacquainted with you, would, in my mind, unavoidably make. It never would have been written, were it not in reference to M[r] H. L. Hunt's letters, especially where he said that even a grant of £100 per annum must be conditional, and not as a matter of justice, but one of *sympathy and humanity*, at the same time giving you as his authority for what he wrote.

I related, fairly as I could, the entire question between your

[1] A draft.
[2] The second paragraph of number 70.

brother & yourself to Mr Hazlitt; and as I believe that what he may have said on the subject will be of some weight with you, I ought not to refrain from informing you that his opinion perfectly coincides with mine.

I remain, dear Sir,
Your's very sincerely,
Chas Brown.

· 74 ·

TO JOHN HUNT [1]

ALS: British Museum.

Dear Sir,   Florence   7th May 1825.

The disappointment you express at the proposal you last made not being accepted was unavoidable, owing to the want of the most essential documents. Among these a copy of the Deed of partnership would be the principal guide to Mr Leigh Hunt's decision. I am surprised you conceive it has nothing to do with the matter. In a question so long the subject of debate which hinges on the primary agreement, and on which agreement (to speak plainly) you and I do not more widely differ and you and your son though in different ways, I am at a loss to imagine what can have to do with the matter in a greater degree. That this Deed never would have been entered into but for the security of Mr Whiting may well be the case; but by no means lessens its importance; and it is impossible to suppose that any clause contained in it was adverse to the previously understood agreement between yourself and your brother. The addition you mention to the usual stipulations, was not the only one of the kind, according to an Extract which Mr Henry L. Hunt transcribed verbatim for me. A copy, not the Deed, was requested; to transmit the Deed itself would be incurring unnecessary risk; it had surely better remain as at present in your custody. Your delaying to make your

---

[1] A draft.

brother acquainted with the contents of this Deed, for the reasons you state, or indeed for any reasons whatever, I cannot understand.

Surprised as I was at your not complying with the request for a copy of the Deed, I was equally so at an item among the deductions from the profits of the Examiner for last year. This is of no small consideration. In August last [2] I pointed out several errors in the Accounts, and some of them were grounded on the belief that the debt to Messʳˢ Magnay & Cᵒ was chargeable on the Examiner, agreeable to a passage in one of your letters to that effect. Mʳ Henry L. Hunt answered me by stating that it never was any other than a private debt of your own, which of course tended to explain away those particular errors. But now I find you deduct from the profits of the Examiner £208 as a payment to Magnay & Cᵒ. It follows therefore that either those errors still exist in the Accounts, or that your nett profits on the Examiner for the last year were not £541. 3. 8, but £749. 3. 8.

Had it been in my power to adjust this question to the satisfaction of all parties, few things would have afforded me more pleasure; but it must necessarily be carried before arbitrators. Your sentiments upon the propriety of such a measure have been frequently and forcibly given; yet though, in that letter where you declare yourself not a proper judge on your own cause, you assure your brother that in all money concerns between you, (should there be any difference of opinion), the points should be adjusted by any just person he might name to look into them; and to whom all your books and accounts should be submitted, — I say, that notwithstanding this handsome offer on your part, I beg leave to suggest it may hereafter be more satisfactory to both parties, that each should appoint his own arbitrator, with power in them to choose a third, in case their opinions do not coincide. On turning to the correspondence, I perceive that on 30ᵗʰ Decʳ last,[3] I demanded, in Mʳ Leigh Hunt's name, an arbitration, and that your son, in answer, declared your readiness; — *"My father is quite ready to arbitrate, if desired, — what just man can refuse?"* When I repeated the demand in my following letter,

[2] In number 61.
[3] In number 66.

on 12th Feb^y,[4] no further answer was sent; probably owing to the wish on your part to settle it with less trouble, as I am conscious of having entertained the same wish myself. However, as the matter now stands, and as you are prepared, I shall take an early opportunity of writing to the gentleman on whom, with his consent, Mr Leigh Hunt has fixed for his arbitrator.

As I am certain that no arbitrators can enter on their duty without first requiring the Deed of Partnership, and that, on application, they will furnish your brother with a copy of it, in order that he may be enabled to present the best statement in his power before them, — (for, after all, he will be at a disadvantage owing to the distance,) — I leave it to yourself to consider whether it will not be adviseable to furnish him with a copy beforehand, if for no other reason than to save as much time as possible. In the mean while I shall, as far as at present lies in my power, prepare the statement, from the file of letters and copies of answers on the subject.

I remain, Dear Sir,
Your's most truly,
Chas Brown.

I showed the postscript of your letter to Mr Marriott Hunt, but at the same time I mentioned that I could not immediately draw on London, and that when I did it must be at 3 months date.

[4] Number 70.

· 75 ·

TO LEIGH HUNT [1]

ALS: British Museum.

Dear Hunt,   Florence. 8th June 1825.

I return you Mr J Hunt's letter, and hasten to give the opinion you ask of me respecting his demand of "what it is you wish to be done; and, if an Arbitration be desired, what it is that you deem it right to submit to such a tribunal."

The general answer to this is, that you wish nothing but what is just; and that, after having exhibited the entire history of the affair, with all its bearings, before the Arbitrators, you will willingly abide by their award.

If however, as it appears, you are urged to state your specific claim, I know not how you can answer him on that point, until you are aware of your own situation; that is, until you possess a copy of the Deed, which Mr Novello will certainly forward as soon as possible. We can then confer with Mr Reader, who will not only give us the legal, but will assist us in the equitable interpretation of that document. I mention the word *equitable*, as your brother has an idea that I have advised you to advance claims contrary to equity.

An accusation of having been your ill-adviser was never what I feared or cared for, except from myself; and, as you well know, the responsibility I felt on your account induced me to seek the opinions of Mr Hazlitt and Mr Kirkup. If therefore I am your ill-adviser, I neither stand singly, nor have I been wanting in prudence.

Instead of complaining of my having repeatedly alluded to errors in the Accounts, insisted upon as trifles, it would have been more to the purpose had your brother mentioned whether he was right or wrong in deducting the payments to Magnay & Co from the profits of the Examiner. If he was right, then there may

---

[1] A fair copy that, after Brown made some changes in the final paragraph, became a second draft. The first draft of the letter is also preserved in the British Museum.

be errors in the Accounts to the amount of about £800, as I showed in my letter of 20th Augt last.[2] This he ought to have understood.

Any displeasure expressed personally towards myself, in a matter of right and wrong between others which I have discussed with the best intentions towards both, is in one point of view nothing to me; and I am sorry to add that your brother's extraordinary conduct and anger has made it little to me in any. I certainly do not think that he understands either the business or himself, so much as he thinks he does; and I regret that, in consequence of this, he has lost his temper.

Your's most sincerely,
Chas Brown.

To /

Leigh Hunt Esqr

· 76 ·

TO MARRIOTT HUNT (?) [1]

ALS: British Museum.

[September 1825]

The party is calculated at six persons,[2] therefore Mr Marriott Hunt will have to pay a sixth part of 82 Louis, and also a sixth of all contingent expences on the road, including presents for service &c.

Mocali [3] says the usual present to the Vetturino is 5 Louis, and I told him the man would be paid something more, in case

---

[2] Number 61.

[1] Finally returning to England, the Hunts left Florence on September 10. They did not reach London until October 13 (Clarke, *Recollections of Writers*, pp. 228–230). This is apparently a note to inform Marriott — who was quite deaf — of his share of the expenses of the trip from Florence to Calais.

[2] Actually there were ten — Hunt, his wife, seven children, and Marriott — but they counted as six "because of the number of children" (Hunt, *Lord Byron*, II, 389).

[3] Either the father or the employer of the vetturino, Gigi (see the next letter and the opening of number 80).

his civility should deserve it, — or something less, should he prove uncivil or disobliging.

CB

· 77 ·

TO LEIGH HUNT

Address: Inghilterra. / To / Mr Leigh Hunt, / Care of Mr Hunter,[1] / N° 72 St Paul's Church Yard, / London.

Postmarks: FIRENZE; AT.; AUTRICHE PAR HUNINGUE; FPO OC 6 1825

ALS: British Museum. Brief extracts are given by Richardson, *The Everlasting Spell*, p. 62.

My dear Hunt,   Florence. 24th Septr 1825.

I was delighted to read your little letter from Modena; it was full of good news, and now I am hopeful that Mrs Hunt will not feel the fatigue of the journey a tithe so much as any of us expected.[2] Kirkup joins me in congratulations. The letter reached me nine days ago, and none since; I suppose there will be one to-day at the Post.

There is so much to tell you of and concerning your affairs, that I must begin immediately on business.

Morandi[3] brought me in a bill of 42 Crowns, and *without* calculating for the window broken by the wind. I refused to pay for the recovering (in any sense of the word) of his old chairs; then I cut off as much as I thought could not fairly be demanded. The end of it was that I paid him 30 Crowns. I have taken great pains in examining into the dilapidations and deficiencies, nor do I think I have paid too much. He was a little restive, but altogether conducted himself decently.

---

[1] Numbers 78–81, 85, 88, 89, 94, 95, and 106 are also addressed to the care of Rowland Hunter, bookseller, the successor in business to Joseph Johnson (1738–1809), who published Priestley, Horne Tooke, and Cowper, among others. Hunter had married Mrs. Kent, Marianne Hunt's mother, at least as early as 1803.

[2] See the first note to the preceding letter. Mrs. Hunt gave birth to her eighth child, Jacintha, soon after they arrived.

[3] Hunt's landlord.

Nesti has been paid the following bills: 4th May Pauls 58. 4; 2nd June Pauls 21. 7; and 25th June Pauls 11; — making together Pauls 91. 4,[4] for which he has given me a receipt, engaging to refund, in case M[rs] Hunt can send any of his receipts for the same bills.

M[rs] Lambardi's bill amounts to 237 Pauls, about double what I expected; for Thornton told me I had only to pay for the horse, and the two last weeks of washing; now the bills are from 22nd July, more like two months. I have not yet paid her, as I wish to understand how I am to act respecting the linen that was missing on the last day. She insists upon it that every article was there, as she counted them with her own hands, and that if any thing is missing, either from her linen or from Marriott's, it must have been stolen from your rooms. Let me know what I am to do.

Passeri's bill is not from 11 to 13 Crowns, as M[rs] Hunt imagines; it proves to be 27½ Crowns, without including the last orders for shoes which were not delivered. I told him the difference was so great from your account, that I must needs wait to hear from you on the subject; in the mean time I have paid him 13 Crowns in part.

Molini's [5] bill is already paid in books, though the Edgeworth is not sold; he objects to the price I demand, and to the pencil marks and one ink mark in the volumes, executed, I presume, by your good self. Excluding him therefore, I shall have to pay on your account, together with expences for carriage to Leghorn &c, above 100 Crowns.

Your furniture has been all wheeled into town, and it stands in a room in Landor's house, where it must remain till the beginning of November when I remove to my new house,[6] where I shall have it valued. I must again ask you to reconsider the matter of your two favourite sofa's. They will occupy, in space, above two tuns, and the expence of ship carriage to London, with Arno carriage here, will amount to far beyond their worth, at least £5; add to which, the large sofa cannot be taken to pieces,

---

[4] An error for 91. 3. On the values of Tuscan money see number 67, n. 2.

[5] Giuseppe Molini, bookseller and publisher. A prospectus of "Molini's English Magazine," a compilation from English periodicals that Hunt planned to establish in Florence, is preserved in the British Museum.

[6] In the Piazza del Duomo, where he lived until the fall of 1828.

and is not strong enough to bear the stowage in a ship, unless in a frame of carpenter's work. Landor says there is not the slightest doubt but that it will be smashed to pieces on purpose! You and Mrs Hunt must consider whether it will in any way be prudent to let me send it; — indeed on the score of prudence there can be no question, as you can purchase two small beds in London for much less than the expence of sending these, together with the sum they may fetch here. As I have your other goods, I shall not be in want of it myself, — but I am resolved to keep it, till I hear further from you, and even if you forbid it to be sent, I will not permit either of them to pass into unhallowed hands.[7]

I am sorry to tell you there is not water enough in the Arno for the floating down of your "roba." We must wait till the rain pleases to come. It was absolutely necessary to order cases to be made by the carpenter; — the chest you talked to me about did not hold a third of your books, and when full, gave signs of opening in the back, — so I unpacked them. Every thing is ready, and marked LH N° 1 to 5, containing as under:

N° 1   A large case, cont^g all your books, a writing desk, & two or three blankets.

"   2   A case, cont^g the 101 views of Rome for Mr Clarke,[8] the portrait of Mr J. Hunt, your picture frames (one glass broken) and drawings, a counterpane, two blankets and a pair of shoes.

"   3   Marriott's trunk.

"   4   A box, cont^g Marriott's medicine chest, a bunch of keys he left behind, some blankets &c.

"   5   A box, contents unknown, packed by Mrs Hunt.

There! have I not been a very industrious, a very busy fellow? And just as I finished the account of my doings, in came your letter from Voghera, and I see you had nearly arrived at Asti. I calculate you will sleep to-night in the good city of Lyons. A good

---

[7] Brown later bought them (see number 85). On returning to England he sold the larger sofa (which according to Trelawny had belonged to Shelley and had been given to Hunt by Mary Shelley) to Seymour Kirkup. Kirkup sent it to Trelawny, who in turn gave it to W. M. Rossetti. It is now owned by Mrs. Rossetti Angeli, of Woodstock, Oxford (*Letters of Trelawny*, pp. 260–261, 267, and Grylls, *Trelawny*, p. 243).

[8] See number 87.

Veturino is a blessing on a journey greater than fine weather, and I wish you joy on having one.[9] I'll call on Mocali, as you say. Mrs Hunt ought not to have been frightened, — God bless us! can't she endure the cracking of a pannel? — but that's idle talking, — glad I am she remained well for two days after. Maria [10] is effectually separated from her infamous family, and, at least for the present, as effectually from Kirkup. Hitherto the Police has been acting in a most determined manner against him, with something, as appears, like personal animosity, though that is impossible. I am afraid, very much afraid, I shall lose his company in Florence, owing to all this roguishness. I shall call, when I'm a little at leisure, on Mr Sam Castelnuovo.

When you see Mr Colburn, don't forget to ask him about the "Italian Chat". I see plainly how it may be managed as suitable to the "Original Papers"-part of the Magazine, and I am preparing for it accordingly. I shall give all sorts of *anecdotes* that have come under my knowledge, notices of work {in the} Fine Arts and Literature, and extracts from {the It}alian Newspapers and Magazines, making every part of it as piquant and Italian and short as possible. And pray ask Mr Colburn, with my comp^ts, why he has not informed some body that he does not intend to pay me less than 16 Gn^s a sheet; [11] say something to that purpose, for he had better not make me write unwillingly, — not for *his own* interest.

When I returned, first after you left us, to Majano, I expected the rooms would look desolate and melancholy, — but they did not, — I suppose because I had prepared myself for it. But I had an odd twinge when I saw your goods packed in the carts and ready to move from the door, — it seemed as if you had all died of the plague, and that I was left Executor.

Kirkup sends his remembrances, and I send my own. All your friends here have desired me to give theirs' when I write,

[9] His name was Gigi. Hunt describes him in *Lord Byron*, II, 390–391: "as pleasant a little Tuscan to drive us as I ever met with . . . as honest a rogue, I will undertake to say, as ever puzzled a formalist. He makes us laugh with his resemblance to Mr. Lamb."

[10] Kirkup's mistress. She is called "Maria" also in numbers 79 and 94, and "Marina" in numbers 89, 96, 102.

[11] That is, a guinea per page, the "largest pay given" by the *New Monthly Magazine* (see number 62, n. 5).

— matters of course. Mʳˢ Landor does not yet recover her strength properly.[12] I drank some caudle at Reader's the other night, and the lady looked as if nothing had happened. In my next letter I shall write about Mʳ John Hunt. Your's most truly,

Chaˢ Brown.

· 78 ·

TO LEIGH HUNT

Address: Inghilterra. / To / Mʳ Leigh Hunt, / Care of Mʳ Hunter, / Bookseller, / St Paul's Church Yard, / London.

Postmarks: FIRENZE; Toscana; I.T.; FPO OC 17 1825

ALS: British Museum.

My dear Hunt,   Florence. 3ʳᵈ October 1825.

I have received another of your letters from Turin, or rather from St Ambrogio, since I wrote to you on 24 Septʳ. I thought you would like Turin. De Martini, whom you admire so much, is one of the famous dancers of Italy; she is also famous for the number of her presents from lovers, and for making them quarrel together, — not the presents, but the lovers.[1]

According to your orders I have opened two letters from Mʳ John Hunt. The first is dated 13 Septʳ. He says he thinks it most possible the Deed contains matters contrary to the understanding between you and him. It does not appear to me to contain any matter contrary to the understanding as stated by himself in former letters; but Mʳ Reader's opinion is more in your favour than I expected, and than I have frequently expressed to Mʳ John Hunt, when I was aware of nothing beyond his own statements. In an after paragraph he seems to have misunderstood part of Mʳ Kirkup's paper of "proofs &c". He says he is ready to

---

[12] She had given birth to Charles Savage Landor on August 5.

[1] "At Turin was the finest dancer I ever saw, a girl of the name of De' Martini. . . . [She] is a dancer all over, and does not omit her face. . . . she is beautiful both in face and figure. . . . I never saw any thing like it before; and did not wonder, that she had the reputation of turning the heads of dozens wherever she went" (Hunt, *Lord Byron*, II, 399–400).

answer *all* questions, either to an arbitrator, or to *yourself*. It is
certain he has made a mistake in imagining he is called upon to
perform any thing "noble and generous" to his own detriment;
those words which I wrote in Aug[t] last year, and which in giving
an extract I was obliged to repeat,[2] were used in a far different
meaning, and which I need not have used at all; but it will be
well to explain to him that it never was your intention to claim
more than your due. The second letter bears no date, — indeed
it is not a letter; but a paper headed "Proofs that L. H. has forfeited (not *given away*) his Proprietorship." In these proofs there
are many errors, chiefly of omission, nor can M[r] Kirkup and
myself perceive how they bear upon the question. In one part he
says, "Had L. H. been asked (before the framing this Deed) —
If you withdraw your services from the Paper, are you entitled
to the half or any of its profits? — what must have been his reply?"
This may be in part answered by another question: — Had J. H.
been asked, at that time, — If L. H. withdraw his services, after
twelve years, when by his abilities, and his abilities alone, the
Paper shall have become an established property, will he not be
entitled to a share in the profits? — in other words, if L. H.
creates a valuable estate, wanting no more for its continuance
than cultivation, is he not entitled to a rental? There is however
another answer; you never did withdraw your services; ill health
prevented you from performing your services; you did not even
withdraw them when you wrote for the Liberal, for at that time
you stated to him you thought it better for both parties, not to
write in the Examiner at that time, to which he made no objection. You did not withdraw your services; it was he who refused
to admit them, suddenly, without notice, and giving as a reason
for such refusal your endeavour to benefit *him* as well as yourself
by exerting yourself solely for a time in the Liberal. He says —
"J. H. declares, that it was distinctly understood, that L. H. was
to give the Paper his literary services for the half of its profits, —
what else had *he* to give?" You may reply to this that you have
always been ready to perform your part, except when ill health
or certain considerations unobjected to by him intervened. I remark that J. H. has said nothing in his "proofs" of having per-

[2] A passage from number 61, quoted in number 70.

formed his part of the Contract, not only stipulated in the Deed, but acknowledged formerly both by himself and his son, — viz, — to be printer of the Paper free of expence, — and what else had *he* to give? Now during his two years' imprisonment [3] I think he could not have performed his duties, and that probably the expence for another in his place was charged to the Paper. In making the Statement I find it necessary to have the following questions distinctly answered:

1st   What is the precise meaning of being printer free of expence?

2nd   Has J. H. been at all times printer free of expence?

3rd   If not, when did he cease to perform his part of the contract?

4th   How much has been charged, and for how many years, to the general Account of the Paper for the expence of a printer in his place?

Again, as I ought to be acquainted with the exact sum due from you to J. H., and as I perceive in the Accounts of 1821, — "Add one third of Loss on Reflector,[4] never before charged, £300," — I wish, or I cannot well do my part in the Statement, to have these answered:

5th   Was there £300 Loss on the Reflector for L. H.'s share, neither more nor less?

6th   Why was he not debited for it before 1821?

7th   Is L. H. credited for his contributions in the Reflector, at so much per sheet, equally with the other contributors?

It is also necessary that another line in the Accounts should be explained, — "Allowed for remainder of Liberal of all Nos (8285) £300." I know not whether this allowance may or may not be objected to on your part; certainly it is not quite 8¾ per No. However, an answer to the following question is requisite:

8th   How many out of the last 8,285 Nos of the Liberal have been sold, and what is the amount of the Sale?

In a passage among the "Proofs &c" J. H. says — "That Accounts were supplied to L. H. up to a certain time, is no proof of

[3] In 1813–1815.

[4] Hunt's *Reflector, a Quarterly Magazine, on Subjects of Philosophy, Politics, and the Liberal Arts*, four numbers of which were issued in 1811–1812.

his proprietorship. They were furnished *until it was seen that no equivalent was given to J. H., or likely to be offered.*" What impression this avowal may make on the Arbitrators remains to be seen. It is certain, however, from this passage, that he harboured the intention, secretly from you, and as far back as 1821, of taking the entire profits of the Examiner to himself, or of obtaining, through your connections and personal exertions, an equivalent for your half of the profits. I cannot understand it in any other way, and yet he continues to complain of, what he calls, the "offensive passage."

Mr Reader's opinion, both in an equitable and legal point of view, is, without a doubt on his mind, entirely in your favour. As a dry matter of law, it is far more in your favour than I imagined, and more than I would recommend you, in fairness, to urge, or than you would urge. He has inquired of me whether J. H. has always performed his part of the contract as printer *free of expence*, which I am not yet able to answer.

As J. H. so frequently mistakes that passage of mine [5] where I say, — "I know not whether this would be fair and just, or noble and generous, but I am inclined to believe in the latter," it would be well to let him know that, in his acceptance of the terms I there proposed, it is a long time since I thought it otherwise than "fair and just", and that I have little doubt but that the award of the Arbitrators will bestow on you better terms, in their view of the fairness and the justice of the case.

Perhaps you will choose to have all or some part that I have said in this letter copied out and sent to your brother, asking for explicit answers to the eight questions; and perhaps it will be as well to send it.

My head has become so occupied with this affair, that I cannot well turn round my brain to other matters. I have sent an Article to the New Monthly on my walk to Siena, a very gossipping affair of about six pages.[6] You will, I hope, soon let me know about "Italian Chat", and about the so much per sheet which Mr Colburn intends to pay me. I have obtained every possible informa-

---

[5] See n. 2 above.
[6] "A Walk from Florence to Siena" appeared in the November issue, 14 (1825): 463–469.

tion for Mr Novello's brother.[7] To-day it has begun to rain, and in a day or two I hope the Arno will be navigable. My boxes of books [8] are lying at Leghorn, and can't come, owing to this provoking want of water. Kirkup desires to be remembered to you and all. I am going to write an Article on Cenino Cenini,[9] with Kirkup's assistance in painting-knowledge. Mr Wakefield's address in town is N° 70 Old Broad Street; [10] he hopes to see you at his country-house, but I can't direct you to it. I want a transalpine letter from you.

Your's most faithfully,

Chas Brown.

4th Octr. Giuseppe has returned from the post, — no letter from la V. S.

· 79 ·

TO LEIGH HUNT

Address: Inghilterra. / To / Mr Leigh Hunt, / Care of Mr Hunter, / Bookseller, / 72 St Paul's Church Yard, / London.

Postmarks: FIRENZE; Toscana; I.T.; AUTRICHE PAR HUNINGUE; FPO NO 1 1825

ALS: British Museum. Brief extracts are given by Richardson, *The Everlasting Spell*, p. 62.

[7] Francis Novello, bass singer at the Portuguese Embassy chapel, where his younger brother Vincent was organist. On the death of his Italian father-in-law, he and his wife inherited an estate that, after the executor took his share, was represented as too small to live on. The Novellos felt that the executor (a Signor Raggio, of Sestri Levante, near Genoa) was deceiving them, and Vincent had asked Brown to look into the affair for them (Vincent Novello to Hunt, March 14, 1825, British Museum).

[8] See number 80, n. 4.

[9] Cennino Cennini (ca. 1365–1440), Florentine painter. Brown wrote the article and sent it to England later in the month (see the end of the next letter), but apparently it was not printed.

[10] The directories list Francis Wakefield and Company, stockbrokers, at this address.

1821					
Feb^y	21	Paid Willoughby –	£5.	8.	–
,,	28	Mr Fry's bill ———	27.	10.	–
,,	,,	Tomb's last bill ——	25.	–.	–
June	1	Mr Fry's bill ———	15.	18.	9
July	24	A Bill &c (Green Kentish Town)	14.	–.	–
Sept^r	1	Mr Fry's bill ———	16.	2.	6
,,	30	Mr Novello, for the instalments	144.	–.	–
,,	,,	To Mr Novello ——	10.	–.	–
1822					
May	31	Paid Servant from Plymouth ——	1.	4.	6
,,	,,	Mott's[2] (linen-draper) bill ———	30.	18.	5
Oct^r	11	Paid I. Green Carpenter ————	5.	–.	–
,,	15	Mr Miles'[3] Bill ——	50.	–.	–
,,	,,	Mr Rodd's[4] bill ——	30.	–.	–
1823					
Feb^y	3	Paid I. Green, Carpenter, his balance	10.	–.	–

Florence.

20 Octr 1825.

My dear Hunt,

I have given you every thing connected with p a y m e n t s to tradespeople from Mr J. Hunt's Accounts.[1] Your letter arrived yesterday from Paris, — Paris! — how odd it sounds! — and so Paris is "a noble and chearful place." God help you! — mend you! I mean. I had no such idea of Paris, and therefore never thought of writing to you there; — no, the fact is, it was not worth while, as I must have written so very soon after you left us. You will find two let-

---

[1] For the accounts, see number 61, n. 19.
[2] John Mott, retail linendraper, of 8 Gray's Inn Passage.
[3] John Miles, surgeon, of 23 Throgmorton Street.
[4] George Ramsay Rodd, surgeon and obstetrician of Hampstead.

April		Mr J Bennett,[5] K Town ————	. 17. 6	
"	28	Paid Mr Reynell,[6] on Acct of Indicator	35. —. —	
May	23	Paid Appleyard, do 100. —. —		
July	29	Paid Mr Wilkinson Tailor ————	7. 16. —	

ters from me, this the third, at Mr Hunter's. I heard of you, *before* your letter came, in Paris, — that eternal Paris, — I suppose I shall hear of nothing for a twelvemonth but Paris. Mr Johnstone met your son and Marriott in Paris; so I made up my mind that as they were in Paris, every one of you had arrived safely in Paris. Your next letter will be from London. Then there will be nothing for a long time but London. Smoky, nasty, splashy London; foggy, cloggy, boggy London; rainy, drainy, stainy London; greasy, squeezy, uneasy London; droppy, sloppy, moppy London; always cloudy, always crowdy, very dowdy London; kissing-Molly, what a folly! melancholy London.[7] I hate London. I can't bear that you should leave Florence for London. The Devil will make a "fritto" of you for going to London. To think for to go for to travel to London, and at your age too, when you ought to have known better, and to leave this charming, delightful Florence, — and here am I in love! At least I begin to suspect as much, for I woke in the middle of last night, and could not go to sleep again for thinking of my dear Euphemia. To be caught at last! — is it not an uncommonly foolish — sensible sort of thing? There's Kirkup cocks his eye at her, not wickedly, but artistly, and declares she has the most beautiful eyes, forehead, nose, mouth, chin, cheeks, neck and all that, and such a figure, such a shape! She says she is eighteen, — I willingly yield her up

---

[5] A bookseller and stationer.

[6] Nos. 1–22 of the *Indicator* were printed by Charles H. Reynell, of 45 Broad Street, Golden Square, who also printed the *Examiner*, the *Liberal*, and other of Hunt's works. He was John Hunt's brother-in-law.

[7] Compare Hunt's description of Shacklewell written to Novello after he returned to England (Clarke, *Recollections of Writers*, pp. 232–233): "that dirty Shacklewell, that wet Shacklewell, that flat, floundering and foggy Shacklewell, that distant, out-of-the-way, dreary, unfriendly, unheard-of, melancholy, moping, unsocial, unmusical . . . foolish, faint, fantastical, sloppy, hoppy, moppy . . . plashy, mashy, squashy . . . Shacklewell."

twenty. She is going, (or talks of it,) to teach embroidery in a Convent, — the jade! She wants me to marry her, — jade again! But what a sweet voice she has, let her talk of what she will! Yet she is false hearted on one point, I am sure, for she pretends to be "tanto innamorata di me!" — this won't do. Her father, a bill-broker, a fellow with a hard lined face, is going to be married again, and she is in a pucker about it. I think I've made her a very handsome offer, — to be governess to Charley,[8] or my house-keeper, — which ever title she likes best, — and if neither of those pleases, why I must be her "amico" in a private way, for I'll have nothing to do with priests, — or I must be unhappy, and cut a weeping willow twig, and hang myself in it. I wonder how it will end. If I could spy a fault in her, I should be tolerably recon-ciled, touch my hat, and walk away. The jade sings too. I have known her now pretty nearly a week, and she is never to be found alone. Something has been done in the way of letters to be sure, and something more through the good offices of a petticoat friend, but there's nothing decisive, and I have no patience in these matters. What a fine name she has! Euphemia! there's certainly something in a name,[9] — and no doubt that is the reason she speaks so well. I wish you could see her. Maria is not a jot more free than she was. The cause of this persecution is now discovered, — just as I said from the first, — the Magistrate is her damnable sister's "amico." She goes to-day to the President,[10] and will state that fact among other vile things. Then the lawyer has been traitor, trying to keep her entirely in his power, retarding every thing as much as possible, and making love to her! — a fellow at least as fat gutted as Falstaff, and with a fistula in one of his leering eyes. Kirkup is enraged on all sides. I am afraid he will leave Florence. He sends his remembrances, and says he shall write to you, and send music. All the Landors are very well, — the little one growing out of all cess. They too told me {to re-m}ember them to your worship when I should wri{t}e. Carlino

---

[8] In 1827, when Kirkup moved in with Brown, his mistress Maria (or Marina) was established in the house as "aja [governess] del bambino di Signor Carlo Brown" (see the first extant paragraph of number 89). Beyond the details of the present letter nothing is known about Euphemia.

[9] Alluding to *Romeo and Juliet*, II.ii.43.

[10] President of the Tuscan Buon Governo (state police).

complains against the whole affair of going to England, wishes there was no such place, and wants Henry and Swinburne. He lately made a sad mistake, — he told a gentleman that you were gone, and that papa had *stolen* your furniture. I got your letter, a post or two beyond Lyons. I'm glad you were pleased with "Les Charmettes".[11] Would you believe it possible? — we have had but one rainy day since you left us, and it is not possible to waft your things to Leghorn. It now appears set in for rain, but does not actually begin. All Tuscany is crying out upon it; mills are stopped, wells are dry, water (in most of the villas) costs a paul a barrel, and the farmers cannot work their ground for sowing. Kirkup requests you'll not talk of him & his Maria together in England. Give my love to Wife and children, — all I can spare from Euphemia. Let me hear from you of all sorts of things. In a few days I shall be on the move.[12] The front room, with the fire place, on the ground floor, will be my favourite; there I shall have all my books and prints, — I'll hide the walls with them. It will be but a hop skip and jump into the garden. I've a great deal of "Italian Chat" ready, and have written to Westmacott & Severn for chat from Naples and Rome. Last post I sent off an Article on Cennino Cennini.[13] Landor has made me a present of his "Conversations." [14] We hear nothing of Hazlitt, and I see nothing of his in the Chronicle; [15] — where are he and his? I've been wondrously merry, I mean "allegro", for the last fortnight, and so I shall proceed, if Euphemia will allow me, — the jade!

Your's most lovingly,
Chas Brown.

[11] Rousseau's house near Chambéry.

[12] See number 77, n. 6.

[13] See the end of the preceding letter.

[14] The first two volumes of *Imaginary Conversations*, published by Taylor and Hessey in 1824.

[15] Hazlitt arrived back in England on October 16 (Howe, *Life of Hazlitt*, p. 348). His *Notes of a Journey through France and Italy* (1826) first appeared serially in the *Morning Chronicle*, September 14, 1824–November 16, 1825.

. 80 .

TO LEIGH HUNT

Address: Inghilterra. / To / Mr Leigh Hunt, / Care of Mr Hunter, / Bookseller, / 72 St Paul's Church-Yard, / London.

Postmarks: FIRENZE; Toscana; I.T.; FPO DE 6 1825

ALS: British Museum.

My dear Hunt,   Florence. 24th Novr 1825.

Your Cases and Trunks have been shipped on board the Amphitrite, Captn Brightman, and I must not longer defer sending you the Bill of Loading, so I accordingly enclose it. I have waited in the hope of answering your first letter from England. We have had no news of you since you arrived at Paris, except through Mocali, who has heard of his Gigi's [1] having reached Calais with all his family. There has not been a little anxiety on your account. I in particular, having fifty fears about your first step into London, know not how to make choice of the least of my apprehensions. Your silence is entirely owing to that villainous climate; it is certain there is something in the nature of the atmosphere that uncommonly depresses all attempts at writing to friends abroad; so as I thus account for my not hearing from you, I shall proceed, satisfied in my clever discovery, to any other subject. First and foremost: as soon as I got into my new house, your goods were removed from Landor's, and valued, article by article. The valuation stands thus: for Marriott's furniture 72 Pauls; for your furniture 592 Pauls; and for the two Sofas (which are or are not to be sent) 150 Pauls. This valuation is beyond my expectations, as it must be beyond your's, when you recollect you thought of paying Morandi for repairs with every stock and stick of it. I must tell you it is valued not as to a dealer, but as to an individual in want of it. If you wish it, I'll copy the list of all the articles, with the prices to each. In removing from Majano two of Marriott's chairs were stolen; neither I nor my servant can imagine how, — but certainly they are gone and irrecoverable.

---

[1] The Hunts' vetturino.

Marriott will have to pay you his proportion of freight and charges; I think the 72 pauls, which will be carried to your account, will, as nearly as possible, settle it. M^r C Clarke is not to pay you for his proportion for the Case & the freight &c, — he pays Mr Mancur,[2] and I deduct the sum from your Account. I find that, after paying Passeri and Mad Lambardi, our Account together will nearly balance; you shall have it, when I know the exact charges for lighterage, shipping &c from Johnstone, and when I know what Mollini does.[3] There won't be many pauls difference on either side. I am waiting to learn whether I am to pay Passeri & Mad Lambardi their long bills, or whether they ought not to be paid. According to this Bill of Loading, the freight is charged at 2 shillings per cubic foot & 10 per ct primage, — double what I expected; and as there are 72 cubic feet in the large sofa, make your own calculations. My boxes of books have come; [4] there were six copies of Bacchus in Tuscany,[5] which shall be disposed of thus, — to Landor, Kirkup, Lord Dillon,[6] Castelnuovo, Severn, and myself, — is that right? Roscoe's Novellists [7] for Thornton, — very handsome four volumes, and a very faithless translation, even to deplorable ignorance of the Italian, — what am I to do with them? There are a few other books for you, of no great value, except another copy of the "Day in Stowe Gardens",[8] which I've a great mind to send to Severn. Then there are some letters for you and Marriott, — they shall be sent to you by Mr Hogg, when he returns from Rome in Jany. Yes, I've had Mr Hogg here, and glad I was to see him; and he will be with me again on his way back.[9] Now I've settled your business, I'll sing

[2] See number 87.

[3] Brown sent the account in number 85.

[4] Hunt told Elizabeth Kent on January 4, 1825 (*Correspondence of Leigh Hunt*, I, 234–235), "Mr. B[rown] . . . thinks of sending for all the books he has left in England." The books subsequently named in the present letter were ones that Hunt suggested "could come in the same box without any expense."

[5] Hunt's *Bacchus in Tuscany, A Dithyrambic Poem, from the Italian of Francesco Redi*, published in 1825 by John and H. L. Hunt.

[6] Henry Augustus Dillon-Lee, thirteenth Viscount Dillon (1777–1832), "a rather crack-brained literary man, in poor circumstances, and living mostly abroad" — Vicary Gibbs, *The Complete Peerage*, IV (London, 1916), 362n.

[7] *The Italian Novelists*, 4 vols. (1825), selected and translated by Thomas Roscoe.

[8] A collection of stories by Mary Sabilla Novello, published in 1825 by John and H. L. Hunt and dedicated to Leigh Hunt.

[9] Thomas Jefferson Hogg (1792–1862), Shelley's friend and biographer, stopped

a stave on my own. I have drawn to-day on Colburn for £25, which I have well earned; but in my letter to him I avoid mentioning how much per sheet I am to receive, — and indeed it would be of no use, as I'm yet ignorant of the precise quantity printed, — for Mancur won't let me into that secret. You must let me know whether Colburn will give me a guinea a page, — he ought to do it, and I shall be glad to hear the news. Last Saturday I sent off N⁰ 1 of "Italian Chat",[10] and perhaps you can tell me if it is liked, and how much it is liked, and whether it is thought it could be improved, — I thought it would prove very amusing. As Roscoe says not one word of "Gonnella the Court Fool," I sent that Article; and indeed it hath little of Bandello in it, except facts; and those he took, every one of them, from Bartolomeo del Uomo;[11] — but you need not mention my immediate authority. I must tell you one droll mistake, among a thousand, of Roscoe's; he causeth a Nobilissima to employ herself in "cooking viands" instead of setting down to *needlework*, mistaking the word "cucire" for "cuocere"! You can have no idea of the warm comfort of my parlour, — nor of my warm in-door coat, — nor of my out-of-door cloak, — Gad! I defy cold this winter. Then I dig and work in my garden till I'm quite in a lily dew. As for the house, — its a very fine house, — but so many rooms, and windows to curtainise, that I'm put to an outrageous expence for furniture, — your's is scarcely visible in its scatter-about. Kirkup has not yet begun to furnish his rooms, as he is yet beriddled as to {his rela}-tions; soon that love affair, in my opinion, {will be s}ettled to his satisfaction; the Police are yielding, and I'm in great hopes not to lose him. He now thinks well of it, and certainly hopes to stay, for this morning he bought a hearth-rug. He sends his kindest

in Florence from November 2 to 10 on his way to Rome, and from January 1 to 7 on the return trip (Hogg's *Two Hundred and Nine Days*, London, 1827, I, 305, 327, and II, 158, 169).

[10] He later sent off two more installments (see number 85), but apparently none was printed.

[11] "Gonnella, the Court Fool of Ferrara," *New Monthly Magazine*, 16 (1826): 162–167. Bandello wrote about Gonnella in *Novelle*, IV.3, 18, 21, 24, 27 (according to the numbering in *Le Quattro parti de le novelle del Bandello*, ed. Gustavo Balsamo-Crivelli, Turin, 1910–1911), and in the dedication to IV.24 he mentions "la vita di esso Gonnella" by "Bartolomeo de l'Uomo Ferrarese," written "in prosa con stile molto elegante." Bartolomeo's work is no longer extant; see Letterio di Francia in *Giornale storico della letteratura italiana*, 81 (1923): 57–58.

remembrances. The Landors and every body are very well in this excellent Florence. The strangest piece of news that I can tell you is that Landor, within the last week, has been to TWO BALLS! — one given by Mr Hare,[12] and the other by Lord Dillon; — besides which, he lately went to a Musical Conversazione. I hear he is quite gay in his new element, joking and laughing *ad libitum* among the flounced and feathered company. Carlino, thank ye, is very well, and behaves very well. He is always talking of Henry and Swinburne. I long to hear how you and your's are going on, — now you have ceased to *go on*. Love to your Wife, and remembrances to them all. Your's most sincerely,

Chas Brown.

I answered your's from Paris immediately, giving the list you desired.[13] Tell Mr Novello it would be well if he were to write either to me or to Sig Giorni at Genova, about the Sistri affair.[14] I've another letter from Giorni this morning; he has taken a good deal of pains, and Italians are eager to have their trouble acknowledged, — besides, he wishes to know whether he is or is not to act, — and besides, Mr Novello ought to write to CB.

. 81 .

TO LEIGH HUNT

Address: Inghilterra. / To / Mr Leigh Hunt, / Care of Mr Hunter, / Bookseller, / St Paul's Church-yard, / London. / Angleterre

Postmarks: FIRENZE; Toscana; I.T.; FPO JA 19 1826

ALS: British Museum.

My dear Hunt,   Florence. 7th January 1826.
One murder is found out, — it is certain that a letter from Dilke has miscarried. I suspect that one from Mancur has not gone the right road; and it is almost certain that the large packet you were to send between 11th and 18th November has been

---

[12] Francis George Hare (1786–1842), a close friend of Landor in Italy.
[13] See the preceding letter.
[14] See number 78, n. 7.

stolen, for I have not received it. You must know I have had but one note from your worship since your arrival in England. I shall address this to Mr Hunter's care, as I suppose you have left Hadlow Street long ago; [1] and I've no idea of your precise direction at Box-hill. To-day I went, as usual, to the Post-office, and, as usual, those vile words "Niente, Signore," sounded in my ears; so I returned home to despatch a short letter to you, before it is too late for you to return an answer. I am much in the same situation as you were this time last year, not knowing what to be at with Colburn. You promised to send me word whether he would or would not pay me at the rate of 16 Gn^s a sheet, and unless I am clear on this point, how am I to manage my bills on him? I have spent a good deal of money on my new house, and only wait to hear from you in order to make myself still more comfortable. But that is not the worst part of the story, for here is a poor fellow waiting for me to advance him some Crowns, which I dare not do till I know how I stand on my own bottom. Pray then have the kindness, *in less than a week after the receipt of this*, to send me a letter, telling me either that Colburn agrees or refuses to pay me 16 Guineas a sheet, or that he will give no direct answer, or that you do not like to ask him the question, — in fact, let it be a letter giving me all the information you can on the subject, for it is of purse-importance. I should wish to know, at the same time, whether my "Chat" pleases you and the Editor. Do, pray make it a matter of business for my sake.

Mr Hogg has come back from the south, and he left us this morning for the north. The letters to you and Marriott, which came in my box of books, I have consigned to Mr Hogg's care, having broken the seals; they are tied up together in a brown paper parcel.

Has it never struck Mr Novello that he has left me in an awkward situation with Signor Giorni, who has done every thing he could? and not a word, no answer of any kind is sent, not even thanks, which surely he deserves, and which I ought to be able to return him, on the part of Mr Novello.

---

[1] The Hunts were still in Hadlow Street (see the address of number 83, and Clarke, *Recollections of Writers*, p. 233). They moved to Highgate before August 1 (Clarke, p. 234).

I am writing for the Magazine very much out of spirits. After all my pains I conjecture the "Chat" will do me no good; and in addition to my knowing the amount of pay, I should be glad to be assured that I am considered as a monthly contributor of other Articles, — that is, that the Editor will put them in as long as I furnish them. You that must know all about it could tell me. I care not for compliments, unless they come from the Mag Proprietors.

I have heard of you from Dilke, who wrote you that note at my request; he says Mrs Hunt has a little Englishwoman,[2] — give mama my congratulations. Mr Hogg has also told me that you are in good health and spirits, — but these are sorry ways of hearing from you.

This is scrawled in haste for to-day's post, as I must not run the chance of having your answer a day too late.

Your's most sincerely,
Chas Brown.

Oh! I forgot! Mr Hare has written to Landor that the parcel intrusted to you has not been delivered.[3] That was five weeks ago, and I have heard nothing since, not liking to touch on the subject with Landor, for he was in a fever when he told me.

[2] Jacintha Hunt.
[3] Julius Charles Hare (1795–1855), brother of Francis, supervised the publication of *Imaginary Conversations* in London. The parcel contained "additions to the Conversations which were of such importance that he [Landor] was afraid that without them the publication would be dropped altogether" (Super, *Landor*, p. 188).

· 82 ·

TO ROBERT FINCH

Address: All' Ornatmo Signore / Il Signor Roberto Finch, / Gentiluomo Inglese, / Roma.

Postmarks: FIRENZE; 16 GENNAIO

Endorsements: Rec^d Jany 16° 1826. Ans^d D°; Brown.

ALS: Bodleian Library. Extracts are printed by Nitchie, *The Reverend Colonel Finch*, pp. 89–90.

My dear Sir,   Florence. 12th January 1826.

    Before I received your letter Sig. Palmerini [1] had mentioned to me that he was seeking for an opportunity to forward some books to you, and I had waited on Mr Hogg [2] to ask him if he would take charge of them. "With pleasure" was the answer, so off I went to Sig. Palmerini; who having opened the parcel, and seen what sort of books they were, thought it adviseable, as they are not of a pocketable size, not to attempt to forward them, unless by some German gentleman whose trunks would be exempt from examination. Then came your letter, which I carried immediately to Mr Hogg's hotel; he was out, I called again, he called on me when I was out, then called again, (this was yesterday,) and as I was engaged at that hour, 4 o'Clock, he went by himself to Sig. Palmerini, when he was not at home, and the answer was he would return at 10 at night. Mr Hogg called again on me to tell me this, and I engaged to go at 10, receive the books, and carry them to his hotel before 11. I went, was there at $\frac{1}{4}$ after 10, and could not by all the ringing in my power get the door answered. The night was got up in imitation of the famous deluge, and I rung, and rung, till I was downright rude, if any one was there to hear me, and it was downright useless, if they were all out, all dead, or all asleep. The end of this mischief is that Mr Hogg has

---

[1] Niccolò Palmerini, Florentine bookseller and art dealer, a longtime friend of Finch.

[2] John Hogg, who was traveling south to spend the winter and spring in Rome at the same time that his brother, Thomas Jefferson, was returning to England (see the preceding letter).

left Florence this morning at 6 o'Clock without the books. This I am so sorry for, that I've penned a long story in justification, — though to tell you the truth, I don't know why you should be so eager for such naughty books.[3]

I suppose you have heard of M[r] L. Hunt's arrival in England. He is going on in a very prosperous manner, though M[rs] Hunt, who never will have done, brought him an eighth child soon after they arrived.[4]

Kirkup desires me to say he is happy to hear of you and your's, and wishes me to say every thing that is kind in return for your remembrance of him. He talks of taking a trip to Venice this Carnival, — I hope it's nothing more than talk.

Master Carlino, many thanks to you, is very "pleasant." We have an English Preparatory School here, and I have tried it with him for this last twelvemonth with great satisfaction. In the spring of 1827 we are both resolved to go to Rome, pay our visits, go to Naples,[5] and then return to our dearly beloved Florence.

I am indeed sorry to hear that M[rs] Finch is not quite well and hearty. My best regards to her, and my best love to Miss Thompson.

You have put me in an agony, — "a horrible murder, and the fall of part of the Pincian hill!" I must know the particulars. Pray send them, for my sake, for the sake of my "Italian Chat," and for its readers' sake. My N° 3, which must be sent off about 20th is sadly behind hand. "If I provoke you," quoth your Worship, you promise to send me grand news. I do provoke you, — I dare you to do it! Is that enough? At your leisure hours, if you have any, you could really do me and the state some service. Is it true that half Palermo has been destroyed by an earthquake? If so, I should relish some account of that which *does not* appear in the Newspapers. Ha! my dear Bianca Cappello![6] Would you believe it? — L. Hunt persuaded me not to proceed with it, saying as how that

---

[3] In a letter to Finch of January 20 (Bodleian Library), John Hogg describes them as "Antipapistical books."

[4] Marianne "had done" after the birth of their ninth, Julia Trelawney Leigh Hunt, in December 1829.

[5] They went with Dilke and his son in September–October 1826 (numbers 85, 88).

[6] See number 56, n. 18.

such sort of romances were not the thing. I'm now sorry I listened to him; and intend to turn my researches to some account in giving a short history of her, which is quite a romance by itself. Such a romance I sent off lately! — very short, but very shocking, — a horrible Dwarf; — there are love, murder, madness, a shrieking dream, the Carnival at Rome, banditti, Cardinal Gonsalvi,[7] a mysterious mask, an awful spy, and death by a slight wound in the left shoulder. You can no doubt fill up the particulars, and thus understand the tale in all its due horrors, which doubtless will be vastly "pleasant," and therefore, leaving you in the full enjoyment of them, I remain, Dear Sir,

> Your's most truly,
> Chas Brown.

· 83 ·

TO LEIGH HUNT

Address: Inghilterra. / To / Leigh Hunt Esqr, / N° 30 Hadlow Street, / Burton Crescent, / London. / Angleterre

Postmark: FIRENZE

ALS: British Museum.

My dear Hunt,   Florence. 24th January 1826.

    I received your letter on 10th inst, and am now prepared on every point. In the first place it will be as well to see how M^r J Hunt's questions can be answered. 1st "Why should not Mr J. H. be paid for the portion of Editorial duty he performed for Mr L. H?" Because J. H. undertook that duty of his own accord; because had he not acted in that manner, he would not, according to his own account, have done any thing; and because such a payment would be grossly unjust and illegal. 2nd "Why should not Mr L. H. return the half of the sums paid to others for the labour he did not perform, such sums being paid by the concern?" This is a mistake. In the account for 1821 (and perhaps in former years) L. H. had charged against him, separately from the con-

---

[7] Ercole Consalvi (1757–1824), minister of the Papal States.

cern, sums paid to others, or at least to another, for labour performed for the Examiner. There are two payments to Mr Gorton am^g to £105 during that year; and L. H. must be credited for one half of that amount, or it must be proved that an Editor is compelled to furnish writing for every part of the Paper, which is not the fact. An Editor's duty is not, unless stipulated to that effect, to furnish original Articles. 3rd "Why, he asks, should not the lowest rate of interest be charged to Mr L. H. for such advances?" Provided both parties act up to the strict letter of the law it may be charged; and then, as will be shown below, the interest will be acting against Mr J. H. before the close of 1829. But it is a question whether any interest can legally be charged except from 1st Jany 1824 when Mr J. H. stated the exact balance in his own favour.

In reply to his attempt to prove that you dissolved the partnership by receiving £100 per annum together with payments for your literary aid to the Paper, I shall only say I have written much to prove the contrary, and that I have proofs to the contrary under his own hand. It is well indeed that the Deed does exist, — though I alluded to *proofs in his letters*, — but I will not trust myself to write what I think of this attempt against you.

Now to his definition of a "Printer free of expence." It is, he says, to perform the usual duties without charge, but he declines stating what those duties were. By his account they were not only nothing, but worse than nothing; for it appears the Paper was printed, *"as a cheaper course,"* by Mr Bensley,[1] and since by Mr Reynell. What! does he confess that his stipulated share of the labour for the Paper put the concern to an expence? The fact, I believe, is this: the materials were sold, he dismissed his journeymen, and ceased to be Printer free of expence. Did it never strike him that while he was contending you had forfeited your claim to the profits by withdrawing (as he erroniously called it) your services as Editor, that he was in the same predicament, having withdrawn his services as Printer? It is true, he took upon himself other and doubtless more essential duties, owing to your ill health at the time. But all that he has performed for the last four years, all his attention to the interests of the Paper, including the suc-

---

[1] Thomas Bensley (d. 1833), who with his son Benjamin, at Bolt Court, Fleet Street, also printed the second edition (1817) of Hunt's *The Story of Rimini.*

cess he has achieved by lowering the price to 7d, were surely not too much in return for the sums of money he has received, year after year, from a work raised into importance solely by your talents. For he cannot pretend to say that the Paper owed any thing to its establishment to him. Talent, and talent alone could have established it; while for its continuance it wanted attention. It is an Estate formed by yourself, not by him; and now he hopes to enjoy the entire fruits of it, without even paying a rental. For my part, though he calls it an "unworthy act" to refer to the Deed of Partnership, I think his share from the first, as equal to your's, was far too large, as by that document he is bound to be Printer free of expence and nothing more; and I shall refer to that Deed, with the opinion Mr Reader sent me on the case, in order to show what your claims strictly are. This Deed, which M^r J H makes so light of, had better be considered betimes by him. He is bound by it to pay you an equal share of the profits with himself; and not only to pay you, but to pay your heirs the same share, or to pay it to any person to whom you or your heirs may choose to sell it, after giving three months notice of the sale, according to the terms of the Deed. Your heir, or your assign is not bound to find an Editor free of expence, nor are you *bound* to be Editor during your life time and possession of it. I will copy Mr Reader's words, — in answer to my question of — "in the event of L. H's *refusal* to perform the duties of Editor, what would be the consequence?" "If I am correct in the interpretation of the Deed, Mr Leigh Hunt has no right to refuse giving his personal superintendance of the Examiner; and, in case of his doing so, his partners would be entitled to institute proceedings against him, and bring their complaint to the decision of Arbitrators, as is directed by the Covenant. But he has still his share of the Newspaper, of which he cannot be dispossessed." I put this question, as one of the strongest nature I could think of against you, and the answer is favourable. You, we well know, never *refused*; on the contrary, it was ill health, by J. H's admission, that caused you to leave England. Afterwards, you still believing yourself considered by him on the same footing, *he refused you*, and would not consent that you should have any thing to do with the Examiner. My next question to Mr Reader was, "In the event of incapacity on the part of Leigh

Hunt to perform the duties of Editor, from sickness or otherwise, would he cease to be a partner, or would he be liable to the expence of paying for another Editor in his place, or would he still continue partner without any deduction?" Mr Reader had previously said that even a direct refusal on your part to continue as Editor could not dispossess you of your partnership, and then he says, — "But if from ill health, or any other cause, Mr Leigh Hunt should be incapacitated, and consequently excused, from performing the duties of the office, is he to be compelled to pay for an Editor? I incline to think not. The words of the Deed refer exclusively to his own personal services, and intimate nothing about providing an Editor." Afterwards, in conversation, Mr Reader expressed himself in a stronger manner on this point, (more in your favour than he had written,) upon consideration that in the event of your selling your share, the purchaser would have nothing to do in the provision of an Editor, — he would not, according to the Deed, be permitted in any way to interfere, except in the examination of the Accounts, and in his receipt of his share equally with J. H. I am no lawyer, but the words of the Deed are so plain, that I understood them beforehand precisely in the same manner as Mr Reader explained them. Besides, it was Mr Reader's opinion, that any complaint against you for non-performance as Editor free of expence, must be backed by proofs that he, J. H., had always performed by himself, or deputy, (for the Deed allows a deputy,) the duties of Printer free of expence, — and that was my reason for putting, through you, a question on that point to him. In point of law therefore, I conceive Mr J. H. must yield, and all that you want of him is to act with justice. The Deed cannot be overthrown; there it stands for you and your heirs against him and his heirs, as long as the Examiner exists, and so it ought to be, for the property was of your making. I need not call his conduct, as you tell me a Solicitor in London has called it, "unjust, illegal, and preposterous," — I am quite content in his not having it in his power to pursue such conduct against you and your young and numerous family. Let it come to an Arbitration, I'll not spare him. I will, even without the Deed, array his own letters against him, together with the positive facts of the case, till he and those who were previously his friends will be startled, —

245

but not he and his friends with the same feelings. But this is foolish; I wish that he should act well, and that neither he nor you should be injured. Let us examine the case as it stands, taking your claim against him, and your debt to him, equally into consideration; — 1st according to the letter of the law, as appears in the Deed, and then (2nd) what is the fair and equitable interpretation. Now debiting you for the monies you have recd, and you always enjoying £100 per annum till the end of 1829, I will suppose the balance against you as he states it on 1st Jany 1824 to be £1790. 19. 10; when from this sum I must deduct on Cr side the half of the sums paid to Mr Gorton in 1821, and the half nett profits, after paying Mr Whiting, for the years 1822 & 1823, which will be £250 per annum, — a round sum, which may or may not be correct, but he has afforded no better guide. Your half profits are for 1824, £457. 2. 10 after deducting the annuity to Mr Whiting. During the last year I am informed the sale of the Examiner has increased, as well as the profits by advertisements; however, as I cannot do otherwise, I will take the profits at the same amount; and for the years following to the end of 1829 still at the same amount. Your account with J. H. will then stand as under:

Dr				Cr
To Balance 1st Jany 1824 —— £1,790. 19. 10		By half of £105 pd Mr Gorton 1821 ——— £52. 10. –		
" Cash recd in 1823, 1824, & 1825 on Acct – 269. 6. –		" share of nett profits 1822 & 1823 ——— 500. –. –		
" do £100 per ann from 1826 to 1829, four years ——— } 400. –. –		" — do — do — from 1824 to 1829, six years, £457. 2. 10 per annum ——— } 2,742. 17. –		
Balance — 835. 1. 2				
£3,295. 7. –		£3,295. 7. –		

The nett profits for these four years to come may be more or less (an equal chance perhaps) than £457. 2. 10 per annum. From this it is scarcely fair, in such a calculation, to deduct as I have done so much as £200 per annum to Mr Whiting; it ought rather to be the interest on the sum for which an annuity to that amount can be purchased at his period of life. Here no interest is taken into calculation; but if it were, and during the last years the balance of interest would be against J. H. will not the above balance on the Account *in your favour* cover all such claims of that nature? It may be urged that he may hire an Editor, and charge the expence to the joint account; true, but still it will be far from affecting the proposition you formerly made, viz: to receive £100 per annum until the end of 1829, and £200 per annum afterwards to you and your heirs, upon condition on his part that the whole of the debt should be cancelled, and on your part that the Deed of Partnership should be cancelled. Had I the means of making a more exact calculation, so that I could rely on every item, till the end of last year, (and the want of them cannot make a very great difference either way) I would show, with regular interest columns, and allowing (say) £200 per annum for an Editor, that at the end of *1839* he (J H) would be *indebted to you* to a large amount. My advice to you is, under all the circumstances, to renew your former proposal as above stated, taking care that the annuity is properly secured to you and your heirs, on the Examiner; and not to ask for more, though by the strict letter of the Deed, more might be obtained. If he refuses your proposition you have then *two* things to choose; 1st either to refer the question to Arbitrators, who by the by cannot give an award against law; or, 2nd, to sell your property in the Examiner, pay J. H. out of the pro{ceeds . . .} and purchase (so I advise) some property with the remainder for the {. . .}[2] What I have stated, (the proposal on your part as formerly made,) will b{e . . .} fair interpretation of the agreement between you; without urging the {. . .} means to their extremity, you will leave him uninjured in the conce{rn . . .} and secure a certainty (as far as the Examiner's sale is certain) for {. . . if on the} contrary, you choose to let the matter rest, till such time, (about tw{. . .} debt will be nearly liquidated, you will come in for the half nett pr{ofits . . .} possibly £500 per annum & more on Mr Whiting's

---

[2] A large rectangular piece has been cut from the right-hand side of the third page, and across the page there is a hole made by cutting away the seal.

decease, without its being in his power, by the te{. . .} a sixpence from you & your heirs. Again I say, that under all the circum-stan{ces . . .} adhere to the first proposal. Yet should he reject it, be it understoo{d . . .} obtain th{e u}tmost I possibly can from the Arbitrators, and in {. . .}me, — indeed I am not clear but that I require {. . .} of an arbitration, and I do not believe Mr J. H. w{ill agree} to any {thing with}out one, be p{ar}ticular in stating that not only {. . .} question is to be brought before the arbitra-tors, but also the examination of th{e . . .}

You can send a copy of the above, the whole or pa{rt, just as you} choose, to Mr J. H.; and don't destroy this letter as I have no copy. {. . .} thoughts upon it, and done my best, — so Kirkup thinks.

I have paid Mad Lambardi the balance, she asserts {. . .} day she herself counted every article in the basket, & accompanied it to {. . .} Passeri's bill, so as to check it exactly with Mrs Hunt's account, and {. . .} him, and make him explain; though the two stories look very much {. . .}

Landor set off to Rome yesterday morning,[3] on a {. . .} the children are quite well. He desired to be remembered kindly to you {. . .}[4]

*   *   *

Mr J. H's non-acceptance of that bill was spite. You ask me about the £30; you sent him the Bacchus in Tuscany, and drew £30 on the strength of it. This was afterwards, *not immediately*, objected to. He said he could not find a purchaser of the Ms at that sum. You wrote to him you would not print it on your own account, and desired him to find a purchaser if he could. Then, without saying a word to you, he printed and published it himself. Now, what right had he to do so, unless he conceived he had bought it for the £30? He must have regarded it as his property; and if so, at what price? If under £30, why did he not procure your per-mission? Why did he not write to you that he could only afford

---

[3] He went with Francis Hare, and stayed in Rome for a month (Super, *Landor*, pp. 186–187). Sharp, p. 152, says that he "bore a special letter from Brown to Severn."

[4] Here and at the asterisks just before the signature a third of a page is heavily deleted (by someone other than Brown) and the text illegible.

such or such a sum, leaving the sale to your decision, if the terms were under your demand? He has chosen to act in this instance, as in many others towards you, on his own *will*. I did not notice this £30 in the Account I have drawn up, because I was not certain of the correspondence upon it, — and you may have made a mistake in relating it to me, though by his letters I can scarcely imagine that to have been the case. As for his changing the date of the year in the Dedication,[5] it is not so much as he has done in his correspondence with me, respecting various items in the accounts and Partnership.

* * *

Your's most sincerely, Chas Brown.

· 84 ·

TO C. W. DILKE

Address: Inghilterra. / To / Chas Wentworth Dilke Esqr / Navy Pay Office, / Somerset house, / London. / Angleterre

Postmarks: FIRENZE; Toscana; I.T.; FPO MY 15 1826

Endorsement: Brown 2 May 26 [1]

AL: Keats House, Hampstead. Printed by Richardson, *The Everlasting Spell*, pp. 197–198.

[May 2, 1826]

* * *

Severn [2] will certainly be in Rome; I wrote to him {to say that} I was fishing for you,[3] and that I had hopes, and he has answered me in a sentence of joy on the occasion. Whether you are in three

---

[5] It was originally dated January 1, 1824 (see number 65). John Hunt — the dedicatee — changed the date of the year to 1825.

[1] Another hand has penciled, "Ought I to ask the old Lady to dine I mean Mrs Browne."

[2] Two thirds of the first leaf is torn away. This beginning passage occupies the lower third of the first page, and the next passage ("The £50 . . .") begins on the lower third of the second page and continues on to the third. A small strip, containing perhaps only the signature, is torn away at the bottom of the third page.

[3] To come to Italy (see numbers 85, 88).

or four, or possibly in two, the expence of travelling *post* will be much the same as crawling on in a "voiture", — rather less indeed in *amount,* only you will be a less time on the road, and therefore not *kept* so long for your money. You must hire a carriage at Calais, or you must buy one (as I did)[4] and sell it again at half price or as you can. I'll give you facts. Six months ago our banker, Mr Johnstone, went with *three* other persons from Florence to Paris; the carriage was his own, so no expence was on that

*   *   *

The £50 is not due from you till next November, nor can I possibly want it before.[5] Pay it to Mancur, and he will either give you a receipt, or return the bill which I left with Skynner. Pay him also the money from Keats.[6] I never heard of his having any hopes from Chancery.[7] The return of this money is as if I had *found* it, for I never much calculated on it, and latterly not at all, notwithstanding what you wrote about Geo Keats. By good luck I have not destroyed the Account between me and poor John Keats. The balance in my favour, on 22^d Decr 1819, was £6. 4. 1, agreed to by his initials. After that time, the Account is as follows, — for it is proper I should send a copy of it:

1819	Dec^r	22.	Balance ———————	£6.	4.	1
1820	Jan^y	1.	Examiners ————————	2.	10.	10
	„	„	Half Wine & Spirits bill	5.	9.	6
	„	8	Boot-maker's bill ———	3.	6.	6
	March		Dr Bree —————————	4.	4.	—
	„		Coach hire ———————	.	3.	—
	„	22	Board 3 months ———	15.	—.	—

---

[4] In number 41 Brown says that he traveled to Turin "by post."

[5] Brown had lent him the money in 1822 (see the first paragraph of number 125).

[6] George Keats, who had authorized Dilke to pay the bill itemized in the present letter. Dilke's grandson wrote to Milnes around 1875 (*KC,* II, 337), "I have the original bill for 75£ with the details — claimed against George Keats — by Brown in 1826 & paid by my grandfather" (see also n. 8 below).

[7] In 1823 George had applied for his share of a sizable fund left in Chancery for the Keats children by their grandfather John Jennings (Gittings, *The Keats Inheritance,* esp. pp. 32, 36, 38–39). By the date of the present letter he still had not received the money (see *More Letters and Poems of the Keats Circle,* ed. Rollins, p. 34, and *KC,* I, 298). Neither John Keats nor Brown ever knew of the existence of this fund.

May	4	Sundries ———————	.	6.	6
"	"	One Week's rent in advance at Kentish Town }	1.	1.	–
"	6	Board 1½ month ———	7.	10.	–
"	"	Loan ———————	50.	–.	–
"	"	Half wine & Spirits bill	5.	18.	–
1821 March	6	Mr Rodd's bill ————	13.	11.	–

115. 4. 5

Less received of J K 6th Feby 1820 ———— 40. –. –

£75. 4. 5 Balance due.

You may mention that he and I always had a running account together.[8] The above is an exact copy, with this exception, — I have omitted to charge interest on the £50 loan, though it is entered in the Account, because it was interest I had actually *paid* to Skynner for that *identical* sum which I had borrowed from him to lend to Keats, before I set off on my second trip to the Highlands. But as it is unpleasant to my feelings to mention any thing about interest, especially as if that is once begun upon it would raise the amount to nearly £100, I would rather omit it altogether. I never saw Miss Keats, — for which her guardian is answerable, — yet though I never saw her, my congratulations on her marriage,[9] and my wishes for her welfare and happiness are not the less hearty; — have the goodness to tell her so.

*   *   *

[8] Dilke "mentioned" it indignantly in his notes on Milnes's *Life* (Forman, 1952, p. li): "What Mr. Milnes means by a 'generous protector' I know not — assuredly it had nothing to do with money. When John Keats died Brown sent in an account to George for board, money lent, and *interest* amounting to about £72 — which by George's order I paid."

[9] Keats had written to his sister Fanny in October 1819 (*Letters*, II, 225–226), "I am sure you will take pleasure in being a friend to Mr Brown." Fanny married Valentin Maria Llanos y Gutierrez on March 30, 1826.

· 85 ·

TO LEIGH HUNT

Address: Inghilterra. / To / Leigh Hunt Esqr, / Care of Mr Hunter / Bookseller, / St Paul's Church Yard, / London. / Angleterre.

Postmarks: FIRENZE; Toscana; I.T.; FPO JU 12 1826

ALS: British Museum.

[May 29, 1826]

D^r   Leigh Hunt with Chas Brown   C^r

1825				Pauls	Cra	1825				Pauls	Cra
June	1	To	Balance, as per Acc^t delivered . . .	1,978	4	July	2	By	Cash . . . . (£45 at 42½)	1,893	4
July	2	"	Cash	690	–	Aug^t	30	"	d^o	2,000	–
"	"	"	d^o paid Lambardi & Nesti	150	–	Sept^r	8	"	d^o	1,750	–
"	13	"	d^o	240	–				Balance	13	6
"	30	"	Charges on box of books	90	–						
Aug^t	1	"	Cash paid Lambardi & Nesti	150	–						
"	4	"	d^o	590	–						
"	6	"	Rent paid Morandi . .	357	–						
"	30	"	Cash	600	–						
Sept^r	1	"	d^o paid Lambardi & Nesti	182	6						
"	8	"	d^o . . d^o . . balance . . .	564	4						
"	"	"	Trunk . . .	35	–						
"	"	"	Cash	20	–						
"	10	"	Postage of a packet to London . .	9	4						
			Pauls	5,657	2				Pauls	5,657	2

Septr	10	To	Balance, as above	13	6	Octr	24	By	expences, charged to C. Clarke . .	48	–
"	12	"	Porterage at Villa Morandi	3	4	Novr	26	"	Furniture at valuation . .	592	–
"	16	"	two Packing cases	48	–	"	"	"	do (M. Hunt's) at do	72	–
"	17	"	Cash paid Nesti	91	4	"	"	"	Two Sofas, pro tempore, at do	150	–
"	"	"	do paid Morandi . .	300	–	"	"	"	Books, £5. 13. – at 42	237	3
"	19	"	moving goods to Florence . .	22	6	"	"	"	do (Cecilia &c) 17s at 42	35	5
"	20	"	Cash paid Passeri, in part	130	–	"	"	"	do sold to Molini . . .	110	–
"	26	"	do " Lambardi, do . .	150	–				Balance	42	6
Octr	24	"	Moving Cases & trunks from the Villa to the lighter in Florence	21	3						
Novr	25	"	Lighterage to Leghorn, and shipping	95	5						
"	26	"	Comn on appraisement of Furniture	9	–						
"	"	"	Molini's bill	150	–						
1826											
Jany	18	"	Lambardi, in full . . .	92	2						
April	2	"	Passeri, do .	145	–						
"	"	"	Piatti,[1] for a Boccaccio .	15	–						
			Pauls	1,287	6				Pauls	1,287	6

April	2	To	Balance, as above	42	6	By 14 vols unsold of Miss Edgworth's works . .	

[1] Guglielmo Piatti, publisher and bookseller.

Mems: The Balance due to C. B. is 42 pauls and 6 crazie; but, to
meet that, there is the value of Miss Edgeworth's works,
still unsold. They have been for a long time offered for
14 crowns; as that sum cannot be had, they are now
offered for 10 crowns.

In comparing Mrs Hunt's Account and Passeri's bill together, he appeared to charge for two pair of shoes too
much, and for soling six pair of shoes too *little*, — CB
therefore paid the amount. The two pair of shoes were
not those which Mrs Hunt mentioned were returned. The
first item in Passeri's bill was 25 pauls, a balance due on
a former Account.

CB paid Piatti's bill of 15 pauls without question, — he
hopes he has not done wrong. It appeared a true story.

CB has entered the value of the two Sofas (pro tempore),
but if they can be sent by some good opportunity to London, CB will take advantage of it.[2]

My dear Hunt,   Florence. 29th May 1826.

I heard of you about a month ago, and that you were not very
well, — this has made me anxious. By the same means I heard you
were in Hampstead, but whether living there, or only on a visit, the
deponent [3] did not think it necessary to specify. However, to avoid
blunders, I shall conclude it probable you have left Hadlow
Street, and direct this to Mr Hunter's care. Your last letter was
begun on 5th Decr and ended on 24th, and I answered it at considerable length, chiefly about Mr J Hunt's resistance, on 24th
Jany; [4] this I mention to avoid any mistakes, in case my letter, or
one from you has miscarried. I hope that affair is concluded as it
ought to be, and that J. H has been brought to his senses without
being medicined by arbitrators. Carlino is very well, and growing
stout and strong, with bright eyes and rosy cheeks. For the last
fortnight I have been rather quisby; [5] I left off wine and was at

---

[2] Brown did not send them (see number 77, n. 7).

[3] Probably Dilke, in the letter that Brown answered on May 2 (number 84).

[4] Number 83.

[5] "Queer, not quite right" (*New English Dictionary*, whose earliest example of
the word as an adjective is dated 1853).

first the worse for it; four days ago I was, on a sudden, disgusted at the taste of meat, — so I ceased to eat meat; now I am remarkably well, and in high spirits, living on bread, butter, cheese, fruit, vegetables, and puddings, and drinking water! So, I've turned Bramin! My servant, Maddalena, (who was Shelley's servant,[6] when he lived in Florence,) never fails in a Catholic joke as she puts my "magro" [7] on the table. Kirkup is at Venice, astonished at St Mark's Square, and at the city, and all it contains. Landor and family are very well, — they live in a villa, beyond Bellosguardo, — he has often desired me to send his remembrances. Lord Normanby [8] has been giving his theatricals here this spring; I went, and saw Lord D{illon} play one of the Monks in Bertram! [9] this gave me a horrid pain {in} my internals, because decency forbad me the relief of a hearty laugh, — it was really very comic. He pops in upon me about once a week, and I once left my card at his house. I have (in Feb^y) been to Milan, and stopping at the Peacock in Parma, I saw Thornton's name written on the wall, and Marriott's on a fire-screen, — the latter was diffuse, touching his stay in Florence &c, and a frenchman had written some strange observations beneath on his uncalled for communications. I shall go with Carlino to Pisa next month to see the Illumination. Dilke and his son [10] will be here in Sept^r, — news that makes me wild; then I intend to go with him to Rome and see Severn, who, I am happy to say, is succeeding to our wishes. I had a great deal of company last Thursday at my five windows [11] to see the procession of the Corpus Domini, and was sorry your children were not there, especially as we had such a store of cakes. Landor is anxious to know if there is a portrait of Shelley; he begs you will urge Mrs Hunt, in case there should not be one, to make one, either in clay,

---

[6] Perhaps the "German-Swiss who speaks Italian perfectly" mentioned by Mary Shelley in a letter of December 28, 1819 (*Letters of Mary Shelley*, I, 91). The Shelleys were in Florence from October 2, 1819, to the following January 26.

[7] Food allowed on fast days.

[8] Constantine Henry Phipps, first Marquis of Normanby (1797–1863), author, politician, and a cousin of Lord Dillon.

[9] Charles Robert Maturin's *Bertram, or The Castle of St. Aldobrand*, produced at Drury Lane and published in 1816.

[10] Charles Wentworth III, later Sir Charles (1810–1869). Brown outlines his "rambles with Dilke & Co" in number 88.

[11] Brown's house faced the Cathedral.

or in paper, as a profile; [12] — will you answer this? — he is with me at this moment, just walked into town, pressing me to press you. My garden is beginning to look gay, and to comfort me with its trees, — and the orange and lemon blossoms send forth a fine rich odour. It is impossible for me to write for the New Monthly without a proper understanding on the subject. Up to this moment I know no more than an African if my "Italian Chat" has been published, — I sent three numbers, and hearing nothing, I could not go on writing in the dark. If not published, why have they not been sent to Mancur? There is no apology, — it is absolutely unfair and ungentlemanly in the Editor to keep me writing on without knowing whether the articles are or are not approved of. Possibly I may pull Mr Campbell's nose. Then, for this year, I sent "Gonnella" which I see has been printed; [13] but as the Articles are seldom specified in the Advertisements, in their new system of puffing, I have no idea whether my "Luciano & Giustina" or that on the "Misericordia" [14] has been printed. You will do me a great favour in letting me be acquainted with the *yes* or *no*, in answer to each of these doubts. At the same time give me information, for the which I am hungry, about what you are doing in the Mag, and what elsewhere, and how Colburn behaves to you. And let me know how your children are, and how Mrs Hunt is, and a million of other matters. Remember me kindly to her. If the "Chat" has been utterly disregarded, perhaps you will have the kindness to show the 3 Articles to the Editor of the Morning Chronicle,[15] as specimens of what I can furnish from Italy, and to ask him what he will be willing to pay me for a continuance of them. I have been damnably puzzled and vexed, and, what is worse, disappointed of certain pence. If any thing better than the Morning Chronicle scheme should strike you, pray tell it me, or rather do the kind thing towards me, and tell me afterwards. Carlino sends Henry a thousand kisses and compliments. Gianetti is all gratitude towards

[12] Marianne Hunt had made a cut-paper silhouette of Shelley within a year of his death, and a sculptured bust sometime afterward (White, *Shelley*, II, 520–521). Super, *Landor*, p. 546, thinks Landor's request may have been inspired by T. J. Hogg's recent visit and by his own trip to Rome, where he perhaps saw Shelley's grave.

[13] See number 80, n. 11.

[14] "I Fratelli della Misericordia — The Brotherhood of Mercy," *New Monthly Magazine*, 17 (1826): 503–509. Apparently "Luciano & Giustina" was never printed.

[15] John Black (1783–1855).

you for the Shakespear, and is endeavouring to translate Macbeth,
— we had a confab of an hour the other evening about the proper,
or at least the best, method of translating this line — "When the
hurly burly's done," [16] — but we could hit upon nothing to the
purpose. He certainly understands Shakespear very well. Mem:
whenever you want a glass of lemonade, you have merely to step
into my garden, pluck a lemon, call for a knife, a tumbler, water,
and powdered sugar, and "ecco fatto!" — pray don't be cere-
monious on this score.

Your's most sincerely,
Cha[s] Brown.

. 86 .

TO ROBERT FINCH

Address: Al Gentiluomo Inglese / Il Sig. Roberto Finch, / Roma.

Postmarks: Pisa; 22 GIVGNO

Endorsements: Rec[d] June 26° 1826.; Brown.

ALS: Bodleian Library. Extracts are printed by Nitchie, *The
Reverend Colonel Finch*, pp. 90–91.

My dear Sir,   Pisa. 19th June 1826.

As the worthy ironmonger sends his salutations to your Worship, I take the opportunity of sending my best compliments to
the ladies. Pray, how had Miss Thompson succeeded with her
green China? I'm a little jealous on this score, as I am making some
myself, and hate to be surpassed, though by the best and cleverest
of all possible ladies.

Of course you have seen the illumination here, so I shall only
tell you I was highly pleased with it, and that the night was clear
and still for the occasion, no doubt expressly got up by S. Ranieri
himself.[1] My everlasting boy is with me, and we shall return to
Florence in two or three days.

---

[16] I.i.3. Various translations read "Allor che al fin del marzial tumulto," "Al-
lorchè un tal tumulto non sarà più inteso," "Quando il tumulto sarà finito," "Allor
che, cessati i clamori," "Quando cessi dell' armi il frastuon," "Quando la zuffa sia al
fin combattuta."

[1] St. Rainerius (d. 1160), patron saint of Pisa. The illumination celebrated his
day, June 17.

When I left Florence all the town was agog about a hermit, who was saying prayers with a beard a foot and a half long, and performing miracles an age and a half too late, all on the top of a hill to the south of Fiesole, about five miles off. I had not time to pay so long a visit, though as curious as others to see the would-be Saint pop down on his knees to run over the litany, which, I was told, is his method of receiving company. Since I came here, I've heard a little more about him. The odour of his sanctity smelled so strongly at Ponte a Sieve, that the people there, not many days since, became tumultuous on his account. The miracle that had the best effect was that of the Angels' providing him with sand for the building of his little chapel in a wood. Now, whether this was specially offensive, as it represented the blessed orthodoxical Angels as belonging to the Order of Masons, or whether it was merely thought necessary to put a stop to the farce, I know not; but lo! the holy Hermit has had an action brought against him for having vaunted of working miracles, or of their being worked in his favour, — it's all the same. When I return, I must busy myself in this matter, for it will be worth witnessing, as of course the Angels will turn Advocates in the cause, — and then I shall know, what I never yet could comprehend, the precise meaning of an Angelic discourse.

I've just heard a bit of romance. Did you know an able and (they say) an honest lawyer here of the name of Scaramucci? Well, he died yesterday, and the Pisans are sorry to lose him. Now for the romantic part of the story. He pined away, and sighed his last, absolutely for love of another man's wife, the husband not being agreeable. This is very wrong. Here is a man put to death, purely because another man is not agreeable; — the lady was perfectly so, but that was not enough.

Will you have another spice of gossipping? You had better say "Yes!" for you can't help yourself at this distance. A Mʳ Grant of Leghorn,[2] one of Shylock's *good* men,[3] has married his woman-

---

[2] John Grant, merchant, of Grant, Pellan and Company, Leghorn. In 1822 he kept Shelley's ashes before forwarding them to Rome for burial, and in 1823 he apparently was Trelawny's financial agent (*Letters of Mary Shelley*, I, 191; Sharp, p. 130; *Letters of Trelawny*, p. 42).

[3] See *The Merchant of Venice*, I.iii.12-17. T. J. Hogg (*Two Hundred and Nine*

servant's daughter, having been honoured with a gracious dispensation from Rome, "con patto però" that all the children shall be Catholics. I like this, — it is so extreme; and I like the account of the wedding-feast, — it would have been wrong, on such an occasion, not to have it very splendid.

I have not heard for some time of Mr Leigh Hunt; the last was that his health was not good, and that may account for his not having written to me; — though I rather imagine there is something in the English atmosphere adverse to letter-writing, for I find all my friends there, except one,[4] most infamous in their correspondence.

So, you are mightily occupied, — and that's a good thing; and I am mightily idle, — and perhaps that's a better. Every man to his taste. Mr L. H. put me out of conceit of my Bianca Cappello, and so I cut her. At last I've discovered he was in the wrong, and so I've a will to be at her again; and so I've procured a letter to a learned Abbate, who is to overwhelm me with historical facts; and so, I suppose, I shall not be able to breathe under them; and so I shall be so-so again.

Have you read Lord Normanby's Novel, "Matilda, a tale of the day?" [5] Colburn has given him £700 for it! There is not much stuff in the novel, but it is written with a sort of vivacious ease and cleverness, with now and then an admirable bit, — but I can't tell why it is worth that sum of money, — Colburn can, no doubt.

There's a wedding about to take place in this house; and certainly Gordini is playing the part of uncle much better than most men play that of father. He deserves to be as happy as he is. I wonder where such a money-making man got at so much philosophy.

Your's most sincerely,
Chas Brown.

Days, I, 298) says that "the number of Jews [in Leghorn] was so great . . . that I left the place with real pleasure."

[4] Probably Dilke, who was planning a trip to Italy.

[5] Published by Colburn in 1825.

· 87 ·

FROM C. C. CLARKE [1]

ALS: British Museum.

19th June 1826

My dear Sir, On Saturday last I paid into the hands of Mr Mancur £5. *11. 6* for the Rossini's views of Rome you were so kind as to resign to me.[2] I am greatly pleased with my bargain, and this feeling should have induced me to have been more prompt in discharging my obligation to you in the more worldly and tangible sense of the word. The truth is, that though I *got* the prints, I *for*got my duty to pay for them. I request you to pardon me; and at the same time accept my best thanks for your kindness. You will be sorry to hear that our friend Novello is sadly out of health — but I will leave all the news to be told by our mutual friend Hunt (who I am pleased to say is in fine feather, and fiercer a great deal than the most "wrathful dove")[3] and whom, I am sure I should be paying you both a poor compliment, if I did feel and aknowledge you would prefer having to chat to you. So, fare you well my dear Sir, and believe me to be your's truly and obliged Charles Cowden Clarke.

[1] Since it is among Hunt's papers in the British Museum, this is probably the unforwarded letter that Brown refers to in number 106.

[2] Luigi Rossini's *Le Antichità romane, ossia raccolta delle più interessanti vedute di Roma antica* (Rome, 1820–1823). Clarke had requested Hunt to get him a set of these engravings in December 1824.

[3] *2 Henry IV*, III.ii.171.

· 88 ·

TO LEIGH HUNT

Address: Inghilterra. / To / Leigh Hunt Esqre / Care of Mr Hunter, / Bookseller, / St Paul's Church Yard, / London. / Angleterre

Postmarks: FIREN[ZE]; Toscana; I.T.; FPO NO 13 1826

ALS: British Museum.

My dear Hunt,   Florence. 29th October 1826.

Let me first look at the date of your last letter, — oh! the 22nd August! — not quite ten weeks ago. Now don't you think this delay of mine is serving you with a little of your own sauce? — that I have been guilty of it with malice prepense? You no doubt suspect me, — though no, — I give you credit for being more generous. If however you should have entertained so pestilent a notion, learn, to your confusion, that I did not receive said letter of 22nd Augt till nine days ago! It arrived here in due course, but unluckily I was on my rambles with Dilke & Co to Rome, Naples, and Pæstum, so the letter remained quietly in our Post Office till my return. For these last nine days I can account tolerably well, having had some ugly letters to write upon an urgent matter of business, and a melancholy one (at least for me, though I hope she will find it otherwise,) to my sister in-law, whose father lately destroyed himself. As I disliked the man himself, and as she was aware of it, nothing could be more drearily difficult than for me to write to her on this subject. Indeed I felt it so fearful a task, that I went to it in the midst of heavy sighs, and I accomplished it by resolving not to rise from the table till it was done; for I was compelled to write, she wished me to do so, and she and I are great favourites with each other; [1] and what was worse, she had a great love for her father. Now, if you please, we'll chat of something else. The Dillons set off this morning for England, — is that news? I met him yesterday, when he inquired where you lived, intending

---

[1] Possibly, therefore, she was the wife of Septimus Brown, the married brother nearest in age to Brown.

to call on you. I could only say you lived in a snug cottage at Highgate, — this was awkward, — I ought to know your exact address,
— nay, if it were but for my letters, as I am again compelled to
direct this to Mʳ Hunter's care. Miss Dillon is no more! — she is
now Mʳˢ Spencer,[2] and has made a good match of it, they say. She
and her "sposo" have set off on a trip to Rome. Landor and family
are very well, — they have returned into the city, and live in Via
Pandolfini. It was amusing to see him and Dilke together, each by
the side of his double; and, no doubt by sympathy, they seemed
to take a liking for each other.[3] Dilke has left his son with me for
two years; it was far from a pleasant parting, you may suppose,
when I tell you he always felt a cut in the heart at parting from
any body, — "figurativi" what he must have felt as he bade good
bye! and God bless you! to an only son for two years![4] I wonder
he did it. Oh! Dilke, to whom I read that savage sentence (against
yourself) in your letter, desired me to say he could not possibly
call on you, as you requested, before he set out, because he was
then within two days of setting out, with fifty thousand things to
do, all left, as usual, to the last. Kirkup will soon be back again to
Florence. I've managed that at last. Mʳ Geo. Hayter,[5] a great friend
of his, is with him in Parma; they'll come on together, I hope, in
about a week. Gianetti is at Pisa; the last he spoke to me about
you was a supplication for a small portion of my next letter, for
him to scribble on to your worship. I found Carlino very well,
when I returned from the South; and I am happy to tell you my
servant Maddalena has proved herself a very trustworthy person,
so much so that I have not a fault to find with her on the score of
honesty and regularity of conduct; the only point wherein she
annoys me is that she has no taste in setting out a table; — it is in
vain to teach her, — the next day every thing is forgotten, and all
the dishes are squinting at me; you must know I am a little more

[2] An error for Stanley. Lord Dillon's eldest daughter, Henrietta Maria (1807–
1895), married Edward John Stanley, afterward second Baron Stanley of Alderley
(1802–1869), in Florence on October 7.

[3] Many years later Dilke referred to Landor as Brown's "crack-brained friend of
Fiesole" (Forman, 1952, p. li; Bodurtha and Pope, p. 9n).

[4] In 1819 Dilke had "continually in his mouth 'My Boy,' " and had moved from
Hampstead to Westminster in order to educate him (*Letters*, II, 84). The boy remained with Brown for only eight months.

[5] Later Sir George (1792–1871), portrait and historical painter.

particular than usual on this matter, as I am now in possession of an uncommonly handsome service of real China. As for Carlino, he is a jewel; I think him clever, but I can't swear to that; but he has a most affectionate heart, — as a small proof of which he sends to you and your wife 100,000 kisses each, and to each of your children, especially Henry and Swinburn, 3,000; I give his own numbers, and leave you to count them as you will. We are very happy, and very merry together. Dilke says I'm a boy, — and that when I was a boy, I was an old man! Gad a'Mercy! what a monster does he make of me! Then seeing me flounce at this, away he flings himself into a compliment, protesting I am all wisdom in being a boy at my age, and that I was quite an idiot when I was younger; — this I call boxing one cheek and patting the other. By the by, now I think of it, though it never occurred to me before, that Dilke, that eternal Dilke, is using me very ill, because forsooth! he is a grave, fat, comely, old gentleman. Mem: I'm not so fat as I was, much handsomer than a twelvemonth ago, and shan't be forty till 14ᵗʰ April next, — while you have been (for how many years, eh?) a venerable senior between 40 and 50!! [6] My love to your Wife, and I thank Heaven, I'm too far off to have my ears smacked by her fair — (I might say, in one sense, unfair) — hands, — for truth is truth, as parish registers can certify. A thought comes across me, — quite a new one, — that the best comfort of wifedom (alias husbandom) is that one has, always close at hand, a champion, whom nobody in decency can challenge to the fight, ready to attack any person who whispers the slightest word against the pre-eminence of said *one*. Mem: Mʳ Landor is just now with me, and he desires to be well remembered. But it is high time to leave this gossipping, and to proceed to business. Know then, in the first place, you have not written to me like a precise man of business, — at which who can be astonished? — however such is the fact, and I'm a little in the dark as to your meaning. 1ˢᵗ Your friends advise you not to renew your offer to your brother, — good, — I was partly of their opinion, and am now more so. 2ⁿᵈ You say it must be referred to arbitrators (that is, my statement) that it may be settled whether it should be finally arbitrated, or settled by law. Now this, begging your par-

[6] Hunt had just turned forty-two.

don, is not to be understood; for arbitration is law, its award being as legally binding as any verdict in a Court of Law; and to have arbitrators to fix upon whether a matter is to be arbitrated is a strange course, for which I must make two statements, — one certainly unnecessary, and of no avail. If you mean that it may be thought that an action at law is more adviseable than arbitration, then I ought to wait for your determination, — but I believe arbitration will be fixed on. 3ʳᵈ If you and your friends resolve not to renew your offer, what has prevented you from demanding from your brother an arbitration, (which he and his son have declared he is ready to accede to, should it be thought necessary,) and from demanding of him to nominate, without delay, his arbitrator, specifying your own, and also from setting about to prepare a regular Arbitration-bond, which he and you must *sign*, or the award will not be binding on either party. Again, you must take care that power shall be given, in the bond, to the Arbitrators to examine and settle the Accounts. Those who know more than I do of law, can manage all this, — I merely know the matter in the rough, — and they will, no doubt, give as large power as possible to the Arbitrators. As for me I am prepared to commence the Statement, nay more, I am prepared to *conclude it at ten days notice*.[7] All I wait for is to know if it is to be carried to arbitration, if he J H does not fly off from his promise when it comes to the push, and who are the Arbitrators. You may answer to this, — "Never mind, — make your statement, — and we'll use it if it should be wanted." No, don't tell me so; because no man on earth can do a thing so well, nor take such pains, nor go to his task with spirit, when there is a doubt on his mind whether it will or will not be of use; — and surely I ought, in this instance, to do my very best. I long to begin, if only for the p{lea}sure, the actual pleasure of it, when certain of its being acted on{.} How will his and his son's contradictions (not to use a harsher term) appear when brought together in a string, and what volumes do they utter in your favour, not only in the general claim, but in respect to the Accounts. I am strongly of opinion, and I thought I said or hinted as much, that his statement of the present profits (nett) of

[7] Apparently Brown began the statement (number 91) in February 1827, but did not send it until the beginning of July (see the next two letters).

the Examiner is incorrect. There is a minor matter of business between *you and me*, which ought to be settled. I wrote you (in my last, I think)[8] that I had a balance against you of Pauls 42. 6; since that time Miss Edgeworth's works have been sold by Molini for Pauls 100, so of course I am become your debtor for Pauls 57. 2, which at 45¼ make £1. 5. 4. I forgot to write to Mancur in my last to pay you this, but, at the bott{om of} this sheet, I'll give you an order on him. If you do not[9]

* * *

There is no space for my travels with the Dilkes, otherwise I could spin you a yarn concerning our visits to Naples and Pæstum. But, thank Heaven! I *can* afford a few lines about Severn. Know then, I found him well in health, in high spirits, painting for ever with every one's applause, and with plenty of commissions for pictures; and what is yet better, beloved by every one, — nay honoured. I would not stay at the inn with the Dilkes while we were in Rome, but chose to be with my dear Severn, — and a happy time we had together. He says he'll come to Florence in April, and has some floating notions about a visit to England for a few months.

Your's ever, Cha[s] Brown.

[8] Number 85.
[9] The lower fourth of the second leaf is cut away.

· 89 ·

TO LEIGH HUNT

Address: Inghilterra. / To / Leigh Hunt Esqre / Care of Mr Hunter, / Bookseller, / N° 72 St Paul's Church Yard, / London. / Angleterre.

Postmarks: FIRENZE; Toscana; I.T.; FPO MR 6 1827

ALS: British Museum.

[February 19 (?), 1827]

*   *   *

[Could] ¹ you not afford half a line about him? ² Sir, he is worth more than any two letters that ever were written, — mind that! I suppose you did not know he was in Florence, — whew! he has been here ever since new year's day, — he and his. We've gained the victory at last, — tantara-ra, ra-tarra, — tantarrirrirra!!! Here he is, the police all graciousness, the "genitore" a greater black-guard than ever, Marina in our house as "aja del bambino di Signor Carlo Brown",³ and we sit down five to

*   *   *

20th Feby. I must begin this morning more seriously, — if I can. In the first place, let me seriously remonstrate with you on not giving me your address at Highgate; you let me know where it is, but that's not enough, — has the house neither name nor number? — you compel me to trouble Mr Hunter again. And how is Miss Kent? ⁴ Give my Carlino's love, and my own particular, to your Wife and children.

I have written so much on the question between you and your

---

¹ About five sixths of the first leaf is missing. The text given here begins near the bottom of the first page, and then (after the asterisks) skips to the lower sixth of the second page. The bracketed date for this fragmentary first part is purely a guess.

² Kirkup.

³ See number 79, n. 8.

⁴ Elizabeth Kent (d. 1861), Marianne Hunt's sister, author of *Flora Domestica* (1823) and *Sylvan Sketches* (1825).

brother, that with what is already done, and with another bushel of thought, I shall easily make out the statement. It will be divided thus: 1st a plain history of the matter; 2nd an argument as a matter of law; 3rd as a matter of justice; 4th as a matter of feeling; and 5th as a matter of accounts between you both, taking into consideration your debt &c. I only wait for orders, — and I *wait for them,* and to hear that the Arbitration bond is signed by both parties, because, even now, I look upon it as probable that your brother will offer to yield. His natural obstinacy may prevent him, but the question is whether that will not be overcome by his feeling he has not a leg to stand upon, together with the fear of what may be said in the Statement. Of course I shall not spare him; every thing that has happened *must* be put down, — and I shall do this without putting my constructions on his conduct, leaving that office to the Arbitrators, and to whomsoever may read it. I shall deal in facts, — his once favourite facts. The Jew shall have his bond.[5] Tell Marianne I shall be careful not to talk of *rescuuing* the partnership, especially as I was the first person to cry out against the phrase; and tell her also she has sent me one very good hint, that promise to over{come all} possible argument on his part; — I have noted it. {What you} have written about is also of use, — and so are a f{ew o}ther things you have mentioned. I think myself strong on all points, armour proof, and certain of victory. At the same time I am not vain enough to think it impossible I may commit some monstrous oversight or blunder in the statement, so I shall consult with Kirkup on it from first to last. I cannot imagine a better Arbitrator for you than Dilke. When he was here, I declined entering on the subject, lest it should be said that he commenced his office as a prejudiced judge.

Respecting your Memoirs,[6] — know I had heard of them long before you told me. They will be very interesting as far as Shelley, Keats, and Ld Byron are concerned. I can't promise so much for the remainder, where you speak of the living. There every reader will, and with justice, suppose you guilty of partiality. You will describe people as they have behaved to you, not their general

[5] *The Merchant of Venice,* III.iii.4ff.
[6] *Lord Byron and Some of His Contemporaries,* published by Colburn in 1828.

character. If you do otherwise, you will be different from all men else. As for myself, since you have threatened me, Sir, — I must tell you that every thing in my favour, coming from you, will give me pleasure; but the pleasure will by no means be increased by passing through a printer's dirty fingers, and by being read by ten thousand scoundrels. Then again, the living are rarely satisfied, and always dissatisfied at something. Every body has some particular dislike, or will fancy he has, when his character is intended to be spoken well of. For instance, you fell out with what Hazlitt meant as a compliment; [7] and I should fall out with being called amiable. I would lay a wager you have already called me so, — I would as soon you called me lovely! Besides, the world is not good natured enough to read memoirs in favour of the living; — the good must be dead, or imaginary characters. Let us hope that portion of your Memoirs is *short* & sweet.[8]

The Landors are very well. He is very angry at Colburn.[9] He desired me, whenever I wrote, to remember him to you.

You have given me an odd dream, a *waking* one.[10] I have supposed that you and I set up the "Companion",[11] — I with the drudgery and what money I could spare, — you with your everlasting talents, — and that we became amazingly rich. This of course supposes me in England, with fifty other suppositions. Dreaming is mightily pleasant.

Your's most sincerely,
Chas Brown.

Notwithstanding what I have said, I shall *begin* the Statement in a day or two, so as not to keep the Arbitrators waiting long for me.

[7] Hazlitt had written about Hunt most recently in *The Spirit of the Age* (1825) and *The Plain Speaker* (1826). See his *Complete Works*, ed. Howe, XI (1932), 176–178; XII (1931), 16–17, 38–39.

[8] See Brown's reaction to the published work in number 95.

[9] "Presumably for delays in the publication of further volumes of the *Imaginary Conversations*" (Super, *Landor*, p. 195). After Landor broke with Taylor and Hessey, Colburn issued a second edition of the first two volumes (1826) and the first edition of volume III (1828). James Duncan published the fourth and fifth volumes (1829).

[10] A common phrase in the period, but Brown is probably thinking specifically of "Ode to a Nightingale," l. 79.

[11] Later (see the opening of number 96) Hunt did establish a periodical called the *Companion*.

· 90 ·

TO LEIGH HUNT

Address: Inghilterra. / To / Leigh Hunt Esqre, / Care of Mr Johnson,[1] / Bookseller, / St Paul's Church-Yard, / London. / Angleterre.

Postmarks: FIRENZE; Toscana; I.T.

ALS: British Museum.

My dear Hunt,   Florence. 3 July 1827.

I wrote on 19 June.[2] There has been no second letter from you. I enclose the Statement.[3] Where you and your friends think I might have said more, or written in stronger language, any addition may be made, on another sheet of paper, by way of annotation, with reference to the numbered paragraphs. Only take care that nothing is said to commit yourself, for this is not the time for concessions.

I leave it also for you and your {fr}iends to consider if it would not be giving your brothe{r} an advantage over you to let him see your Sta{te}ment before he makes out his own; and if it would not be better to let him know no more of this than in a general and indistinct manner.

The vouchers are necessary for you in{deed.} I have therefore sent all letters and papers bet{ween us} to you (except copies i.e. Copies of my letter of 20 Augt 1824,[4] of the Deed, of my letter of 19 June last, and of the Statement, — nothing else.) packed up in one parcel {to the} care of Mr Dilke. His son, who left Floren{ce for} London a few days since, took charge of th{em.}

You will gratify me by letting me {know} that the letter of 19 June and this Statement {have} arrived safe.

When you gave back the letters you bor{rowed} of me (from

---

[1] Number 96 is similarly addressed to the care of "M^r J Johnson." Perhaps Hunter's establishment, at 72 St. Paul's Churchyard, still bore the name of its previous owner, Joseph Johnson (see number 77, n. 1).

[2] The letter is no longer extant.

[3] Number 91.

[4] Number 61.

your brother) I found, after you {left,} that one or two were missing. Can you find {them?} I wish you could find that one, excusing hi{mself} for not sending the Examiner Accounts, (see {. . .)} as it is of importance. If it is lost, don't say {a word;} don't let him hear that possibly it is lost. Is {not} Mrs Shelley a witness? — did she not read that letter?

Sad news for you! Think what a na{me} you must have left behind! Why, folks have hanged you in effigy, — here, in this good city of Florence! There you hang! — I see you at this moment, — and Severn opposite to you; they certainly are two very nice drawings by Kirkup,[5] and very nicely framed and glazed. Love to all.

Your's most truly, Chas B{rown.}

· 91 ·

CHARLES BROWN: STATEMENT OF A QUESTION OF PARTNERSHIP
(1827)[1]

MS: University of Iowa.

Statement of a question of Partnership in the Examiner Sunday Newspaper between John Hunt and Leigh Hunt.

Paragraph 1. Some time in December 1808 John Hunt and Leigh Hunt established the *Examiner* (see deed of Partnership.) Leigh Hunt's talents made it a valuable property.

Par. 2. On 1 January 1809, within a month after its establishment, James Whiting was admitted as a partner with them, he paying to them £800. Each of the three partners possessed an equal share in the proprietorship and profits, to him and to his heirs. John Hunt agreed to print the Newspaper gratis; and

---

[5] See Sharp's frontispiece for a portrait of Severn by Kirkup. The drawing of Hunt apparently has not survived.

[1] Enclosed with the preceding letter. As early as October 1826 Brown was "prepared to *conclude it* [the statement] *at ten days notice,*" and on the following February 20 he planned to begin it in "a day or two" (numbers 88, 89).

Leigh Hunt agreed to edit the Newspaper gratis. (see Deed of Partnership.)

Par. 3. After about ten years, James Whiting renounced his share in the partnership, upon an annuity being secured to him of £200. This renouncement, it is stated, took place in 1819.

Par. 4 Leigh Hunt, possibly before 1819, signed a paper, to what effect I cannot exactly state, but I believe it was giving up his *public* proprietorship. He was promised, at the time, a counter paper as his security; John Hunt never fulfilled that promise though repeatedly reminded of it. Whatever the paper was, however, the fact of John Hunt's leaving, for the following years, up to 1 January 1822, duly carried to the credit of Leigh Hunt one entire half of the nett profits of the bussiness, constituted him a partner, after signing the paper, as firmly as a regular law Deed. Besides, no valuable consideration was paid to Leigh Hunt for his share. My sole reason for alluding to this paper is that it is alluded to in the Correspondence between the brothers; for I am aware that John Hunt cannot bring that paper forward, not only on account of its invalidity, but because he gave the following assurance to Leigh Hunt, in a letter dated 8th Decr 1823: "Be assured that the paper you allude to, in which you renounced your proprietorship, if it exists at all, will never be brought forward in resistance of your claim. It was designed for a particular object which it answered.["]

Par. 5. In 1821 Leigh Hunt's health was in so declining a state, that he could not write so much for the Examiner as former-ly; yet still, up to the end of October, (he sailed for Italy early in November,) he wrote 31 Articles, and contributed 17 more, written by others at his request; that is 47 [2] in 43 weeks

Par. 6. As Leigh Hunt was advised on account of his con-tinued bad state of health, to reside for a time in a warmer climate, and as Lord Byron and Mr Shelley had invited him to Pisa, to join with them in a literary work, Leigh Hunt proposed to go to Italy, and John Hunt made no objection to it whatever; on the contrary he gave his consent, and afforded assistance to-wards the voyage.

[2] A slip of the pen for 48. The "others" were Brown and Richards (see number 61, n. 8).

Par. 7　Leigh Hunt, besides the reestablishment of his health, entertained hopes of advantage in a pecuniary point of view, not only for himself, but for John Hunt. It was Leigh Hunt's intention and wish equally to divide all pecuniary advantages, arising from his connexion with Lord Byron and Mr Shelley, with John Hunt.[3] In the end it happened so far otherwise, that Leigh Hunt enjoyed the proprietors profits arising from the *Liberal*, (the work established by Lord Byron and him) and that John Hunt enjoyed the profits in printing and publishing it, together with the profits arising from printing and publishing all Lord Byron's works,[4] and consequently the Establishment of himself and Son as Booksellers; for which great advantages John Hunt, as he has frequently acknowledged, was indebted to Leigh Hunt.

Par 8th　Leigh Hunt sailed for Italy early in November 1821. He was driven back by contrary winds, and eventually detained on the coast of Devonshire for some months. So far from not being considered as a partner at that time, John Hunt pointed out to him the propriety of preparing 16 articles for the Newspaper previously to quitting England, in order that his writing appear, as it generally had appeared, from week to week before the public until other articles could be forwarded by him from Pisa. Leigh Hunt engaged to prepare these 16 articles, but, from increasing ill health, he was unable to prepare more than 9 (See file of Examiner for 1822.).

Par 9.　On 24th Feby 1822, while Leigh Hunt was ill on the coast of Devonshire, John Hunt lowered the price of the Examiner from 10 pence to 7 pence.

Par 10　Oweing to various mischances, Leigh Hunt did not arrive at Pisa until June 1822. In a few weeks after his arrival Mr Shelley was drowned. One of the consequences of this misfortune was, that, losing his coadjutor in the Liberal, Leigh Hunt found

---

[3] On October 10, 1822, Hunt wrote to his brother (Brewer, *First Editions*, p. 120), "I wish to have no profit that I ought not to have, and you every profit that you ought to have. You understand me." Brown suggests in number 61 that Hunt's "expressions were indistinct and therefore misunderstood."

[4] Brown makes this point for the first time. Besides the *Liberal*, which contained "The Vision of Judgment," "Heaven and Earth," "The Blues," and the translation of a canto of Pulci's *Morgante*, John Hunt published *The Age of Bronze*, *The Island*, *Don Juan*, VI–XIV — all in 1823 — and *The Deformed Transformed* and the last two complete cantos of *Don Juan* in 1824. When he was prosecuted for publishing "The Vision of Judgment" Byron paid for his defense.

he could [not] do justice to that Work, which promised to be extremely lucrative, and to the Examiner at the same time. He therefore wrote to John Hunt [5] that he thought it was, for the interest of all parties, adviseable for him to confine his exertions, for a short time, to the establishment of the Liberal. John Hunt in his answer to that letter, made no objection to this proposition.

Par 11. At some time in 1823, Leigh Hunt, not having as was usual, received the last year's Examiner's accounts, wrote for them; when John Hunt excused himself from sending them, on the ground of the profits being so trifling, that it was not worth while to send them. Be it remarked, that this excuse was the farthest in the world that he did not regard Leigh Hunt, at that time as a partner; and be it further remarked, that John Hunt afterwards stated that the nett profits on the Examiner for 1822 and 1823 were £1400, of which, after deducting the two years annuity to James Whiting, there remained £500 for Leigh Hunt's share for those two years that is, £250, (or nearly so, I conceive,) for 1822, the year as asserted of trifling profit.

Par. 12. It must appear improbable, from the facts above stated, that John Hunt could have considered that Leigh Hunt had forfeited his share in the partnership from 1st Jan[y] 1822; nevertheless John Hunt ceased, from that date, to carry to Leigh Hunt's credit his half of the profits. But it must appear almost impossible, that John Hunt, having considered that such a forfeiture had taken place, should have retained Leigh Hunt's share of the profits, on the pretended ground of their being trifling, & never should have hinted at the alledged forfeiture till 19 Sept[r] 1823; nevertheless it was not till that day that he wrote to Leigh Hunt asking him his "opinion as to the extent of his claim &c," and, at the same time, forwarding him a general account of the previous year without any sum being carried to Leigh Hunt's credit for the profits on the Examiner. This startling letter was follow'd by another, dated 21st Oct[r] 1823, in which John Hunt plainly tells Leigh Hunt he will not, unless compelled, allow him to be a partner in the Examiner, giving his reasons for this determination, and talking of an allowance to be made to him, the amount of which he proposes shall be settled by Arbitration.

[5] In the letter cited in n. 3 above.

Par 13. Had Leigh Hunt been duly warned that, by quitting England, he would have forfeited his share in the partnership, he would not have quitted England; or had he afterwards been warned that he must of necessity continue to write for the Examiner, he would have abandoned all idea of the Liberal. John Hunt might have guessed this.

Par. 14 It may be worth while to enquire why John Hunt delayed to threaten Leigh Hunt with a forfeiture of partnership, until 19 Septr and 21 Octr 1823. At that time John Hunt knew that Leigh Hunt was destitute of all means of support except from the Examiner, because the Liberal (the last three numbers of which were not profitable) had ceased; he also knew that Leigh Hunt had not any money, in Banker's hands, or elsewhere, for his immediate support; and, be it noticed, he forbore, in those letters, to offer any relief to Leigh Hunt until the question should be decided. At that time John Hunt knew that Lord Byron had sailed for Greece, and might have supposed, as was really the case, (for even I was in Rome,) that Leigh Hunt was, in addition to his utter destitution, without a friend to advise him, or to assist him, in a foreign country, with a sick wife, and seven children, the eldest not thirteen years old, and the youngest a new born infant. Nay more, at that time John Hunt knew (see his letter of 3 Octr 1823) that Leigh Hunt had again fallen into a bad state of health, and consequently was unable to earn a subsistence for his family. Add to all which, at that very time, John Hunt was enjoying the advantages of being Lord Byrons publisher and Bookseller, — advantages to which he was indebted solely to Leigh Hunt, and for which he has expressed himself with thankfulness, saying "I hope it is not in my nature to forget the person who originated the benefit."

Par 15. But could John Hunt deprive Leigh Hunt of his share in the partnership? I contend he could not, according to the deed of partnership. I contend he could not, either, in law, in Justice, or in Good feeling, according to the facts I have above stated; and I further contend he could not, according to the deed of partnership. In that deed there is no clause of forfeiture of partnership [6]

[6] The question, says Thornton Hunt (*Correspondence of Leigh Hunt*, I, 245),

· 92 ·

TO ROBERT FINCH

Address: Robert Finch Esqre / Rome.

Endorsements: Rec^d April 18º 1829.; Brown.

ALS: Bodleian Library.

My dear Sir,   Florence. 10 April 1829.

Permit me to introduce to you Miss Cobbett and Mr Ja^s P. Cobbett; [1] and should you have it in your power, during their short stay in Rome, to be of any service to them, you will confer a favour on me, and, what is of more importance, a pleasure on yourself, which you will immediately comprehend upon becoming acquainted with them.

With best compliments to the ladies,

I remain, ever,

Your's most truly,

Chas Brown.

"was . . . submitted to arbitration, with an award in Leigh Hunt's favour; and his brother, influenced unquestionably by third parties, continued estranged from him for some years, until they were called together again by the sheer prompting of natural affection, to find that the grounds of quarrel had been the result of misconstruction on both sides."

[1] See the first paragraph of the next letter.

· 93 ·

TO ROBERT FINCH

Address: Robert Finch Esqre / Rome.

Postmarks: FIRENZE; 16 AP[RILE]

Endorsements: Rec^d April 16° 1829. Ans^d March 18° 1830.; Brown.

ALS: Bodleian Library. Part of the first paragraph is printed by Richardson, *The Everlasting Spell*, pp. 67–68.

My dear Sir,   Florence. 14 April 1829.

It is little to say that I take on myself the responsibility of introducing to you Miss and Mr Cobbett Junr,[1] because I am certain you will thank me. To you and me they have an interest, exclusive of themselves, on account of their father, who has effected more, in a political point of view, than any other man of his age. They have also interested me, inasmuch as, by their general conduct, and their veneration for their father, they give the lie to the million slanders that the venal press of England has poured forth against him, as an unworthy man, and a domestic tyrant; for though I never put faith in any of those slanders, it is pleasant to witness their direct contradiction. You will find his son and daughter good and sensible beings, without show, affectation, pretence, or presumption. Miss Cobbett is a greater favourite of mine than I have yet told her. They talk of making a fortnight's stay in Rome; but it appeared uncertain whether that fortnight will take place before or after their visit to Naples.[2] They left this on Saturday.

[1] One of William Cobbett's younger daughters, either Eleanor (1805–1900) or Susan (1807–1889), and his son James Paul (1803–1881). They had arrived in Florence on February 26, and departed for Rome on April 11 (carrying Brown's letter of introduction, number 92). James Cobbett subsequently published an account of their trip, *Journal of a Tour in Italy, and also in Part of France and Switzerland* (London, 1830), in which, under the dates April 3 and 4 (pp. 141–148), he quotes at length from Brown's 1826 article on the Misericordia and prints a detailed account of prices in Florence from a list that Brown had allowed him to copy.

[2] Actually they spent three weeks in Rome, visited Naples in the middle of May, and then returned to Rome to stay for two more months.

I seldom hear news of you, or of the ladies. Some time ago I heard you had been ill. If so, I am sorry for it; but I am not bound to give credit to it without a regular bulletin.

Soon after I had heard your friend, the Professor of "Borgo Allegri," so violently abuse plebeians, the common herd, the dregs of society, the refuse of humanity, base-born wretches, to be ruled by the lash, or, if they presume to murmur, by the sabre, — I was tempted to inquire, for he gave a fair challenge, who the said Professor was; when it turned out exactly as I had foreboded, — to wit, that he himself had but just emerged from the class of men whom he loaded with contumely, his brother having been a vetturino, not of the most respectable order, and his father something below that rank, — though I have now forgotten whether he was cobbler or what. It is a pity a man, like this Professor, a learned man, should have so little discretion, policy, and common sense. Had he not talked in that strain, I should have honoured him the more for having raised himself by his abilities, and sought his acquaintance. As it is, I seek him not.

You well know the English society of this good city. In addition to other accomplishments, it is now their fashion to lay bets upon every possible question. They will crowd, ladies and all, to the Cascine to see two men run a race, one with a third on his shoulders. If this were solely from the love of fun and frolick, it would be respectable; but it is nothing better than gaming. Opulent men and Noblemen are striving to outreach their neighbours in a bet; they talk of their gains in a worse style than a shopkeeper would; and they glory in taking others in, while they cry shame on the poor Italians who cheat them of a paul in their several vocations. I have therefore been much pleased with the conduct of a German Baron here; his name, I believe, is Rosenburg; for he, by his gentlemanly feeling, has thrown a reproof on our English. Mr Baring [3] betted with him a hundred Louis, or Naps, that he could not walk to Pisa in four and twenty hours. The German won his bet; and then, what did he? Instead of pocketing the sum, like a fellow, with a gentleman's coat on his back, who strives to turn his acquaintances to profit, he received

---

[3] George Baring, youngest son of Sir Francis Baring (1740–1810), founder of the banking firm (*Letters of Trelawny*, pp. 135–136).

the money, and gave it, merely deducting his own expences, in charity. It is true that, according to the opinions of many, he showed little charity, as the money was bestowed on Convents. That is another question. He gave it away, agreeably to *his* ideas of charity. At any rate, he scorned to profit by his feat, like a common prize-fighter, or a bravo.

I'm not a good newsmonger, — so you must not expect me to shine in that character. The newest thing I can think of at this moment is that Kirkup is, and has been for some time, very industrious. Morgan, living in the same house with me, has just popped his head up into my floor, and sends you his compliments.

Give my kindest remembrances to the ladies; and tell Miss Thompson I am sorry that her commission to forward letters from our Post-office came to nothing.

Your's most sincerely,
Chas Brown.

· 94 ·

TO LEIGH AND MARIANNE HUNT

Address: Inghilterra. / Leigh Hunt Esqre / Care of Mr Hunter, / 72 St Paul's Church Yard, / London. / Angleterre. (*readdressed to*: Woodcote Green / Epsom)

Postmarks: FIRENZE; Toscana; I.T.; FPO AU 24 1829; NOT PAID; AU A 24 1829

Endorsements: Brown; Rc^d 9th August [1] / Ans. the day of its arrival

ALS: British Museum.

My dear Hunt,   Florence. 9th August 1829.

Now that the weather is a little cooler, I'll write to you, Mrs Hunt, and my mother. I will not pen letters during the excessive heats, unless on business, or some compulsory matter. Either you mistook Trelawny, or he mistook me; I can't determine which,

---

[1] An error (see Brown's date and the postmarks) for August 24 or 25.

as he is at present at Ancona.² I never was angry at your not writing, because I never expected that, after a time, you would write; and all I told Trelawny was to remind you of my having foretold as much to yourself, just before you left Italy, while you were in the midst of resolutions to be an admirable correspondent. Do not imagine I can be such a fop as to be displeased at a friend's not writing for my pleasure. So much for apologies, which I neither like to give nor to receive. It is much more gratifying to deal in thanks; I am quite at home there; and therefore with all my heart I thank you for the books you have so kindly sent.³ They are not yet arrived, and Molini is bankrupt, but I shall have them notwithstanding. The best I can at present do in return will be to answer your questions about your friends and acquaintances here. In the first place, I am sorry to tell you that Kirkup has been very ill, for some months, with an affection of the liver; he is now a little better and a little stronger. Maria still lives with him. Before this illness he had been very industrious at his painting. Severn is wondrously happy; last September he was wived, and last month he was daughter'd.⁴ When he writes, he is brim full of delight, either about his painting or his wife, — and truly I like them both very much. They were married here, and they were with me every day for a week, so I saw a good deal of her. She was a Miss Montgomery. Landor and I are now old friends. He and all his family are in excellent health. Not long ago, partly owing to a mistake, he was banished from Tuscany. Down he sat and wrote an expostulatory letter to the Grand Duke, beginning in this way, — "Highness! I know not how to write a petition; and if I did, I would rather die than write one." The letter was very clever, and very manly. He fulfilled the awful sentence of the law by taking a trip to Lucca and Massa; when "Highness" ordered the sentence to be annulled, and he returned

---

² Trelawny moved in with Brown in February, went to Ancona in May, returned to Brown's house later in August, then moved to his own villa south of Florence in November (numbers 95, 96; *Letters of Trelawny*, pp. 116, 125).

³ See the opening of number 96.

⁴ Severn had married Elizabeth (d. 1862), daughter of Major General Lord Archibald Montgomerie (d. 1814) and ward of Lady Westmorland, at the British consulate in Florence on October 5, 1828 (Birkenhead, *Against Oblivion*, p. 151). Their first child was Claudia Fitzroy Severn (d. 1874).

to Florence roaring with laughter.[5] You ask me about Castelnuovo; I never saw him but once, when I gave him your book; it strikes me that some one told me the house was bankrupt. Now and then I take Maiano in my walks; your habitation remains just as you left it, even to the broken windows; I don't think any body has lived there since. La Signora Ristori is also much the same as when you last saw her; but her present Cavaliere has forbidden her to come to my house, — upon which, to set his mind perfectly at rest, I will not go to her's. Among all your inquiries you don't say a word about your Genoese Giuseppe. Alas! you may go into mourning for him. Soon after you left us he set up a wine cellar, in San Michele, close to where you had a flask of wine broken over your white trousers.[6] It seems he loved his profession too much, so much that he was in the habit of locking himself up in his own dearly beloved cellar; when, in about a couple of months, he there got, literally, dead drunk. Nobody missed him, — not even his wife, I suppose. However, in a few days, he contrived to revenge himself on us for our indifference, — at least on the passengers near his cellar door, and that most offensively. Come, let us leave him for a little fresh country air. You must know that now, living on the south of the Arno, I find the country at Bellosguardo, Arcetri, and other places, a thousand times more beautiful than at Fiesole and Maiano. It is not because the latter are farther off; for Carlino and I seldom find eight or ten miles too long a walk. You know nothing of Tuscany beyond a short stroll from villa Morandi, — you were never even at Settignano, where, near the ancient statue of Septimius Severus, there is a view of the most beautiful kind; nor did you ever go up to the old castles on the hills above your villa, nor visit the curious excavations in the hill which has given Florence its stone buildings; — you know nothing but that eternal walk from Florence to Maiano, and a few square yards about it, while I am acquainted with every

[5] Other accounts of Landor's banishment (for insulting the president of the Buon Governo) are given by Forster, *Landor*, II, 217–220, and in *Papers of a Critic*, I, 19–20. Landor published his letter to the Grand Duke, Leopold II (1797–1870), along with a defense of his conduct, in "High and Low Life in Italy," *Monthly Repository*, 1837, 1838; see Landor's *Complete Works*, ed. T. E. Welby, XI (London, 1930), 86–90.

[6] On his last day in Italy. See Hunt's *Lord Byron*, II, 387–388.

high road and by road all around me. On this account I cannot take you with me in my walks, otherwise I would tell you much of and concerning certain favourite spots. You had but one, — positively but one, — that cluster of wood in a hollow, where Westmacott cut a chestnut twig; [7] I am happy to tell you it remains in its old state, — not the twig, (for that was lost at Milan,) — but the scene. Of course I defer talking of ill fortune as long as I can, because it is painful, — and I, for self and friends, am all for pleasure; otherwise I would have, (before this,) noticed what you and Mrs Hunt say of your various disappointments. Yet, what can I say? — nothing, but that they grieve me, and that I hope you will meet with brighter days. When I was a card player I observed that I was certain of enjoying extraordinary good luck after a run of bad cards; and I have since thought that the world, with its flashes of good and evil, is much like a card table. May you, for the future, turn up an honour every deal, and win the game. From what I hear, there is no method of making much among the booksellers except by novel writing; therefore I am glad you are to write novels. [8] If ever it should happen that I am persevering, I'll write a novel, and it shall be, though I say it, a good one. Why, I have it all in my head; and, I assure you, it is one of the best that was never written. Write novels, — let sentiment spring unobtrusively out of character and incident, and you will succeed to your utmost wishes, and I shall roar out, "Let tales be trumps, he said, and trumps they were!" [9] So be it. The other half of this sheet of paper you are not to read, unless your wife should have the artifice to persuade you that nothing but the most innocent friendship is intended towards her by,

> Your's most sincerely, Chas Brown.

My dear Mrs Hunt,

With a thousand thanks for your letter, and a thousand and one for the profiles, (which are not yet arrived,) [10] I continue my

[7] In May 1824 (see Westmacott's letter in Sharp, p. 142). Hunt's "favourite nook," in the Vale of the Belle Donne, was on the grounds of Landor's new villa (see the opening of number 106).

[8] See the next letter.

[9] *The Rape of the Lock*, III.46 ("Let Spades . . .").

[10] At least one was presumably a profile of Shelley for Landor. Apparently Brown never received them (see numbers 85, 96).

pen to inform you of certain matters touching me and mine, which I did not think fit to tell your husband. Indeed your letter is a fair challenge to talk and expatiate on home. Know then, in the first place, that Kirkup and I have not the same home.[11] We separated from our inability to find a house suitable for us both; and it was absolutely necessary I should leave the house on the Piazza del Duomo, as there was no other bed chamber for me but one on the ground floor, which I discovered was unhealthy, as a complaint in my eyes could testify, and which I always ceased to have if I slept three nights away from that ground floor. I have been nearly a twelvemonth at N° 1905 Via Maggio, and had scarcely taken possession before I found out, what is not generally known, that it was the house of Petrarch! Many enthusiasts would think its extremely provoking that it should be one of the most modern looking houses in the city. However I am assured the walls were Petrarch's, and there is not a doubt of his having possessed a house on this site, the only one he or his father had in Florence.[12] Trelawny has been living with me, and will again when he returns from Ancona. This Petrarch's house is very comfortable, but I never shall be completely happy till I live in a villa surrounded by a garden. By an odd chance the villa most to my mind is that of Galilei at Arcetri, where the Dominicans annoyed him, and where Milton visited him. It is probable I may move into that villa next year.[13] With this view I am making love to the owner, a spacious lady of sixty, whose husband, (now in Heaven, poor man!) bought it out of pure veneration to the memory of Galilei; — think of that for a Tuscan farmer! Don't be jealous of this spacious lady. I assure you, on my honour, nothing has hitherto passed between her and me in any way improper, — unless it be the money I paid her for a barrel of Certosa wine. You inquire about Carlino; — know then it is confidently asserted that he is uncommonly like me; yet he is fair, slender, and tall for his age, —

---

[11] Kirkup and his mistress had come to live with him at the beginning of 1827.

[12] Actually Petrarch's family left Florence two years before the poet was born.

[13] He "cut the town" and moved into a villa, perhaps this one, in March 1832 (number 107). Milton mentions visiting "the famous *Galileo* grown old, a prisner to the Inquisition, for thinking in Astronomy otherwise then the Franciscan and Dominican licencers thought," in *Areopagitica — Works*, ed. F. A. Patterson, et al., IV (New York, 1931), 330.

all of which I am not. He sends love for love to Henry and your-self. He is strong and saucy, and has been very healthy since last year, when he had that frightful disease, the hooping cough, which, at one time, I thought would have put an end to his being, but sea bathing saved him. He had been four years at Miss Smith's school, when I took him, at Xmas, under my tuition; not that he learns so well with me as with her, but long walks upon the hills are of more use than books. Your hub says that Thornton is an author, and you say he is an artist; I suppose he is both, and I hope he'll suc-ceed in both.[14] Remember me to him, and to all who remember me. As it generally happens, you in England talk more of coming to Italy than we Italians talk of visiting England. Certainly I have no great wish to be found on the other side of the Alps; neverthe-less I think, in about a couple of years or so, I shall be on a pilgrimage to my old friends.[15] Mentioning old friends puts me in mind of Madam Lombardi,[16] whom I saw some time ago, when she talked to me of buying another house. "Really," said I, "you have made soap and water answer very well in this world." "Why Sir," she replied, "God Almighty has been very *good* to ME!" Kirkup has just come in, and desires to be remembered to all your family. Of course you will not allow Mr Hunt to read this letter; but pray ask him, from me, if Colburn would *engage* to purchase a novel in two or three vols *to be* written by me. If so, I imagine I should be industrious enough to write mine.[17] If Colburn wants a notion of it, let him understand that the scene would be in Florence about three hundred years ago, immediately after the destruction of the republic.

With best wishes, I remain,

Your's most truly, Chas Brown.

[14] According to the *Dictionary of National Biography*, Hunt intended to make Thornton "an artist, and with this view . . . [Thornton] passed some time in a studio. He soon, however wearied of the scheme, but he obtained work as an art critic."

[15] He did not visit England until 1833 (number 108, n. 1).

[16] Signora Lambardi, Hunt's washerwoman in Florence.

[17] The novel about Bianca Capello.

· 95 ·

TO LEIGH HUNT

Address: Inghilterra. / To / Leigh Hunt Esqre, / care of Mr Hunter, / 72 St Paul's Church Yard, / London. / Angleterre. (*readdressed to*: Epsom)

Postmarks: FIRENZE; Toscana; I.T; FPO SE 28 1829; NOT PAID

ALS: British Museum.

My dear Hunt,   Florence. 14 Septr 1829.
    The answering my letter by return of post [1] was an extraordinary flourish on your part. Lest you should, at some less flourishing period, be put too much to shame, I refrain from taking up my pen to inform you &c, until five days after the arrival of your letter, though its cheerfulness might have, otherwise, induced me to keep up the ball without a moment's pause. Think of my provident charity! It really gives me great pleasure to find you writing in so much better spirits. This I ascribe to two causes: 1st the novel being finished; and 2nd its turning to good account.[2] I have no doubt of your making more by novel-writing, if you choose to stick to it, than ever you made by the Examiner in its most glorious days. There is doubtless a third reason for your happy mood, — you and your family being in good health. You tell me not to let your novel-authorship get wind; I do not, for I have only talked of it to Trelawny, who, as he lives with me, must know it. But why not tell me its name, and its subject? — the secret would not be the worse kept. In a novel a man may give vent to all his opinions, without offence, through the mouths of his characters; which is of use to most people, but absolutely necessary to you.[3] In other works, — for instance, your Ld Byron, — I

---

[1] See Hunt's endorsement on number 94.
[2] *Sir Ralph Esher: or, Adventures of a Gentleman of the Court of Charles II*, 3 vols., not issued by Colburn until January 1832. Hunt expected to be paid for it at the *New Monthly Magazine's* rate of a guinea per page (Brewer, *First Editions*, p. 153).
[3] In his *Autobiography* (ed. J. E. Morpurgo, London, 1949, pp. 416, 418) Hunt calls *Sir Ralph Esher* "a fictitious autobiography," and says that it was represented

wish I and others were at your elbow when you wrote it; for
there are some things I would have had omitted, some changed,
and the whole of your obligations to him put in quite a different
light; so that, I think, you would have stood on higher ground,
defying your enemies. Don't think I am going to play the critic
on the three vols; [4] however, you surprised me when I saw your
friends' names at full length, — you used to put their initials only;
and, to give you a slap, I was angry at your publicly noticing my
grave face, — my curse.[5] Had I a hump-back, would you have
called every one's attention to it? It is only different in degree; de-
formities, defects, and peculiarities are of the same class, though
of distinct species. Few have the courage to complain of these
notices, either in company or in books, as it calls their good temper in question, and holds up their vanity, and therefore many
think it all fair. Now I do not, and I have that courage. This I do
because you complain of something Landor has written. He never
talked to me of having aimed any thing at you; nor have I seen any
thing that could be so construed; but I have not seen his last
volume.[6] I hope he has not, because I hate the present literary
fashion of being personal. He never told me he disliked what you
have said of himself and family; but, had it been my case, I should
have been half mad, if only on account of exposing the privacy of
my fire-side. Hazlitt, on these matters, is atrocious; I have learnt
to detest, to loathe his "Spirits of the Age." Landor has purchased
a handsome villa, gardens, and podere, — a mile in circuit; it is
Villa Gherardeschi, near Fiesole, in the hollow, below the Doccia.
He says he has paid a great deal for air and water,[7] — but he has

---

as a novel against his wishes. G. H. Lewes observed in 1840 (Blunden, *Leigh Hunt*,
p. 277) that the work lacked "intellectual ventriloquism — all the characters speak
L. H. more or less."

[4] Perhaps Brown refers to both the first edition and the second (two-volume)
edition of *Lord Byron and Some of His Contemporaries*. Later in the month (see
the next letter) he received from Hunt the second edition, which with the
Companion also made "three vols."

[5] Hunt wrote (*Lord Byron*, II, 388), "the grave face of Brown (who had stayed
all night, and was to continue doing us good after we had gone, by seeing to our
goods and chattels,) was not so easily to be parted with. I was obliged to gulp
down a sensation in the throat, such as men cannot very well afford to confess 'in
these degenerate days.' " Brown can hardly have been angered by this tribute.

[6] The fifth volume of *Imaginary Conversations* (see the next letter).

[7] "Landor was rather fond of saying that he got the place at a bargain, but
the vendor had no cause for complaint: Landor paid him 8,600 *scudi fiorentini*

them both good. Kirkup is much better. Mrs Severn, and, consequently, the infant, have been ill; but, by the last Roman news, they are well. You mistake when you imagine we have cribbed your summer in addition to our own. We have certainly had hot weather; but it began late, and was pretty well over when I wrote to you. Trelawny returned soon after; and on 30th August, he, in Florence, burnt an old chair in my chimney piece to obtain a little warmth! I was walking at that time, buttoned up close. About a week ago we thought we had a second summer; — no such thing, — it soon turned to clouds, rain, wind, and cold. You wrote to me in a high wind, and I write to you in another; — "go to, there's sympathy." [8] With so little sun, for even our hottest weather was generally cloudy, I despaired of eating ripe fruit. Yet, I know not how, the grapes are wonderful this year; — I have just eaten above three pounds of the most delicious that can be imagined. After all, our summer, bad as I think it, is better than ever I saw, except once, in England. We live in an odd Eastern fashion; speaking of myself, — without coffee and smoking, — it stands thus: I rise ad libitum; at eight I take a mouthful of bread, and two of milk and water; at twelve I dine; sometimes I have tea, — at two! then I walk, or read, or write, till eight, when I sup. You would willingly lay down rules for health,[9] — I know an infallible one; eat, drink, sleep as your inclinations lead you; walk or sit, as ditto; but watch your bowels, — they are the *leading strings* of our system. Now I'll put you into a violent passion; — I have been studying Mother Rundell and Father Kitchener,[10] — and the result is this in my store room; — 200 Tuscan pounds weight, including cherry brandy, of preserves; of sauces, various, 2 gallons; mushroom ketchup, 2 bottles; d° powder 10 pounds; ditto pickled 2 quarts; mixed pickle 2 gallons; pickled wallnuts 3 quarts. I know that, as you read this list, you are stamping your feet, and tearing your hair, calling me lost! lost! lost! Yet, it is very odd, if any body

for the property, which less than two years before he had purchased from the Count Gherardesca for 6,400 *scudi*" (Super, *Landor,* pp. 208–209).

[8] *The Merry Wives of Windsor,* II.i.7.

[9] In *Lord Byron* (I, 27) Hunt says, "The great secret in . . . almost all moral as well as physical cases of ill, is in diet. If some demi-god could regulate for mankind what they should eat and drink, he would put an end, at one stroke, to half the troubles which the world undergo."

[10] Maria Eliza Rundell, *A New System of Domestic Cookery* (1808), and William Kitchiner, *Apicius Redivivus; or, The Cook's Oracle* (1817).

happens to dine with me at our early hour, I only find a certain portion of the list lost! lost! lost! — without a word of abuse; and Trelawny, who loves sweet and poignant touches by turns, when he hears me boast of my store, puts on a frown, and reminds me there is a long winter before us, shaking his head at the notion of my being *out*, before the next season is *in*. Mem: brandy peaches must now be put in practice, or he will frown at me throughout the winter. Now after having thrown you into this violent passion, I will be equally provoking by telling you of your presumption, — you pretend to have walked in Tuscany! — nay, what is worse, what is most unpardonable, you pretend to have visited Arcetri. Set your soul at rest on that score. You never visited Arcetri. It seems that you fancied such a thing, when you went with Landor to Bellosguardo, a most inferior place, to see old Smith, who is as young as ever, only that he grows deaf, and won't own it, and is more dirty. Bellosguardo has not a handsome tree of any sort, owing to the clay-soil. Arcetri stands higher, has a rich soil, — is beyond and above the Poggio Imperiale, — has a tower, where Galilei took his "osservazioni" as the peasants there call it, and whence there is one of the most commanding panoramas I ever saw. Do you confess your ignorance? What! tilt with me, of and concerning the vicinities! What! attempt to palm on me a pilgrimage to my future, (quondam Galilei's) dwelling! — it is unbearable. I wonder you're not ashamed of yourself; — but, perhaps, by this time, you are. Then, how could you have been at Settignano, and not see the great statue, staring every one in his face, just beyond the piazza, of Septimius Severus, with the elephants' heads at the four corners of the pedestal, and the inscription, saying — I forget what. Oh! you confess you've not been to the old castles, — well, that is a virtue! One day when I went to the upper castle, I pulled out my luncheon of crust, because it is delightful to eat it in the high air, when out rushed a large Dog from the castle, now inhabited by tanners. To stop his furious barking I threw him a corner of my luncheon; upon which he came up to me, wagged his tail, *licked my hand*, and begged strenuously for more. I gave it him; eat more; gave more; till at last, finding my own crust grow scanty, I popped the remainder in my mouth. The *moment* this was done, before I could bite it, he flew at me like a tiger. I have never liked dogs, indiscriminately, since. I had a switch in my hand, and had the pleasure, for a minute, of proving the ungrateful scoundrel to be a coward. A woman came out to relieve me. I expatiated on the brutality of her dog; — "Che!" quoth she, "è il suo naturale!" I offered her two crowns to let me hang him. "Che!" quoth she, "vale più di dieci!" When I told Landor, the friend of dogs, of this, he swore he must be a Florentine, — it then being his humour to abuse Florentines! Carlino sends his love to all, but to Henry in particular. (It blows so hard at this moment, that there is a crash on the other side of the way of windows breaking, and we dare not open a door, the windows being open for air, without great precaution, and some strength, lest the slam should tear off the hinges.) ((Talking of slams I have latterly recommenced whist, and, as usual, I, with my cold blooded calculations, beat all the table.)) I can't conceive why you call your wife my Thisbe; — do you mean to say I am Bottom, — with a large B? Give my love to her, not in a whisper, but so that the neighbourhood may hear it; and I give you leave to kiss her twice during the next month. I ought to have left a corner to answer her corner, but you have so occupied me in this sheet, that I find I must have a pair of sheets for her. Your's truly CB

· 96 ·

TO LEIGH HUNT

Address: Inghilterra. / Leigh Hunt Esqʳᵉ / Care of Mʳ J Johnson / Bookseller / St Paul's Church-yard / London. / Angleterre. (*readdressed to*: Knights Cottage / Cromwell Lane / Old Brompton)

Postmarks: FIRENZE; I.T; FPO [. . .] 1829

ALS: British Museum.

My dear Hunt,   Florence. 28 Novʳ 1829.
    About a fortnight after I last wrote to you, on 14 Septʳ, Molini sent me the two Vols of Byron and the "Companion." [1]

---

[1] The second edition (1828) of *Lord Byron* and the *Companion* (1828), a periodical that ran from January 9 to July 23, 1828.

I should of course have acknowledged the receipt of them earlier, and repeated my thanks, but of course I fancied I should soon hear again from you, and you of course have not written another word. That's a very savage sentence, I must confess, from one who ought to be particularly civil. Will you have the truth of it? I took it into my head, from your silence, that I had offended you in my last, by protesting against your public notice of a private man's grave face. Was I right? If so, I don't think you are quite right; for the devil's in it if, among our few privileges, we may not say what we like and dislike. I have inquired of Landor if he had been quipping you as a biographer of the dead; and he, with a most negative and astonished face, declared that such a thing never entered his head, and that there is not a passage in his "Conversations" that can lead to such a notion. Here his memory failed him; for yesterday I read his last vol, and found the passage in Izaac Walton's talk about Donne; [2] — however, that Conversation, I believe, was written more than two years ago. He further added, "So far from thinking of quipping him, I had determined to speak of him, or of one of his works, in the best way I could, — which I have done, where I speak of his "Indicator." [3] He also desired me, when I wrote, to wrap up his remembrances to you. In case I should not have told you before, let me now tell you he has bought a handsome villa and podere near Fiesole, in the vale under the Doccia. I like your "Companion" as I like all that sort of writing of your's, — or almost as much; for, taking it as a whole, it does not delight me so much as the "Indicator." This, I conjecture, arises from its noticing several passing occurrences in England, which cannot greatly interest a Florentine, — though very likely that very thing made it the more acceptable to the Londoners. The papers which pleased me most were "Chapelle's trip," and "Walks home by night in bad weather", — the last I pronounce inimitable, — I walked with you all the way, and was an Englishman again. The books came separate, not in a parcel; and it was in vain for me to demand a packet which you spoke of,

[2] "Izaac Walton, Cotton, and William Oldways," the final conversation in the fifth volume (1829) of *Imaginary Conversations.*
[3] In a note appended to "Leofric and Godiva," the next-to-last conversation in the same volume.

and the silouettes which Mrs Hunt was so kind as to send; [4] — tell her, with my love, that the rogues know their value, and won't give them up; and Mem. the vols of Byron want his silouette and your portrait,[5] — how came that about? Kirkup is perfectly recovered; and, moreover, is again a widower, Marina being married to an actor, who bears a good character, is young, and picks up a pretty penny by playing Stentorello.[6] What a lucky fellow Kirkup is to get rid so well of two incumbrances! — for a mistress, after awhile, is generally an incumbrance, tied to a man almost as firmly as a wife, — without their interests being mutual, and without (as the world goes) the respectability, — which last I care very little about, — yet it is something. There are such things as mistresses who are a thousand times better than wives, but I've never met with one that w{as} not all for self, — nor, in my opinio{n}, has Kirkup. The best mistress that ever I heard of was Hayter's, — the painter's; and she poisoned herself here in Florence. He was surprised to find that society, particularly the female part, and the *married*, put its own construction on the case, without asking a question, and turned him adrift; so that he was compelled to quit Florence for Rome, — where again every door was shut against him, — and then he wisely went out of Italy. Another Englishman attempted to murder his wife, in an odd way, here in Tuscany. He came to her with a knife, saying, "My dear, I must rid you of such a wicked monster as I am!" — "For God's sake, don't lay violent hands on yourself!" — Oh, no, my love, — don't be afraid of that; I'm going to rid you of an infamous husband by sending *you* to Heaven, — it's a duty I owe you, my sweet soul!" She ran for her life, and saved it. He, being never sober, staggerred in the pursuit. There's an incident for your next novel, — quite original certainly. Pray is your first novel out? — whisper the name of it in my ear, — and let me know when I may talk about it. What else have I to say? — Oh! I've again turned to whist, and go to parties, — am invited every night throughout the winter, and only go three times a week, — there's moderation! Col. Wardle is here,[7]

---

[4] See number 94, n. 10.

[5] The frontispieces to volumes I and II.

[6] A mask of the Florentine theater representing a poor half-starved wretch.

[7] Gwyllym Lloyd Wardle (1762?–1833), soldier and politician. He had saved Hunt and the *Examiner* from government prosecution in 1809.

— he has me every Sunday, — I like him much. Trelawny abuses me therefore (i.e. for whisting), — he has left me to live in a villa a couple of miles from the Roman gate, on the top of a considerable hill.[8] Your's most truly Cha[s] Brown.

· 97 ·

TO C. W. DILKE

Address (mostly torn away): {Cha[s] Wentworth Dilke} Esq[re] / {Navy Pay} Office / {Somerset} house / {Lo}ndon.

Postmark: [F]IRENZE

AL: Keats House, Hampstead. Printed by Richardson, *The Everlasting Spell*, pp. 198–200.

My dear Dilke,   Florence. 17 December 1829.

In answer to your favour of 31st July 1824, or rather in second answer, for the first I sent on 6th Sept[r] 1824,[1] I beg leave to inform you, — but first I must wish you a merry Christmas and a happy new year, the usual beef, ham, turkey, plum pudding, mince pies, and a bowl of punch of my own making; — ditto to wife, — ditto to Wentworth,[2] and ditto to all I know; — Carlino tells me he wished to say all that, but he is too late. Now for my second answer to your favour of 31st July 1824. No, I can't come to that yet; for I've a story to tell first. (I think, if I had studied it, I could not have commenced my letter with a more astounding interest; — but let that rest.) A few days ago, I received a letter from Galignani in Paris, asking me for Keats's autograph, and telling me they were on the eve of publishing his works. I had heard of this, wished to communicate with them, and was told the volume was published,[3] — so, with regret, I remained silent. It appears, however, I was in time. I have answered them in a manner to make

---

[8] Trelawny describes the villa in two letters to Claire Clairmont, December 10, 1829, and March 8, 1830 (*Letters of Trelawny*, pp. 131–132). His three-year-old daughter Zella had recently come to live with him.

[1] See numbers 60, 63.

[2] Dilke's son.

[3] *The Poetical Works of Coleridge, Shelley, and Keats* (Paris, 1829).

them wish for my pen, and Keats's Mss, — now, perhaps, too late to enter into an arrangement with them. Be that as it may, (your father's favourite expression,) I am resolved, seeing that Keats is better valued, to write his life.[4] I can find time for it and Trelawny's work together,[5] — with a spice of fagging, to which I have not the slightest objection. In doing this I shall want the letter from George to you, of which you gave me a loose account in the said letter of 31st July 1824, — or a copy of George's, — and that as soon as convenient. Fact is, your account of the business was, as I thought at the time, though I was willing to take the best side, lame in the extreme. I think his may be a better story, and therefore wish to see it. Besides, upon taking it into my head it is time to write Keats's life, I read a packet of letters, in which I found a few things against your statement, (if statement it may be called,) and a letter from Abbey, addressed to Keats, upbraiding him for having given or lent, (no matter which,) all his money to George. Then again, I have one of Abbey's Accts Current with Keats,[6] wherein there are two or three matters which I cannot reconcile with what, you say, George asserts. There are also, taking them in their general tenour, documents much against George. You will guess from this that I do not think George has been calumniated, unknowingly by Keats, and afterwards by me, in repetition. You will give me credit for wishing to see things in the best view, if I can. Then, be not fearful that I will make a cruel use of the letter from George; quite the contrary; all that I want is authority for stating that Keats's generosity to Tom when under age, and to George after 21, diminished his fortune, or rather finished it, — or something to that effect, — I mean that it shall not be a

---

[4] Brown's "Life" of Keats, published first by Bodurtha and Pope in 1937 and then by Rollins in *KC*, II, 52–97, is mentioned many times hereafter in these letters.

[5] "I am actually writing my own life," Trelawny told Mary Shelley on March 11. "Brown and Landor are spurring me on, and are to review it sheet by sheet, as it is written" (*Letters of Trelawny*, p. 117 — see also pp. 120, 133, 140–141, and *Letters of Mary Shelley*, II, 40). Brown not only "reviewed" but actually rewrote *Adventures of a Younger Son*, according to Carlino (*KC*, I, lix), who adds that "Trelawny recognized Brown's assistance, by dividing with him the proceeds of the two editions [1831, 1835] that were published." For other details see number 107. Brown also rewrote a letter to the *Literary Gazette* for Trelawny, and was to have a hand in his life of Shelley, which, however, because of Mary Shelley's disapproval, was not written during Brown's lifetime (*Letters of Trelawny*, pp. 143, 117, 118n).

[6] For Abbey's letter and the account see number 108.

stigma on George, — you understand me of course. Now, taking
the uncharitable side, in answer to George's saying he ever avoided
mentioning to Keats his poverty, — I have proofs to the contrary;
and proofs of George's extravagance, in a letter from Keats to him,
and to Abbey.[7] I know that Keats himself never was extravagant;
that he well was aware of the value of money; that he could well
understand an account, — though latterly (though I would not
permit it) he wished to avoid examining any; that he, as he told
me, impoverished himself by lending money to George before he
was of age, and that George repaid him in the lump, without an
account, which Keats believed he kept, and therefore Keats did
not; and moreover that this sum, paid on George's first going to
America, was not to Keats, or to my mind, satisfactory. All this is
between ourselves. I only want George's own statement, word for
word, — not, as you see, for any harsh purpose.

If, in any letters from Keats to you, there should be some passages worth recording, (for his entire letters, unless on very particular occasions, ought not to be printed,) let me have them, —
with the *dates* of the letters, — for the dates are of importance to
me.[8]

Do you remember advising me never to mention Keats's origin
to Hunt? I never did. He learnt it, I suppose, from Clarke, a little
while before he wrote the Account of Keats. Think what a use he
has made of that information; — "his origin was of the humblest
description; he was born at a livery stables in Moorfields &c."[9]
Now I can state all that affair, without telling a lie, in a more
decent manner.[10] Thank heaven, there is damned bad grammar in
Hunt's indecency! As the world goes, (though you and I would not
have cared if Keats had been the hangman's bastard,) such bald
and untrue words may have a bad effect, — for they are untrue, as
far as *humblest* is concerned, and even as far as *a* livery stable*s* is
concerned; he, Hunt, ought to have known better, because, though

[7] Keats's two letters (mentioned again in numbers 98, 101) are not now known.

[8] Because Brown wanted to trace "the development of his mind as a poet"
(numbers 102, 106).

[9] *Lord Byron*, I, 409.

[10] In his "Life" of Keats (*KC*, II, 54) Brown wrote simply that "John Keats was
born in Moorfields on 29th October 1796. His father was a native of Devonshire,
and married a daughter of the proprietor of an inn."

it is true a God was born in a manger, his admirers, or worshipers, or priests would rather he had been born in a palace. I hate Hunt's account of him, though every sentence, I verily believe, was intended to his honour and fame; but what does that matter when he manages to make him a whining, puling boy? The truth is, Hunt seems to be so much impressed by his illness, that he forgets he was ever in good health. How odd, — Hunt must make some vile mistake.

I ha [11]

*   *   *

· 98 ·

TO FANNY BRAWNE

Address: Inghilterra. / Miss Brawne, / Wentworth Place, / Hampstead, / near London. / Angleterre.

Postmarks: FIRENZE; I.T; FPO DE 29 1829; 10 F-NOON 10 DE 29 1829

ALS: Keats House, Hampstead. Printed by Williamson, pp. 87–88 (with a facsimile, plates XLIX–LI), and in Forman (1952), pp. lx–lxi.

My dear Miss Brawne,   Florence. 17 December 1829.

Without any apology for our long silence, let me hope you are in the best health, that your mother is better, and that Margaret is never ailing; [1] to which I add a merry Xmas and a happy new year to all. Now, with these good wishes, I may begin.

A few days ago I received a letter from the Galignani in Paris telling me they are on the eve of publishing the works of Keats, and asking for his autograph. [2] I sent it to them, with a letter stating it was always my intention to write his life, and annex it to a Tragedy of his, [3] together with some unpublished poems in

---

[11] About half of the second leaf is torn away.

[1] Brown did not know that Mrs. Brawne had died suddenly on November 23. Margaret was Fanny's younger sister.

[2] See the preceding letter.

[3] *Otho the Great.*

my possession, whenever his countrymen should have learnt to value his poetry. I also told them I believed that time was arrived, as needs it must, sooner or later; but that I was fearful it was too late for me to enter into any arrangement with them. Whatever their answer may be, I am resolved to write his life, persuaded that no one, except yourself, knew him better. Leigh Hunt's account of him is worse than disappointing; I cannot bear it; it seems as if Hunt was so impressed by his illness, that he had utterly forgotten him in health. This is a dreadful mistake, because it is our duty to his memory to show the ruin his enemies had effected; and I will not spare them. It is not my present purpose to enter into any criticism on his works, but to let it be simply a biography; and, to make that as vivid as possible, I shall incorporate into it passages from letters to me, and to his brothers, — which last are in my possession; together with passages from particular poems, or entire ones, relating to himself, always avoiding those which regard you, unless you let me know that I may, without mentioning your name, introduce them. There are, however, two of his letters which I wish to give entire; one written when he despaired of Tom's recovery, the other when he despaired of his own.[4] This latter one is of the most painful description; therefore I wish it to be known, that Gifford and Lockhart may be thoroughly hated and despised.[5] The question is whether you will object to it; I think you will not. Though much of it regards you, your name is never once mentioned. Then again, those poems addressed to you, which you permitted me to copy, — may I publish them? It is impossible for me to judge of your feelings on the subject; but whatever they are, you are certain that I shall obey them. To my mind, you ought to consent, as no greater honour can be paid to a woman than to be beloved by such a man as Keats. I am aware that, at a more recent period, you would have been startled at its being alluded to; but consider that eight years have now passed away; and now, no one, if you do not, can object to it. Besides, Hunt has alluded to you, and what more will it be

---

[4] The first (now lost) is probably the letter that George answered on March 18, 1818 (*Letters*, I, 247–248). For the second (to Brown, November 1, 2, 1820) see *Letters*, II, 351–352. No letters from Keats to his brothers were included in the "Life."

[5] See number 26, n. 3.

to give his poems addressed to that lady? [6] Your name will still remain as secret to the world as before. I shall of course scrupulously avoid intimating who you are, or in what part of England you reside.[7] As his love for you formed so great a part of him, we may be doing him an injustice in being silent on it: Indeed something must be said especially as Hunt has said something. We live among strange customs; for had you been husband and wife, though but for an hour, every one would have thought himself at liberty publicly to speak of, and all about you; but as you were only so in your hearts, it seems, as it were, improper. Think of it in your best train for thinking, my dear Miss Brawne, and let me know your decision.[8] I have turned it in my mind a great deal, and find nothing, — to confess the truth freely, — against it.

Three months ago I heard you were at Bruges, on a visit to your aunt; [9] but I suppose you are, by this time, returned. Give my kindest remembrances to Mrs Brawne and Margaret. Carlino and I lead very comfortable, happy, healthy lives, with short lessons, long walks, and, now and then, a game at romps, or a "ballo grande" at the Opera. Believe me always

Your's most sincerely,

Chas Brown.

[6] Hunt wrote about the love affair only in the most general terms (*Lord Byron*, I, 439–440) — for example, "[Keats's] trouble was secretly aggravated by a very tender circumstance, which I can but allude to thus publicly, and which naturally subjected one of the warmest hearts and imaginations that ever existed, to all the pangs, that doubt, succeeded by delight, and delight, succeeded by hopelessness in this world, could inflict."

[7] Brown mentions her twice in the "Life" (*KC*, II, 54, 71) as "a lady" and "the young lady in Hampstead who had won his heart." By the time that he wrote these words (1836), Fanny had married and was living on the Continent.

[8] Fanny granted his requests. A draft of her immediate reply, December 29, is printed in Forman (1952), pp. lxii–lxiii.

[9] Mrs. John Gould, with whom Fanny had spent the summer (Richardson, *Fanny Brawne*, pp. 117, 157).

· 99 ·

TO C. W. DILKE [1]

Address (*partly torn away*): {Cha^s Wentworth Dilk}e Esqre / {Navy Pay} Office, / {Somerset} house, / {Lon}don.

Postmarks: FIRENZE; I.T.; FPO FE 9 1830

Endorsement: Brown Jany 10 (? — *the rest missing*)

AL: Keats House, Hampstead. Most of the first extant paragraph is quoted by Bodurtha and Pope, pp. 15, 96.

[January 10 (?), 1830]

*　　*　　*

In writing Keats's life, in order to salve over his "low origin" as Hunt calls it,[2] as a good patrimony is the next best thing, (even in the eyes of aristocrats,) to a good parentage, I wish to know from you if I am correct in saying this: "Property in the funds to the amount of about £10,000 was bequeathed among them; £2,000 to each of the brothers, and the remainder to the sister." As you know all about this, you can answer me without difficulty.[3] Respecting Keats himself, you must excuse me when I say I think you never rightly understood any thing of him but his poetry. How could you say that, after his illness, he sunk something from his high feelings of {g}enerosity? Why, from the moment he was taken ill, he had not {th}e means of proving his feelings of generosity to the amount of a penny.

*　　*　　*

in France and England. Deaths are numerous here among old and young; those who chance to have any latent unsuspected disease

---

[1] The upper half of the second leaf is all that remains of this letter, and the second digit of the date in Dilke's endorsement is partly torn away. If Brown mailed the letter on or soon after January 10, it took about twice the normal time to reach London (see the last postmark). From what remains of Dilke's date, however, 10 is a better guess than 16 or 18.

[2] See number 97.

[3] Dilke did not reply, and Brown let the passage stand in his "Life" (*KC*, II, 54–55). See *KC*, II, 175, and Bodurtha and Pope, p. 96, for Dilke's later comments on the question.

are the sufferers. A few days ago the weather, at last, broke; and a few days hence, if the thaw should be quick, and accompanied by rain, we may have the Arno overflowing the city, owing to the prodigious quantity of [snow]

*　　*　　*

· 100 ·

FROM JOSEPH SEVERN

Address: To / Charles Brown Esqr / (Inglese) / Poste Restante / Firenze

Postmarks: ROMA; 22 GEN[NA]IO 1830

Endorsement: J. Severn.

ALS: British Museum. The first three paragraphs are printed in the *Athenaeum*, August 30, 1879, p. 271, in Forman (1883), IV, 373–375, and (from the *Athenaeum*) by Sharp, pp. 161–162.

My dear Brown　　　　　　　　　　Rome Jany 17th 1830 —
　　Your letter [1] found me in all the glorious confusion of re-moving. — I recognized it as from you and so put it into my pocket to read in the first quiet moment. — I am glad I did so, for its contents affected me much, altho' it was agreable new's for every thing about poor Keats is melancholly. — I am content that this reverse in the fate of his works, gives you the occassion to pay a true tribute to his memory, such as I have ever long'd should be done, and such as I know you quite able to do
　　I feel, that if you can get over my defective writing and promise me (which I know you will) not to expose it to the public as mine (for I am not a little proud of Keats as my friend) that I can supply you with ample materials, which I will write spon-tanously — not only as to facts which I have witnessed, but also as to my own feeling & impression of his beautiful character — I will not expect or oblige you to use any thing I write but as you see

---

[1] "Towards the end of December, 1829, Brown wrote to Severn, begging for his practical aid in the Keats Memoir" (Sharp, p. 159). The letter is no longer extant.

fit, — but I shall expect that you destroy these papers when you
have used them as I feel they *must* contain invectives against
many persons whose enmity or even notice I am little anxious to
have —

Respecting the portrait I feel differently and shall be proud
to make my appearence before the public as the unchanged friend
of Keats, loving his memory now he is dead, as I did himself and
his works when he was alive and this is an honor that no one shall
share with me not even the engraver, for I will take up the graver
once more, and fancy myself inspired to give his resemblance to
the world, faulty as it may be, yet done with all my heart & soul.
— I think the miniature will make a good engraving, and have
already imagined the style of the thing and long to be about it. —
It would be necessary to have the one in colours [2] to engrave from,
which can soon be had from England as it is such a trifle; — not
that I think yours [3] defective in any respect, but it is a great advantage always to engrave from colour's when it [is] possible. —
I take it one great reason why the Italian engravings are so stoney
and lifeless *is* because they are copied from mere black & white
drawings wheras there exists a singular power in engraving in the
insertion [?] of colours. — So pray write immediately for the
original in colours, and I will commence the moment I receive it.
— It may come by the Courier quite safe —

It is a very singular fact this Mrs Severn had just set about
making you a copy of Keats picture which I have here,[4] and as her
progress is so very surprising I have not the least doubt that it will
be worthy your acceptance. — It is to be the same size. — She has
compleated a copy of Romulus & Remus by Rubens [5] which would
surprise you — the fact is she has a real good & pure taste in Painting, and [6] is of the greatest service to me in the advice I get from
her about my own doings. — You will be glad to know that we
have removed to a very beautiful & convenient house, aye beyond

---

[2] The miniature exhibited at the Royal Academy in 1819 (*Letters*, II, 48;
Parson, *Portraits of Keats*, p. 52), at this time in Fanny Brawne's possession
(number 102), and now in the National Portrait Gallery.
  [3] Brown's India-ink copy of the miniature (Parson, p. 113).
  [4] Perhaps the reminiscent portrait of Keats reading (see the end of number 30).
  [5] In the Capitol at Rome.
  [6] *Written* as.

any thing we had expected to find. — I have two Studios with real work lights, one with screens [?] to show my pictures. — We are going on very comfortably, our little daughter Claudia is growing and is very interesting, I am very happy in my married life and would not change it for any of your bachelor liberties. — My Painting flourishes, as I have much more time for it. — I have painted 7 works since last summer. — one of which was the Warrior & Lady for Lord Lansdowne.[7] — Prince Leopold [8] has not yet paid me for my Fontain picture I wrote to Kirk [9] some time since but he has not answerd me yet — I hope he is quite recoverd — he knows our new house to [be] 152 Via Rasella where M[rs] Seymour lived. — It is really a beautiful house, and my Studio is the finest light possible we pay 165 Scudi a year, which sum includes many fixtures — large looking glasses &c — We have taken a lease of 10 years M[rs] Severn who is very well begs her kindest remembrance to you and a Kiss to Charley — Our little Claudia is a love and we delight in her. — We have been a little gay this Winter — but now "chiudiamo bottega — tho' dont mistake and think M[rs] S. is a gay woman, for she is not. — "Think what a wife should be & she is that —" adieu remember [10] me most kind[l]y to Trelawny, was he married in Greece or not? [11]

ever Sinc[e]rly you[r]s
J. Severn

[7] Henry Petty-Fitzmaurice, third Marquis of Lansdowne (1780–1863). In 1892 the painting was in "the present Lord Lansdowne's collection" (Sharp, p. 156).

[8] Of Saxe-Coburg (1790–1865). He was elected King of the Belgians in the following year.

[9] Kirkup.

[10] *Written* rembember.

[11] Early in 1829 Kirkup had told Severn (Sharp, p. 158), "they were all lies about his [Trelawny's] marriage in Greece, &c., &c." But according to his biographer, H. J. Massingham, *The Friend of Shelley* (London, 1930), pp. 252–257, Trelawny did marry Tersitza Kamenou, sister of the Greek leader Odysseus, in 1824. The marriage ended in divorce after the birth of Zella in June 1826.

· 101 ·

TO C. W. DILKE

Endorsement: Brown

ALS: Keats House, Hampstead. Printed by Richardson, *The Everlasting Spell*, pp. 201–205.

Florence.   20 January 1830.

MEM: *I give you warning this is the most unpleasant letter I ever sent you! — to my feelings.*

My dear Dilke,

Many thanks for your early reply to my letter; [1] and I should have felt doubly thankful if you had found George's letter, and sent it, or a copy. I am, at present, at a standstill; — though not on your account, as your information respecting that letter will merely influence one paragraph; for others are tardy.[2] Yet, if you can find, and will send the mass (which you mention) of facts, documents, and writings, I shall esteem it a high favour. My motive for writing Keats' life is that he may not continue to be represented as he was not; possibly I ought to add another motive, — that of revenge against Gifford and Lockhart, — aye, and Jeffrey.[3] I did intend to sell it, but from what you have said, it is likely I may refuse to touch a penny of its profits, if any there should be. Your letter, relating George's defence, is strange indeed; when I first received it, willing to believe the best, I either did not strictly examine it, or I acquiesced to broad assertions. another and a better reason is, I did not know I had it in my power to refute it.[4] Now I put it under a keen scrutiny, backed by staunch

---

[1] Number 97.

[2] Besides Dilke, Fanny Brawne, and Severn, Brown had also asked Richards for help in the memoir (see the next letter).

[3] Francis Jeffrey (1773–1850), editor of the *Edinburgh Review*, whom Brown (*KC*, II, 60) charges with the "irreparable disgrace . . . of having neglected his self assumed duty as a careful examiner into the literature of the day" (he did not notice Keats's poetry until August 1820).

[4] This sentence ("another . . . refute it.") is written in the margin and marked for insertion here by means of asterisks.

documents, and have no hesitation in declaring that if that is his defence, and if you believe in it, you have been grossly imposed on. You will not allow John (to speak in their Christian names) to have had capacity to judge or know any thing of money affairs; therefore you contend his evidence goes for nothing. I recollect, when balancing an account of my brother James's property,[5] he looked over me, and pointed out an error, of such a nature as required a merchant's eye. When I expressed my surprise at this knowlege of his, he said something to this purpose, — "I detest my own accounts, because they are bad; but I have learnt Accounts, and, when mine are worth looking into, I shall be a good accomptant." The reason for his having signed Abbey's balances wrongly was his entire faith in Abbey's honesty, of which he has often spoken to me, together with his averseness to canvass his small means. He knew enough of Accounts to see (what you assure me of) that George was not capable of being a man of business, — which I have under his own hand. However, I shall not have to press John's knowledge on this point much into the service.[6] You say I have not authority for stating that John's generosity to George finished his fortune. No? Have I not John's positive and often repeated word to that effect? And have I not their guardian's information, both verbally and written? These authorities, with the world, would be deemed sufficient. But, you contend, the one's evidence is unavailing from his ignorance, and the other's from his character, — though it is difficult to imagine what purpose could be answered by a deception of this nature. In addition to these authorities I have mark you![7] that of George himself, as contained, by powerful implication, in his own defence, as given by you. The defence sets out with declaring that, at the time George first went to America, (June 1818) John was indebted to George, had not one shilling, and received £300 from George. Upon this setting out the greater part of the defence rests. Let us examine it. 1st *John was indebted to George*. In another part of the defence this debt is made out to be more than £100. Did it never strike you how im-

---

[5] James had appointed Brown one of his executors.

[6] Compare Brown's earlier remarks on Keats's knowledge of money affairs in numbers 63, 64.

[7] The words "mark you!" are written above the line.

probable it was that George, considered the most expensive of the brothers, especially in dress,[8] could have maintained his capital entire, lived on the interest, (£60, I believe,) and out of that small sum, and the £100 he says he earned from Abbey, lent more than £100 to John? Without canvassing this improbability, for there is no occasion for it, I compel George to accuse himself of a vile falsehood. Here is a passage from a letter written by him to John, on 18th March 1818: — "I am about paying your's and Tom's bills, of which I shall keep regular accounts; and, for the sake of justice and a future proper understanding, I intend calculating the probable amount *Tom and I are indebted to you*; [not underlined in the original; I have done so, merely to draw your attention to the words.] something of this kind must be done, or, at the end of two or three years, we shall all be at sixes and sevens." [9] This is positive proof. When a man is convicted of falsehood at starting, his defence, by most persons, would be thrown aside; particularly on a point where he could not be mistaken; and they would act rightly, for, it will be seen, as might be expected every part of his defence rests on falsehood. 2nd *John had not one shilling*, — that is, in June 1818. Now I have before me Abbey Cock & Co's Acct Current with John.[10] This is undeniable, indisputable evidence, because they acknowledge themselves debtors to him on 4 June 1818 for £500. Had it been in their favour, you would be at liberty to question it, but not when against themselves. On that day there was due to them from John no more than £31. 9. 2, for tea, chocolate, and cocoa, furnished to him George and Tom at various dates, during the previous three years. George paid all his tradesmen's bills at that time; so did John, as I recollect he told me, — besides, I knew him to be quite free from debts, when he lived with me, up to that period. For this

[8] Fanny Brawne, who thought George "extravagant and selfish," advised Fanny Keats on May 21, 1821, "whenever you have your money in your own power . . . be warned by what has already happened — and remember he [George] is extravagant at least every one says so" (*Letters of Fanny Brawne*, pp. 33–35).

[9] For George's letter see number 108. Brown's words following the italics are written in the margin and connected with the text by means of asterisks. The brackets here are an editorial addition.

[10] The account is transcribed in number 108. Abbey, Cock and Company (Richard Abbey's firm) were merchants and tea dealers at 4 Pancras Lane, Cheapside.

purpose, it seems, John drew out £140, — part of which, possibly, went to pay Tom's bills. There therefore remained belonging to him, clear of all debts, £336. 16. 11,[11] taking into Account the balance of interest in his favour of £8. 6. 1. This sum, at the least, was his at that time, instead of not having one shilling! I say *at the least*, because the round sum of £500 does not look like the last of property; it implies there were yet some gleanings. But enough, — I have proved that George, for a second time, is guilty of falsehood in his defence. 3ʳᵈ *John received £300 from George* before he first went to America. Here I am the principal evidence. Immediately after our leaving George at Manchester,[12] that is, on our first day's walk towards the Lakes, John told me that George had repaid the monies, furnished to him, when under age with — (I am nearly certain,) — £70 or £80; — but I am certain I am not ten pounds wrong. This John did not believe was sufficient, and regretted that George had not kept, as he had expected, a regular account. John told me further, how unlucky it was for him to be the eldest of two brothers, who could not live on their incomes; and mentioned that he had expended a good deal for Tom in his illness, taking him to Margate, (before we knew them,) [13] and afterwards to Teignmouth; [14] add to which, there was George's and Tom's pleasure jaunt to Paris, the trip to Lyons, and the money lost at the "rouge et noir" table in the Palais Royal,[15] — how much, I forget, but far too much for their circumstances. John did not mention all this *against* his brothers; he loved them too well; he mentioned it as a fact, speaking all the while affectionately of them. He complained of his elder brothership, not of them [16] All this was in confidence, and I have never spoken of it till now that it is become necessary. I was undoubtedly of opinion that George had not fairly repaid him, and I never liked George

---

[11] That is, £508 6s. 1d. less £140 and £31 9s. 2d. According to the copy of the account in number 108, however, only £302 7s. 7d. remained. Keats had withdrawn an additional £30 (June 19, 1818), and the 1815–1818 expenses for tea, etc., given there seem to amount to a few pounds more than Brown's £31 9s. 2d.

[12] They left George and his wife at Liverpool (not Manchester) on June 24, 1818.

[13] In August 1816, April–May 1817.

[14] In March–May 1818 (actually Keats joined Tom there).

[15] In September 1817.

[16] These two sentences ("John . . . them") are written in the margin and marked for insertion here with asterisks.

afterwards. For, besides the above, I learnt that George had been extravagant; it was Abbey's alleged plea for dismissing him from his counting house; and I have a letter from John to Abbey, never sent,[17] (possibly from its being torn,) wherein John hopes that Abbey will consider George cured of "his careless and extravagant propensities." Now, it is impossible that John could have related this on our walk to me within two or three days after having received £300 from him; and it is equally impossible that I should have dreamed it. We talked over it for miles, and it has never been off my mind. Then again, where were the £300? Not in Abbey's hands, or they would stand in the account; they could not be included in the £500, because no merchant or man of business whatsoever lumps two sums, received from different sources, in one; the £70 or £80, I think, John told me he had left in the hands of Tom, which is probable. Were the £300 locked up in a box at home? — no, for it appears John continued to draw on Abbey for his expences. But what ought to set this question to rest is that George had need of all the money he could scrape together for his American scheme, and John had £336 at least, say two years' provision; so there was no immediate necessity for making this handsome present; there would be time enough after George had established himself and was thriving; in the mean while the money was of importance to George, and not to John. The story refutes itself at every turn. For the third time I accuse George of falsehood, and believe that those who read this will own he is convicted of it. Thus, all his defence, resting on his being John's creditor for more than £400, becomes shameless; and John, in all likelihood, was, even at that time, his creditor. I will now examine into a few other bold assertions of his; and you must not be weary of me; but as I am weary of charging him with falsehood, I now leave that to you. 4th He says that on his return to America, he arrived with exactly £700. Then, forgetting his arithmetic, in his haste to depreciate Tom's estate and prove that he, a creditor for more than £400, only borrowed of John £170, he makes it out that he could not possibly have left London with more than £440, — unless indeed some kind friend there made him a present of £260, and paid his passage! 5th You make him say Tom's estate, after

[17] It has not survived.

paying the Doctor's bill, and the funeral expences, was reduced to about £1,100, but you meant, as I see by the after sums, £1,200. Tom's fortune was equal to George's, which was about £1,600, and the stocks had not fallen. So, Sawrey's [18] bill, (a moderate one, though I forget the amount,) and the Undertaker's, (under £28,) amounted to about £400! — 6th George says he left £100 with John, when he went, for the second time, to America. John, after taking leave of him in town, came to me at Hampstead,[19] pulled out a packet of notes from his pocket, placed them in my hands, and told me that was all George had left him. I counted them instantly; they amounted to £40. He and I then sat down to calculate how much he owed, and we found it to be about £60; so he was left by George about £20 in debt. — 7th George says that, on his return from America, he found that John had used £100 of Tom's estate. John told me he had not touched a penny of it, and that George took it all, except the £40. John was certainly in the right, as I can pretty well prove. It was in 1819. On 2 and 3 April of that year he drew £106. 7. 7. out of Abbey's hands, as per Acct Current, being the remains of the £500 and interest. A considerable portion of that sum (£106. 7. 7) went, as I know, to pay bills; with the remainder he went to the Isle of Wight. There I joined him; we then went to Winchester, where he received £40, a loan returned from a friend.[20] We lived as economically as we comfortably could; and, as I said, he was, at the end of the year, about £60 in debt. Now, how could he have spent £100 in addition to those sums? Indeed I am sure he never had it, — he could not.

I have done with his defence. Minor delinquencies I omit. My refuting it has filled me with disgust. I hate him more than ever, and feel tempted to put these documents to a vindictive use. Once or twice I was on the point of throwing this paper in the fire; but I wished to prove the knave a knave; and I am anxious to disprove any idea that may be entertained of my having either rashly or wantonly spoken against him. If you imagine there are any who hold such an opinion of me, let them see this letter; but

---

[18] Solomon Sawrey (1765–1825), surgeon and writer on venereal diseases.

[19] On February 6, 1820, according to the account in number 84. George left on January 28.

[20] Haslam.

I beg the favour of you to *show it to Miss Brawne & Mancur* the two to whom I have most spoken against George. I own myself mistaken when I said that George had taken from his brother, according to my calculations, somewhere about £700; the mistake arose from my not asking John whether the sum he named was money or stock, — (it turns out to have been stock,) — from my not being aware of a prior and separate claim on the part of the sister on Tom's estate for £100, and from my having understood that John, to the last, when George took all had still a balance in Abbey's hands of a small amount; — then it would have amounted to about £700. But whether that sum or half the sum, the crime was the same, — leaving his brother worse than destitute, — in debt. I now calculate the sum he took was full £425, without taking into account that Tom's estate was indebted to John for the money he had advanced to Tom; so that probably it would amount to £600, — for Tom cost him a great deal.[21] — but it is useless to explain the calculation. I'd rather write a second letter on other subjects, which I will, as an envelope for this.[22]

Your's most truly, Cha[s] Brown.

· 102 ·

TO JOSEPH SEVERN [1]

[February 1830]

*   *   *

It was about four years and a half ago [2] that George Keats sent to Dilke a defence of himself, refuting the "cruel charge" (as he called it) which I had made against him. Dilke sent me the purport of it, with a request that I should make you and others acquainted with it. I did so, for I had no evidence by which I could contradict

---

[21] The words "without . . . deal." are written in the margin and marked for insertion here with asterisks.

[22] The second letter has not survived.

[1] From Sharp, pp. 160–161, who dates it (p. 159) "Late in February" 1830.

[2] Actually it was nearly six years ago (April 1824). Dilke sent Brown "the purport" of George's letter in number 60.

his bold assertions; though, as I told you in Rome, when you put the question to me, I had no faith in his defence. Now, see the danger of villainy, and by what unlooked-for chances it is laid bare. Having a bundle of papers which belonged to Keats, part in his own handwriting, I lately opened it, on the supposition the papers might assist me in the Memoirs. They were chiefly letters between Keats and his brothers. I threw George's and Tom's aside; but, after awhile, as if by an invisible hand, a passage in one of George's own letters was turned towards me, which gave the lie direct to the groundwork of his defence! I then searched further, and found an Acc^t. Curr^t. of Abbey's; when, by these two documents, I was instantly enabled to prove that every tittle of his defence was false, most impudently and atrociously false. I have sent these proofs to Dilke,[3] requesting him to promulgate them among our acquaintances, that I may be no longer suspected as a rash accuser. How he, who has been so positive in George's favour from the first, will take it, I know not. I expect his answer every day. You may rely on my obeying your orders respecting the papers you have promised. You knew Keats before I did, and perhaps you can give me some account of the development of his mind as a poet. He himself has talked to me a little on this subject; but, if possible, I would have further information. When did your acquaintance with him begin? Nearly two months since I wrote to Richards for assistance; [4] no answer. If I knew how to direct a letter to Haslam, I would apply to him; can you tell me his address? or will you write to him? When I asked you about the terms for engraving, it never entered my head that you would offer to engrave his miniature; if you can spare time, this offer of yours is admirable. Respecting the original, in Miss Brawne's possession, I am afraid you cannot have it. Were I to ask her for the loan of it, I believe she would send it; and that belief makes me the more delicate in asking for it; besides, I cannot run the hazard of its being lost on the way. No, Severn, I do not feel myself authorised in making that request. I will send you my copy, and the drawing I made from your representation of him a little before his death, together with that foolish little painting I

[3] See the preceding letter.
[4] The letter is not now known.

have promised in a short while.[5] I have been very much occupied in Mrs. Medwin's affairs,[6] battling with bankers, and lawyers, with my hands day after day full of documents in Courts of Law; let this be my apology, especially when I tell you I have been of service to that ill-treated lady, with whom every one in Florence sympathises. I have had much conscientious responsibility on my head, little able to think of anything else. To return to Keats: Dilke urges me, as a proof to the world of my friendship for Keats, and as the only proof that I am not book-making, to declare, from the first, that I will not accept of one penny of the profits which may arise from the Memoirs. I never thought of profit, rather of loss, as I expected to pay a large sum for the engravings. To my mind Dilke's advice is good; and I intend, you willing, to set out with a declaration that the book is an offering to his fame by you and me, both refusing to partake in the profits. The only question then is, who is to have them? Should there be any, ought we not to present them to his sister? It is true she does not *want* them, and therefore we might dispose of them in some other way, something still conducive to his fame, what say you? — what have you to propose? [7] Give my love to Mrs. Severn, and say I am eternally obliged to her for the copy she is making.[8] I am equally surprised and rejoiced to hear of her excellent painting. Carlino also sends his love, with ten kisses to Claudia. Shall we make up a match between them? Their ages are suitable, — ask Mrs. Severn what she thinks of it. Kirkup is very well — all very well. Did I tell you Marina is married? I cannot, literally *cannot*, answer your question about Trelawny. I'm turned whist-player.

> Yours most sincerely,
> Charles Brown.

[5] See number 100 (for Severn's miniature and Brown's copy), number 37, n. 13 (Brown's copy of the deathbed portrait), and the opening of number 104 (the "foolish little painting").

[6] See number 106, n. 6.

[7] See number 104 for Severn's reply.

[8] Of a picture of Keats (number 100).

· 103 ·

TO C. W. DILKE

Address (partly torn away): {Inghilter}ra. / {Chas Wentworth
D}ilke Esqre, / {Navy} Pay Office, / {Somer}set house, / London.

Postmarks: FIRENZE; Toscana; FPO AP 13 1830

ALS: Keats House, Hampstead. Printed by Richardson, *The
Everlasting Spell*, pp. 206–209.

My dear Dilke,   Florence. 31 March 1830.
    You have wounded me to the quick. I could not have believed
that any one I am acquainted with, far less you, would treat me,
both in matter and manner, with such injustice. To make these
words good, I must use many more.
    When you sent me George's defence, you told me it was quite
conclusive, in your judgment, and in that of others that had read
it, to prove the "positive fallacy of the cruel charge against him." [1]
You, and certainly most of the others that had read it, knew that
I had promulgated this cruel charge. Add to which, in that defence the impossibility of my having heard such a charge from
John Keats was urged as far as the nature of the subject would
admit. I therefore stood convicted, by you and others, of having
made a cruel charge against a man, of the fallacy of which you
and those others were convinced, while, possibly, some suspected
I never had grounds for making it. You requested me to convey
the spirit of the defence to Mr Hunt and any other likely to have
heard of the charge. I could not believe in it, but, having no evidence in contradiction, I was compelled to accede, and make the
defence, fully and faithfully, known to Mr Hunt, and four others
in Italy, of which I took care to inform you. Though my case was
a hard one, and though the defence rested on nothing but mere
assertion, I was convinced of the goodness of your motives.
    After wearing this stain on my character for more than five
years, documents come into my hands by which I am enabled to
prove that, root and branch, every tittle of George's defence is

[1] Brown quotes from number 60.

false. I do so, saying it is a most unpleasant and disgusting office to me, but necessary, and send the letter to you,[2] requesting you will show it to Mancur and Miss Brawne, and to any others who may have entertained thoughts prejudicial to my character, as one guilty of having spoken indiscreetly against another. What is your answer? You say it is "unintelligible," (assuming that I had given no reason for it, though it stared you in the face,) that I should "inflict" an unpleasant letter on you, "unasked for, unnecessary," stirring up your "gall and bitterness with facts and figures". This implies I had no right to send you such a letter; — I had. You made yourself an agent between George's character and mine; you forwarded his defence to me; I had a right to forward my defence to you in return; and more, — you were bound to act in the same manner, at my request, towards me, as I was bound, at your request, to act towards you. Instead of this, you say not one word of your agreeing to state to those, who were convinced of the fallacy of my cruel charge, the grounds of my defence; you content yourself with telling me you will show my letter to Mancur, when you see him, letting me know, on another page, that you have not seen him these six months, and that you suppose it out of all possibility that he should call on you. Now I request you will send it to him by the post, or back again to me. In respect to your not showing it to Miss Brawne, your reason is good; provided neither you, nor your wife, gave George's defence to her, or offerred it, or spoke of it to her, — otherwise you are unjust. When George's character was to be made fair, backed by mere assertions, it did not appear that mine ever entered into your head, — all was tenderness for him; when mine was to be made fair, backed by incontrovertible documents, nothing but George's character is spoken of, — all is anger at me. You set[3] yourself up as umpire, — act uprightly! George's facts, dates, and figures, without a document, were all in all sufficient, convincing to all; mine, with documents, are "ingenious, quite conclusive to those who do not know they are erroneous, — to me" (you go on) "they only prove how ingeniously a man may satisfy himself that error is truth, and confirm an old opinion, not of mine, but of

[2] Number 101.
[3] *Written* sat.

most people's, that to build up an error *solidly*, there is nothing
like facts, dates, and figures." [4] Why did you not apply this old
opinion to George's defence? Considering you had been convinced
by his unbacked facts, dates, and figures, would it not have been
more to the purpose to pluck out the soul from any one of mine?
You cannot do so, without doubting my word, which would be
less offensive than disregarding it, because I can easily send you
attested copies of these documents. How easy is it to speak positively! — how difficult, when that positiveness is called in question,
by positive facts, dates, and figures, to do otherwise than sneer!
You care not, you say, one farthing what I believe of George; — or if
you did, what then? — but you ought to be careful that the world,
— our world, — believes nothing against me without reason. The
hope you express, never once noticing my character, that you may
hear nothing further on this subject, by no means strengthens my
faith in your perfect knowledge of George's immaculateness. You
have it in your power, you aver, to prove every thing in his favour,
— do it then, and I will bow to him, honour him, make him every
amends in my power. I shall be rejoiced to find, by conclusive
evidence, that my Keats's brother did not behave as I believe he
did, that he did not borrow money without an acknowledgment,
and then declare himself a creditor, — and that my Keats was not
so weak and shallow as to accuse a brother of what he never committed; for this knowledge I would willingly sacrifice that part of
my character, which you allow to be attacked, — I would confess
myself indiscreet, defaming, — heinous, if any one insisted on the
epithet; but it is enormous to expect that I should forfeit one
iota of my good name in order to uphold that of the swindler of
my friend. Instead of telling me you care not what I believe of
George, you might have said, — I care not for you. Yet, even then,
I should have answered, — Care for me or not, care for your own
honour; you, the active party in declaring me guilty of having
made a cruel charge against another, are bound to examine, care-

---

[4] Perhaps Dilke was thinking of Sir Arthur Wardour's words in Scott's *The
Antiquary*, ch. V, "[Mr. Oldbuck] never has any advantage of me in dispute, unless when he avails himself of a sort of pettifogging intimacy with dates, names,
and trifling matters of fact, a tiresome and frivolous accuracy of memory which is
entirely owing to his mechanical descent. . . . It leads to an uncivil and positive
mode of disputing."

fully examine into every particle of evidence which I may produce in my favour. You have, virtually, accused me of defaming George; this you have done, publicly as you could, short of printing; be rational enough to examine if the accusation you have made is, or is not grounded on a mistake.

You seem to think I ought to rest content with your bare assertion against me. It is, however, impossible to put faith in your infallibility on this subject; for which I will give a few reasons. I was never aware of your being skilful in matters of account; and, judging from some self-convicting errors of account in George's defence, whether unperceived by you, or committed in your version of it, you are not skilful. Your late knowledge of the Keatses' affairs in Chancery does not necessarily imply, as you assume, that you are well acquainted with all their affairs of twelve years standing; [5] nor do I perceive how John's, George's, and my want of that Chancery-knowledge should have prevented either of us from understanding other matters; nor why, because an explanation to George of those Chancery affairs occupied sixteen foolscaps, he could not clearly acknowledge himself his brother's debtor in one explicit and entire sentence, which you miscall "broken sentences." George's assertions in his defence did not pretend to rest on any thing but his intimate acquaintance with his own and his brother's affairs, which passed with you unquestioned; but, when a paper is discovered wherein he has condemned himself by striking at the root of that defence, you declare he knew little more than nothing of his affairs, which is not sufficiently consistent for an infallible man. Then again, your memory is not good; I have more than once told you that John's information to me of his brother's having taken from him all his money, without an acknowledgment, was clear, distinct, and often repeated, and you call it "the ambiguous givings out of John." For these reasons I cannot appeal to you as an oracle, to which you have but one claim, that I know of, — enigmatical positiveness. Add to which I cannot recollect you ever gave up any one of your positive opinions; so that, if my memory serves me well, I ought not blindly to yield to any one of them, knowing

[5] Dilke boasted to Severn in 1841 (Sharp, p. 199) that he knew "more of Keats's affairs . . . than all the Keats[es] put together."

you, like many men, to have been positive on the wrong side.
     Now I come to the [6]

*   *   *

sheer rudeness, and, terming it so, I am content. But I call,
seriously, on you to make your words — "most cruel severity" —
good, or to explain how you had been inadvertently led into error.
Trusting you will either do the one or the other, I remain,
                                        Your's truly,
                                        Cha[s] Brown.

With thanks for your consent to lend me £50, I have already
arranged the business otherwise.

· 104 ·

FROM JOSEPH SEVERN

Address: To / Charles Brown Esq[r] Inglese / Poste Restante /
Firenze [1]

Postmark: ROMA

Endorsement: J. Severn.

ALS: British Museum. Extracts are printed in the *Athenaeum*,
August 30, 1879, p. 271, in Forman (1883), IV, 375–377, and (from
the *Athenaeum*) by Sharp, pp. 162–163.

My dear Brown —   Rome April 15th 1830
     I have been so full of pressing occupations about the Exibi-
tion at the Capitol here, that I have [2] not had a moment to thank
you for your kind present, or even answer your last letter — I like
your tree much [3] — 'tis full of nature, perhaps I like it better as
you have done [it] for me, but be assured there is a good deal to

---

     [6] Half of the second leaf is torn away.
     [1] After writing the address, Severn added "forw'd [?] by Robert Finch Esq[r],"
and then deleted it, no doubt because Finch had already departed for Florence
(see the next letter).
     [2] *Written* have have.
     [3] Presumably the "foolish little painting" mentioned in Brown's "last letter,"
number 102.

be vain of in it — the colour particularly — perhaps the composition of it might be more picturesque. — I shall put it in a collection of presents we are making in a pictoral way. — You will no doubt have heard of our Exibition which includes the works of most of the foreign schools now here — I was appointed on the part of England to arrange the works — It is a very interesting thing and attracts great attention. — A Lottery is to succeed the exibition — The subsc[r]iption is 6 Crown's a year — it will select one or two Works in Painting — You will be annoy'd to hear that my last picture "Ariel" on the Bats back,⁴ was excluded, because it was a naked figure — As the work is universally thought to be my "Capo d'opera": this affair has given great displeasure and will injure the exibition — I must also tell you that this picture is painted for Mʳ Finch, who has very generously given me two thirds more than the price I ask'd for it. — Viz — 30£ was the sum I asked of him & he has given me 50£ — He is an excellent hearted man — and I am not a little glad to have pleasd him. You ask me what shall be done with the profits of our work to poor Keats memory — Now I have thought a good deal of it & am going to propose — *That we erect a monument to his memory here in Rome* to the full extent of the money arising from the sale of the work — I have consulted Gibson,⁵ who says that for 200£ something very handsome may be made. — I have a subject in my mind for the Basso Relievo which I think I once mentiond to you before ⁶ — It is Keats sitting with his half strung lyre — the three Fates arrest him — one catches his arm — another cuts the thread & the third prononces his end — This would make a beatiful basso relievo — and as the grave stone is so unworthy him, and so absurd (as all people say) — and as the spot is so beautiful, I hope you will agree to it. — Gibson seemd very much taken with the idea of placing a work of his on this spot. — I knew Keats as far back as 1813 ⁷ — I was introduced to him by Haslam — he was

---

⁴ Called "Ariel Aflight" by Sharp, who reproduces (facing pp. 210, 272) studies for the picture. In 1871 it was owned by James T. Fields, of Boston (Sharp, p. 273). For more details on the exclusion of the picture see number 106.

⁵ John Gibson (1790–1866), sculptor, whom Severn had known since 1821.

⁶ On January 21, 1823 (see Sharp, p. 124), when he proposed "a little Monument to Keats . . . in Hampstead Church."

⁷ Severn first wrote "1812." Either date is much too early: he met Keats (who was at Guy's from October 1815 to July 1816) probably in the spring of 1816.

then studying at Guy's Hospital, yet much inclined to the muses — I remember on the second meeting he read me the Sonnet on solitude in which is the line "To start the wild bee from the Fox glove bell." — He was at that time more playful in his manner — the world seem'd to have nothing to do with him — Poetry was evidently at that time his darling hope — he dislikd the Surgery & complained that his guardian Mr Abbey forced him to it gainst his will — He was introduced to Mr Hunt I think in 1814 or 15 which wrought a great change in him — It confirmed him in his future career and I think intoxicated him with an excess of enthusiasm which kept by him 4 or 5 years — perhaps until you knew him.[8] — This was injurious to him, as Hunt and others not only praised his works and spoke of them as faultless, but even advised him to publish them — Now, merit as they then had, they were not fit things to offer to the world, and I have always thought, that, that publication was in a great measure the reason poor Keats did not sooner acquire the power of finishing his works. — At the same time he got a kind of mawkishness also from Hunt, which to my thinking was a fault and which he got rid of when he came to live with you — Yet that first volume gives a good idea of his beautiful character — of one, who on his death bed, acknowledged that his greatest pleasure in almost every period of his life had been in watching the growth of flowers & trees. — and it [was] thro' this medium that he was so profound in the Greek Mythology — At my first acquaintance with him — he gave me the compleat idea of a Poet — 'twas an imagination so tempered by gentleness of manner and steady vivacity, that I never saw him without auguring on his future success — At that time he had no morose feeling or even idea — he never spoke of any one, but by saying something in their favor and this always so agr[ee]ably & cleverly, imitating the manner to increase you[r] favorable impression of the person he was speaking of. — At that time he was not well acquainted with painting, but soon acquired a very deep knowledge of it — indeed I used to observe that he had a great power of acquiring knowledge of all kinds — for after a few years he used to talk so agreably on Painting & Music that I was

[8] Another confusion of dates. Keats met Hunt in October 1816 and Brown less than a year later.

charmed with him and have often spent whole days with him devoted to these things. — The only differrence in his personal appearance at first was — that he had not that look of deep thought, but as I said his look & manner were more playful
How long shall be occupied on this work — I would like to know that I may be ready with the Engraving — the original minature I should like to have had — for yours good as it is will render my engraving a mere copy from a copy — yet I am content and anticipate that I shall succeed — I think the picture well calculated for an Engraving. —

I have just began on a new picture for Sir M. Ridley [9] — The subject is "Vintagers returning" — The father puts his Infant son on the Ass laden with grapes [10] — The mother dances before it, a boy of 10 years preceds the group dancing & beating the Tamborine — there are 7 figures — the child I make look like a little Bacchus sitting on the tubs of grapes — the group has just advanced in a shady point of the road and the sun-lit trees throw them out. — I make progress in my painting that is I paint with greater facility. — The change in my life is very favorable to my pursuits — I cannot be happier. — My dear wife was made for me in the stati[o]n that I am in — she is an invaluable help to me — You have heard of the loss we have in Lady Northamton [11] — She was a dear & valuable friend to us both — I was just about beginning [12] their picture of the Siccilian Mariners Hymn [13] — The body set off today from Rome followd by 60 carriges. — believe me ever Sincerly

J Severn —

I do not know Haslam's address — he knew Keats before I did —

[9] Sir Matthew White Ridley (1778–1836), M.P., of Heaton and Blagdon, Northumberland. The picture was "Italian Vintagers Returning," exhibited at the Royal Academy in 1832 — Graves, *The Royal Academy of Arts,* VII (1906), 81.
[10] *Written* graves.
[11] Margaret Maclean Clephane, wife of Spencer Joshua Alwyne Compton, second Marquis of Northampton (1790–1851), died on April 2.
[12] *Written* beggning.
[13] A study for the "Sicilian Mariner's [*or* Mariners'] Hymn" is reproduced by Sharp, facing p. 167.

· 105 ·

TO ROBERT FINCH [1]

Address: Robt Finch Esqre

Endorsements: Rec^d April 22° 1830.; Brown.

ALS: Bodleian Library.

Dear Sir,   [April 22 (?), 1830]

   I wish you would come and dine with me, tomorrow or next day, at any hour you choose. Welcome to Florence.

                       Your's most truly,
                        Chas Brown.

· 106 ·

TO LEIGH HUNT

Address: Inghilterra. / Leigh Hunt Esqre, / Care of Mr Hunter, / 72 St Paul's Church-Yard, / London. / Angleterre. (*readdressed to*: Cromwell Lane / Old Brompton)

Postmarks: FIRENZE; I.T; FPO JU 15 1830; 4 EVEN 4 JU 15 1830; TP Rate 2

ALS: British Museum.

My dear Hunt,   Florence. 1 June 1830.

   Your letter came when I was annoyed by some plaguing reflections,[1] and therefore it was doubly welcome. It strikes me I have 101 things to talk about; so I had better begin with your friends here, lest they should be lost in the crowd. Landor sends

---

  [1] Written on an invoice form headed "GRAND HÔTEL DE MAD^ME HOMBERT / rue Porta rossa, Palais Torrigiani, prés du Cabinet litteraire / et de l'Etablissément des Bains à Florence." Obviously Brown called on Finch at his hotel and, finding him out (or possibly not yet arrived), scrawled this note on the readiest piece of paper at hand. Finch's diary (Bodleian Library) shows that he arrived in Florence on April 21, and dined with Brown on the twenty-fourth.

  [1] Concerning the quarrel with Dilke.

his remembrances, and desires me to say he often thinks of you, which, I suppose, is the fact, since he often talks of you. I have not yet told you, for I was not aware of it at first, that in the grounds to his villa is that favourite nook of your's, — that deep dell with the Africo running through it, very cool and green, and full of chesnut trees, whither you took Westmacott, and where he cut a walking-stick, which, by the by, to his great grief, as he wrote me, he lost at Milan.[2] There's a circumstantial sentence, worthy of Pompey Brun! — however, it will serve to make you understand where Landor lives, where there is work going on at the rate of fifty things at once; oh! such planting and transplanting, such watering, such nursing of flowers, and such choice grafts! In conclusion, when the conclusion shall arrive, he will make it a beautiful place, in spite of the poverty of the ground. Kirkup is very well, quite recovered from his last year's illness, which was long and serious. He sendeth his remembrance. He has just finished a copy from his own "Shylock giving the keys to Jessica," and greatly surpassed the original. He is now beginning a picture of Cassio, Desdemona, and Emilia, with Othello and Iago in the back ground, — "Ha! I like not that!"[3] — an admirable subject. Severn continues as uxorious as ever. If he goes on writing to me so much in praise of his wife, I shall, in revenge, make love to her when I go to Rome next October, which is my intention. His last picture, they tell me, is far superior to all his others; it is "Ariel on the bat's back." It was painted for Finch, at a fixed price; but the moment it was finished, *he objected to the price.* "O, fie! Mr Finch!" I think I hear you say; and, at the same time, I think you ought not to say any such thing; because his objection was that the price was too low, and accordingly he gave him about half as much again for it. Didn't I take you in there? Finch was here lately, and dined with me, — just the same as ever. Since his mother's death he has been a much richer man,[4] inhabiting an enormous palace in Rome, splendidly furnished, and giving grand dinners off a service of plate, and driving about like an

[2] See number 94, n. 7.
[3] *Othello*, III.iii.35.
[4] On the death of his mother in the spring of 1827, Finch inherited "about £1,300, the house and stables in Great Ormond Street, the books, bookcases, and plate" (Nitchie, *The Reverend Colonel Finch*, p. 25).

Ambassador. But there is an odd story about that picture: it was sent to the Exhibition in Rome, and sent back again as improper. The first notion was that a naked figure was not approved of, but that seemed preposterous, — only think of our little Ariel being pronounced indecent! No, the heinousness of the picture was at last made known. The priestly directors, not being acquainted with Ariel, mistook him for Uriel; upon which they voted that a representation of that blessed angel riding on one of the incarnations of the devil was scandalous, infamous, blasphemous. Moreover, they strongly suspected that the peacock's feather, which Ariel holds above him like a canopy, (a beautiful invention to reduce the fairy and the bat to their proper diminutive size,) was a covert ridicule against the Catholic faith. Now, does not this look like a fiction of mine or of some other's? — upon my word, I am assured that every word is true. If it were not for laughing, I could moralize on this to some effect; and if it does not make you laugh, you are not your mother's son, — nay worse, you are turned Catholic, unable to relish a joke at your pastors and masters. All this talk about artists brings me naturally to Thornton; I heartily wish him success, and look forward to seeing him pass through Florence to Rome, having gained the gold medal and the pension, like Severn. I am glad you are so happy with John; he and all the rest of them must be grown quite out of my imagination. My Carlino is tall for his age, clever, and very affectionate, remarkable for truth telling, but, when he takes a thing in his head, most difficult to turn from his will. I educate him at home, and encumber him with few lessons; he has taken to reading as much as Thornton when a boy. Tell Hazlitt, with my rems, it is not likely I can find a traveller willing to take a trunk to England, and that books alone, from the hindrances in Piedmont or Lombardy, would be a strong objection; if he likes, I will send it by sea, — in that event he must direct me to whom I am to consign it.[5] He can perhaps do a great favour to me, or rather to Mrs Medwin, in whose misfortunes I have interested

---

[5] See number 72, n. 3. Hazlitt (who died on September 18, 1830) never received the books. At least one of them, a copy of Bacon's *Advancement*, was taken by Brown or his son to New Zealand, whence, some years after Brown's death, Carlino sent it to Sir Charles Dilke, who bequeathed it to Keats House, Hampstead. See Payson G. Gates in *South Atlantic Quarterly*, 46 (1947): 249.

myself.[6] She was a young widow with about £10,000, which Medwin has squandered, she believing all the time her money remained in her own name, and that he had £900 a year of his own. She is here with two little children. I have protected her from the brutality of a banker's proceedings against her for a considerable debt contracted by Medwin; and she looks up to me, — or rather *down* on me, for the poor lady lives in a convent above Fiesole; — for assistance, as far as my knowledge of accounts can give it; — I was battling in a Court of Law for her against that banker, and gained my point! Now she is anxious to turn every thing of value into money, and I hope to get something for a Ms of Burke, given by him to her first husband.[7] Hazlitt, who so well knows Burke, is most likely to be of service. I am told it has *never been published*. It is in his own handwriting. Its title is, "Observations on the criticism contained in the Monthly Review for November 1790, on the Reflections on the 'Revolution in France &c' by the R^t honble Edmund Burke." It will fill about half a sheet in the New Monthly. Colburn, I imagine, would give something handsome for it to publish it there, and it may be of value merely as Burke's Ms. Does Hazlitt, or do you think I can sell it for Mrs Medwin for £25? In such a cause I need not urge you to do your best, and to do it speedily. You must know I am employing myself in writing Keats's Memoirs, at greater length than your's,

[6] Anne Henrietta, born Baroness Hamilton of Sweden (1788–1868), wife of Shelley's cousin and biographer Thomas Medwin (1788–1869). Medwin had deserted her in the summer of 1829, and the Florentine bankers Donato Orsi and Company were suing in his absence for the recovery of loans amounting to 30,000 lire (Ernest J. Lovell, Jr., *Captain Medwin, Friend of Byron and Shelley*, Austin, 1962, pp. 236–241).

[7] According to the *Dictionary of National Biography*, she was by her first marriage Countess of Stainfort or Starnford (Lovell, pp. 205–206n, gives some other forms of the name — Stainforts, Stamford, Starnfold). Concerning the manuscript, H. C. Robinson noted in his diary, October 8, 1830 (Dr. Williams's Library), "Mr Brown lent me yesterday a MS — Observations on the review of Burke's Reflections in the Mon: Rev: Nov: 1790 . . . Which Mrs Medwin wants to sell And wch She declares to be in Burkes own hand — I doubt the fact — The letters are very disjointed . . . [and] in sev^l places the writer has rubbed out with the finger what was written, which is the trick of a boy at school or Woman, not of a man — The thoughts or rather the doctrine is certainly Burkes — If the article be his, it confirms what I have heard before that B's first writings were meagre; — That he wrote & re-wrote. And that his good things & fine things were added successively." Robinson quotes several sentences from the MS, and then adds: "all this has been better said by B: in his printed works . . . . The MS has I fear no value and wo^d scarcely be bo^t by any one."

and Severn will ingrave his portrait from the miniature I have.
If there should be profits, we intend to employ them in erecting
a handsomer monument over his remains. What I stand in need of
is an account of Keats when a school boy; and if I knew C. C.
Clarke's address, I would write to him for information on that
point. As you stopped a letter from him to me,[8] I really think you
are bound to induce him to send one, giving me all he can of his
boyish disposition, and of any thing else while at school; — in one
word, I want to make out, as far as I can, the developement of his
mind. Both he and Tom have talked a little to me on this subject.[9] Can Clarke tell me in what parish Keats was born? for I
think you have given a wrong birth day,[10] though you have his
authority. I have written about this to London, but, for want of
a clue to his parish, I am unanswered.[11] In searching into a bundle
of letters and papers, which Keats left behind him, I found two
damning documents against George's defence of himself, when
accused of having taken his brother's money. You must remember
the letter Dilke sent me here on that affair, and how it placed me
in the awkward situation of having indiscreetly spoken against
another's character. Well, I wrote to Dilke, giving him *proofs* in
an Account Current, and in a letter in *George's own hand writing*,
that every word of that defence is a falsehood, and asking him to
do me justice among our mutual friends in England.[12] This he
took in high dudgeon, refused to interfere, and treated me with
the most haughty insolence that ever fell to my lot to bear; —
indeed I can't bear it. Fact is, Dilke is the most positive man I
know, and I never knew him retract his positiveness. Aware of

----

[8] Probably number 87.

[9] In his "Life" (*KC*, II, 55–56) Brown gives an "account of the sudden developement of his [Keats's] poetic powers [that] I first received from his brothers, and
afterwards from himself."

[10] October 29, 1796 (*Lord Byron*, I, 409), a date that Brown followed in his
"Life" (*KC*, II, 54), adding, however, "I cannot be certain of this date. While I
was in Italy, and since my return, friends have in vain endeavoured to discover
the registry of his baptism. One of his schoolfellows informs me that he thinks
Keats must have been born a year earlier." Keats was baptized at St. Botolph's,
Bishopsgate.

[11] Brown wrote this and the preceding sentence ("Can Clarke . . .") in the
left-hand margin, marked them with an asterisk, but did not indicate where they
were to be inserted. Their position here is arbitrary.

[12] See number 101.

this, I had forborne to twit him on that theme, letting the facts stand for themselves. It was to this correspondence that I alluded when I said I had been annoyed by plaguing reflections; for the whiffing away a friendship, of thirty years,[13] in rageful words is as grievous as it is foolish. I hear, which I did not know when I first wrote, that, not long since, he lost an old friend [14] by conduct very similar to what he has inflicted on me. Dilke, I am afraid, has boasted too highly of his superior discernment, to withdraw a peg, much less the whole. I have been told that I am positive; I'll keep a watch on myself; I see that such a humour may lead a man to trample on all around, rather than say, "I am in the wrong," — or "I have been deceived." I was about to begin my letter with thanks for your promise of the new novel,[15] and lo! they come in at the fag end. Mem: I have been led astray. I dare assert it is an excellent novel, because you have taken pains with it, and are dissatisfied, — the pains you have taken have created the dissatisfaction; this is the reason why authors are enamoured of their worst offspring; we like what has given us least labour; and where we have laboured most, we are most aware of imperfection. This reminds me, in the fullest pride of humble authorship, that I have made a strange discovery into the character of Shakespear. A good deal is written 60 pages,[16] and so delighted and convinced was Landor, that he used to visit me nearly every morning to hear how I was going on. To give you an idea of it, the title is, "To the Lovers of Shakespear, a dissertation on his character, drawn from his Works." At first thought, you, like others, will, I dare say, think this puerile; but, had I you at my elbow, you would, I hope, say otherwise. What I have drawn from his plays *astonishes myself* because, being a complete dramatist, he never speaks in his own character. (Oh! could you send me Ayscough's Concordance?) [17] Then his Sonnets, — there I have made a discovery, a key to the whole, which Landor declares incontrovertible, — it is a

[13] In 1833 Dilke wrote (*KC*, II, 10) that their "intimacy & friendship *was of five & thirty years standing*" at the time of the breaking off.

[14] Perhaps Mancur (see numbers 103, 125).

[15] *Sir Ralph Esher.*

[16] The words "60 pages" are inserted above the line.

[17] Samuel Ayscough, *An Index to the Remarkable Passages and Words Made Use of by Shakspeare* (1790; 2nd edn., 1827).

discovery of which I am almost ashamed, *as* no one else discovered it before me, — the *as* is queer, but I feel it so. Landor swears, out and out, that no man ever understood Shakespear like myself; this is the greatest compliment, true or not, that ever I have received; but, true or not, I am almost as proud of it as if I had been the author of his worst play.[18] Since you were here he has been my Bible; — and, deuce take Carlino's taste, he will read any thing but Shakespear! Don't let my pen forget to attack you on a most atrocious circumstance: you recommend exercise to me; propose a horse as my legs are lazy; and infer that I am fat-suffocative. Now hear me: in my walks I am often fearful of wearing out Carlino's strength; I am the jest of my friends for walking so much; I know every high and by road for four miles round Florence; no one, except Landor, *exceeds* me; if he really does; I walk gallantly, and therefore remain "within reasonable compass." [19] Besides which, I like carriage drives to carry me into new parts whither I may wander all the day. I am astounded at your suspicions! I am egrigiously hearty, strong, young, and over-bearing, so make my love to your wife, and believe me

Your's sincerely, Cha[s] Brown.

I have read Moore's Byron (the 1st part) [20] and think it wretched, canting stuff. I am afraid it must prove a bad life, let who will write it. How came you to say of Campbell's letter that it "was written as if he was drunk, which he very likely was?" Is it not the fact that you heard me say *those very words* to three or four here? Give my best regards to M[rs] Hunt. O, Lord, I had forgot! I have sent her my *love* on the other page. I have thoughts of visiting England next summer, or the summer after next. Our summer this year is glorious.

---

[18] Brown dedicated *Shakespeare's Autobiographical Poems* (1838) to Landor, saying, "To you I first communicated at Florence my explanation of Shakespeare's SONNETS. The interest you felt, and your desire that I should publish the discovery, have induced me . . . to enter on the . . . task." He also showed the manuscript to Robinson, who entered the main points of the "discovery" in his diary, October 7, 1830 (Dr. Williams's Library), and "promised not to *talk* abo[t] [it] . . . before his book appears."

[19] *1 Henry IV*, III.iii.26.

[20] The first volume of Thomas Moore's *Letters and Journals of Lord Byron: with Notices of His Life* was published on January 15.

I won't be punctilious about your answering my letters; but if you have a spare half hour, I shall be happy.

I write here [21] merely to prove how wonderfully well filled is this sheet of paper; and to say that, notwithstanding my lengthiness, many matters are left unsaid.

· 107 ·

TO JOSEPH SEVERN

Address: Al Pittore Inglese / il Sig. Giuseppe Severn, / Nº 152 Via Rasella, / Roma.

Postmarks: FIRENZE; 6 OTTOBRE

ALS: Harvard. A long extract is printed by Sharp, pp. 170–171.

My dear Severn,   Florence. 3 October 1832.
    You did vastly wrong in sending me a scolding letter, because I have the best excuse in the world for not having written to you for a long while; which is, that not having written to any one for a long while, I could not presume to make you an invidious exception. Besides, a hard working gardener like myself has scarce time to write a note, or he is worn off his legs and arms, or his hands are too rough and tough for a slender goose quill. If you answer that my neglect is sheer idleness, then you have the greater reason to pardon it, because it has brought me into scrapes with ten others, all highly piqued at my silence. Think of eleven letters of apologies for not having written! — surely my punishment is great. I begin with you, on account of your being the greatest grumbler, — is not that kind? By the by, it was a long while before your scolding letter came to hand, owing, as usual, to your obstinacy in addressing a letter to a house in Florence; and, what was worse, to a wrong house, for you know very well I cut the town eight months ago for ever, and that I live everlastingly in a villa.[1] I am positively afraid of telling you the name and situation

[21] Opposite the address on the fourth page. The other postscripts are written in the margins of the first and second pages.

[1] Perhaps Galileo's villa (see number 94), the location of which corresponds to the subsequent description here.

of the villa, lest you should address your letters there; — is it not easy to write "Poste restante?" Should you send me a friend from Rome, bid him inquire of Johnstone the banker for my address, — that's better than trusting to your discretion. Suffice it to say I live within half a mile of the walls, have a good sized garden, unstared on, where I work away at my flowers, of which I have many choice specimens, and that I, perched on a hill, have one of the most beautiful views in the neighbourhood. On the other hand, my flower purchases have been abominably expensive, for already I have above 200 garden pots, great and small, to attend to, and my ranunculuses, anemonies, hyacinths, irises, jonquills, tulips, and narcissuses, have just cost me a mint of money. However, I am wonderfully happy among them, watching their growth. Woodhouse lived with me here for seven weeks, and he got so well in health, he was quite a credit to the place. He left me about a fortnight since for Venice and England. I like him much, and hope he will come back again. The bas relief he gave me of our Keats delights me; [2] never was any thing so like, it seems quite a piece of magic. Trelawny went to England in the spring. Every one ascribes "the younger son" [3] to him, but I believe he still denies it. Have you read it? I am told it runs off like wild fire. At the head of every chapter are one or two quotations from Byron, Keats, and Shelley, — from *no one else*; and Woodhouse and I think his lordship does not look over grand in such company. Woodhouse also thinks that these quotations, in so popular a book, will be of great service to the fame of Keats; and indeed they are chosen, in number 53 great and small, with much care, — some great friend of Keats must have done all this, don't you imagine so? [4] Woodhouse has promised to send me certain dates and other particulars, which no one would ever send me,

[2] A copy of the medallion portrait by Giuseppe Girometti (Parson, *Portraits of Keats*, pp. 151–152). Many years later Carlino gave this copy to Alfred Domett (Sharp, p. 263).

[3] *Adventures of a Younger Son*, published in 1831.

[4] Trelawny wrote to Mary Shelley on October 28, 1830 (*Letters of Trelawny*, pp. 135–136), "I have selected mottoes from the only three poets who were the staunch advocates of liberty, and my contemporaries. . . . Brown, who was very anxious about the fame of Keats, has given many of his MSS. for the purpose." About sixty lines of *Otho*, "King Stephen," and "The Cap and Bells" appeared for the first time among the fifty-four (rather than fifty-three) quotations from Keats.

and further has made me promise to write a life of Keats in my quiet country nook during this winter. Now I have changed my mind about his portrait; it must be from that medallion. What a pity it is you know nothing of flowers, — how can you be so ignorant and live? Otherwise I'd talk to you of my perfection of a volkameria, perfuming half my garden with its hyacinth-scent, with its second crop of blossoms on it at this moment; and of my noble metrosideros now in full bloom, of my verbena splendour, in bloom for these five months back, with a scarlet that would cut out all your painter's shop, and of Carlino's gardenia, — but you know nothing. O lord! I've another excuse for neglect in writing, — I've been studying botany, with its crack-jaw words. But don't believe I'll ever treat you so again, for I'm resolved to return to my old plan, that of answering every body within a week; so you may trust me, and don't seem offended. Carlino desires to learn news, bribing you with love and kisses, about Claudia and Walter.[5] Give my love to your wife, and keep her best kisses to yourself, — moderation is every thing. Kirkup has gone with Lord Wenlock (some write it Wedlock, on acount of his extraordinary connubial constancy,) [6] into the country, and with, as I was sorry to hear, a slight return of his former liver complaint; — he has made a masterly likeness of Carlino at 12 years old, — who, by the by, runs on in music, I hope well, — but to *keep in time* is his difficulty.   Your's most contritely,
Chas Brown.

I've not said a word about your painting, because I'm hardly recovered from your scolding, — I scarce know in which you most excel, — besides, you can't talk with me about flowers.

L. Hunt is earning 12 Gn^s a week for writing in the Sun Newspaper,[7] — so I hear.

[5] Severn's first son, born on October 12, 1830.

[6] Sir Robert Lawley (1768–1834), created Baron Wenlock in 1831. He had been married since 1793. Carlino (*KC*, I, lxii) tells that "When Sir Robert Lawley was made Lord Wenlock . . . he said he hoped Brown would make an exception [to his vow never to put legs under a lord's table] . . . but they drifted apart."

[7] The *True Sun*, to which Hunt contributed theatricals.

· 108 ·

WILLIAM DILKE: NOTES ON THE BROWN-DILKE CONTROVERSY
OVER GEORGE KEATS (1833)

Endorsement by C. W. Dilke: This was Brown['s] charges ag^t GK abstracted by my Brother when Brown visited England[1] & from Browns papers.

MS: Keats House, Hampstead. The account is printed in *Keats-Shelley Memorial Bulletin*, no. 14 (1963), p. 34 (in facsimile), and by Gittings, *The Keats Inheritance*, p. 78.

Charles letter[2] is dated 31st July 1824. — "Convey the spirit of what follows to Mr Hunt & any other likely to have heard of the charge" — "quite conclusive in my judgment & of others that have read them". — The letter however is not written intemperately or tauntingly when taken together & read calmly & deliberatively as I have had now an opportunity of doing. —

Mem: of Brown's.

G. states, 1st went to America (June 1818) John had not one shilling, but was indebted to him 400£.

On these grounds he builds his defence & they are thus proved untrue. Abbey Cock & Co's acc^t with John proves that exactly in June 1818 he had in their hands 468– 10. 10 & so far from John being indebted to George there is G's letter (18th March 1818) or 2 months previous, acknowledging himself then a debtor to John —

As to the assertion that John rec^d 200£ from Tom's estate it is impossible for he p^d all his bills in the spring of 1819 & had (see the acc^t) 46– 7. 7 rem^g, besides which in the summer he rec^d 30 or 40£, a returned loan from Haslam, & when G. left England a 2^d time in the winter following he owed about 60£, less 40, the only sum &

---

[1] Sharp, who saw many papers of Brown that are now lost, says (p. 174) that Brown visited England in 1833. Apparently he left Italy sometime after meeting Milnes at Landor's in April or May (Milnes, *Life*, I, ix; Super, *Landor*, pp. 237–238), and returned by September 17, when he wrote to Severn from his villa outside Florence (Sharp, p. 174; the letter is no longer extant).

[2] That is, Dilke's letter, number 60.

no more placed in his hands by George. This same 40 John lodged with Charles Brown, telling him he had lent his brother every farthing else. — Charles Brown once [?] said the sum lent by John to George was about 700£, he thinks however the sum fairly made out would amount to 500 — What he asserted in England he also wrote to George in America whose answer, far from denying the charge at that time, while his brother was supposed to be alive may be seen dated Louisv^{ille} 3^d March 1821.

> John died February 1821
> Tom   "   Dec^r ——1818. —

John K. in account with Abbey Cock.

D^r					C^r —			
1815	June 9th — Sundries	1. –						
	Dec^r — Tea. ——	1			1818			
1816.	Sundries ⎫				June 4th By Cash —— 500			
	Cocoa ⎬ 10				Decr 31 Interest —— 8– 6. 1			
	Tea ⎭				1819			
1817	d° ⎫				April 3^d			
	d° ⎬ 12							
	d° &c ⎭							
1818.	Tea &c.— X^3							
	June 19: — Cash —— 30							
	20: d° ——— 140							
	July 9th — George							
	Keats —— 30							
	Aug. 8th Cash per							
	Post ——— 30							
	Oct. 27. Cash —— 20							
	Decr 9. Himself — 20							
1819.	Febr^y 18th d° ——— 20							
	Mar. 1 d° ——— 6							
	" 15th d° ——— 60							
	" 25 – d° ——— 10							
	Ap^1 2 d° ——— 60							
	Bal^{ce} —— 46– 7– 7							
	508– 6. 1.				508. 6. 1			

April 3^d 1819 —

---

^{3} "X" (which may be "1" with a line crossing it) has to stand for £11 18s. 6d. if the account is to balance. But in any event something is amiss in the copy. In number 101 Brown says that as of June 4, 1818, Keats's debt for tea, etc., amounted to "no more than £31. 9. 2." The account is discussed by Norman Kilgour in *Keats-Shelley Memorial Bulletin*, no. 14 (1963), pp. 35–36, who suggests that the £140 withdrawn on June 20, 1818, was intended for George Keats, and by Gittings, *The Keats Inheritance*, pp. 49–51, who thinks that the initial £500 credited to John on June 4, 1818, was really George's money rather than John's.

Pancrass Lane [4]

18: March 1818. — To John Keats. Teignmouth Devon —
"The enclosed 20£ will reach you before you are quite aground, I am about paying yours as well as Tom's bills, of which I shall keep regular Acc[ts] & for the sake of justice & a future proper understanding I intend calculating the probable amount Tom & I are indebted to you, something of this kind must be done or at the end of 2 or 3 years we shall be all at sixes & sevens — let me know when you want money — I have paid Hodgkinson [5] who desires his best rem[s]"

———

M[r] John Keats.   Pancrass Lane Aug[t] 23[d] 1820.[6]
Dear Sir — I have yours of Sunday & am exceedingly grieved at the contents — you know that it was very much against my will that you lent your money to George. In my settlement with him M[r] Hodgkinson omitted a 50£ bill which he had drawn from America & not then due, so that he got this 50£ more than I knew of at the time.
Bad debts &c — & therefore it is not in my power to lend you any thing. I remain D[r] Sir
                    Yrs Richard Abbey

When you are able to call I shall be glad to see you, as I should not like to see you want "maintenance for the day". —

———

Sir   Louisville 3[d] Mar: 1821 [7]
I am obliged for yours of Dec[r] 21st informing me that my Brother is in Rome & better. The coldness of your letter explains itself.[8] I hope John is not impressed with the same sentiments, it may be an amiable resentment on your part, and you are at liberty to cherish it; whatever errors you may fall into thro' kindness for

---

[4] For the full text of this letter from George, see *Letters*, I, 247–248.

[5] Abbey's junior partner. Joanna Richardson in *Keats-Shelley Memorial Bulletin*, no. 5 (1953), p. 30, suggests that he was Cadman Hodgkinson, like Abbey a member of the Pattenmakers' Company, who died aged seventy-three in 1832.

[6] For the full text see *Letters*, II, 331.

[7] For this letter to Brown see *KC*, I, 222. Brown's of December 21, 1820, has not survived.

[8] The remainder of number 108 is copied in another hand.

my Brother however injurious to me, are easily forgiven. I might
have reasonably hoped a longer seige [9] of doubts would be necessary to destroy your good opinion of me. In many letters of
distant & late dates to John, to you, & to Haslam unanswered, I
have explained my prospects, my situation, I have a firm faith that
John has every dependance on my honor and affection, and altho'
the chances have gone against me my disappointments having
been just as numerous as my risques, I am still above water &
hope soon to be able to relieve him.

I once more thank you most fervently for your kindness to
John. and am Sir

Your ob^t Hble Servt
George Keats —

· 109 ·

FROM JOSEPH SEVERN

Address: To / Charles Brown Esqr / Poste Restante / Firenze

Postmarks: P ROMA; 18 MARZO 1834 (*another illegible*)

Endorsement: Joseph Severn

ALS: British Museum. Long extracts are printed in the *Athenaeum*, August 30, 1879, pp. 271–272, in Forman (1883), IV, 377–
379, and (from the *Athenaeum*) by Sharp, pp. 163–164.

My dear Brown   Rome March 14th 1834
Now I dont know what you'll say to the request I am going
to make, that you come off to Rome without a moments delay
and bring Keats Tragedy with you — There are here 5 Englishmen who have all been together at Cambridge, they are devoted
admirers of Keats, and as they are really clever fellows, I must
confess myself gratified with their attentions to me as the friend
of Keats. — Now you must know that they have been acting, —
two of them are first rate, and they made me join them in the 4th
act of the Merchant of Venice as Gratiano, when I was so much

---

[9] *Written* longer, seige.

331

struck with one (M^r O Brien) [1] as the very man for Ludolph in Keats's Otho. — His voice and manner of reading remind me most forcibly of Keats himself,[2] — When I mentioned to them the Tragedy they were all on fire to be at it, but I did not see any hope until I heard from Captn Baynes [3] who is also an Actor that we could easily have the beautiful private Theatre here. — I then recollected how much some years since you would have liked to have had the Tragedy acted in Rome when there were private Theatricals,[4] and I think how much more you would like it done now by *devoted admirers of Keats good actors and handsome young men* into the bargain. — I assure You that I think it would be well done and as they are all you[ng] men of rank, it would certainly be a good report to its forthcoming. — Should you not be able to come yourself — nor even Charley to play the Page cannot you send me the M.S.S by the return of Post I will be particular that no copies be taken in Any way. — [5]

Now I wonder what you will say to all this, is there any possibility that you throw cold water upon it.

And now I am going to wrangle with you — Here I have heard and heard of Keats life which you are doing, I have written & written to you about it, and now I hear nothing more, now, when the world is looking for it, and the Tragedy — Why, you would be astonished, were you to know the many who come to me as the friend of Keats, and who idolise him as another Shakespear, — 'tis an injustice to withold these two works any longer — I remember you said "the public should never have the Tragedy until they had done justice to Keat's other works" — *The time has come,* AND I FEAR THE TIME MAY PASS. — These yong men read and recite Keats to me until I think him more beautiful than ever — (I am dying for them to see the tragedy) Then there is another point — the Public is wrong about Keats himself — Ld Byron & L. Hunt have most vilely lead them astray — I persuade myself that Keats

[1] Stafford Augustus O'Brien, later Stafford-O'Brien (1811–1857), a friend of Milnes at Cambridge.

[2] Compare Woodhouse's remark to Taylor (*Letters*, II, 164), "you know how badly he [Keats] reads his own poetry."

[3] W. G. Baynes, who joined Severn's circle in 1824.

[4] See the end of number 64.

[5] See Brown's injunction at the end of number 14.

life will be a most interesting subject. — If you will go on I will send you every thing I can think of, and I am sure I can supply much — if you will not, I mean to defy you and try and write his life myself which I am sure will make you look about you — How can you be wasting your time, rewriting the lies of that Vagabond Trelawny, when you should be writing for Keats who has the 1st Claim — How rejoiced I am that Trelawny ran away with all the money, *how right I find it according to the tenor of his whole book* — the book is a very good book but it ought to be Keats's — Now tell me what you have to say by way of excuse — It cannot be save that you do not know how high Keats fame has risen — that if he is not the Poet of the million,[6] he is more, for I would say that judging of the talents of his admirers and their rank as scholars, that his fame is a proud one — So now my dear Brown I send this off Saturday Evg youll have [it] Tuesday Morg and I shall receive the Tragedy Saturday —

believe me Sincerly Yours
J. Severn

Mrs Severn sends her love to you & Charley who must be a fine lad and able to do the Page — do come and have Lamb & green Peas with me on Easter Sunday — Do Mrs Severn is preparing the room for you, and will have no refusal — There are three Ladies who act also

Rem[em]ber me to Kirk [7] and tell me how he is, and what he is doing — I will write him soon, rem[em]ber me also to Mr Landor, and any other friend I may have in Florence — We have had a beautiful Winter & a lovely spring —

---

[6] Severn had told Haslam in July 1820 (*Letters*, II, 306) that *Lamia* "will even please the Million."

[7] Kirkup.

· 110 ·

TO W. S. LANDOR [1]

Address: Post restante, Florence.

[April 4, 1835]

*   *   *

It was scarcely possible for me to make such a reply as your letter required before I quitted Florence. As we have a day's rest here I avail myself of it.[2] . . . but there are certain words, which, once uttered, whether directed towards myself or my friend, cancel every obligation; nor can I affect to feel their power lessened on account of their being uttered by the wife of my friend.[3] . . . It commenced by upbraiding you for conduct excessively bad to-wards herself; but her own statement, as well as your answer, certainly proved that you were blameless, and I ventured to point out her mistake. Unfortunately no attention was paid to either of us; and still more unfortunately — [4] . . .

    I am ashamed to write down the words, but to hear them was painful. . . . I am afraid my patience would have left me in a tenth part of the time; but you, to my astonishment, sat with a

---

[1] From Forster, *Landor*, II, 307–309, who supplies the fragmentary address given in the headnote, dates the letter "from Genoa on the 4th of April," and explains: "In April 1835 Landor had left his villa, and was in Florence waiting a letter from Armitage Brown, at this time on his way to England. A few nights before his departure, when bidden to his last dinner at the villa, he had been present at the scene that had driven Landor from Fiesole; and in justification of this extreme step an account of what he witnessed had been asked from him." On this incident, which occurred late in March, see Super, *Landor*, pp. 251–253. Apparently Brown left Florence for England almost immediately afterward (Sharp, p. 176; Super, p. 560). Landor permanently separated from his wife three months later.

[2] Forster paraphrases the omitted passage: "He grieves to have to be ungracious to one who had uniformly treated him with the utmost courtesy and kindness."

[3] Forster: "He then describes language used in presence of the elder children, which had constituted the unpardonable offence, and which he declares to have had no provocation."

[4] Forster adds: "But the story is an old and familiar one, that it is the very consciousness of our own injustice which will make us add to the injury we inflict, and that, by doing all we can to aggravate the wrong we commit, we seem to justify ourselves for committing it."

composed countenance, never once making use of an uncivil expression, unless the following may be so considered, when, after
about an hour, she seemed exhausted: "I beg, madam, you will, if
you think proper, proceed; as I made up my mind, from the first,
to endure at least twice as much as you have been yet pleased to
speak." After dinner, when I saw her leave the room, I followed,
and again pointed out her mistake; when she readily agreed with
me, saying she was convinced you were not to blame. At this I
could not forbear exclaiming, "Well, then?" in the hope of bearing back to you some slight acknowledgment of regret on her
part: but in this I was disappointed. You conclude your letter
with "I feel confident you will write a few lines, exculpating me
if you think I have acted with propriety in very trying circumstances; and condemning me if I acted with violence, precipita-
tion, or rudeness." For more than eleven years I have been intimate with you, and, during that time, frequenting your house, I
never once saw you behave towards Mrs. Landor otherwise than
with the most gentlemanly demeanour, while your love for your
children was unbounded. I was always aware that you gave entire
control into her hands over the children, the servants, and the
management of the house; and when vexed or annoyed at anything, I could not but remark that you were in the habit of requesting the cause to be remedied or removed, as a favour to
yourself. All this I have more than once repeated to Mrs. Landor
in answer to her accusations against you, which I could never well
comprehend. When I have elsewhere heard you accused of being
a violent man, I have frankly acknowledged it; limiting however
your violence to persons guilty of meanness, roguery, or duplicity;
by which I meant, and said, that you utterly lost your temper with
the Italians.

*   *   *

· 111 ·

TO JOSEPH SEVERN

Address: Rome. Italie. / Al Pittore Inglese, / il Sig. Giuseppe Severn, / Via Rasella, / Roma.

Postmarks: P[L]YMOUTH JY 27 1836; LONDON 29 JULY 1836; C PAID 29 JY 29 1836; ANGLETERRE PAR CALAIS; PONT BEAUVOISIN; CORRISP^{ZA} ESTERA DA GENOVA; T.F; 11 AG 1836

ALS: Harvard.

My dear Severn,   Laira Green. 6 July 1836.

Following your good example, I sit down to answer your letter on the day of its arrival; but I know not when it will be finished, — but be that as it may. I very much like your account of the new altar piece,[1] — and am again to lament the being bereaved of a parish church, otherwise I might give it a hoisting. A new edition of Keats's poems may be published, but any additions, from his Mss, are forbidden by his heir at law, George Keats; it was plainly told to me, if I attempted it, an injunction would be served;[2] Mr Milnes thought he had not the power to do so, but that gentleman, after an inquiry, has altered his opinion. In a former letter surely I gave you an account of house expences in Plymouth;[3] — I did not? — well then, in the hope of luring Captn Baynes hither, I will now. Not knowing the markets in Rome, I can make no comparison with them; but, taking one thing with another, I find that living here is cheaper than at Florence. Bread is the same; meat (all

[1] "The Infant of the Apocalypse Caught up to Heaven," commissioned by Cardinal Weld as a present for the Pope, to be placed in the Cathedral Church of San Paolo fuori le Mura (Sharp, p. 168). A study for the altarpiece was exhibited at the Royal Academy in 1838 (see number 116, n. 3).

[2] In number 114 Brown says that an injunction was threatened in 1835, but George Keats did not write to Dilke between November 1833 and March 1836 (*KC*, II, 22). In spite of the injunction Brown published Keats's sonnet "If by dull rhymes" in the *Plymouth, Devonport, and Stonehouse News*, October 15, 1836.

[3] The letter is mentioned by Sharp, p. 177, but is now unknown. Brown arrived in England at the end of April or beginning of May 1835, took a house in Plymouth, and then perhaps a year later moved to the cottage in Laira Green, two miles northeast of Plymouth (Sharp, pp. 176–177).

kinds round) much the same; tea and sugar are a little dearer; poultry and game are, considering the size and quality, much the same; fish is very cheap, while in Italy it was my most expensive luxury; milk and butter are both cheaper and better here; fuel (coals instead of wood and charcoal) is greatly cheaper; and servants' wages are low with us, — I pay for an excellent woman servant of all work £6 a year, and £1 for tea and sugar, — in Florence I was obliged to have a man, who cost me £15 a year in wages, the women there being good for nothing as servants. On the other hand, those who must have wine in England, though the duty is lowered, must buy it at an extravagant price, compared with that of Italian wines swallowed on the spot. The house I live in is extraordinary, being extra parochial; but poors' rates and taxes are not what they were. The house I had in Plymouth was on a small scale, 2 parlours, 5 bedrooms, a kitchen, and scullery, — all small; for that I paid £19 a year rent, £2. 1. – poors' rates, £1. 8 window tax, and a pound or two will be claimed from me for the passed year's lighting, watching, watering, and paving. Tell Captⁿ Baynes all this, and tell him honest and happy human faces are to be had here at every turn; after living so long among those down looking Italians, (or, if they look up, they do so with a sinister expression,) these manly and womanly english countenances are a delight. Then again, I am content to let the scenery of the south, albeit few admired it more than myself, live in my memory, and, for the future, enjoy the woodland and meadowland of my native soil. It was but yesterday when we and our neighbours, leaving Laira Green well nigh empty, set out on a pic nic to Bickleigh vale; the gemmen walked, the ladies donkey'd, the cart brought up our provisions; what an enchanting place! — what woods! what quiet nooks! and what a river is the Plym! — so gentle, so clear, so winding, and so begirt with green banks and flowers! We had a glorious day of it, all happy, chiefly in vying with each other to make all happy, and we returned in the evening, tired, but still laughing away fatigue. We were not once asked for our passports, and not even a policeman came civilly about us to guess at our proceedings. Imagine the cloth laid on the grass, and kept firmly in its place, by a veal pie, a chicken and beef d^o, two currant and raspberry d^o, a mug of clouted cream, a dish of sliced beef, a d° of sausages, a d° of cucumbers, — and all that! — do you not chuckle and lick your lips at the thought of it? Not that we had no troubles, — for the sound of distant thunder alarmed a girl who had heard sad stories of the effects of lightening under trees, a lady tore her gown with a bramble, one donkey would not cross any sort of brook, my sister in law [4] was horror struck at the suspicion of a wasp's nest in the bank, and a boy was popped at in the face by an effervescing cider bottle, — and oh! oh, fie! my boy cracked his trowsers right across his head's antipodes!!

27 July. It is high time to banish this sheet of paper from my portfolio. I have been, and am still annoyed by workmen, building an extra bed-room, and a green house, with sundry jobs. The green house is to be my grand delight. Then I have attended the hanging of the pictures at our Institution,[5] — not a bad show, — a few good modern ones, and several good ones by old masters, — there is one Rembrandt superlative, — a Sir Joshua, — and some others. After all, I have hung up your miniature of Carlino,[6] that the series, if of interest, may be complete. Kirkup's portrait of you is there.[7] My copies of your miniature of Keats, and of the sketch you made of him shortly before he died, and Girometti's study for the cammeo for Woodhouse are there.[8] Do you recollect a little nephew of mine at Hampstead, whose portrait you took as a study for Falstaff's Page? [9] — wonderful to say, he is grown up to a fellow of eight and twenty! Severn! — you and I are waxing old! — don't tell your wife! Well, that same nephew is a surgeon, is married, and has a child and three quarters, — and has come to live at Plymouth.

---

[4] The widow of John Armitage Brown, apparently now living in Plymouth with her son, the nephew mentioned below (see n. 9). Brown made a colored pencil sketch of her in 1837.

[5] The Plymouth Institution, founded in 1812.

[6] Severn's two miniatures of Carlino (aged three and six), now at Keats House, Hampstead, are reproduced by Joanna Richardson in *Keats-Shelley Memorial Bulletin*, no. 5 (1953), p. 49.

[7] See the end of number 90.

[8] See numbers 100 (for Brown's copy of the miniature), 37 (the deathbed portrait), and 107 (Girometti's medallion).

[9] "Falstaff" is mentioned in number 45. The nephew was John Mavor Brown, who, according to Brown's great-grandnephew R. A. Walker (in a letter to L. A. Holman, December 23, 1932, now at Harvard), married Louise Dunnage and had three sons and two daughters. He later moved to Kineton, Warwickshire.

He will be ballotted for at our Institution, and must give us some botanical lectures. By the by, I study and have long studied botany. I tell him our Institution has forwarded many in their professions, and that he ought to be as impudent a member as his uncle. Give my love and Carlino's to your wife; and tell your little Romans [10] there is one in England, besides their relations, who is glad to hear they look and behave as they ought, — and who would be glad to pay his admiration personally.

Your's most sincerely, Cha[s] Brown.

· 112 ·

TO JOSEPH SEVERN [1]

Laira Green,
26th November, 1836.

When I received your last letter,[2] nearly three months ago, I resolved not to answer you in a hurry, though now, upon looking back, I am astonished at so much time having passed. How could I write to disturb the pleasant dreams in which you then were? You were resolved on a fine monument to Keats, and I utterly disapproved of it. If his Poems should induce his countrymen, otherwise uninfluenced, to erect a monument to him, my joy would be great; but I cannot approve of such an honour, in a questionable shape, by his *personal* friends, paid to him *as a poet*. Still, looking on the intention in its best point of view, I do not perceive it can do his fame any harm, — which, at first sight, I thought I did perceive. The impropriety of a relation or a friend [3] as a subscriber to or furtherer of national feeling, of a national tribute, I feel so strongly, that I am afraid thousands of others will feel the same. On this ground, while I sincerely thank you for referring the subject of a bas-relief and other matters to me, conjointly with yourself, I must decline having anything to do with

---

[10] By now there were four: Claudia, Walter, Ann Mary (b. 1832), and Henry Augustus (b. 1833). Another son was born later this year.

[1] From Sharp, pp. 178–179.

[2] Of July 13 (Forman, 1883, IV, 379–380; Sharp, p. 165, following the *Athenaeum*, August 30, 1879, p. 272, dates it July 10).

[3] Severn had suggested George Keats and Woodhouse as subscribers.

the monument, — except on one point. This point is that not one word shall be there except those contained in his dying request — "Here lies one whose name was writ in water." Swayed by a very natural feeling at the time, I advised more,[4] but now I am convinced of the error, the sort of profanation of adding even a note of admiration to his own words. If a dying friend, a good man, leaves strict orders for the wording of his epitaph, he should be obeyed, if good faith is in the world. I have long repented of my fault, and must repeat what I said to you in Rome, "I hope the government will permit the erasure of every word, with the exception of those words to which he himself limited his epitaph." The memory of Keats has been one of my greatest pleasures, but lately it has been mixed with pain, — for I have been occupied in writing my life of him, and, consequently, been turning over letters and papers, some full of hope, others of despair, and my mind has been compelled to trace one misfortune to another, all connected with him. I knew this task was my duty, and, from the beginning I had from time to time made, I found it a painful one. Therefore to compel me to my duty, I boldly put down my name at our Institution for a lecture, on 27th December,[5] on "The Life and Poems of John Keats." Now that it is advertised, the card printed, the members looking forward to it, there is no retreating: it must be done. About one half is done. Probably I shall afterwards print it in a Magazine, there to rest as a voucher for his admirers; possibly I may print it in a small volume by itself; in either shape you must have it. My first lecture was given about a fortnight ago,[6] "The Intellectual History of Florence." I was aware of the interest of the subject, but the unusual hand-applause and the high compliments bestowed on me were unexpected. After the "Life of Keats" I shall give no more lectures this season.

* * *

[4] See number 35.
[5] He gave the lecture on December 29 (see the next letter).
[6] On November 10 (lectures were given on Thursdays).

· 113 ·

TO LEIGH HUNT

AL: Harvard. Printed in *KC*, II, 26–28.

Laira Green, near Plymouth.

My dear Hunt,   21st Decr 1836.

After a long silence on both sides, when a letter does come, there is generally something particular in it. Be patient, — you will come to it presently. Many a resolution and many an attempt have I made to write a life of our Keats, but the pain as often made me defer it. Still I felt it a duty; and, last summer, when the card of winter lectures was to be printed at our Literary Institution, of which I am a member, I boldly put my name down for a "Life of Keats" on 29th Decr. Thus I compelled myself, in spite of pain, to fulfil my duty. So, to-morrow week, in the evening, from seven to ten o'Clock, you may imagine me reading my paper to about a hundred gentlemen, explaining any question I may be asked, or discussing his merits as a poet, or reading his posthumous poems. Afterwards it will be published, though in what work, or by itself, I am yet in doubt. Now I am unwilling to do this without first acquainting you. There may be something you may wish were introduced, of which I am ignorant. Mine is a most plain un-varnished tale,[1] and rather short. None of his living friends are mentioned by name except yourself and Severn. Indeed I feel so cautious about mentioning the living,[2] that I prefer telling you beforehand, and subject to correction, what I have said of you. In the first place you are mentioned, without comment, as having been the first to notice his poetry, which you did in the Ex-aminer;[3] then, when I left him to go to the Highlands a second time, I say, — "It was his choice, during my absence, to lodge at Kentish Town, that he might be near his friend, Leigh Hunt, in

---

[1] *Othello*, I.iii.90.

[2] See Brown's remarks in numbers 89 and 95 on Hunt's speaking "of the living" and giving their "names at full length" in *Lord Byron*.

[3] On December 1, 1816, pp. 761–762 (see *KC*, II, 56–57).

341

whose companionship he was ever happy." [4] After this, I speak of your kindness in a word; and in a letter of his, there is another word to the same effect.[5] To tell the truth, this does not quite satisfy me; but I had fallen into a most unadorned and matter of fact style, oppressed, all the while, by a head-ache, — uncommon for me — or I was crying like a child. Then, I have thought, the more simple the more powerful are the words. One thing I think of doing, and I will do it, unless you object to it; the introduction of your letter to Severn,[6] when we feared Keats was dying; it arrived too late; Severn showed it to me, and I was so touched by it, that I took a copy. There was a letter from Shelley,[7] inviting him to Pisa; you begged it from me, and you had it; can you send me a copy of that? Are there any letters from him to you, which you wish to be published? I open the life with my favourite passage in "Adonais".[8] I know not what the London Bookseller's answer may be, but I am anxious to get it off my mind; so, do not you delay letting me know what you like, or what you dislike, or sending me copies of letters, — otherwise you may chance to be too late.[9]

*　　*　　*

[4] *KC*, II, 74.
[5] *KC*, II, 78.
[6] See number 26, n. 1. Brown omitted the letter from his "Life."
[7] *Letters*, II, 310–311.
[8] Lines 370–383.
[9] The second leaf of the letter is missing.

· 114 ·

TO LEIGH HUNT

Address: Leigh Hunt Esqre / 4 Upper Cheynè Row / Chelsea.

Postmark: PLYMOUTH JU 10 1837

ALS: British Museum. Extracts are given by Edmund Blunden, *Shelley and Keats as They Struck Their Contemporaries* (London, 1925), p. 83, and Bodurtha and Pope, pp. 18–19.

Laira Green, near Plymouth.

My dear Hunt, 10 June 1837.

The swift answer you require is here. I have all Keats's un-published poems, to which you are most welcome, piecemeal or at "one fell swoop;" [1] but I send none to you at present, for the following reason: — Geo. Keats has empowered Mr Dilke to lay an injunction against the publication of any of his deceased brother's works. At least such was the case two years since,[2] and I have heard nothing to the contrary. If Mr Dilke will consent to the printing, in your new periodical,[3] of some of Keats's *minor* poems, such as sonnets, and other short pieces, I will gladly and immediately send some to you. To print them without his consent would but subject you (so it appears) to an injunction.

I have the "Life," which was read at our Plymouth Institution in December last. As I conceived it my duty to write it, I have pleasure in its existence; but my intention of publishing it is not so eager as it was. 1st I must not give his unpublished works, nor can I refer to them effectually till they shall be published; — this, however, is not much. 2^d By the experience I had at our Institu-tion, and by what I read in the works of the day, I fear that his fame does not yet stand high enough. 3^d I had rather a cool reply on the subject from Saunders and Otley.[4] And 4th I would almost rather it were published after my death than it should disturb my

---

[1] *Macbeth*, IV.iii.219.
[2] See number 111, n. 2.
[3] The *Monthly Repository*, which ran from June 1837 to April 1838.
[4] Publishers at 50 Conduit Street, Regent Street. They issued several works by Landor in the 1830's.

tranquillity, from attacks, whether against him by his revilers, or against me — for I know not what. It had a remarkable reception at our Institution; but, I have been told, less on his account as a poet than on account of its interest as a piece of biography, read by the friend of a young poet — no matter who it was. It also exalted me as his friend; a compliment which I had endeavoured to avoid, but possibly the endeavour had directly the contrary effect of what I intended. Among other parsons Coleridge's son was there,[5] and he was the only person (as well as parson) present who had *read* his poems, — he was enthusiastic in their praise. There were two parsons, one a regular and the other a dissenter, who angered me a little, — but it was of no importance; — I paid one in his own coin, and will pay the other by degrees; — you can well imagine that an exposure of the Tory critics [6] on Keats must necessarily make many a parson spiteful.

Now let me, since you have a good opinion of your new speculation, congratulate you on it. I never have seen the "Repository." I hope you will soon raise it into more general notice, and that I shall have to wish you joy on its success. This I call kind-hearted, after your wishing me in London! — and in the turmoil of literature too! You may be too busy, but get some one to write me how the "Repository" goes on. Do not, if possible, make too great, or too *lasting* a sacrifice in borrowing money for the purpose. As it is not in my power to lend money, I can preach moderation to lenders. I heard from Kirkup lately, — he was very well. Last year he married off his third M^rs K [7] to a Florentine Marquis, — a Medeci! [8] Remembrances to all at home.

> Your's most sincerely,
> Chas Brown.

As you are near at hand, you can best make the needful inquiry of Mr Dilke.

---

[5] Coleridge's second son, Derwent (1800–1883), is listed as a corresponding member from Helston in *Transactions of the Plymouth Institution* (Plymouth, 1830), p. 354.

[6] In *Blackwood's* and the *Quarterly Review*.

[7] That is, his third mistress. Kirkup did not marry until 1875, when he was eighty-seven.

[8] Perhaps the Marchese Luigi de' Medici-Tornaquinci, Landor's landlord in the 1820's (Super, *Landor*, pp. 157, 197).

· 115 ·

TO JOSEPH SEVERN [1]

Laira Green, near Plymouth,
My dear Severn,   26th October, 1837.

It is now ten months since I wrote to you, and all this time I have had no news of you or yours. My faculty of hope is tolerably strong; but when I found the cholera had ceased in Rome, and still you did not write, I became uneasy, till last night I tossed about in bed in downright fear.[2] Pray write immediately. Keats's "Life" remains unpublished till called for; I am sorry to say there is no call for it at present, so it may remain quiet till I am "quietly inurned." [3] I have done what I conceived my duty, and I can leave it to another generation, if, after my death, he should be then more considered by the many. I cannot bear the thought of its being printed and received as of little interest except among a few. Sometimes, however, I think of printing a limited number, and of not selling one; and sometimes my purpose is to lodge it in the British Museum, to be referred to at any time, by anybody. It is, of course, short, as I am not permitted to use for publication his posthumous poems. . . . Last Thursday I gave one lecture on Shakespeare, and to-night I am to give another.[4] In that one already given I brought forward very strong circumstantial evidence from his works that he must necessarily have visited Italy, about 1597, I having first proved that he had sufficient means, with prudence, to meet the expense of such a journey. By the bye, from some late discoveries, irrefragable ones, I can calculate that, at the age of forty-four, he was possessed in lands and money, of £6500 in our present money, or £1300 of his time. I was listened to with deep interest; [5] but neither that, nor the question of his

[1] From Sharp, p. 184.
[2] For Severn's account of his activities during the plague of 1837 ("the cholera year") see Sharp, pp. 179–183.
[3] *Hamlet*, I.iv.49.
[4] In *Shakespeare's Autobiographical Poems* (London, 1838), p. 102n, Brown tells that "Three papers, parts of this volume, were read at the Plymouth Institution." The lecture of "Last Thursday" (October 19) became the chapter "Did He Visit Italy?" (pp. 100–118).
[5] Forster, *Landor*, II, 387–388, says that Brown "does not seem to have made

learning in the classics, could raise a general discussion. Every man would have it understood he knows a great deal about Shakespeare, but if he is led into deep water, he is silent.

*   *   *

. 116 .

TO JOSEPH SEVERN [1]

London,

My dear Severn,   2nd June, 1838.

Here am I, lured from my quiet cottage to the turmoil of a city, for the sake of publishing a volume,[2] which may, in its consequences, bring disquiet into my cottage. One good thing, however, has accrued: — I have seen your four pictures in the Exhibition.[3] My praise is worth nothing, as I am an interested party; but they are much praised by those who know nothing about you. They are well placed. Your "Crusaders" seems to be the chief favourite; though I prefer the Venetian scene. The composition of the former is most striking. Imagination, which we rarely see now-a-days in painting, is in your painting; not a dreamy one, like Fuseli's,[4] but one that makes your treatment of a subject gain imperceptibly on the beholder. The colour fully keeps its pur-

---

much impression with these lectures, until, with the view of proving that Shakespeare must have had ample means for visiting Italy, he undertook to show that at the age of forty-three the great poet was worth nearly seven thousand pounds: when a burst of glad applause, sudden as a pistol-shot, shook the lecture-hall. [In *Shakespeare's Autobiographical Poems*, p. 102n, Brown gives a similar account.] Brown mentioned this to Landor as quite a good anecdote in the history of human nature, showing the delight of those west-country folk at the rewards bestowed, even in his lifetime, on the author of *Othello*; but Landor declared with his hearty laugh that it showed only how much better than a wilderness of *Othellos* they comprehended seven thousand pounds."

[1] From Sharp, p. 186.

[2] *Shakespeare's Autobiographical Poems*.

[3] At the Royal Academy. Severn's pictures were "The Infant of the Apocalypse Saved from the Dragon" (see number 111, n. 1), "Ariel," "The First Crusaders in Sight of Jerusalem" (called by the *Athenaeum*, May 19, p. 363, "a work of great merit"), and "The Finale of a Venetian Masque at the Summer's Dawn" — Graves, *The Royal Academy of Arts*, VII (1906), 82.

[4] John Henry Fuseli (1741–1825), Anglo-Swiss historical painter, professor and Keeper of the Royal Academy when Severn studied there.

346

pose with any of the best around them. Wilkie must be merely painting for money, — his are sad fallings off. Turner is like a kitchen-fire in the dog-days.[5] Going from the Exhibition to the National Gallery,[6] I became intoxicated with admiration; and I endeavoured to account for part of their — the old masters' — superiority. Beyond any modern they contrived to give a roundness to the figures; somehow, it seems as if, by turning the frame, we could see the other side of the limbs. How this is managed I know not, but occasionally I perceive they adopted a bold, harsh outline, which, I thought, contributed to the magical effect. This, together with the depth they gave to their pictures, seems to me the grand secret: reflect on how it might be done. . . . Dilke is altogether unpleasant towards myself. He is dogmatical, conceited, and rude. Success has turned his brains. For the last fortnight I have kept from his house, except in paying two visits of mere civility; and though I will not again quarrel with him, I would rather not henceforth be in his company: it is a nuisance to my better thoughts. My forthcoming volume is on Shakespeare. It is printed at my own risk. I say nothing of its contents, as I shall send you a copy by Mr. Crawford,[7] who will set off for Florence in about two months. Charles Richards prints it. I have dined with Haslam, who lives like a most prosperous man. He has a wife and daughter,[8] the latter a nice girl of about sixteen; he sends remembrances, and no reproaches for not writing. In this town, this city of humbug, I am hurried and flurried in all sorts of ways. I am sick of the eternal wheels, sick of the eternal streets, and abominably sick of the process of printing. Away I go to-morrow, leaving the last proofs to the care of the printer.

*   *   *

[5] Sir David Wilkie (1785–1841) and J. M. W. Turner (1775–1851). Reviewing the exhibition, the *Athenaeum*, May 12, pp. 346–347, said that Wilkie's "The Queen Holding Her First Council" was "the object of most general attraction," and that "Turner is in all his force this year," though generally "the artists to whom we have been accustomed to turn for our chiefest pleasure, have fallen below their usual standard."

[6] The "new" National Gallery, adjacent to the Royal Academy, had opened to the public on April 9 (*Athenaeum*, April 7, May 12, pp. 257, 347).

[7] Identified in Sharp's index and by Rollins, *KC*, I, 241n, as the Crauford who commissioned copies of Raphael by Severn in 1823 and 1824 (see number 64, n. 9).

[8] Mary (the second Mrs. Haslam) and Annette Augusta (probably the daughter of the first Mrs. Haslam).

· 117 ·

TO JOSEPH SEVERN

Address: Joseph Severn Esqre / 19 Brook Street / London.

Postmarks: PLYMOUTH AU 23 1838; C 25 AU 25 1838

ALS: Harvard. Sharp, pp. 186–187, prints all but the last two sentences.

My dear Severn,   Laira Green. 23^d Augt 1838.

You puzzle me with your unadvised comings, your threatened goings, and your unthought of stayings.[1]

I enter heart and hand into all your good purposes about Keats.[2] You do me injustice in thinking I am remiss or lukewarm. His memoir has been long ready, and I am anxious it should be published. Here are the difficulties in publishing the whole of his poems. Moxon [3] told me that Taylor, like a dog in a manger, will neither give a second edition, nor allow another to give one. But now, I believe, his copywright is out. George Keats threatened any one with an injunction who should publish the posthumous poems; this indeed stopped me in the intended publication of the memoir. Dilke, George's agent, however, told me, when I was in town, that George wished to obtain from me those posthumous poems, by purchase, if they could not be otherwise obtained.[4] My reply was most conciliatory on this point, putting all thoughts of profit aside. I desired to publish a few here.[5] Dilke told me he knew of no objection *now* to my publishing the whole.

---

[1] "In the summer of this year Severn made a flying visit to London," returning to Italy shortly after the date of this letter (Sharp, pp. 165n, 188). In number 150 Brown calls the trip "your Coronation visit" (Victoria was crowned on June 28).

[2] Severn had written on August 21 (Forman, 1883, IV, 381; Sharp, pp. 165–166) to inquire about Brown's progress on the Keats memoir and tell about new plans for a monument.

[3] Edward Moxon (1801–1858), co-owner of Keats's poems with Taylor after 1845 (*KC*, II, 128–129) and publisher of Milnes's life of Keats in 1848.

[4] See *KC*, II, 23, 30.

[5] Brown published twelve poems by Keats in *PDWJ* between July 19 and November 22, 1838, and a fragmentary stanza in an article on July 4, 1839 (see Richardson, *The Everlasting Spell*, pp. 210–211, for a list of the poems). See also number 111, n. 2, above.

Thus it stands. A publisher, whoever he may be, would desire explicit allowance, lest he might subject himself to an injunction; and he, a stranger, would be the fittest party to apply to Dilke and, if necessary, to Taylor. I know not where Woodhouse's papers are,[6] but I have every thing, from which a proper selection should be made, as some poems are trivial, or some parts are, and some were written when he was unskilled. The former difficulties may now be easily overcome, and I hope soon to hear from you that a respectable publisher is taking it in hand. Perhaps mine, Bohn in King William Street,[7] will be glad to enter on it.

When in town I doubted the behaviour of Dilke, as he is subject to violent fits of ill temper. I doubt nothing now. It was all malice prepense. My fault has been in not lauding his literary talents, which was out of my power. I could praise his talents in obtaining success,[8] but no more. My conscience has undone me with him. Two days since I wrote him a declaration of war, because I would not be treacherous like himself; and I told him plainly he was generally regarded as a blockhead, quoting Charles Lamb's adjective, — for a particular sort of a blockhead, — a dilkish blockhead. Thus during the winter I can, without remorse, draw him at full length in a novel.[9] He is a capital character for one. Because I rarely show my teeth, he thought I was unable to bite.

Mind you come here on your way to Paris. You can go every mile of the way by steam. Give me warning of your approach, lest I should be flitting on some little excursion.

I wrote to you at Rome a kind message from Haslam. You have seen him of course. Thos Richards, the eldest son of our old friend, wrote to you at the Academy in order to learn your ad-

---

[6] Woodhouse died on September 3, 1834, leaving to Taylor, among other things, "all papers I have in the handwriting of Keats or relating to him and all manuscript copies of his Poetry whether yet printed or not; and all copies of his letters and all other papers whatsoever connected with him" (Blunden, *Keats's Publisher*, p. 199). Many of the papers are now in the Harvard and Pierpont Morgan libraries.

[7] James Bohn (1803–1880), of 12 King William Street, West Strand, publisher of *Shakespeare's Autobiographical Poems*.

[8] As editor and proprietor of the *Athenaeum* since 1830.

[9] He did, in the unfinished "Walter Hazlebourn," now at Keats House, Hampstead (see Richardson, *The Everlasting Spell*, pp. 90–92, for extracts). His "declaration of war" has not survived.

dress for me. He writes he has neither seen you, nor heard from you. His brother,[10] a godson of mine, is on a visit here. See Thomas at 100 St Martin's Lane, at the printing office.[11]

Your's most truly,

Cha[s] Brown.

· 118 ·

TO LEIGH HUNT

ALS: British Museum.

My dear Hunt,   Laira Green. 20 Sept[r] 1838.

I hear your drama [1] is actually forthcoming, and, as before, I promise success, grounded on its scenic treatment, for more is not yet in my knowledge. If you have not already another subject on your mind, you ought to have one; and, supposing it possible you have not, I send you two, which have been furnished to me by my friend here, Col[l] Smith.[2] This gentleman, of whom M[r] Macready [3] can afford you much delightful information, begs me to say he will, in case you should dramatize either of the legends, send you every fact, you may deem necessary, respecting the manners and customs in domestic life during the feudal times in France of that period. A dramatist, I hold, should select a story involving new combinations of feelings and passions; and, in this light, I was particularly struck with both the legends. The first I give took place at Begard, near Corseul in Bretony; on the borders of the celebrated forest of Broceliand, famous in the romances of the Round Table Cycle. Its era is 1373–6. The following is taken from a Ms by the Colonel; but further information can be obtained from *Tristan le Voyageur* by Marchangy.[4]

---

[10] Sidney Richards.

[11] Where he was in business with his uncle Charles.

[1] *A Legend of Florence*, produced at Covent Garden on February 7, 1840, and published by Moxon in the same year.

[2] Lieutenant Colonel Charles Hamilton Smith (1776–1859), F.R.S., F.L.S., artist, writer on many subjects.

[3] William Charles Macready (1793–1873), the actor.

[4] Louis Antoine François de Marchangy, *Tristan le voyageur, ou la France au XIVe siècle*, 6 vols. (Paris, 1825).

"Yeolinde de Malestroit and Giran de Tresumel et Plemangât are the subject of a romantic tale of love and murder. The lover carried off the lady at the feast before hir wedding to another. Her father pursued them in the dark, and fell, unknown to his daughter, by the hand of Giran. He concealed her in his castle; but, feeling that the slayer of the father must not wed the daughter, he put off the ceremony. The poor creature, ignorant that she was an orphan by her lover's hand, wondered, pined, and vowed a pilgrimage to be performed by herself alone. She departed, and died on the road of a broken heart. The lover sought her to no purpose, till supernatural warning brought him to the Abbey of Begard, where he beheld her funeral and *his own* in preparation. He fled, but lost his way, so that next morning he found himself again at the Abbey Church-door. Forth came a Knight; it was the brother of his beloved. This brother, believing not only that Giran had slain the father, but also had been guilty of abandoning Yeolinde, challenged him instantly. The lover drew his sword, but only made a semblance of defending himself, and was consequently pierced to the heart. When his body was brought into the Church, the Abbot said he had received an unearthly warning to commence the service the evening before, and therefore was quite prepared. Giran was buried by the side of the wretched Yeolinde. This story created extraordinary interest and commiseration."

Lest you should not immediately perceive that which, I think, constitutes its value, I will say a few words on it. Here is no repulsive villainy, no evil passions. On the other hand, the tale is full of the strongest passions, leading through woful errors to death. The scenes at Giran's castle between the lovers would be strangely natural and effective; he with his affection unabated, nay heightened, while his marital love is utterly chilled; she horror-struck at his inexplicable and sudden coldness. It may be necessary, should the authority be wanting, to invent a character for the baffled bridegroom at the first, as well as other circumstances, so as to make the audience well acquainted with all the family in the first act, which might be most interesting in itself. The supernatural agency should, to my notion, be retained, but it must be skilfully managed. One way is by the father's ghost appearing, or rather *not* appearing to Giran and the Abbot, — that is, *not* appearing on the stage, — though with due preparation, why not?

Now I must return to the Colonel's Mss for an introduction to the second legend.

"On the site of the village of Savasse, in the present department of the Drome, in Dauphiny, there stood the city of Mergalant, probably as old as the Ligurian period before the Roman conquest. It was finally destroyed by the Saracens in the 7th century. The vicinity is highly picturesque, and full of chivalrous records. The forest of Acquabella, or Acquebelle, is celebrated for the beauty of its trees, and the verdure of the grass, nourished by numerous rivulets. Here also at the hamlet of Lene, originally Helene, a ruined tower is pointed out, standing on a rocky ridge, half hidden in trees, oaks, elms, and chesnuts. Within this structure tradition relates that a young lady was imprisoned under the pretence of leprosy. — See De la Croix. *Essai sur la statistique de la Drome*; also Marchangy, who relates it, in his own way, from De la Croix." [5]

With this notice for authorities the Ms stops; but as well as the Colonel can recollect the legend, it is as follows.

Helene, who gave the name to the hamlet, was left a young orphan, her father dying a Crusader in the Holy Land. Her uncle, in order to possess the Lordship, persuaded her she was a leper, frightful to behold, and dangerously infectuous, upon which she consented to live secluded in the tower. Of course the little polished steel or silver mirrors were out of her reach. Her attendant, or jailor, did not act severely, merely performing the task assigned to seclude her and to reiterate the progress of leprosy on her face. She even had the enjoyment of a small garden. Somehow (I know not how) an aged Knight Templar was admitted, while he was escaping from the extermination of his Order in France, 1306–7. Having seen her and heard her story, he went his way, and soon died, but previously he had made a young Knight acquainted with the discovery. This young Knight also gained admittance, by

---

[5] Nicolas Delacroix, *Essai sur la statistique, l'histoire et les antiquités du département de la Drôme* (Valence, 1817). In his second edition (Valence, 1835), Delacroix merely mentions the story, referring (pp. 520, 608) to Marchangy (see the preceding note), 2nd edn., VI (Paris, 1826), 10–59, for details.

bribery or what not. He saw her most beautiful, and told her so. Gradually she became aware of the deception practised on her, and gradually her young heart throbbed with joy to think she was not hideous, not an outcast, not infectuous to the world, and she loved the youth, who showed he loved her, for the tidings. (None but L. Hunt can paint such a scene exquisitely.) She was reinstated in her feudal rights by her lover; they were to be married; but first it was his duty to join some enterprise, some war. Thus separated, the uncle, hoping to get rid of Helene another way, intercepted all letters & messages between them; till she, believing herself forsaken, died. He returned, but only found her monument.

The authorities given may afford more particulars. I do not like the unmitigated sorrow (with the exception of one gleam of joy) attending poor Helene. Either, by some error of her own, we should be partly reconciled to her fate, so as not to leave us unallayed pain, or the tale should end, after a fearful fate seemingly impending, in her happiness. Here is villainy enough; and too much, unless the uncle be kept in the back ground.

Carlino will set off tomorrow for London, — a good opportunity for sending what may not prove worth postage. And now my hand is in for a lengthened letter, I will say something about the *Examiner*'s neglect of my volume. Last Sunday it complained of the "sullen silence" of the press towards Macready, — it has done the same itself towards me. Any notice would now, I conceive, be too late, and therefore now I complain. There must be a reason for the "sullen silence", though I cannot see it. The most provoking thing is that I had counted on my favourite *Examiner*, and even gave orders to advertise the volume, after its notice, in no other paper. I cannot comprehend it, because every notice, good or bad, has owned that my *discovery* is complete, except that in the *Athenæum*, which, ignorantly as well as spitefully, (unhappy Dilke!) implies it must be a "conjecture" *after* using these words, — "we have neither time nor inclination to test his speculations." [6] After the wild guesses of a full century have been wasted

[6] The *Athenaeum* reviewed *Shakespeare's Autobiographical Poems* on July 21, pp. 508–510. Dilke told George Keats in September (*KC*, II, 33) that "formal civility" between Brown and himself "terminated lately because we did not flatter him about a silly book which he was pleased to publish."

on the "Sonnets", surely my discovery, allowed by many Magazines and Papers, deserved to be examined by a literary examiner,
not for my sake but Shakespeare's. There are also other speculations acknowledged, — that of the bequest of a bed in the Will for
instance, — which should be important enough for a notice; the
want of which, in a Paper standing high as a literary one, and of
an immense sale, will (I shall hear from my publisher) be injurious.
I write to you the more freely on this subject, because I have heard
from Severn what you said of the volume. A few days ago I wrote
to Landor, telling him that, like himself, I could not ask either
an editor or a critic to favour me, yet I could not understand why
the *Examiner* should refuse to give any sort of opinion. I am, as
I said, in a state of surprise, viz — [7]

Hoping you have all been grumblingly well during this cold
apology for a summer,

I remain,

Your's most truly,

Chas Brown.

· 119 ·

TO CHARLES BROWN, JR.

Address: Mr Carlino Brown, / Care of Mr Richards, / 100 St
Martin's Lane, / London.[1]

Postmarks: PLYMOUTH OC 1 1838; C 3 OC 3 1838

ALS: Keats House, Hampstead.

My dear Son,   Laira Green. 30th Septr 1838.

This Elizabeth will drive me mad, unless I can first drive her
out of her vagaries. Having little to do, she has taken it into her
foolish noddle, by way of amusement, to dispose things in the
house according to her taste. She has been even rummaging my

---

[7] Here Brown has sketched a face "in a state of surprise."

[1] Beneath the address Carlino has scribbled "Charles" (thrice), "Myers Miers
Miurs Myurs," "Charles Brown," "Ludovico," "Pistrucci," "Lodola," and the names
of six days of the week, Saturday through Thursday, with their early October
dates, 6–11.

cupboards for articles to set off a mantlepiece. Every thing I want is somewhere hidden by her unfair hands. Your bed-room furniture is all displaced to please herself; that and every thing else must be put back again in their proper places, or she will lose her place. I have just made the discovery, while she is taking her Sunday jaunt. If my present mind lasts, I'll give her warning.

Every one has been asking about your safe arrival,[2] and I was glad to give the good news. I now look forward to other news, — that of your having found some situation to your mind. Any situation under a first rate engineer will be worthy of your attention; but under a person who is inferior in his profession, even what may appear a good situation will, in all probability, be only loss of time. Before you fix with any one, seek the advice of some one capable to advise on such a point, — Mr Lloyd's friend for instance,[3] or some such person.

Addis's furniture was sold by auction two days ago.[4] I bought the Cacti, and some odd things. They will be off before you receive this letter

Should you go to Midhurst,[5] bring me my "Apochryphal New Testament", and the volume of "Tillotson's [6] Sermons".

Should you see Mr Mat^w Snook at Chichester, bring me my "Guida di Firenze." [7]

Tell Leigh Hunt when you next see him that I shall be happy to hear from him per post.

Should you go to Ashford, give my best remembrances to all the Sulivans.[8] Before you go, you had better write to learn if they are or are not at home; otherwise you may be at fault.

I believe I gave you Severn's address. Be sure you call on him soon; and let me know when he thinks of coming to the west.[9]

---

[2] Carlino had left for London on September 21.

[3] Brown had known a man named Lloyd in Florence. He was at Brown's when H. C. Robinson dined there on October 7, 1830 (MS diary, Dr. Williams's Library).

[4] Timothy Addis and Son, lightermen, etc., Freeman's Wharf, are listed in Pigot's *Commercial Directory* for 1838 as a "removal" "occasioned by the destruction of the Royal Exchange."

[5] To visit his uncle William Brown.

[6] John Tillotson (1630–1694), archbishop of Canterbury.

[7] Perhaps the *Guida della città di Firenze e suoi contorni con la descrizione della I. Er. Galleria e Palazzo Pitti con pianta, vedute, e statue* (Florence, 1828).

[8] See the address of number 122.

[9] According to Sharp, p. 188, Severn had already returned to Italy.

Mr Far [?] and family are next door till their shipment. Poor Mrs Berry comes here dolorous at Mitty's ill temper. She will leave a bad odour behind here. She was disappointed at the sale, — things were not run up high; then the vessel arrived, to be ready for her on exactly the appointed day, which is provoking. Even her two favourites now complain. No one can approach her with impunity.

I am beginning to set my green-house in order; it will make a fine show this winter. Give my spiritual love to Sidney, — a different sort of love to Mrs Staples, — and kind remembrances to all friends. Uncle and brother Tom,[10] it seems, are at Brussels, — for how long?

Your affectionate father,
Chas Brown.

I sent no letter by you for Mr Wilson. Of course, go where you will, you must buy your own candles.

Except that I have not quite got rid of my cold, I am very well.

· 120 ·

TO CHARLES BROWN, JR.

Address: Mr Carlino Brown / Care of Mr Richards / 100 St Martin's Lane / London.

Postmarks: PLYMOUTH OC 8 1838; C PAID 10 OC 10 1838

ALS: Keats House, Hampstead.

My dear Son,   Laira Green. 8 Octr 1838.

You seem to have cause for relinquishing the pursuit of a civil engineer in London. Sorry I am that it is so; but still you need not fall out with the profession, carried on elsewhere. It is a pity that, after having to a certain extent qualified yourself for it, you should throw your former studies aside. Again, I do not believe you would be long happy in an independence acquired by a certain number of hours, daily followed up, in uninteresting work,

---

[10] Sidney, Harriet (see number 121 — "Mrs Staples . . . nata Richards"), Charles, and Thomas Richards.

monotonous drudgery like that of a horse in a mill. Should I be mistaken in this, which I may be, all the willingness and exertions on my part could not, I am convinced, obtain for you a situation similar to that of Henry Hunt. He has obtained it, politically, through his[1] father's name as an old reformer; not that the government would have bestowed on the son even that, did it not fear the cry of shame for not, in some way, rewarding the father for his long services and sufferings in the cause.[2] You could have hardly pitched on any M. P. less likely to forward your interest than M[r] Milnes; I have no claim on him whatever; and if I had the greatest, he could do nothing; he is an absolute Tory, votes constantly against Ministers, and is industrious in acting and speaking in the house against them. Would Ministers give him any thing? — would he ask it? Even M[r] Bewes,[3] as Capt[n] Howell tells me, could obtain nothing of the kind from them; they care little for him, because he *must* vote for them, or his constituents would displace him; all they have granted him is a petty office or two, for his immediate friends, local offices in the town, so as somewhat to oblige his constituents more than himself. Pray do not lose your hopes, your time, your energies in a vain pursuit. Rather inquire if there are not good prospects in France as an engineer. There none but englishmen are employed; and you, with your partial knowledge of the language, and with your present acquisitions, may well succeed. Endeavour to find out some persons in London interested or acquainted with engineering in France. Should your funds be running too low to allow you to remain a few days more in London for this purpose, M[r] Skynner will let you have a pound or two more on my account; for I think it eligible, now you are in London, to make such an inquiry. It is natural you should desire to be independent; it is fit, in order that you may be happy, to have a pursuit; and, in this

[1] *Written* this.

[2] Apparently from about 1836 to 1852 Henry held a Treasury appointment at £100 a year (Brewer, *Holograph Letters*, pp. 216, 330; *Letters of Mary Shelley*, II, 168). Hunt himself was granted a pension of £200 a year in June 1847 (Blunden, *Leigh Hunt*, p. 297).

[3] Thomas B. Bewes, liberal M.P. for Plymouth from 1832 to 1841. Carlino (*KC*, I, lx–lxi) tells that Brown "wrote very effectively in the 'Plymouth Journal' during an election [in July 1837], in support of M[r] Bewes, also some doggerel verses, and political skits, that were very telling and successful."

view, though against my comfort, I would not oppose your leaving me for N. S. Wales, should nothing else nearer home offer itself. But the first thing is to make every inquiry where you are, and the next thing is not to be hurried in a choice, nor easily thwarted in your views.

Owing to the dying state of Mr Woolcoombe's [4] brother, it fell to my lot to sit in the chair and open the Session last Thursday. No one ever enjoyed dignity less, for I was not well, and the great chair seemed to make me worse and worse. As I walked home, I wondered what could be the matter, since I had been scrupulous in my diet, in order to get rid of my cold. In the morning I felt very ill and in pain, when suddenly came an attack of the *European* Cholera Morbus. I suspected it, as it has been rife in Plymouth, killing a few, especially, as I hear, the young. Captⁿ Howell was very kind. The disease is shocking while it lasts. I had no strength, nothing but pain, with violent retching and purging. Last night I thought myself recovered, and to-day I am quite well. This Cholera has travelled from the town to us. Elizabeth has had a slight attack, so has Captⁿ Trader, and Captⁿ Branch a severer one than mine. Mrs Dechamp has also been attacked. I am now strong enough to walk into town to put this into the post, and the walk will do me good. Unless Fanny [5] earnestly desires to see you, I agree with you that, for your reasons, you had better not go. Still let it be made known to her, through James when he returns, that, should she prefer to live with me, I shall be happy. The reason why I informed James of your proposal was because, though inefficacious and wrong, it was to your credit with your cousins; [6] and because, lest you should

---

[4] Henry Woollcombe (1777?–1847), former mayor, alderman, and recorder of Plymouth, founder and perennial president of the Plymouth Institution. As "Senior Vice" (number 128) Brown presided in his place over the first meeting of the 1838–1839 session, October 4.

[5] Brown's niece Frances Joanna Brown, the fourth child of John Armitage Brown. From the present letter and numbers 122, 126, 141, it appears that while on a visit to Brown she became pregnant (perhaps by "that Dudley" of number 122) and went to France to have the child, and that Carlino, who once considered marrying her, continued "flirtations" in spite of the scandal. According to R. A. Walker (in a letter to L. A. Holman, December 23, 1932, now at Harvard), she later "married a man called Hodging Lloyd and they had children, one of whom was . . . a doctor."

[6] Chiefly Fanny's two brothers, John Mavor Brown and James Armitage Brown (the James mentioned above and in number 122).

repeat it, *all* your cousins should beforehand know precisely in what light I regard it, and no further. I am glad you were not here when I was ill, as Elizabeth was extremely attentive; and I have told you all about it that you may not be uneasy. Indeed I fancy it will, after awhile, be of more service than not. Give my best remembrances to every one we know. Your letter came only last night, — so I answer quickly.

Your affectionate father,
Chas Brown.

Laira Green news. Captⁿ Howell is resolved to be off next spring. Captⁿ Trader talks of being off at Christmas. The Berry's will be off very soon, — a sale is to take place in a few days. Captⁿ Branch is seeking for a purchaser. The Addis's are six days sail off. All this induces people to think the place is an unhealthy swamp.

· 121 ·

TO CHARLES BROWN, JR.

Address: Mr Carlino Brown, / at Mr J. Robinson's, / 10 Northumberland Court, / Strand, / London.[1]

Postmarks: PLYMOUTH OC 27 1838; C PAID 29 OC 29 1838

ALS: Keats House, Hampstead.

My dear Son,   Laira Green. 26 Octr 1838.
    I send a copy of the following paragraph from the Newspapers, as perhaps you have neither seen nor heard of it.
    "Mr Stephenson, the celebrated rail-road engineer,[2] has been engaged by the Florence and Leghorn Railroad Company to make the requisite surveys and plans for that line. Two English

---

[1] Carlino has added "From C. Brown Esqre Senr to" above Brown's address, and "From Plymouth to" opposite "London." At various places around the address he has scribbled "Carlino Brown" (thrice), "Charles" (six times), "Charles Brown" (five times), "Brown," "Carlo Rugieri" (twice), "Civil Engineer," and "Mio Caro Padre." The address is presumably that of a rooming house. The directories list John Robinson and Son, makers of artificial legs and arms, at 35 Northumberland Street, Strand.
[2] George Stephenson (1781–1848).

359

engineers have already arrived at Florence to commence the pre-liminary works."

Now an inquiry into this may lead to great good. Your present acquirements, and knowledge of the language and of the people, may well be considered more than equivalent to a premium. Thus also you would be introduced into the practical part of engineer-ing. Many questions are to be solved: Is the Florence Company English or Tuscan? Is Mr Stevenson in London? Is the railroad decided on? or is it merely a thought?

Were you once to make yourself useful in Italy as an engineer, a large field would be open to you. The next rail-roads would be from Leghorn to Rome, from Rome to Naples, and from Milan to several parts of Lombardy.

In my haste to send this I forgot that this is Friday, our no-post day.

It is advertised that the Brunswick will take her last trip, for the season, from Plymouth to Portsmouth, on Thursday, 15th Novr. I tell you this, though I do not wish you should come by her during this the most stormy season of the year. An outside place per coach would be but a few shillings dearer.

Remember me to all the Richards's, and to Mrs Staples, (nata Richards).[3] Should you see Mr Stephenson you can very honestly tell him you are perfect in the knowledge of the colloquial idioms (which I am not) among the working classes of Tuscany; this would be a great advantage. Make known to him also your acquire-ments in mathematical pursuits and in the theory of engineering. Should he not be in London, learn, if possible, his address; you can then write to him, or I can. In fact do every thing in your power to obtain a situation, for which you seem peculiarly eligible.

The interest that is making for you in a public Office may be sincere, but beware of being led on from week to week in hope, to be disappointed at last.

Your affectionate father,
Chas Brown.

[3] Harriet Richards.

· 122 ·

TO CHARLES BROWN, JR.

Address: Mr Carlino Brown, / Robert Sulivan Esqre, / Ashford, / near Staines, / Middlesex.

Postmark: PLYMOUTH NO 13 1838

ALS: Keats House, Hampstead.

My dear Son,   Laira Green. 11 Novr 1838.

This I write in preparation, to be sent off on the receipt of the forthcoming letter from you.

At this distance, and not well versed in such questions, I could have no definite reply to make to your letter of the 1st. Having read it with great interest, I waited for more information. You, together with your friends, must judge if going as a common apprentice in a first rate manufactory is the most eligible for you. I feel obliged to Mr Rendle [1] for his advice. What would be the premium as a common apprentice? — you have said nothing of that.

I have written to Fanny at the request of James. Though I have said nothing more to her about returning to my house, you need not apprehend that she and you will be living with me together; for I have told James that I wish no more than one at a time. Throughout this late disastrous affair, from the first false step, she has proved the truth of my old assertion, which you could never accede to, that she is sadly deficient in common sense. I have done the utmost in my power for her, especially in the propitiation of her brothers, and in that I completely succeeded. I can do no more, but preach patience and prudence to her now, as the only means of retrieving her fault; and such was the burden of my letter to her, which was sent yesterday. Yes; I also said much against any notion on her part of a further acquaintance with that Dudley, — a convicted liar, not only to her, but in what he stated to James. [2]

[1] James Meadows Rendel (1799–1856), Plymouth engineer.
[2] See number 120, n. 5.

Laira news is that the Traders will be off to the town at Christmas. Miss Trader does not want a slate. Your young friend Talker has been dismissed by Fryer [3] for want of steadiness and many irregularities, — nay, something worse than those. I have of course only heard Fryer's story; but from that it appears the lad is plunging himself into misfortune, owing to idle company and to a disregard for truth. I am sorry for it.

I wrote to you stating the last voyage of the Brunswick according to advertisement. Capt[n] Howell says she is already laid up in *Portsmouth* for the winter, where she is, not here, to be lengthened six feet. The Sir F Drake does not go; but the Irish Steamers are advertised as usual from London to Plymouth. I told you I wished you to come by land; however, you may do as you please, as the autumn gales seem to have spent themselves, and Capt[n] Howell declares he thinks there is no danger.

If not inconvenient, see M[r] L. Hunt before you leave town. Yesterday morning he had a letter from me with an article on the emperor Paul.[4] I want to know his opinion of it, and what he thinks of doing with it. Make him write; and then give my remembrances.

I cannot discover which Article I was particularly to read in the Morning Chronicle you sent.

Should you see M[r] T Richards, beg him from me to keep an eye on the new *Pictorial Shakespeare*; [5] for I have a suspicion the

[3] John Hubert Fryer, chemist and druggist.

[4] Paul I of Russia (1754–1801), who was strangled by conspirators when he refused to abdicate. On November 17 Hunt wrote to Robert Bell (*Correspondence of Leigh Hunt*, II, 326), offering the article to the *Monthly Chronicle* and quoting the following sentence from Brown's now-lost letter mentioned above: "If the *Monthly Chronicle* would print my *Paul*, entire and signed, or with something from the editor equivalent in authenticity to a signature, I should be content; but I do not think it likely." Bell replied to Hunt by return mail (the letter is in the British Museum): "It is a curious narrative, & would be most acceptable but that it is not quite so new as the writer appears to think. . . . You will find the main incident stated in the third volume of the History of Russia in the Cyclopedia, the variations being so slight . . . as hardly to justify the publication of M[r] Brown's paper as a document throwing new light upon the subject. Besides the condition he stipulates for is inadmissible." Brown subsequently resolved to introduce the materials into "Walter Hazlebourn." The uncompleted manuscript of that work (Keats House) breaks off just as a new character, the governess of the Grand Duke Michael, is beginning her narrative of "all that I personally witnessed connected with the death of Paul."

[5] *The Pictorial Edition of the Works of Shakspere*, 8 vols. (1838–1843), edited by Charles Knight.

editor is making use of my volume. If so, — acknowledged or unacknowledged?

Our West of England Mag is improving. In the third number my *Orlando Innamorato* looks stately.[6] We have had admirable lectures on lead and iron at our Institution. When I learn that Mr Sulivan (not Sullivan) has returned to Ashford, I intend to write to him. Mr Soltau[7] is elected Mayor; I delivered your message to Mrs Soltau, when she chanced to pay me a visit. I have given an evening *spread* to our neighbours, including Misses Jane and Margaret Renfry, — the other two were prevented from coming; talkative Jane was dumb as a fish the whole of the evening, much to the surprise of all of us. I must soon invite the new comers, who are rather dull, and very sickly; — I have met them at the Howells'.

By your account I scarcely expect your letter to-night. However, I shall go to Plymouth with this for an immediate answer; when, if necessary, I shall add a postscript.

Your affectionate father,
Chas Brown.

13th Novr. I thought you had calculated badly. On *this* evening I found your letter at the post. I have a suspicion that one of my letters, wherein I mentioned the Brunswick, and my disinclination to your return by sea, has miscarried, owing to my having paid the postage; so, I shall leave the postage of this to you. I shall be happy to see H. Hunt. Give my best remembrances to Mr & Mrs Sulivan, and to Tom, — if I must call her by that unfeminine name. I don't see your prosperity in so clear a light as yourself; but no one, of course, can wish it more certain. Hoping for the best news, I remain, at Fryer's shop,

Your affectionate father,
Chas Brown.

N. B. No dogs permitted at Laira.

---

[6] A translation of forty-eight stanzas of Boiardo's *Orlando innamorato*, Canto I, in the November issue of the *West of England Magazine*, pp. 161–171 (reprinted in *Some Letters*, pp. 122–138). Though it ended "To be continued in our next," no further installments were printed. Milnes, *Life*, II, 50, says that Brown "left behind him a complete and admirable version of the first five cantos," but it has not come to light.

[7] George William Soltau, merchant and consul for the Portuguese, mayor of Plymouth in 1838–1839 and 1841–1842.

· 123 ·

TO CHARLES BROWN, JR.

Address: Mr Chas Brown Junr / Robert Skynner Esqre / 42 Mortimer Street / Cavendish Square, / London.

Postmarks: PL[YM]OUT[H] JA 2[7] 1839; C 29 JA 29 1839

ALS: Keats House, Hampstead.

My dear Son,   Laira Green. 27 Jany 1839.

I answer your last letter immediately. You say, — "I want to know if you can put up with the expence of £3 to go to Liverpool, the sum of £3 to be deducted from the income allowed me during the first six months." Does this merely mean, — Can I afford to advance you £3 to be repaid within six months? If so, I can afford the advance; but I cannot afford you more than £60 a year in all; for I keep but £90 for myself, — exclusive of that which I earn by writing. In looking into my accounts I was obliged to ask for my loan to Mrs Brown,[1] and it was quickly repaid. I am sorry you have not met with better success hitherto; but it appears to me you are impatient. Would it not be better, instead of adding to your expences by travelling on an *uncertainty*, to rest quiet awhile? — at any rate so as to save money enough for it before hand? Possibly you may be enabled to fix yourself at Birmingham or Liverpool by letter. If not, wait awhile in London to look more about you, to inquire further, and to be *ready* to start upon any thing eligible that may offer itself. You are and always have been too much in a hurry; and in such a humour, take care you do not tie yourself down to something below what you have a right to expect. I am unable to advise you upon the means of getting forward in your chosen profession; but Mr Skynner, I have no doubt, can give you good advice, and he will surely be kind enough to do it. Recollect that, even with Mr Rendle's advice, you went, the last time, to London, assured you could instantly place yourself where you wished, and recollect also that I doubted it. My doubts are stronger against the Provinces than they were in respect to

[1] Probably Jane Elizabeth Brown, the sister-in-law mentioned in number 111.

London. Having a sufficient income, why need you be in a fevered hurry? As for your other question, in case you should leave London, how are you to receive your money? — that must be settled with Mr Skynner. I cannot spare my *Plymouth Journal*, and an extra one would cost me, as a favour, 2d a week, which I do not think is worth while paying. I have no high opinion of my Articles, but May[2] is delighted, and is always hoping I will continue, he being somewhat afraid I shall be finding it irksome. I don't trouble my head about them till Sunday night when the *Examiner* appears, and on the Monday my *Article* is finished; so the job does not occupy me much. During the remainder of the week I work a little every day at my Novel, which goes on, but not fast. When I get more in the heat of it, its speed may increase. I am now 18 years old, and shall soon set off to St Petersburg. As I proceed, characters accumulate, and I foresee my pages will soon be in a bustle. There is not more than one character yet introduced which is not drawn from an individual, — though Walter Hazlebourn himself is certainly not *myself*, — but I take the liberty of putting him in many of my situations. I begin to see my way more clearly, and am so much in earnest that yesterday I bought ruled paper enough for *three* volumes, — yet I know not whether it will swell to more than *two*, or whether the matter will require *four*. It must work out *its own* extent. Pray call on M^r C Richards directly, and tell him, with my best compliments, if he has not already disposed of my *Death of Paul*, I request he will put it into your hands. Mind you keep it safely. If not disposed of, I will introduce it into my novel.[3] Let me know the result, that I may manage accordingly. Remember me kindly to the Skynners, the Richards', the Staples', and the Hunts, — in fact to all possible friends. I am remarkably well, with my brain full of the personages and incidents of my novel. I foresee I shall meet with M^r & M^rs A at St Petersburg, — and that the latter will be horribly mischievous towards poor Walter.

Your affectionate father,
Chas Brown.

[2] Daniel May, of 32 Bilbury Street, Plymouth, bookseller, stationer, and proprietor of *PDWJ*, to which Brown was at this time a regular contributor.
[3] See the fourth note to the preceding letter.

I seldom write so long a letter, — I can't afford it. Should you receive the *Death of Paul,* — try to enclose it to me in a *frank,* cutting off the *letter part* to Leigh Hunt, so as to decrease its weight. Mr Skynner will pay the postage of this on my account. I never attempt to impost a paid letter by a servant

· 124 ·

TO CHARLES BROWN, JR.

Address: Mr Charles Brown, / N° 5 King's Row, / Pimlico, / London.

Postmarks: PLYMOUTH FE 7 1839; C PAID 9 FE 9 1839

ALS: Keats House, Hampstead.

My dear Son,   Laira Green. 7 Feby 1839.
    The letter I received yesterday gave me more pleasure than I can express. Your hopes, months ago, of getting into a government office did not appear to me of a nature to produce a reasonable reliance. Now you have written that those hopes are accomplished. This happens also precisely at a period when you discover the great difficulty, if not impossibility, of pursuing your favourite profession. For that, as it seemed to be the means of your happiness, I was willing to make any sacrifice in my power; and against it, I was unwilling to urge my secret disinclination. Now I can speak out. You know what my opinion is of the feelings of a gentleman; — with me, they are solely confined to the mind. In this view, I looked forward to your inevitably associating with the working journeymen, if only in your duty; and I could not forbear entertaining serious thoughts that the effect, sooner or later, would be detrimental, in my estimation, to your character. In a public office you will not associate with any but gentlemen; for, should there be exceptions, they will be contemned, and consequently harmless. I have said that a clerk in a public office is a horse in a mill; [1] he is so, but he is a well bred horse, at any rate; and would not your being compelled to work at, or direct some everlastingly

---

[1] In number 120.

repeated piece of machinery, be much the same? You looked forward to five or seven years of suffering before you could arrive at a point whereat you could stop, and be happy. The first was plain enough, but the conclusion was doubtful. In all professions there must be a tedious schooling. A child must learn to walk before it attempts to run, or it tumbles down. If my little income died with me, I might be more strenuous for your election of some line of life, wherein you would be, followed most industriously, in better circumstances than myself. But, in a public office, should the salary, at first, not be sufficient to enable you to live decently and with comfort, I, you know, am ready to add to it, so that it shall be decent and comfortable. On the other hand, to confess the truth, it was a hard case for me to support a son till he was three or five and twenty,[2] — that is, looking at it with one eye; though, looking at it with both eyes, I saw, and told you, how it might be effected, without injuring my income, but at the expence of your future one, though with great anxiety on my part. To avoid this anxiety, I chose to write for a newspaper; which I may continue to do, for both our sakes. Add to which, I laid down a stricter rule of economy, while living by myself. All this I did, and would continue to do cheerfully for your sake, — provided it were really for your sake. In a public office you will have, grant it, — a horse in a mill's work; still you earn a certain salary; you bring grist to the mill, while you work at it; and the grand thing is that you have much leisure time. Now this leisure time is the greatest blessing, or the greatest curse that attends a public-office clerk. According to its occupation, it leads to happiness or to yawning dissipations. Of the latter there is no occasion to speak; but happiness is acquired by a man's having resources within himself, quite independent of others, for the occupation of his leisure hours. You can have reading, and your lathe, or what not, together with a quiet pursuit of mechanical inventions. You have, if you have the will to use them, ample means of becoming rich in happiness. I have known many clerks in public Offices, and the unhappy ones were literally those who spent money for the occupation of their leisure hours. When I have

[2] Carlino, now eighteen, would be twenty-three or twenty-five after a five- or seven-year apprenticeship.

learnt the nature of your office, I may be able to write more. When you write on 12th, I may know every thing. Then I must write to thank Mr Warburton and Dr Black, — to the latter, will it be right to address my letter under cover to Mr Leader?[3] — if so, where does he now reside? Remember me to Trelawny, — him I shall thank in due course. I catch myself writing *long* letters to *you*; — but I can yet afford to send my remembrance to every friend, with reference to Thornton and Henry, — but, in fact, to all. You have many friends here inquiring after you, — Mrs Boulter for one.

Your affectionate father,
Chas Brown.

Tell your Cousin James, when you see him, that, on the whole, I cannot recommend the Pictorial Shakespeare. The wood cuts are square and ungraceful; the text is servilely the old bad one; and — worse than all, — poetry is in double columns! — yet it is a diligently got up work.

Now that I have rarely time to play at chess, I have a good set of men!

· 125 ·

TO CHARLES BROWN, JR.

Address: Mr Carlino Brown.

ALS: Keats House, Hampstead. Part of the first paragraph is printed by Richardson, *The Everlasting Spell*, p. 95.

My dear Son,   Laira Green. 15 March 1839.

Remember me to Mancur, with my love to his wife, if they should be yet in town. Tell him that I have a letter of his, written fifteen years ago, full of detestation against the selfishness and pomposity of Dilke, and that I wonder he can recommend any one to call on him. Were you to do such a thing, or to return his greeting otherwise than with contempt, I must — I could not help it — consider you as ranked among my enemies. No explana-

[3] John Temple Leader (1810–1903), radical M.P. for Westminster, who at this time shared a house with Trelawny at Putney.

tion — nothing could ever after reconcile me to such conduct. If he should accidentally meet with you, and civilly accost you — spit in his face. He never did me but one favour, though he had the power to do many; for that I made him a present to the amount of £11; I have done for him innumerable acts of kindness. In money transactions alone, I have lent him £50 for four years; yet when I asked him to lend me £20 for four months, he stared at me! To crown all, his infamous treachery towards me last year [1] ought to make any friend of mine despise him. Nor, if he could, would he be of any service to you in any of your views; his own selfishness, and his jealousy (long entertained) of me would prevent it. Nor with his piggish son ought you to exchange a salutation. He, pig as he is, sways his father on certain points; and I have traced some of the father's acts against me, in my thoughts, to the son's instigation.

I sent you a "Journal" yesterday; and one was sent to Fonblanque.[2] An exchange is desired. Tell Henry that, if wished by the "Examiner", the exchange of Papers shall be regular. The "Examiner" is not much known in the town of Plymouth, though it is taken in by persons in the neighbourhood.

So, you are writing an Opera! and some one, you don't say who, tells you the dialogue is too common. Here is the difficulty. Dramatic dialogue must be easy as an old glove, yet such as mere conversational folks could not utter. For rules you must read much; Shakespeare, in his comedies, the prose parts, is the grand model; the "Beggar's Opera" next; then Sheridan, though he is almost too artificial, like Congreve, whose dialogue seems like bits cut out of a common place book of good sayings. Goldoni, whoever told you, is poor in dialogue, though rich in character. Moliere is too refined in his comedies of verse — but how can verse suit easy conversation? All this is said to encourage you, to put you in the right path, though I had no more idea of your writing an opera than of my writing an epic poem. Tell me every thing of your pursuits, because they interest me more than any other matter.

---

[1] The *Athenaeum* review of *Shakespeare's Autobiographical Poems* (see number 118, n. 6).

[2] Albany Fonblanque (1793–1872), editor and proprietor of the *Examiner*.

I thought Fanny was at Kineton.[3] She is conceited and with a weak mind, as I always said; and she is with warm passions and coldness of heart — two qualities that frequently go together — to an extent with her that I know not where it will end. Her last letter to me was so full of self-sufficiency and blarney, that you need not fear my taking the trouble of reproaching her, or perhaps of writing to her. I never met with a more affected fool — ugly to boot.

Zella must be a forward girl to write a novel at fourteen or thereabouts; [4] it is almost enough to put one out of conceit in novel writing. I thought it was necessary, for a novel, to have some knowledge and much experience.

Your notion of going to Germany must be considered, and duly. You are too sanguine in your hopes, too depressed in your disappointments. Steering between the two, you may look forward reasonably to getting a situation.

Tell me, if you can, more of Margaret. Is her mother dead? — or her father? — or what?

I like to hear of your taking pleasure. Only beware that you do not exceed your income; if you do, I know not where you can hope for assistance. I live *most moderately,* so as to avoid every species of dilemma. When better days come, then, but not before, we may launch out a little.

Remembrances to all friends,

Your affectionate father,
Chas Brown.

The Howells desire me to send remembrances —

[3] Probably visiting her brother John Mavor Brown (see number 111, n. 9).
[4] Trelawny's daughter, who had come to England in 1836. She was now thirteen.

· 126 ·

TO CHARLES BROWN, JR.

ALS: Keats House, Hampstead.

My dear Son,   Laira Green 16 Ap{ril 1839.} [1]

Little as I have to say, I will not lose the opportunity of saying something through Mr Chapman,[2] who is going to London. Thanks for your letter of remembrance, which was received on 14th.[3] Both the last times I forgot to pay the postage.

You explain yourself honestly about Fanny, but I do not like these flirtations to continue. It is true you gave me your promise not to marry her

This day week Captn Howell &c will be off from their cottage to lodge with me for a week or ten days. I am very sorry to lose them.

So, you think there are no hopes of obtaining a situation. Still you must have patience. You have been so often disappointed, that now, perhaps, your *no hopes* may be disappointed. Always keeping a sharp eye, something may be offered. Even here I have some distant prospect in view for you; but it is hardly worth while to describe it yet; as the *attempt* must depend on many circumstances. Yet, by accident, I have been partly the means of obtaining a promise for May's son of £150 a year! [4] May seeks to provide for no other son, and has offered to use his influence in the same quarter, joined to my endeavours, on *proper occasion*, in your behalf, out of gratitude to me Do not breathe a *hint* of this to *any body*. I tell it to you, as a proof that you need not despair.

---

[1] The year is established by the mention of Captain Howell, who in October 1838 was "resolved to be off next spring" (number 120), and by the reference to May's son, who in number 127 "is already somewhat promoted."

[2] Probably either Thomas or Matthew Chapman, painters of Devonport (see number 133).

[3] Brown's birthday.

[4] In a deleted passage in his memoir now at Keats House, Carlino says that Daniel May, Jr., received an appointment in the Customs as a result of Brown's writings in behalf of Thomas Bewes (see number 120, n. 3). He adds that "an offer was made . . . of an appointment for his [Brown's] son; but the latter declined it, preferring to be an engineer" (compare *KC*, I, lxi).

{You} are in the wrong; — a man with a family, unless {he is in} business, is dreadfully pinched and worn in {the wor}ld; if he has a business, the consciousness of {ha}ving many to provide for excites his industry, and thus he becomes more prosperous than many single men with the same advantage. But what is the use of a man's industry, when he knows not where to apply it properly?

Keep sober and good company; and keep more than free from debt, so as to make up a little bank for yourself in case of need on any occasion.

Your affectionate father,
Chas Brown.

· 127 ·

TO CHARLES BROWN, JR.

Address: Mr Carlino Brown, / Sandrock Cottage, / Midhurst.[1] / P. P.

Postmark: PLYMOUTH JY 1 1839

ALS: Keats House, Hampstead.

My dear Carlino,   Laira Green. 1 July 1839.

I have just finished my Newspaper work, and have a little time to write to you. In the first place, I sent your two trunks by the Brunswick this morning, addressed to your uncle, with this addition — "to be forwarded from Portsmouth by canal." I opened the sea chest to put in the T ruler, the parallel ruler, and a volume (Terence) belonging to your uncle. It opened easily, but it defied our power to lock it again; so I put the key within it, and had it very well corded.

You kept me a long time waiting to hear you had begun your probation.[2] I am glad to hear you are content with it. If you have

---

[1] Carlino was staying with his uncle William Brown.

[2] With the Midhurst millwright Robert Chorley. At the end of a month's trial Carlino entered into a three-year apprenticeship at a premium of £20 per year (number 135).

the true spirit of perseverance, you will become more and more content with it. Wightwick [3] still insists upon it you will be a great man. Now to answer your questions.

The Howells are in Somersetshire, and will visit Plymouth before their departure for France. I am not going to London; but I have some thoughts of visiting Midhurst, after your return from London. Lizzy [4] and I go on remarkably well. The world, thank you, wags on [5] very well with me, — not so my right hand, which I lately sprained in over gardening, and it is worse at this moment just after writing a long Article. It shall be sent to you. There is an odd notice also of mine (a second one) on the Circus here.[6] I cannot write a word more than "remembrance" to your uncle this time.

Leave all books for me with T. Richards, and tell him I expect his visit as promised. Ask Ellen S — if she has remitted that money; I have been plagued about it. Ask if there is a charge for the Index to the Examiner. Ask Mr Caton, Mr Skynner's brother-in-law, with my best compliments, what that liquid poison was which he gave me, when at Clement's Inn,[7] to kill flies withall. May's son is already somewhat promoted, and he is likely to be more so soon. Remind your uncle of those favourite shells promised to me.

There is just arrived, I know not who, a neighbour, with a wife, next door.

My strawberries are now full of fruit, because I had grubbed up so many useless apple-trees. My Sparrmannia was in such a profusion of blossom, that I sent it as a grand show to the Horticultural Exhibition. Wanting you, I keep a cat; a very well behaved young gentleman, for I have — or at least a butcher has — prevented him from following any disgraceful intrigues by day or night; a simple operation, at which he afterwards looked

---

[3] George Wightwick (1802–1872), Plymouth architect.

[4] Elizabeth, Brown's housekeeper.

[5] *As You Like It*, II.vii.23.

[6] Besides the "long Article" (on opponents of progress), the July 4 issue of *PDWJ* contained Brown's "Petriello. Paraphrased from Bandello. Part III. Tale 50th" and a short piece headed "Bridge's Circus."

[7] In 1814 Brown dated the Preface to *Narensky* from 16 Clement's Inn.

no more than highly offended, and he or it was playing about the garden an hour after.

Remember me to all friends in London.

Your affectionate father,
Chas Brown.

. 128 .

TO CHARLES BROWN, JR.

Address: William Brown Esqre / Sandrock Cottage / Midhurst.

Postmarks: PLYMOUTH JY 4 1839; C 6 JU 6 1839

ALS: Keats House, Hampstead.

My dear Son,   July. 6 [*for* 4].[1] 1839

Though dated from Laira Green, this is really written at May's, with an unpleasant pen and thick ink. Your uncle will tell you I am satisfied that you should go to Chorley, and that I have requested he will take my place in fixing you there. Heaven prosper you, my dear boy — and Heaven will, if you exert yourself, giving no cause of offence.

You talk of going to London, or rather your uncle does, at the end of the month's trial. Do me the favour not to go *before* that time, for a particular reason which you will be more than enabled to guess. And, when you go, be careful not to give offence to Mr Stanley[2] or any other of that genus; if you do, all hope will be lost not only with him but with the whole genus. I have many petty commissions for you to transact in London, besides that of the Examiner Index,[3] you careless rogue; but I need not mention them now.

Down with your pride, for you are no longer the son of a Senior Vice! Luney is out as well as myself; — the three elect are Wightwick, Barnes, and Prance,[4] our prodigiously grown fat

---

[1] See the postmarks.

[2] E. J. Stanley (see number 88, n. 2), at this time M.P. for North Cheshire, patronage secretary to the Treasury, and principal whip of the Whig party.

[3] See the fourth paragraph of the preceding letter.

[4] Brown was one of the three vice-presidents of the Plymouth Institution for

magistrate; those three have lads to introduce, I have none. Col[l] Smith and Wightwick have jointly sent up a very grand design for the Nelson Monument. Capt[n] Bowker is neighbourly, but an obstinate old fool I perceive. Branch's, Berry's, and Trader's cottages remain empty. I have a favourite Cat. Present my best compliments to the two fatted calves.

Your affectionate father,
Cha[s] Brown.

· 129 ·

TO WILLIAM BROWN

Address: William Brown Esq[re] / Sandrock Cottage / Midhurst. (*readdressed* [1] *to*: M[r] Carlino Brown / M[r] Richards / N[o] 100 — S[t] Martins Lane / London.)

Postmarks: PLYMOUTH JY 31 1839; MIDHURST AU 2 1839; E 3 AU 3 1839

ALS: Keats House, Hampstead.

My dear William,   Laira Green. 30 July 1839.

As you have kindly interested yourself in the behalf of Carlino, and undertaken to stand in my shoes between him and M[r] Chorley, I call your attention to the following passage in a letter, received the day before yesterday from Carlino.

"M[r] Chorley calls himself millwright and engineer, but he is nothing more than a millwright; so that I must work, after the three years, to obtain all the knowledge I require, which he is certainly not capable of giving me."

I almost fear that more is said here than meant; because, if such is implicitly the fact, how came he to commence even his

---

the 1838–1839 session. The Rev. Richard Luney, M.A., was curator of the Institution's library in 1830, and a vice-president also in 1833–1834 and 1835–1836. The Rev. R. N. Barnes, M.A., lectured on such subjects as "Moral Philosophy" and "Character and Writings of Dr. Johnson." William Prance, also a vice-president in 1830–1831 and 1833–1834, was a town councilor of Plymouth in 1835 and mayor in 1842–1843.

[1] By William Brown, who wrote number 131 across the first page of this letter, which he forwarded to Carlino on August 2.

month's trial without being aware of it? A millwright is doubtless an engineer, and so is a needle-maker; but neither is of that kind to be of future service to my boy, unless he intends to be a millwright. According to his representation, a small premium and a large amount of time will be thrown away for absolutely nothing. By his letter it appears he is most willing, which perfectly surprises me, to enter on his apprenticeship, although, by his account, it cannot be beneficial to him; at least, not much so. At the end of the three years, he will be, in the view of a civil engineer, no better than he is at the present moment. If, therefore, I am to understand the above extract literally, I cannot consent that he should make so great a sacrifice. In case of necessity, will you have the kindness to explain my objection to M[r] Chorley?

Carlino, in a former letter, seems to have a notion that I would prefer his being in a Government Office. He has misunderstood me.[2] I approve of such an Office, but more approve of his being employed agreeably to his talent and inclination. Had I not thought his impending engagement was eligible, I should have written to him ten days ago about an application for a post under M[r] Delabeche, the celebrated geologist,[3] who is appointed by Government to make geological surveys. Not long ago, he wanted assistants. Government has empowered him to engage a limited number of young men at 4s or 5s to 8s or 10s a day — the exact pay I forget, but it is good. The only objection is that such a situation is not permanent, and leads directly to nothing. When no more wanted, the young men may be turned adrift. On the other hand, M[r] Delabeche is a kind hearted liberal man, and with much influence, not likely to abandon a youth, were he partial to him for assiduity and talent. Carlino's mathematical acquirements might make him welcome; and I suppose M[r] D meets with few youths who have even a smattering of mineralogy; that last would have to be [4] learned, and no where better, or so well, than under him.

I want to write to Carlino, but know not whither to address

---

[2] See number 124. Carlino can hardly be blamed for having "misunderstood."
[3] Henry Thomas (later Sir Henry) de la Beche (1796–1855), after 1840 the director general of Ordnance Survey. Among his many works on geology (1824–1859) is a *Report on the Geology of Cornwall, Devon, and West Somerset* (1839).
[4] *Written* would be to be.

a letter. By one passage in his last, it seems he will return from London in a *very* short time; and he says nothing to the contrary. Yet he asks questions, and wants answers. He is yet unused to correspondence. He wishes to know if he may give letters of introduction to a friend of Mr Skynner; — of course he may to Mr Kirkup and Mr Severn; but he has put it out of my power to tell him so, possibly, in time. He has written about the non-arrival of his trunks. They were sent and addressed by me according to his request. Have the kindness to tell him that my written account of his complaint went yesterday, through Mr Blewit's hands, by the Brunswick, to Mr Wheeler at Portsmouth.[5] The trunks were seen safe on board the Brunswick by Mr May Senr.

Your friendliness to Carlino I regard as an obligation to both of us. The account, though not the best, which you gave on 26 June of your own health does not appear to me, in any view, discouraging. As for varicose veins, I have seen lads with them, and have had them myself for these 15 years, owing to a day's walk, on the Siena road, in the heat of the sun, having changed my long stockings for short ones, thereby depriving the calf of the leg of its usual support. But what you say of Mary's becoming of too full a habit, which was observable four years ago, is a matter which requires attention and caution. I suppose my health is very good, for I never suspect otherwise; and any thing untoward or provoking is met by me, not as formerly with irritation, but at its exact value, and no more. Respecting your advertisements, my opinion is, which may have been given before, that, for a Doctor, with or without a degree, you are not enough of a humbug. My love to your wife.

Your's affectionately,
Chas Brown.

[5] John Edward Blewitt, agent for the steam packets *Brunswick* and *Sir Francis Drake* in Plymouth, and Harry Wheeler, his counterpart in Portsmouth.

· 130 ·

TO CHARLES BROWN, JR.

ALS: Keats House, Hampstead.

My dear Son,   Laira Green. 31 July 1839.
   Not knowing for how many days you intended to remain in London, I have written to your Uncle in answer to your last.[1] This is a repetition of your former inadvertency, not telling me, while you ask for answers, how to address a letter. Your Uncle, indeed, some time since, wrote that he supposed you would be in London for a month. If I recollect rightly, I asked you if that was the case. I had as much reason to suppose you had gone to London merely or chiefly for your portmanteaus. Then as you did not inform me to whose care I could direct a letter, I thought at first of answering you with a direction to Midhurst. At length, observing the little word *"yet"* in your postscript — "not *yet* in lodgings," I think it probable, but no more than probable, that a letter may find you at Mr Skynner's. You leave me quite in the dark.
   I told your uncle all about what I did yesterday for your trunks; — it need not be repeated, as he is on the spot to receive them, or to follow up my inquiries.
   From what you have written, I have also explained to him that I entirely disapprove of your sacrifice of three years to study the business of a millwright; and, at the end, be left unfit for an engineer. You must not, however, much rely on a post in a Government Office, to be obtained by your prom{inent} friends. I have told him it would be better, which perhaps I could manage, to place you with Mr Delabeche, who is making a geological survey for the Government, at a certainty per day for an undefined period.
   I should not have run the hazard of this reaching you unless to tell you that you can give introductions to Kirkup and Severn for Mr Skynner's friend.

---

[1] See the preceding letter.

378

Nor will I say a word more, except that I am
Your affectionate father,
Chas Brown.

As I pay postage to your Uncle on your affairs, and owing to your neglect, you ought to pay the postage of this.

· 131 ·

WILLIAM BROWN TO CHARLES BROWN, JR.[1]

ALS: Keats House, Hampstead.

My dear Carlino,   [August 2, 1839]
 I forward to you this letter received from your Father this morning — You will remember that *I* expressed some disappointment soon after you went to Chorley's, at hearing he was *only* a Millwright, when you replied that Civil Engineers preferred taking Millwrights to work (provided they did not call themselves so) because they *"worked to a line"*, and were therefore more eligible as workmen — You observed further, that it would not operate against you, as you should, at any rate, wish to work two years after you left Chorley, with other Engineers, in order to learn what he could not teach you — I at first thought of seeing Chorley and writing to your father this Evening — but finding that he is not expected home till tomorrow Evening, have determined on sending y^r Father's letter to you to answer — It appears you should have told him *when* you intended leaving town, as he feels at a loss *where* to address you, — tho' I certainly think he might have concluded you would not leave town till you heard from him in reply to your last letter —
— Your two Boxes arrived yesterday charged £*1. 9. 10* —
I fully expect being in town tomorrow — Can you call on me at *26 Guildford Street* (Mr Withers's) any time after 6 ºClock —
Your's in haste
Wm Brown

[1] Written across the first page of number 129 (see its address and postmarks).

379

· 132 ·

TO CHARLES BROWN, JR.

ALS: Keats House, Hampstead.

My dear Son,   Plymouth. 3 Augt 1839.
    I have an opportunity by private hand to write a few lines
in a few minutes. Your's of 1st received an hour ago. You seem to
talk of being with Delabeche (not Delabespe) as a land surveyor —
it is quite a different matter, being geological. However, you
need not be with him, though, I suspect, you do not understand
the probable advantages, as I have explained to your uncle. The
account you now give of Chorley is different from your former
account. In some respect you must judge for yourself. I do not see
a sufficient excuse for your not telling me of your whereabout.
You now say you will be in town till you receive my answer —
this is explicit. As a counter-fire, you talk of my not acknowledging M^r S's [1] letter; he knows it was my former stipulation that if
I did not write within three days after my expecting a remittance,
it was a proof that I had received it — this was done to avoid
expence of postage.
    Since writing the above, it seems to me far preferable to go
to the cost of postage than to run the hazard of this being delivered, or rather forwarded, by private hand. The expence of your
living in London, according to your account, ought to be stopped.
I leave you to do as you think best in regard to Mr Chorley, as I
cannot know more than you {h}ave written, and your present
letter contradicts your f{o}rmer one — contradicts it essentially.
You must do as you please, making use of all the foresight and
wisdom you possess.
    I have written *five* Reviews for the next Paper.[2] Booksellers

---

[1] Skynner's.

[2] Notices of Hugh Murray's *An Historical and Descriptive Account of British
America* (vols. XXV–XXVII of the Edinburgh Cabinet Library), the latest *Edin-
burgh Review* (July), *Foreign Monthly Review* (August), and *Dublin University
Magazine* (August), and the third and fourth parts of a work called *Illustrated
Shakespeare for the People* appeared in *PDWJ* on August 8.

seeing their publications noticed with a sort of trading (at least) knowledge, send their volumes, and I am becoming rich in new books. I have silenced the Tory press here, — it is quiet and civil.

Elizabeth goes on well — so does the cat. Last Thursday I advertised for a companion boarder and lodger; [3] this I determined to try, though I do not expect to find an applicant to my mind. My neighbours are all a strange unliterary set — tories into the bargain. I am on the best terms with all, but of what avail? Old Bowker talks often to me of the scoundrel young men who wantonly meddle with other folks' gardens! Miss Renfry is a horrible bore. Several poor people here have been found guilty of harbouring smuggled liquors; a warrant was out against every house in Laira Green; the searchers came not to me or to any of the avenue residents. M[r] May is going to London on business; but I imagine you will be off before his arrival; otherwise he could tell you how young I look.

Love and compliments to the Skynners. I expect to see T. Richards next week.

Your affectionate father,

Cha[s] Brown.

· 133 ·

TO CHARLES BROWN, JR.

Address: Mr Chas Brown, / Sandrock Cottage, / Midhurst.

Postmarks: PLYMOUTH 1839 SE 23 P[Y] POST; Crabtree Penny Post

ALS: Keats House, Hampstead. Brief extracts are given by Richardson, *The Everlasting Spell*, p. 97.

Caro mio Carlino,   Laira Green. 22 Settembre 1839.

La [1] vostra lettera mi è venuta; e spero che l'afflizione non vuol provare stupenda o stupida. Quanto al vostro dazio di due per

---

[3] Richardson, *The Everlasting Spell*, p. 94, reprints the advertisement, to which there was no answer (see the end of the next letter).

[1] "Your letter has arrived, and I hope that your distress will prove neither serious nor tiresome. As to the loan at 2%, I give it willingly, believing that it is for your pleasure, not a matter of necessity; for it is not right, nor does it suit

cento, lo do volontieri, pensando che sarà per il vostro piacere,
non per la vostra necessità; perchè non è giusto, e non mi con-
viene di soccorrere uno che non ha prudenza negli affari di quat-
trini. Vi darò anche più, se volete venire a farmi visita al tempo
della Natività; cioè voglio pagare le spese del viaggio. Ditemi se
il vostro zio vi ha promesso di pagare i venti lire sterlino l'anno
al Sig. Chorley. Voi mi avete scritto di si; ma, nel istesso tempo,
egli mi aveva scritto senza parlarne. Bisogna che io sappia o si o
no. Io trovo sempre occasioni per spendere qualche cosa. Per
esempio, in questo momento ho dato ordine al Sig. Chapman di
tingere in olio la mia casa ed il conservartorio di fuori; un lavoro
necessario, che non posso fare colla propria mano. Cè un altro
regalo per voi — un libro — compratelo e vene pagherò; la spesa
non è grande — dieciotto soldi Inglesi; il titolo è — "The Constitution of Man, by George Combe. The People's edition. Longman & Cº, London." [2] Voi troverete assai istruzione in questo

---

me, to help one who lacks prudence in money affairs. I will give you still more, if
you wish to come visit me at Christmas; that is, I will pay the expenses of the
journey. Tell me whether your uncle has promised to pay the £20 a year to Mr.
Chorley. You wrote that he did, but at the same time he had written to me
without speaking of it. I must know, either yes or no. I am always finding
occasions to spend money on something. For example, at this moment I have
given an order to Mr. Chapman to paint my cottage and greenhouse — a necessary
piece of work that I cannot do for myself. There is another present for you — a
book; buy it and I shall pay you for it; it is not expensive — 18s.; the title is
'The Constitution of Man, by George Combe. The People's edition. Longman &
Co., London.' You will find a great deal of learning in this book. You may also
charge the expense of this letter to my account. I understand little of your profession, and less of your interest with Mr. Chorley. It seems that you wish, after
a little time, to remain with him as his chief man; that you can become his
partner; and that after three years your intention is to work with various
masters. To become his partner will require a goodly sum. Supposing that his
business is really a desirable thing, it would not be impossible for me to find
the money, at least a part of it; but you must keep in mind that every farthing
you take during my lifetime will be your loss in the end, and, further,
that I must always have a moderate income — that is, I must not reduce my
present income; as to the rest, all is yours, since I am not the kind of father who
will do nothing during his lifetime for his son. I think you are strong; but you
have said that your work is quite tiring; write me the truth, then, if your health
or your strength is in the least degree weakened; and since it will be difficult
for you to judge your own condition, the report must be confirmed by your
uncle. Having now something to say that must be read by others in the event
of my death, I had better change language; it is a document to clear my
son of all blame."

[2] A popular phrenological work first issued in Edinburgh in 1828. Brown
published a "Phrenological Note on The Tempest" in *PDWJ*, April 15, 1841.

libro. Potete mettere anche la spesa di questa lettera al conto mio. Intendo poco della vostra professione, e meno del vostro interesse col Sig. Chorley. Pare che volete, dopo un poco di tempo, restare con lui come il suo primo uomo; pare che potete essere il suo compagno; pare che, dopo tre anni, la vostra intenzione è di lavorare appresso diversi maestri. Per essere il suo compagno, ci vuol una buona somma. Sopponendo che il suo negozio è veramente una cosa da desiderarsi, non sarebbe impossible per me di trovare la somma, almeno una parte; ma bisogna tener in mente che ogni quattrino che voi prendete durante la mia vita sarà alla fine la vostra perdita; e di più, che debbo sempre avere una rendita conveniente, — cioè non debbo diminuire la presente mia rendita; quanto al resto, tutto è il vostro, non essendo io un padre che non vuole far nulla per il figlio durante la sua vita. Credo che siete forte; ma mi avete detto che il lavoro è assai faticoso; dunque scrivetemi la verità, se la vostra salute o la vostra robustezza sia nella minima maniera diminuita; e siccome sarà difficile per voi di stare giudice di voi stesso, bisogna che questo rapporto sia certificato dallo zio. Avendo ora qualche cosa a dire, che dove essere letto dagli altri in caso della mia morte, sarebbe meglio di mutare lingua; è un documento per levare ogni colpa dal figlio.

If, by any chance, I should die before you, let this request of mine exonerate you from all blame respecting the mode of burying me. It is my earnest wish to be buried like a parish pauper, the expence being a trifle, something like 9s/–. Let the bearers of the body have a guinea each. Allot £20 for the burial and the poor, saving as much as possible out of that sum for the mere putting me under ground, and divide the remainder, at your best discretion, among the poorest and most deserving of my neighbours. Do not let any foolish pride on your part prevent this. Mr Soltau, the father of our most Worshipful Mayor, was, at his desire, buried in *precisely this manner*. Should my body be thought of use to science, you had better give it to any surgeon, or any anatomical school, and thus save all expence of burial, leaving the whole £20 available for the poor. Keep this as your document. You may read it, with my love and remembrance, to your Aunt and uncle — it may remind them of the poor being preferable to the undertakers; and that it is good to endeavour to be useful to science, that is, to our fellow creatures, even after death. How goes on your uncle's medical or rather dietetic practice? I wrote to him that he is not sufficiently of a humbug, which I thought complimentary, but he seemed to misapprehend it. Why, the great Esculapius himself could not prosper in England unless he were a humbug! When you come at Xmas, do not omit to bring with you my three favourite shells. Once more remembrances to all.

Your affectionate father,
Chas Brown.

N. B. I have no thoughts of leaving this world soon. My health is very good; and, if kept free from medical men, I may last these fifty years.

Not one answer did I receive to my advertisement.

Quanto sarà benedetto il "Penny-postage"[3] da voi e da me!

· 134 ·

TO CHARLES BROWN, JR.

Address: Mr Charles Brown, / Sandrock Cottage / Midhurst.
Postmark: PLYMOUTH 24 OC 1839
ALS: Keats House, Hampstead.

My dear Carlino,   Laira Green. 24 Octr 1839.
    I have just received a letter from Mr Mancur, containing an offer of a situation for you with an English engineer established at Aix-la-chapelle.[1] The situation is described as most advantageous in every respect; but it is useless for me to send you the particulars, imagining you are settled with Mr Chorley. I say — *imagining* — because you have never wrote a word to that effect. Should you be free from engagement — moral as well as legal — for I hold both equally binding; let me know,[2] and then I will

---

[3] The uniform penny rate came into operation on January 10, 1840.

[1] His name was Dobbs. Mancur's letter is quoted at length in number 136.

[2] William Brown's opinion on this point is drafted on the back of the present letter (see number 135).

send the particulars. Should you be fixed with Mr Chorley, write to Mr Mancur, thanking him, to that effect. He seems to imagine you are here with me. His address is No 25 Great Winchester Street, London.

Hindrances are in my way from being able to write more than necessary to-day. All goes on well. Remembrances to uncle and aunt.

Your affectionate father,
Chas Brown.

· 135 ·

FROM WILLIAM BROWN [1]

AL: Keats House, Hampstead.

My dear Charles,   [October 27 (?), 1839]

Carlino wishing me to add any thing that occurs to me while he is gone out riding a favorite poney, — I will just repeat my opinion, that he is not under any moral engagement to remain with Chorley if you have met with any thing else which you consider it more to his advantage to accept, — provided We close the matter with him handsomely in the way Carlino has expressed — The arrangement was, that I should pay him £20. a year for instructing Carlino, by way of premium for three years, — and that if Carlino should leave him previous to the expiration of them, (the case of illness only, I should say, mentally reserved) he should forfeit £10. to him — In regard to the time of paying the £20. Chorley afterwards said to Carlino, he thought it should be paid at the intermediate time of each year, which would be at Christmas; — but I intended paying him only £10. at Xmas, in order to avoid the possibility of my paying £20. for six months, and Carlino's being called on for the forfeit besides, *in case of his happening to leave just or soon after Christmas* — In that view of it, Chorley would now be entitled to the forfeit only, the time

---

[1] A draft, written on the back of number 134 (October 24), of a letter referred to by Brown in number 136 (October 29). Since mail regularly took two days between Plymouth and Midhurst, number 135 was written on October 26 or 27.

for paying the year's prem^m not having arrived — But as I should not consider this any more fair, than my paying him the £20. at Christmas, I feel willing to pay him the £10. unless he should express himself satisfied with a proportionate part of it when Carlino has occasion to enquire what he considers will disengage him from the contract — Carlino seems to have given you a full account of his opportunities here, he at first observed to me, he should not like "to buy a pig in a poke"; but I replied you would of course more particularly describe the "pig" to him, as you represent it "described as most advantageous in every respect." — This comes of course rather suddenly upon him when he has so lately made up his mind to remain with Chorley, but I am quite certain he is not only willing to do so, but desirous of uniting with you in any change that may be thought best adapted to his present and future interests —

· 136 ·

TO CHARLES BROWN, JR.

Address: Mr Carlino Brown, / Sandrock Cottage, / Midhurst.
Postmark: PLYMOUTH 30 OC 1839
ALS: Keats House, Hampstead.

My dear Carlino,   Laira Green. 29 Octr 1839.
   I write, not to lose time, within an hour after receiving your letter. We have now a Post Office here; so I get letters the evening they arrive. Mr Markes [1] calls me the *father* of the measure — how tall are you?
   It seems you are not bound to Mr Chorley, *morally* bound, — I never look on *legal*, that is, knavish binding, unless practised towards me. I do not desire you to leave Mr Chorley, unless it can be done with honour. Nay, it is to be proved by Dobbs' reply that you can leave him *to your own advantage*. I agree to what you and your uncle say; and, therefore, it is fit you should know what Mr Mancur says. The best way is to copy every part of his

[1] Charles Markes, the Plymouth postmaster.

letter relating to the subject. His letter is dated 21st instt from London.

"I have had a correspondence with Mr Dobbs, engineer of Aix la Chapelle *about your son* — he declined answering my letters on the subject, until he could see me; and this morning he favoured me with a call. I mentioned to him that your son was 18 or 19 years old — well educated — could draw at sight — had a decided tendency towards mechanics — and I believed was sufficiently acquainted with practical drawing of machinery as to draw to a scale — but, even if not, could soon by practice, quickness of sight, and attention, make himself decidedly useful. He told me that was good. I added that I believed he had himself made the model of a steam engine; and although these are mere childish feats, yet they weigh something with a man of experience, as showing the inclination. It was at last determined that I should write to you, and that you should address him a letter. *The matter you may almost consider as concluded,* if you and your son are agreeable. You will now learn something further for your information. My second nephew, Richard, now 24 years old, has been with Mr Dobbs for two years, and wishes to leave for a better position in the same town. I was pleased to hear that Dobbs has intrusted him with setting up no less than eight steam engines in different parts of Germany — and, more, that Dobbs has made six or seven Locomotives for the Brussels line of Rail Road, all of which have been made under the superintendence or assistance of Richard. "The fact is" (said Dobbs) he may go where he will in Germany or in England; he is fitted for all engineering; and I, of course, will not stand in the way of his doing better for himself. I can take the son of your friend in his stead, if he possesses the requisite patience, perseverance, and industry." If, therefore, you think well of his chance, write immediately to "Messrs Dobbs, of Aix la Chapelle, Mechanikers"; and, making use of my name, say that you should be desirous of placing your son with them; and that, for the first twelve months, you do not require any salary — and something in a similar position to Richard Mancur — that, at the expiration of twelve months, they may pay him what they think he is worth — and I doubt not the answer will be favourable.

— But if they say, let him remain for two years without salary, close the bargain at once, and send Charles off at once by the Ostend Steamer, with a letter to Messrs Dobbs, and also one to my nephew Richard, who will most likely get him board and lodging with him. Now as to the expence of his living — I should say £40 a year is enough; clothes I can say nothing about; but Charles must make up his mind to wear a Jacket &c &c in the factory. x x x x x Dobbs, an Englishman, is a kind hearted, clever, worthy man; and his factory ranks as high as any in Germany; it is very extensive, and the work is general machinery, and Richard (who understands these matters) says is turned out of hand as well as in England. I look upon Richard's prospects in a few years as brilliant; it all depends upon himself; he has learnt to live upon twelve shillings a week — so much the better. Do not allow Charles too much money — it spoils them from exertion. x x x x Charles must learn the German language; a few lessons &c x x x x The position of an engineer in Germany intitles him to the highest respect, if his education and manners are those of a gentleman.''

The above is a true copy of all that is interesting to you. My first intention was to bid *you* write to Messrs Dobbs, on account of my greater distance for a correspondence; which was the cause of my hurry to finish this letter. But it soon appeared better that *I* should write to Messrs Dobbs; which I have done, requesting them to send their answer to you at Midhurst — and thus more time is saved. I am now writing on Wednesday the 30th, and my letter to them *is now upon the road*. This will be despatched to-day or tomorrow, for there *is now no need* of hurry; and I wish first to say the furniture is arrived. I told Messrs Dobbs that I proposed you should work for them gratis for one year, and afterwards to be paid by them according to your value. I mentioned the cause of delay in my writing, and stated you could honourably quit Mr Chorley, with whom you have been three months. I forgot to say you are above nineteen; but I informed them you are well learned in geometry and algebra. My letter was business-{like} and civil; and I regretted Mr Rendle's absence, else he could give them a professional account of your ability. Should their answer be favourable, it will therefore be addressed to you; and let me hear of it immediately. Should they, as Mancur hints, insist on two years service without pay, yield to the demand forthwith. There is no cold water thrown over my hopes except this — poor Mancur's swans have hitherto invariably proved to be geese.

A walking-stick for me ought to be exactly three feet, less three quarters of an inch, long.

Tell your uncle, with love to your aunt, that I sincerely thank him for the trouble he has taken in this business; and that I agree with him in his opinion of the justice and fairness of the settlement with Chorley — should Mancur's swan, for the first time, not prove a goose.

I now break off, to go into Plymouth and inquire if the chairs are arrived.

Plymouth. 30 Octr. The Brunswick now sails only once a week. It will not come in till Friday.

Your affectionate father,
Chas Brown.

Mr May sells ink and pens — devil take them both! [2]

· 137 ·

TO CHARLES BROWN, JR.

Address: Mr Carlino Brown / Sandrock Cottage / Midhurst.

Postmarks: PLYMOUTH 1839 NO 24 P^Y POST; Crabtree Penny Post

ALS: Keats House, Hampstead.

My dear Son,   Laira Green. 23 Novr 1839.

Not an hour has passed since I received your's of *21st*. This answer will go by to-morrow's mail.

Rest quietly where you are. I cannot comprehend Mr Dobbs' words [1] — "I have advised to refer to a better opportunity for

---

[2] The end of the letter, from "Plymouth. 30 Oct^r," is written with a very heavy pen.

[1] In a letter to Mancur, quoted by Carlino in his letter to Brown. Carlino omitted "him" after "advised" (see the second paragraph of the next letter).

coming over and at the same time a better season of the year."
Whose coming over? — *his* or *your's?* — take it either way, *you* are
not to go over *now*. You say you feel as if sitting on a bag of
lucifer matches; better so, than falling down between two stools.
Mr Dobbs treats my letter as a *wish on my part*, by no means as
the *necessary consequence* of his conversation with Mancur. It
seems to me to be as I feared, of which I warned you when I gave
general reasons for supposing the swan might prove a goose.
Mancur always has been too sanguine; and he may have interpreted Mr Dobbs' words held with him as positive as he has described them, while they were merely intended as complimentarily
speculative. Mancur's proposal to take you with him to Aix la
Chapelle is almost madness — of which he has shown some equiv-
ocal symptoms in his own affairs. I really fear the bird is a
goose. If Mr Dobbs really spoke the words as written by Mancur,
he could not talk like one as if he had received the first notion
of it from *me*. At all events, he *bids you wait his time*. If, as
Mancur says, he desires your services, he will, after my letter to
him, make the fact known to you or to me. My opinion is we shall
never hear more from him — that it is all moonshine, which Mancur has thought to be broad daylight. Your uncle might easily be
deceived, not knowing him so well as I do, by his sanguine and
positive talk. You speak of running about the world as if you had
the seven league boots, or Fortunatus's purse. Rest quietly where
you are; wait, after my proposal, for direct orders. I will write
to Mancur to-night. Should there perchance be any thing, my
letter will further its completion.

Tell your uncle I am sincerely obliged to him for the interest
he has taken in your behalf; and give my love to his wife.

Now that I consider this presumed offer in repose for *a few
months*, I expect to see you at Xmas. If you wish it, I shall be
very glad indeed to see Henry Hunt with you — and say so kindly
from me.

Had you described the chairs before you sent them, I should
have fixed their destination otherwise. At least I had no use for
the round backed ones. Did you take off the castors from the arm-
chair? or were they stolen by the way?

Since penning the foregoing I have finished my letter to
Mancur. The marrow of it is, that I cannot accede to your ac-

companying him to Aix la Chapelle, without a positive written promise from Mr Dobbs; because you must not run the hazard of losing your present situation for an uncertainty. I have also requested him to treat with Mr Dobbs, so as to procure from him an actual engagement. The more I consider it, the more I fear the whole matter is one of Mancur's geese, tricked out swan-fashion. I thought my hint would have tranquillized your ardent hope. Yet I had no right to think nothing {of it}, to your possible injury.

I am tired, and sick of writing.

> Your affectionate father,
> Chas Brown.

· 138 ·

TO CHARLES BROWN, JR.

ALS: Keats House, Hampstead.

My dear Carlino,   Laira Green. 5 Decr 1839.

As this is the first day of the groat-postage,[1] I cannot forbear writing, in order to inquire on what day I am to expect you; though I think it probable you may be taking the same groat's worth of opportunity to give me all the information I require about your visit and other matters.

Since I answered your's of 21st, I have thought it likely you left out the word "him" after "advised" in your quotation from Mr Dobbs' letter to Mr Mancur, as reported by your uncle. This would make the passage sense; and agree with your uncle's words, in a parenthesis — ("Dobbs has written to C") — but that fact, if one it is, you have denied by saying no letter, in answer to mine, has been received by you. I suspect you have not been so nice in your language, or in your copying, as you would be in the making of a cog to a wheel, or of a screw. I still fear, without any abatement, that Mancur has much exaggerated your prospect; and I still remain of opinion that, whether he has or has not, you must not proceed to Aix la Chapelle until after a few months time,

---

[1] The general inland postage rate was (on an experimental basis) reduced to 4d. per half-ounce.

according to the letter from Mr Dobbs — indeed not before he shall sanction it.

Whatever news there may be for you in this part of the world needs not to be now written — it will not grow stale before you arrive.[2]

Love and remembrances to aunt and uncle.

Your affectionate father,
Chas Brown.

Should you go round by London, let me know. Unless necessary, I hope not, as it must be the more expensive way. The Brunswick has been advertising to go *once* a week during the winter; but, possibly, only in case they have passengers or goods enough to make it answer.

· 139 ·

TO CHARLES BROWN, JR.

Address: Carlino Brown Esqre / Care of Leigh Hunt Esqre / 4 Cheynè Row, / Chelsea, / near London.

Postmarks: PLYMOUTH [. . .]; Kingston Penny Post

ALS: Keats House, Hampstead.

My dear boy,   Laira. 31 Jany 1840.

Is that the title you like? — I forget which it was that met with your profound objection.[1] I have not written, purely because I had nothing to say, except that I am as well as a water-drinker can be expected. So, at last my opinion is found to be correct — Mancur's swan has turned out to be a goose. Look upon your hopes of an advantageous situation in America as nothing more than a notion. I suspect your Dr Black is one who loves to make promises, because it implies his great influence with great men, like Mr Lofty in the "Good natured man".[2] Have you seen

---

[2] For the Christmas visit.

[1] See number 143.

[2] Goldsmith's play.

Trelawny? what is his precise address? Without quoting or alluding to you, I have written to T. Richards, introducing certain
facts; that I had gratefully thanked his uncle for extricating me
from the fangs of S & O; [3] that I had offerred his uncle the £25,
which was declined. Many folks have short memories; many
others affect them; the uncle and nephew belong to one of the
two classes. With all my desire to see Hunt's play, [4] and all my
sympathy with your desire, I cannot approve of your neglect of
Chorley. You sacrifice a week for pleasure; and, at the end of the
week you will probably find the performance is put off for another week, or a few days. For some reason, or no reason, I
suspect you want a change from Chorley's. This love of change
is an old complaint of your's. A rolling stone &c. You have always
been most eager to *begin* any thing you liked. Be constant to your
purpose. Let better prospects offer themselves, or, without loss of
time, quietly keep a look-out for them; in the mean while, be
industrious. No play, not even L. Hunt's, should tempt you from
your purpose. Remember me most kindly to him, with my best
dramatic anticipations. If I could witness his triumph, few things
could give me greater pleasure; but you should not think of
pleasure, when your profession stands in the way.

Your affectionate father,
Chas Brown.

· 140 ·

TO CHARLES BROWN, JR.

ALS: Keats House, Hampstead.

My dear boy,   Laira 10 March 1840.
    I know not if I told you that Fanny, on 28 Feb^y, wrote to me
that she would accept my invitation. She promised to be here
during the week. I know not now how to address a letter to her.
Something has prevented her arrival. No further accounts have I
received.

---

[3] The publishers Saunders and Otley.
[4] *A Legend of Florence.*

You will be as sorry as myself to hear that M[r] Child, my tenant, has fled, leaving three quarters of rent due. I can get no account from Bohn. M[r] Richards, by this time, is paid.[1] Tom has proved himself to be a true observer of his uncle's maxims. I think I ought to sell Child's house at once, notwithstanding M[r] Skynner's reluctance. M[r] May has lately been very backward in his payments.[2] I impute no blame to him personally. All I mean is, that unexpectedly I am thrown into pecuniary difficulties. But these, which can be and will be set to rights, in no way interfere with your advantage at the present moment. At your age one pound of assistance is worth more than ten pounds when I shall be under ground — or in M[r] Swain's show-room.[3]

You went on board the San Josef, and were much gratified. I — ditto — ditto. Only there was this difference. I dined on board with the Captain. He was sent to me by Col[l] Smith, that I might prepare his intended pamphlet for the press.[4] Little was to be done. I do it willingly, and gratis. You may imagine I was a welcome visitor. All the models for improvement were shown and explained to me. The first class boys were ordered out, and went through their lessons in gunnery, with geometrical elucidations, and through their various exercises, and I passed some happy hours there, only wishing you had been with me.

Miss Renfry, my horror, has just come to pay me a visit. She will exterminate me. I intended a longer scrawl. M[rs] Bowker is dangerously ill; it is possible and probable she will leave the Captain free for a second wife.

Do not mention *any thing* about Fanny to uncle or aunt. I have just received a letter from him, and will answer it forthwith, and with its due signed inclosure.

Your affectionate father,
Cha[s] Brown.

---

[1] James Bohn, the publisher, and Charles Richards, the printer, of *Shakespeare's Autobiographical Poems.*

[2] For Brown's writings in *PDWJ*. See number 142.

[3] P. W. Swain lectured at the Plymouth Institution on such subjects as "Insanity," "Respiration," "Poisons," "Circulation."

[4] The captain of the 112-gun *San Josef*, whose home port was Plymouth, was Joseph Needham Tayler (1785–1864). His "intended pamphlet" was probably *Plans for the Formation of Harbours of Refuge*, printed and published by Daniel May in 1840.

· 141 ·

(WITH FANNY BROWN) TO CHARLES BROWN, JR.

Address: Paid / Mʳ Carlino Brown, / at Mʳ Chorley's, / Engineer &c / Midhurst.

Postmark: PLYMOUTH MR 30 1840 C

ALS: Keats House, Hampstead.

My dear boy,   Laira. 30 March 1840.

Fanny arrived here a day or two after my last letter to you. She is very well, far different from what I had expected. No news from you; but I suppose all is going on well. Till within these few days we have been much annoyed by Crazy Jane.[1] If Elizabeth is to be credited, she has made her a confidant in the endeavour to gain her purpose over me; and has been weeping in sorrow at my indifference! "I must be cruel only to be kind."[2] Even though you should intreat me to make her your mother-in-law, I should be obstinate. Do not waste your labour in trying to make me as crazy as herself. Ora[3] voglio mutare linguaggio, perchè quest'af-

---

[1] Jane Renfry.

[2] *Hamlet*, III.iv.178.

[3] "Now I want to change language, so that this wretched affair may not be discovered by any spy. It was necessary to inform your cousin [Fanny] of what you said [at Christmas] to Elizabeth, in order to avoid any further revealing of the secret. Almost immediately after your cousin's arrival, Elizabeth spoke to her about the possibility of a rape, trying in various ways to find out how the affair stood. Your cousin, forewarned by me of the trap, did as much as she could to conceal the story. But you can imagine that you are much abused by her, and rightly. I told you in January how much harm you had done in disclosing a thing that otherwise could be no more than guessed at. Now this servant can tell everything, and confirm it with your authority. Fanny says that you have acted dishonorably, and that she herself told you in London that only my servant could throw suspicion on her late visit to France [see number 120, n. 5]. As Fanny has returned to my house, your lack of discretion troubles me considerably. I am also afraid that you have said something about it to the Mays, at least to Daniel. Answer me truthfully on this point, and tell me all that you have disclosed to anyone. I fear too that you have spoken to the Mays about my income — such talk can hurt me with them in our agreement concerning the *Journal* [see the next letter]. In short, knowing that your tongue has been much too long for your mouth, and that everyone speaks of your talent for telling all you know, Fanny and I are in doubt about everything. But the greatest fault is your indiscretion with Elizabeth. Do not say in reply that I had no right to speak

faraccio non sia scoperto da qualunque spia. Era necessario di
avvisare la vostra cugina di quello che avete voi detto alla Liza,
per evitare ogni modo di palesare più il segreto. Quasi subito
dopo l'arrivo, la Liza ha parlato alla cugina della possibilità di
un ratto, cercando in molte maniere di conoscere come l'affare
si è stato. La cugina, sapendo da me la trappola, faceva tanto che
poteva di celare la storia. Ma, potete imaginare che siete voi assai
vituperato, e con ragione. Vi ho detto in Gennajo quanto avete
fatto male di confessare una cosa, che non poteva altrimente
essere più che indovinata. Adesso questa serva può dire tutto, e
sigillare tutto colla vostra autorità. La F— dice che avete mancato
l'onore; e che ella stessa vi disse in Londra che non c'era altro
per la mia serva che mettere in sospetto la sua visità tempo fà
dalla Francia. Siccome la F si è tornata a casa mia, la vostra
mancanza di discrezione mi turba di molto. C'è anche una paura
che ne avete detto qualche cosa ai May, almeno al Daniello.
Respondetemi con sincerità sopra di questo; e ditemi tutto che
avete confessato a qualunque che sia. Temo anche che avete parlato ai May della mia rendità; perchè questo parlare può farmi
del male con loro nel nostro patto del Giornale. In somma, cono-
scendo che la vostra lingua è stata assai troppo lunga per la bocca,
e che tutti parlano della vostra facoltà di dire tutto che sapete,
sianno noi, la F— ed io, in dubbio sopra ogni cosa. Ma la gran
mancanza è la vostra indiscrezione colla Liza. Non rispondete che
io non ebbi il diritto di parlarne alla F, perchè, vi dico un altra
volta, era necessario di metterla sulla guardia contra questa spia
donnesca. Sono il vostro padre affezionato,

Carlo Brown.

Vous [4] avez manqué à *tout*, à l'honneur, à la delicatesse, à tout lien
qui devrait lier un honnête homme. — Vous avez trahi un secret,

---

of it to Fanny, because, I repeat, it was necessary to put her on her guard against
this female spy. I am your affectionate father."

   [4] Fanny adds: "You have failed in *everything* — in honor, in delicacy, in everything that binds an honorable man. You have betrayed a secret, but *you knew*
you could do it without fearing anything, since it was only a question of a
woman. I would not have believed it possible, and at present I am forced to
believe that something worse than indiscretion is involved. In any case you should
have warned me when you knew that I had been invited here. You had no right
to make me suffer thus in your father's house."

mais *vous saviez que* vous pouviez le faire sans rien craindre, puisqu'il ne s'agissait que d'une femme — Je n'aurais pas cru cela possible, et à present je suis forcée à croire qu'un sentiment plus fort que l'indiscretion s'y est mèlé. Dans tout les cas vous auriez dû m'en prevenir quand vous saviez qu'on allait m'inviter — Vous n'aviez pas le droit de me faire souffrir ainsi, dans la Maison de votre père. —

· 142 ·

TO CHARLES BROWN, JR.

ALS: Keats House, Hampstead.

Caro mio fanciullone,   Laira. 17 Aprile 1840.

Non [1] vedo punto la necessità di quello mistero; mandando una lettera a me per le mani di Sig. Silvano; e poi, perchè non avete risposto alla zia che la lettera in vostra tasca era da me? Cosa potrebbe essa fare? e come poteva intendere questa lingua. In vece di mistero sarebbe meglio di non svelare i segreti degli altri. Sono stato un poco offeso in un altro affare. Avete scritto alla vostra cugina quello che ho fidato a voi; le mie opinioni di essa, tirate da un altro; il mio consiglio a voi; tutto che io credei poteva essere ben fidato in mio figlio. E perchè? — per dispetto bambesco! Mene rincresce!

24 April. Many things have withstood my writing for a whole week. I have another bone to pick with you. When I asked you if you had not mentioned to Dan [2] my income, you acknowledged it — saying, "I did not know it was a secret; I suppose you are ashamed of being poor". Here are several injurious mistakes. Every thing is a secret which may do harm by revealment. If

---

[1] "I don't see any need for this mystery — sending a letter to me via Mr. Silvano; and then why did you not tell your aunt that the letter in your pocket [number 141] was from me? What could she do? and how could she have understood this language? Instead of creating mystery, it would be better not to reveal the secrets of others. I have been somewhat annoyed in another matter. You wrote to your cousin what I confided solely in you — my opinions of her, derived from another, and my advice to you — all which I thought could have been safely entrusted to my son. And why? — for childish spite! I am sorry about it!"

[2] Daniel May, Jr.

there is no necessity to tell a fact, which may *possibly* be a secret, it ought not to be told. I am not, or rather I should not be ashamed of being poor, were I so; but the contrary is the truth; were it otherwise, I should be desperately in debt; no one can be poor whose means are equal to his reasonable wants. But, in the opinion of the world in general, an exact account of my income would denounce me as a poor man; and, to the May's, as a dependant man. Such a conclusion will, generally, be *acted* on, instinctively, the Mays not excepted. My first notion of your having declared me, in their notion, poor, arose from their change of behaviour. They took liberties. Before you came here, every thing was done to ingratiate me. Afterwards, and very soon, a liberty was taken by depriving me of the "Evening Chronicle" at the Post Office, stopping it from me. This might be excused; in fact, that trifling liberty, I now recollect, was taken before you came. As time went on, however, I heard such things as "mutual advantage" spoken. Then I never could obtain my money; on the instinctive principle that those who are dependent must, of necessity, *wait*. They have been, and still are in debt to me. Latterly I was attempted to be ruled on the *subjects* of the Articles; and, at last, it came to the *opinions* in the Articles. May, from a mistaken idea of self-interest, began, without the grace of telling me, to resolve against printing any thing against the "National School Society",[3] whose conduct I had frequently exposed. All at once he would not accept my comments on the Society at a particular emergency, advised to this refusal by St John.[4] He would not, he said, any more offend the Churchmen by any thing which could be construed against them. He was induced to this by *promises*, which he thought good "for his family" as he phrased it. In answer, I instantly said — "I do not pretend to find fault with your following your imagined profit; and do not find fault with me for not going on in your *new* path, and for saying that I will write *no more* for *you* till the end of the quarter, the 18 June." He stared like a stuck pig. He asked me over and over

[3] The National Society for Promoting the Education of the Poor in the Principles of the Established Church throughout England and Wales, founded in 1809.

[4] The Rev. B. St. John was an active member of the Plymouth Institution in the 1830's.

again, seeming to think he had not heard aright. I believe he never would have acted in this manner, had he not heard I was with a small income. I never boasted of more than was correct — never, indeed, talked of my income, which made him respect me. As my suspicion of your having blabbed too much arose from their *change* of behaviour, it is not irrelevant to imagine that *you have lost me £40 a year.* It may be otherwise; he may have chosen to change at all risks. At all events, he is astonished at my refusing to write, in the slightest degree, against my conscience; and this, though by *omission,* is a crime equal to *commission,* according to my conscience. I have treated the whole affair with great coolness, and even good humour; so that we continue good friends; and he, I well know, thinks I will not *eventually* keep to the notice I have given. The more fool he — to disbelieve my word, and believe a promise, made to serve a particular purpose, from the Parsons. The Article, rejected by him, will appear tomorrow in the "Independant";[5] it has been *thankfully* received; that Paper is a Radical one. I have followed it up with a Song of 12 stanzas, ridiculing episcopal inspection of Public Schools; which said song I shall send to other Papers — at least the "Morning Chronicle" and the "Western Times" of Exeter.[6] It is really a song that pleases me, each short stanza ending with *inspection,* for which there are so many rhymes. I have no notion that the proprietor of the "Independant" is in want of a writer; but, should such be the fact, and should we agree, I shall not regret the change.[7] With the "Journal" I went half way conscientiously; but with the "Independant" I could go the whole way with more spirit and pleasure. Nevertheless, you have, I conceive, done much harm.

Your copy of the "Constitution of Man"[8] shall be carried by me to Midhurst about the beginning of July. Tell your Uncle & aunt of this, with my love. John Snook dined with me the day

[5] "Inspection of Public Schools," in the *Devonport Independent, and Plymouth and Stonehouse Gazette,* April 25.

[6] Brown's song, "How to inspect Public Schools; being advice from the sanctuary," appeared in the Exeter *Western Times* on May 2.

[7] In a now lost letter written sometime during the summer of this year, Brown told Severn that he was "engaged to contribute weekly a political article to a Liberal Plymouth paper" (Sharp's paraphrase, p. 191).

[8] See number 133.

before yesterday; I did not ask him to trouble himself with it, as I, in spite of your augury, intend to visit Sussex and Hants.[9] Take care of the sundries for me.   Your loving father

Cha[s] Brown.

· 143 ·

TO CHARLES BROWN, JR.

Address: Carlino Brown, / Millwright; / M[r] Chorley, / Midhurst. / Paid

Postmarks: PLYMOUTH MY 5 1840 P[Y] POST; Crabtree Penny Post

ALS: Keats House, Hampstead.

Laira Green.

My dear boy,   5 May 1840.

I am sorry to have offended you in not addressing my letters according to your wish. My mistake was unintentional. Have the kindness to explicitly state in what words I ought to address a letter to you. At this moment my note is addressed as well as I can to please you.[1]

Your affectionate father,
Cha[s] Brown.

· 144 ·

TO CHARLES BROWN, JR.

ALS: Keats House, Hampstead.

My dear boy,   Laira. 17 May 1840.

I sent you one Newspaper with some lines of mine on "Inspection of schools";[1] and, afterwards, another with nothing of mine. I mention this as Newspapers are apt to miscarry. There

---

[9] That is, Midhurst, Chichester, and Bedhampton.

[1] Apparently the desired address, since it was repeated on number 145.

[1] The "song" mentioned in number 142.

are some lines of mine in yesterday's "Independent", "The Church in danger," [2] which I now send. Next week I may have "An excellent new Ballad", called the "Tories' Confession" to the tune of the "Vicar of Bray, Sir," [3] which I can afford to send you, as my Radical verses are published in *two* Papers, one for me and one for you, the "Western Times" and the "Independent".

After May had refused my Article he admitted another, taking the Dissenters' side on the same subject, without his perceiving the bearing, and got himself into somewhat of a scrape with the Church — mine took no side, except against the National Society. May has made a sufficient apology by telling me he thought I was a better judge than himself of what was the best for the Paper. But another hindrance to the continuance of my writing I have chosen to advance — my being compelled to *ask* for my pay, and sometimes to ask in vain. On this point we seem to have split, as he tells me he cannot engage to pay punctually. Can he think that any one, who can write like a gentleman, will consent to *ask* for his due? *I* will not write for his Paper and *ask* for my money — he must pay without my asking for it, and punctually, or I will have nothing more to do with the "Journal". It is plain he has *presumed* it is of importance to me; but I shall effectually take the starch out of him, or fail in the attempt.

There is a "Star Chamber" matter between me and the Institution. I have written a long letter to Mr Woolcombe, complaining of the rude and improper conduct of the Secretary, Dr Moore,[4] to me; and intimating that I may publish the letter. The Institution stands in need of me; yet there is a strong Tory feeling against me, as well as an unchristian feeling; and therefore I expect that Dr Moore will be upheld in not making a due apology. With all my heart! After stating my grounds of complaint to the President, I wrote — "Educated from my childhood as I have been, and accustomed to a gentlemanly demeanour from all, if

[2] This 32-line poem appeared in the Exeter *Western Times* on May 16.

[3] It was published in the *Devonport Independent* on May 23.

[4] Edward Moore, M.D., F.L.S., of 34 George Street, Plymouth, vice-president of the Institution in 1830–1831, secretary also in 1833–1834 and 1835–1836. He lectured on geological and zoological subjects, and compiled an ornithology of South Devonshire. Woollcombe was president of the Institution.

I am to listen to attempted indignities, and be subject to rudeness in the Committee of the Plymouth Institution from its Secretary, much as I desire its welfare, I cannot consent to be a Member of it at so high a price. It is in the power of the Committee to identify themselves with the conduct of their Secretary, or not; it is in their power, therefore, to decide whether I am compelled to send in my resignation from the Society, or remain as heretofore." The whole of my letter was quiet and resolute, much approved of by Col. Smith. Of course the impropriety and rudeness towards me was of an undoubted nature. Still I think they will lose, by rank hatred towards me on the part of the Parsons, their second fiddle (Prideaux being the first,) [5] in their discussions and two promised lectures. A day or two ago Woolcombe met me going out in the avenue. He said he would call on Monday (tomorrow); what he will have to say as a peace maker I know not; but this I know that nothing less than Dr Moore's resignation as Secretary, or his *written* apology, can content me.

Your living in your uncle's house is not a matter requiring my interference, special or incidental. I never believed it would prove agreeable to either party, and told you as much last Xmas. When folks choose to part, let them part friends; which I hope you have done. There is one thing, however, in your change of abode which extremely interests me. I expect to be assured that you will reside in a respectable house, and that you associate with respectable people. My meaning to the word *respectable* is, as you ought to know, not in regard to chintz furniture and all sorts of questionable assumptions, but to good character, undoubted probity, and unfearing sincerity. You have seen more of the world than most of your age — be not deceived! Take no man's or woman's flattering words as a proof of sincerity. Beware of all insiduous claims on your pocket. Never show so much weakness as to be led astray at another's suggestion; every one has suggestions enough, and too many, of his own.

You ask me if your envelopes at 1s/– per 100 are not cheap.

---

[5] The words "Prideaux being the first," are written above the line. The parentheses here are an editorial addition. John Prideaux (1787–1859), for a while a chemist and druggist in East Street, Plymouth, became professor of chemistry in the Cornish Mining School.

I answer by referring you to mine of this letter, which costs 6s/9d per ream, or about 4d per quire. A quire contains 48 half sheets — that is, three for a farthing. Now yours are little more than *two* for a farthing. I therefore think you have paid nearly 50 per cent too much for your envelopes. I thought you were a better calculator.

Your affectionate father,
Chas Brown.

· 145 ·

TO CHARLES BROWN, JR.

Address: Carlino Brown, / Millwright, / Mr Chorley, / Midhurst. / Post paid

Postmarks: PLYMOUTH JU 13 1840 P^Y POST; Crabtree Penny Post

ALS: Keats House, Hampstead.

My dear boy, Laira. 12 June 1840.

Not to conceal any thing from you, I make it known that a letter from your uncle has just arrived, giving me an account of a connection you have formed with a Sailor's daughter — pretty, but somewhat leprous. *Speak not to him of his information*, which I approve; for it is good, and given in good feeling. I see some mystification He is *bound* to suspect the worst; but I am not bound to *imagine* that worst. In fact, the *worst* seems to me that Chorley does not find you so early diligent as usual. Disguise it as you will, I see you wince under the circumstances of your birth. This is a source of pain to me. With reason as your guide, your birth is as good as any one's. If you give way to a morbid feeling, you may link yourself to an ignorant girl; for I do not regard this Sailor's daughter in your Uncle's view, but simply as unworthy in intellect and education — in its widest sense. Youth is apt to folly; be you above it. You know me as just; act, if you will, as you will; I remain the same; never upholding what I believe to be wrong. You are at an age when caution is the most admirable quality, be-

403

cause the most difficult; but if you have a strong mind, overcome difficulty. I cannot uphold deterioration; yet I know nothing as yet; and I verily believe a word from you would dispel this phantom — conjured up by myself more than by your uncle. I shall set off in less than a month, I fancy, for your part of the world. I had your last Sunday's letter. I repeat that I see you have been mystifying your uncle.

Your affectionate father,
Chas Brown.

· 146 ·

TO R. M. MILNES

Address: Richard M. Milnes Esqre / M. P. / Pontefract, / Yorkshire.

Postmarks: PLYMOUTH OC 18 40 P^Y POST; Crabtree Penny Post; B 20 OC 20 1840

Endorsement: Chas Brown.

ALS: Harvard. Printed in *KC*, II, 37–38.

Laira Green, near Plymouth.

My dear Sir,   19 [*for* 18] [1] October 1840.
    I have taken a fancy to rewrite my old Journals of tours to the Highlands, when I set out accompanied by Keats. They are printed, week after week, in a Plymouth Newspaper.[2] The next Chapter will contain a ballad by Keats, written on the road, the first I have introduced, and, as I think you will like it, and like to have it, I will order it to be forwarded to you.
    Possibly, or rather probably, you have not any of his handwriting. I know you will thank me for the inclosure — a rough

---

[1] See the postmarks.
[2] The first four chapters of "Walks in the North, during the Summer of 1818" appeared in *PDWJ* on October 1, 8, 15, 22 (they are reprinted in *Letters*, I, 421–442). Though the fourth chapter (containing the "ballad by Keats" on Meg Merrilies) ended with the notice "To be Continued," no further installments were printed, for reasons given in the next letter. The rest of the work and Brown's "old Journals" are now unknown.

writing of part of his "Lamia" as it was composed.[3] I have nothing but fragments, as most of the originals were scrambled away to America by his brother, after I had made copies of them for the press.

My best respects to your family.

Your's most sincerely,
Chas Brown.

· 147 ·

TO R. M. MILNES

ALS: Harvard. Printed in *KC*, II, 38–40.

Laira Green, Plymouth.

My dear Sir,   25 Octr 1840.

It must appear extremely ridiculous that a few days after I had informed you of my "Walks in the North," interspersed with the posthumous minor poems of Keats, they should be discontinued. They were avowedly doing service to the Paper, and I furnished them without fee or reward; but the proprietor is an impracticable pig-headed man, most gracious and thankful at the offer, till, at the end of a month, when he calculated I had committed myself for the whole series, he turned round upon me, as if I were his shoe-black. To his astonishment, in spite of repentant entreaty, he finds he will have no more. They may appear in another News-paper; in that event, the proprietor will be glad to put down your name as a subscriber for the time.

You ask of me what I am so desirous to give! — a Life of my dear Keats, with all his unpublished poems. As a matter of trade, London booksellers have told me it would prove a most losing speculation, that no one buys poetry and lives of poets, and that very few indeed read any thing but Newspapers. There is, I dare say, much truth in this, and tradesmen are not to be blamed for following their own interest. But after receiving your letter yester-day morning, I thought of the hint of Newspapers, and wrote to

---

³ Two sheets (now at Harvard) containing II.26–49, 122–147, 191–198, plus eighteen canceled and six fragmentary lines.

405

the "Morning Chronicle", asking the Editor [1] if he were inclined to publish a column or two at a time of Keats's life, with, at least, his *minor* posthumous poems. Both you and I may call this *infra dig*; but we must seize on the public ear as we can. I almost expect to receive a "not available" answer, or, haply, none at all. The Life *is written*; and with great pain — more than pain*s*. Recollect, its publication in an ephemeral Newspaper will not injure the after appearance in a volume; it will rather act as an advertisement.

With this subject in my head, I have not yet replied to the most kind part of your letter — a more than [kind] inquiry about my boy. He has now grown into manhood, steady and persevering for the profession of an engineer — good and affectionate to me. On our return to England, seeing his decided turn of mind and talent for mechanism, I performed my duty — with the prospect of our inevitably living asunder — in giving him the best mathematical instruction, which he sucked in like mother's milk. Then, what was to be done? To apprentice him à la mode to a famous engineer was to tie him down, at the expence of £500, to the learning of mechanical drawing, and nothing else, for five or seven years — to his master's profit, not to his own. He rather chose to learn the entire handicraft of the profession; but there was another difficulty; not only a large premium, but the probability (for many cases have occurred) of being kept in the back ground from jealousy, should he evince too much talent. Men of science, after all that has been said against poets, from Sir Isaac Newton downwards, are far more envious than it is thought. At length he fixed on learning what he could, with a small premium, of a Millwright at Midhurst, whom his uncle, who lives there, highly recommended. I went there two months since, and found him hard at work, but complaining that his master gave him inferior work — the old story! The master owned to me his ability, promised to act differently, and, when my back was turned, still kept him back. Carlino has left him, and, at this moment, is working for himself at a machine for cutting tobacco for Trelawny. When finished, he will take it to London, hoping great credit for it, and will be sure, as I last night wrote to him to do so, to call and pay his respects

[1] John Black.

to you. I ought to mention that he has had *more* than a grateful remembrance of you; for, a twelvemonth ago,[2] he asked me if you would not do him a service if you could — and I, for which I may be blamed, replied that I had no *right* to expect so great a favour.

Now permit me to speak of your last born — your "Poetry for the People".[3] The title alone interests me greatly — such poetry is wanted — not such as E. Elliot's [4] to keep alive discontent, justly or unjustly, but to diffuse happiness. I will direct the Plymouth bookseller, Edmund Fry, to request it from your publisher. It will then be sure to reach me. I am very anxious to read it, and very thankful to you.

Pray do not remind me again of George Keats! — I know nothing of him.

I am sorry to perceive you are in mourning — but I hope it is only for the Princess.[5]

Give my best respects to those who know me;

and believe me,

My dear Sir,

Your's most truly,

Cha[s] Brown.

[2] It was more than two years ago (see number 120).
[3] *Poetry for the People, and Other Poems*, published by Edward Moxon in 1840.
[4] Ebenezer Elliott (1781–1849), the "Corn-law rhymer."
[5] Princess Augusta Sophia (b. 1768), sixth child of George III, had died on September 22.

· 148 ·

TO R. M. MILNES

Address: R. M. Milnes Esqre M.P. / Pall Mall / London.

Postmarks: PLYMOUTH MR 14 1841 C; Crabtree Penny Post; A 16 MR 16 1841

Endorsement: Charles Brown.

ALS: Harvard. Printed in *KC*, II, 49–51.

　　　　　　　　　　　　　　　Laira Green, near Plymouth.
My dear Sir,　　　　　　　　　　　　14 March 1841.
　　You have often urged me, as Keats's literary executor, to publish his Poems, remaining in my possession, together with his Life, which has long since been written; and I have, as often, pleaded difficulties in my way. That which arose from his brother George's *veto*, as I was told by his forbidding friend, Mr Dilke of the Athenæum, no longer exists.[1] I desired to give both the Poems and the Life the utmost publicity; but in that I was foiled. At length, after much delay in answering, the Editor of the Monthly Chronicle [2] agreed to print them in his rather unpopular Magazine. But as he is a stranger to me, as I could have no controul, and as I am on the eve of quitting England for ever, I considered it would be my wiser plan to confide in a true lover of Keats, and place the Life and Poems in his hands, to act in my stead. Such confidence I am ready to repose in you, if you will undertake the task — the responsibility — the gratification — or whatever you may be induced to call it. I have thus unreservedly stated why I apply to you, without compliments — for they always look as if they concealed something. Should you consent to accept of the *trust*, I will send you the *Deeds*.
　　I have bought land in New Zealand, with machinery to take

---

[1] See numbers 111, 114, 117. Sharp, p. 191, says that "In the spring of 1841 a letter was received from George Keats, waiving his legal rights, and agreeing to the publication of a 'Memoir, and Literary Remains.'"

[2] Robert Bell (1800–1867). In 1839–1840 the *Monthly Chronicle* printed six items by or about Shelley (White, *Shelley*, II, 409).

thither, from pins and needles up to a Saw-Mill and a steam-engine.[3] Carlino, who called on you when you were out of town at the beginning of February, will sail for the land of promise in a few days, perhaps in two or three days; and I shall follow him at the end of next month, or at the beginning of May.[4] Do not say I am too old for such an undertaking, when I have his young limbs and skill to aid me. He did not tempt me to go; it was my proposition to him, at first an unwilling listener. Yet, as may be imagined, I go for his sake, not for mine. We are partners — he to work and I to keep accounts, shares equal. I put faith, you perceive, in his prudence as well as in his talent.

Your's most sincerely,
Chas Brown the Emigrant.

· 149 ·

TO R. M. MILNES

Address: R. M. Milnes Esqre / M.P.

ALS: Harvard. Printed in *KC*, II, 51–52.

Laira Green, near Plymouth.

My dear Sir,   19 March 1841.

The Ms Poems cannot well be sent by post; you shall receive them by coach, with a notice by post of the day they will be sent.

In the mean time, I send you the Life; as I wish to receive your judgment of it, as soon as convenient. There are but two points, on which I desire to retain my opinion — 1st the propriety, the truth of what I have written against the Quarterly and the Edinburg, and against Blackwood's Magazine — 2nd the *long* history, through Severn, of Keats's painful illness, which should not be concealed, should not be less dwelt upon.

---

[3] Brown had been "cogitating on New Zealand" late in September or early in October 1840 (number 150), and not long afterward he wrote to both Trelawny and Kirkup of his interest in emigrating (Sharp, p. 191; the letters have since disappeared).

[4] Carlino boarded the *Amelia Thompson* on March 20, but did not sail until March 25. Brown sailed in the *Oriental* on June 22.

Yesterday and to-day I have been occupied on this subject,[1] and become fevered and nervous. I feel myself quite unable to fix my attention on these papers, whether in my hand writing or in his, any longer.

I must, however, touch on one topic. You will perceive, I have entirely spared Mr George Keats — not for want of proof. Without giving his name, he is included among those who borrowed *small* sums from Keats. Do you approve of my forbearance? The evidence against Mr George is incontrovertible, but does not lie in a small compass. Mr Dilke, of the Athenæum paper, denies the evidence, and, though he stands alone, has chosen to quarrel bitterly with me for my statement. Yet I have a witness "on this side Heaven too" [2] — Mr Haslam, Solicitor, N° 9 Copthall Court, Throgmorton Street, whom Keats held dearly — I believe they were schoolfellows.

> Your's very truly,
> Chas Brown.

· 150 ·

TO JOSEPH SEVERN [1]

Laira Green,
My dear Severn,   21st March, 1841.

Welcome to England! An impudent congratulation, you will say, from one about to go to the other hemisphere at the beginning of May. I knew you were coming, knew it from others, though I have been strangely kept in the dark by yourself. How could I well reply to your letter of September? Scarcely was it received, when I was cogitating on New Zealand; and when I had made up my mind, and was about to tell you the news, I heard you were expected in England. Did I not tell you that your Coronation visit might come to this? [2] I am certain you have done

---

[1] As Bodurtha and Pope note, pp. 93, 122, the passages in Brown's "Life" beginning "Now that twenty years have passed" and "After twenty years" (*KC*, II, 54, 95) contain last-minute revisions.

[2] Rollins, *KC*, II, 52n, cites *Paradise Lost*, II.1006, "To that side Heaven."

[1] From Sharp, pp. 193–194.

[2] Severn had made a "flying visit" to London in 1838, when Victoria was crowned.

right, not only for your wife's health, and your boy's education,[3] but for your profession. You press me, with your wonted kindness, to go and live with you, instead of pursuing my plans. You tempt me, but I cannot, must not. Had I thought of such a course, while making up my mind to be or not to be an emigrant, I might have concluded otherwise — certainly I should have paused. As it is, the die is cast. Yesterday I took leave of Carlino, who precedes me — he is at present wind-bound in the harbour. Though chiefly for his benefit, it is fair to state that our going was by no means at his suggestion, for he was, at first, very averse to it. Of course I have weighed the consequences of this step with all the ability in my power, and I ought to have the credit of proper deliberation. You *blame* me; but are you acquainted with the country by the best report, with the probable great advantages (not so much, perhaps, in money getting at my time of life, but in happiness), and with the scheme in detail or generally? I think you are not; for those of my friends who have most withstood me have known nothing — nay, they will confound one country with another, one colony with another, one purpose with another. Some friends of this sort have withstood me, and, indeed, teased me. Do not you, my dear Severn, join them, or rather *follow* their example, for they are silent at last. There is doubtless some risk of happiness in any course a man may pursue, however promising; but as it is now too late, pray do not repeat your objections, because you throw a gloom over my cheerful hopes. Your letter, though dated on 18th, did not arrive till last night, when I had taken leave of Carlino. I almost wish you had not arrived so early, because I am now strongly induced to visit London before I go; you need not press me to this, for my inclinations are of themselves enough; you may rely on my going to see you, if I can get rid of business matters and other matters here in time.

I resolved not to leave England and carry away with me the "Life and Remains of Keats." They will be confided for publication to Mr. R. M. Milnes, M.P., whom, I believe, you know. At the close of the "Life" I leave your letters, written at the time, copied verbatim, to tell the sad story of his sufferings. I have attempted to make a selection from his poems, but I find myself too partial

[3] Walter Severn was now ten years old.

to reject any, so Mr. Milnes must exercise his judgment on that point; for I am well aware that a poet's fame is more likely to be injured by the indiscriminate admiration of his friends than by his critics. Mr. Milnes is a poet himself, an admirer of Keats, and, in my mind, better able to sit in judgment on a selection for publication than any other man I know.

The greater part of this letter is for your wife as well as for yourself; so, with my love to her,

I am yours, ever truly,
Chas. Brown.

· 151 ·

TO R. M. MILNES

ALS: Harvard. Printed in *KC*, II, 98–101.

Laira Green, near Plymouth.

My dear Sir, 29 March 1841.

To-day I send to you, by Coach, a parcel containing all Keats's poems in my possession [1] — all that exist, as far as I am aware. Some have been already published in his volumes. Some, perhaps, or rather certainly, ought not to be published, for different reasons — as early attempts, as of too trifling a nature, or as, critically speaking, unworthy of his genius.

A wise selection from a poet's posthumous writings is the best for his lasting fame. Any other Poet's works I can coolly criticize, from Shakespeare downwards, but I feel there is no cool judgment in me while I am reading any thing by Keats. As soon as I begin to be occupied with his Ms poems, or with the Life I have written, it forcibly seems to me, against all reason (that is out of the question) that he is sitting by my side, his eyes seriously wandering from me to the papers by turns, and watching my doings.[2] Call it nervousness, if you will; but with this nervous

[1] Along with the manuscript of his "Life" they are now at Harvard (see *The Poetical Works of John Keats*, ed. H. W. Garrod, 2nd edn., Oxford, 1958, pp. lxv–lxvii, for a partial list).

[2] Compare number 22: "He [Keats] is present to me every where and at all times, — he now seems sitting by my side and looking hard in my face."

impression, I am unable to do justice to his fame. Could he speak, I would abide by his decision.

You were not his dearest friend, were not personally acquainted with him, and the task you have undertaken will doubtless be pleasure, mingled with regret. Implicitly do I rely on your judgment, as a friend to his fame, and as a brother poet; and gratefully do I acknowledge, in the name of Keats, your good will and kindness.

"Lucy Vaughan Lloyd" [3] was written chiefly for amusement; it appeared to be a relaxation; and it was begun without framing laws in his mind for the supernatural. When I noticed certain startling contradictions, his answer used to be — "Never mind, Brown; all those matters will be properly harmonized, before we divide it into Cantoes." As failures in wit, I might point out such Stanzas as 16, 17, & 18; yet there is exquisite wit of a peculiar kind in other parts. And there are many enchanting poetical passages. Probably you will publish the fragment with omissions. What can be better than his description of a London hackney-coach? [4] — yet how much misplaced!

In respect to the Life I have sent, you say — "I should not wish to soften any expressions of indignation at the Reviewers, but I might desire to change some of them"; to which you think I shall have no objection. The word "change" puzzles me. To speak truly, I would have no words changed that would change their purport. If I am wrong in my belief, or if the truth ought not to be entirely told, I am, at any rate, true and honest; if my expressions are sometimes too strong, much allowance will be made for one in my situation. I can enter into another demur which, at first thought, you seem to have entertained, but you immediately answered it yourself — "At the same time, if his first efforts had been successful, there is no saying what effects hope and joy might have had on such a temperament as his." That is precisely the question. His absolute disgust, his horror at what he used to call "shabby and glutinous cares" was joined to a firm spirit of in-

[3] "The Cap and Bells," which Brown (*KC*, II, 72) says "occupied his mornings pleasantly. He wrote it with the greatest facility; in one instance . . . as many as twelve stanzas before dinner."

[4] Stanzas XXV–XXVIII and part of XXIX, first published in Hunt's article on "Coaches" in the *Indicator*, August 23, 1820, p. 368.

dependence. My earnest offers pained him, because he feared for me. When I have put it in this way — "I am certain, Keats, that it would prove a capital speculation for me, if you will agree to let me go in your boat; I risk nothing, for we shall be sure to have a prosperous voyage"; he would look serious, and pleased; but, when it came to the point, he would more seriously refuse to let me enter his boat, with — "No, that must not be; you were very well before you knew me; and so you must remain — you are not a bookseller!"

Severn has arrived just in time for you — has he not? Should you have any questions to ask of me, and probably there may be some, though I cannot guess at them, you should be early in making them known for me to answer, as the Ship in which I am to depart is appointed to sail at the beginning of May. Carlino sailed in the Amelia Thompson on Thursday last (25th) with a moderate and favourable wind.[5]

> Your's most sincerely,
> Chas Brown.

I have not your volume of Poems. When you promised them, did I not say it could be sent through Longman & Co to Mr May, Bookseller, Plymouth, for me?[6] It is possible they are not now in business together; but I must have that vol. any how, by coach, or by post, or through some trading house.

Briefly as you choose, pray acknowledge the safe arrival of the parcel — for its safety is to me momentous.

[5] He arrived at New Plymouth, Taranaki, early in September.
[6] In number 147 Brown had specified "the Plymouth bookseller, Edmund Fry."

· 152 ·

TO R. M. MILNES

Address: Richd M. Milnes Esqre / M.P. / Fryston / Ferrybridge / Yorkshire.

Postmarks: PLYMOUTH AP 10 1841 A; Crabtree Penny Post; FERRY BRIDGE AP 12 1841

ALS: Harvard. Printed in *KC*, II, 101–103.

Laira Green. Plymouth.

My dear Sir,   9 April 1841.

In one sense, I can sympathise in your objection; in another, I cannot. Keats quitted surgery for poetry, one profession for another. A poet writes for public opinion, whether brutal or intellectual. He certainly wrote for it, while he held the opinion of the mob in contempt;[1] but he painfully discovered that in the opinion of those, who ought to have been intellectual, he was held in contempt. Suppose that a soldier or a sailor, a lawyer or a clergyman, were hunted down, month after month, by brute public opinion, so as to rob such a person, undeservedly, of the means of an independent livelihood, might it not break a great heart, while it could not break a great spirit? Such, I know, was the fact with Keats. Should it want confirmation, think of the epitaph he directed — "Here lies one whose name was writ in water." When you take the high ground of a poet's nobility, I can join with you; but I must recollect that a poet is subject, however noble, to the same animal wants and passions as his inferiors. I can scarcely confide in your judgment on this point, because it crossed my mind while I read your objection — "He talks to me that never feared dependence."[2] — excuse me for this, as it was involuntary. To sum up all (as I desire every man should have, and if needful, should express his opinion) pray allow my facts and opinions to stand; and do you, as you may think proper, add to the text your own notes and comments. In this, I think, you will

[1] See *Letters*, I, 266–267; II, 144, 146.
[2] Adapted from *Romeo and Juliet*, II.ii.1 (Rollins, *KC*, II, 102n).

sympathise with me. Not but that I am conscious there was a secondary cause for his fatal attack at my house, on the evening of the very day his brother George left him for America, with more by £20 than Keats possessed, saying, which was repeated to me by himself; — "You, John, have so many friends, they will be sure to take care of you!" — No — I mistake, it was on the evening after that day, that his fatal attack took place,[3] and the words were repeated with bitterness, and he added — "That was not, Brown, fair — was it?" putting me silent from indignation, for alas! the mischief was done! — in keeping his promise (undivulged to me) of assisting him with all the means he had. When I asked Keats why he had kept the promise so secret from me, he answered — "Because I knew you would oppose it, and because your opposition must have been in vain against my promise."

But I am sliding off into a subject, from which I chose to refrain in the Memoir, as irreparable and injurious to the brother, though he has provoked me enough by denying that he owed any thing to John Keats, and though I yet keep proofs to the contrary, besides Mr Haslam's evidence. Mr Dilke, an old friend and schoolfellow, chose to quarrel with me on this point, which provoked me still further; yet still I have been silent.

There is only one other thing I have to say, which appeared, and still appears, unnecessary: it is this — a selection from posthumous poems does not include the altering of a word.

You will find a poem in each of my books of copies from his originals of an exceptionable kind; they were written and copied for the purpose of preventing the young blue-stocking ladies from asking for the loan of his Ms Poems, and, through fathers and brothers, they had the effect.

Your's most sincerely,
Chas Brown.

[3] George left London on January 28, 1820; Keats suffered a severe hemorrhage on February 3. With George's remark about "many friends . . . to take care of you" compare his letter to Keats of June 18, 1820 (*Letters*, II, 296), "you cannot be in better hands than Browns."

· 153 ·

TO CHARLES BROWN, JR.

Address: Messʳˢ Chaˢ Brown & Son, / New Plymouth, / New Zealand. / per Regina.[1]

ALS: Keats House, Hampstead. Extracts are quoted by Hector Bolitho and John Mulgan, *The Emigrants: Early Travellers to the Antipodes* (London, 1939), p. 29.

My dear boy,   Laira Green. 13 April 1841.

The Regina has put back, in want of a heavier cargo, and, as I have heard, has taken our Goods from Bristol per Liskeard; that is, the remainder. I heard of this by accident, but I could find neither Saunders nor Haswell.[2] However, I left at their Office a written order to send you a Bill of Lading per Regina of the extra Goods shipped.

Of course you will choose, if possible, in preference to all others, a section with a water-course for the Mill. Next to that, I prefer a town-section with the boulevard in front for my own house; and it would be best to choose rural sections so that they may be adjoining a high road, and as much adjoining to each other as possible, to make them an estate in a ring-fence, which must be, unless other considerations intervene, more valuable.

It seems probable that the next Ship[3] will not sail till June. All goes on well. Broadmore is engaged to accompany me.[4] I have employed him to examine Huxham's Invoices, and I intend to go on Friday to Powderham, to consult with him on various matters regarding Huxham and the Mill. I have sold this cottage for £225.

Tomorrow[5] I shall wish myself many happy returns of the day in New Zealand.   Your affectionate father,

Chaˢ Brown.

[1] A schooner chartered by the Plymouth Company to carry the baggage and stores of the emigrants who sailed on the *Amelia Thompson*.
[2] Messrs. Saunders and Haswell were the Plymouth Company's shipping surveyors.
[3] The *Oriental*.
[4] "My man, Broadmore" and his wife both went to New Plymouth, according to Brown's logbook of the voyage now at Keats House. Broadmore was with Carlino as late as 1863 (*The Richmond-Atkinson Papers*, ed. Scholefield, II, 26).
[5] His birthday.

· 154 ·

TO JOSEPH SEVERN [1]

My dear Severn,

New Plymouth, Taranaki, New Zealand,
22nd January, 1842.

The Plymouth New Zealand Company have grievously disappointed us, and I intend to proceed, as soon as I can, to return
to England viâ Sydney (as the cheapest way), perhaps leaving
Carlino behind me, at least for a short time. Our letters, it is
surmised, have been opened, and, if found to be unfavourable to
the New Zealand Colonies, they never reach their destination.
We now entertain better hopes of our letters, and should this arrive
at your hands, you will be of essential service in causing it to be
printed in the public papers [2] as a caution to others not to put
faith in representations made by New Zealand companies. No one
letter can contain our grievances; but it is enough to tell you at
present that this place has not a port except Port Hardy, 100 or
110 miles off, in D'Orville's Island, nay, has not a roadstead, and
is so dangerous to approach that, after wrecks and various dis-
asters,[3] ships no more attempt it, and we are left unsupplied,
possibly, at last, to live on the fern root, which would soon kill
me. *I was promised a Port by the Company for my money*, and I
intend to protest against receiving any sections of land on this
coast, and to bring an action against the Company for their non-
fulfilment of the contract between us, I claiming a return of my
money paid to them, together with every expense to which I have
been put, and damages of all sorts which the law will allow. In the
meantime, though much injured in "mind, body, and estate," [4]
I shall not be a pauper, and, looking at your hearty invitation
just before I quitted England,[5] it is my intention, should my

---

[1] From Sharp, pp. 197–198. Brown left Plymouth on June 22, 1841, and
arrived at New Plymouth in November.

[2] As the next letter actually was.

[3] The *Regina* (see the preceding letter) had drifted from anchor and been
totally wrecked upon the coast a few days before Brown landed.

[4] "Morning Prayer. A Prayer for All Conditions of Men," in *The Book of
Common Prayer*.

[5] See number 150.

health and time of life permit me outlive the voyage, to offer myself at your threshhold as your guest, — at any rate, for a moderate period. My health and strength are certainly improved since last month, when I feared I was irretrievably sinking under my grievances; but since that time I happily discovered a document from the Company, perhaps inadvertently granted to me, though a very common one, and that seems to promise me the fullest justice. Without it, I had not anything but verbal promises, verbal representations — which are nothing in a legal point of view.

Think of our being compelled to take shipping to go to our *Port!* the impudence of such an attempt to fulfil a contract is scarcely imaginable. But I have proof that my sections of land were engaged to be at the *Port* of New Plymouth. Accordingly I demand to be conveyed to Port Hardy (the declared Port), and there to take any sections of land; but first the Company must carry land thither, as it is little more than a naked, steep rock; enough of land, at least, for our 201 acres: but though I expressed our willingness, at a public meeting, to go thither, no answer was returned, all looking aghast at the unexpected though reasonable turn I gave to their discussion as to the best means to be adopted for obtaining a Port.[6]

Carlino, I am glad to say, is well and in good spirits. I have written much of my "New Zealand Handbook;" [7] not "New Zealand Guide," because I cannot conscientiously guide any one to it.

Remember me most kindly to Mrs. Severn, and

Believe me, ever yours truly,

Chas. A.[8] Brown.

[6] See the next letter.

[7] Fragmentary passages of the beginning of this work are extant in Brown's logbook now at Keats House, Hampstead.

[8] Brown took the middle name "Armitage" when he published *Shakespeare's Autobiographical Poems.*

· 155 ·

TO E. J. TRELAWNY [1]

Coast of Taranaky, New Zealand,
Jan. 23, 1842.

My dear Trelawny, — Should my health and strength permit me to survive the voyage, you will see me, or hear of my return to England. It is probable that Carlino may not accompany me, but follow me in a short time, in another ship. That folks should be disappointed in their expectations of New Zealand might well be, and yet nobody to blame but themselves; and if such were the case, we could have no just cause of complaint. But the company promised us a port, and do not grant one to the settlement of their New Plymouth. The consequences were (for this coast is extremely dangerous of approach), wrecks and partial losses, together with a dread of sending any vessels to us from Sidney or Port Nicholson, while we have been and now are threatened with famine, unless a man can exist on the fern root, which I cannot. The labourers were the first, about five weeks ago, to convene public meetings for the purpose of considering how best to avoid their threatened fate. At two of these they requested me to preside; but I am sorry to say nothing was elicited except their want of means and want of unanimity. Since that time our stock of course has been diminishing, with less hope of supplies, and our land-purchasers also have had their meetings. At the second I was told that several of the company's agents would attend, so I went and found them there. I found the meeting busy in discussions on the best means, by petition, or what not, of speedily obtaining the construction of a port here. All this they were about explaining to me, when, thinking I held a broom in my hand to sweep away cobwebs and rubbish, I inquired if Mr. F. A. Carrington, the Company's chief surveyor,[2] was present? Upon this he bowed,

---

[1] From *The Times*, August 31, 1842, where it is headed, "From a Correspondent. (Extract from a Private Letter.)"

[2] Frederic Alonzo Carrington (1807–1901), who had the job of selecting, purchasing, and surveying land for the settlement. Scholefield, *A Dictionary of New Zealand Biography*, I, 142, says, apparently without irony, that he "carried

and acknowledged himself. "Then allow me," said I, "to ask you, in your public capacity, where is the Port of New Plymouth?" "It is," he replied, without hesitation, "Port Hardy." Up I jumped, with my question, already prepared in writing, scrawled down his answer to it, and obtained three witnesses to my question and his answer, two of the witnesses being magistrates. "Then," said I, coolly folding up the valuable document and putting it safely into my pocket, "then New Plymouth must be at Port Hardy, to which I and my son declare ourselves ready to proceed, and thus fulfil part of the agreement entered into with the company, for which I have their documents printed and written." All looked aghast and remained silent. "I am aware," I continued, "that Port Hardy is in D'Orville's Island, which is little more than an almost inaccessible craggy steep, yet, to fulfil our part of the contract, we declare ourselves willing to go thither, with all our goods and machinery, in proper ships, we having already paid for our passage in the chief cabin and for freight from Plymouth, in England, to the port of New Plymouth, in New Zealand." "But, Sir, it is an impossibility; there is not land there sufficient for building half-a-dozen houses." "The possibility rests with the company; let them convey thither enough land to fulfil their part of the contract with the purchasers, at least enough for me and my son, no more than 201 acres." "All this must be nonsense, it cannot be — it is not possible." "Of that it is not my business to judge. We insist on nothing but what was specially promised to us by the company — viz., to be conveyed, with our goods, &c., to our proper destination, for the due performance of which we shall forthwith petition his Excellency the Governor.[3] Should the company say 'it is not possible,' we will try if it is more possible for them to return our purchase money, our passage money hither and back to England, our amount of freight, our loss on the goods and machinery we have bought, and our other losses, which I cannot now specify, but which we will, at our leisure, specify before going into a court of law." The meeting was then broken up, no one having recovered from the

out his task with complete success." Years later (1873) he defeated Carlino in an election for the superintendency of Taranaki.
   [3] William Hobson (1793–1842).

state of surprise I had occasioned. This happened only three days ago. By another document in my possession, the company is liable to pay damages to every one of the labouring emigrants who are promised a port to Plymouth in New Zealand; and it is known and (I suppose) commented on that I have explained their claim to them; for already there are symptoms of the company's tyranny, through their agents, being in a course of relaxation. I begin to fear that the boasted capital may fail in satisfying the many claims. Only imagine our being told that we must cross the sea 100 or 110 miles distance to arrive at our port! Was ever anything more impudent?

Make what use you please of this letter, bearing in mind that I wish it to be published in the papers as a warning to others.

Yours very truly,
Charles Brown.

P.S. Premiums of insurance from Sidney to this place, I hear, is 60 per cent; and I hear 90 per cent. is proposed to be asked from Port Nicholson to this place.

156 .

TO ROBERT SKYNNER [1]

ALS: Keats House, Hampstead.

R. Skynner Esqre   N. P. T^y 26 Feby 1842.
Dear Sir,

Two days since, the Timandra arrived here with a large packet of letters for me from England, bearing dates from 15th to 31st Octr last; but not one among them was from you, either with a remittance which might have been or with accounts of the sale of my property, for which you had my Power of Att^y, or with reasons for none of the property having been sold, after more than four months subsequent to my departure. In this uncertainty, I must sell (in a short time) and at very great loss, owing to the want of money here such parts of my investment as will

---

[1] A draft preserved in Brown's logbook of the voyage to New Zealand.

enable me to pay for my passage, or for that of my son (for my life is not to be relied on for the voyage) back to England, — there to go, perhaps, to the Parish for an existence.

I am aware of my letter of 16 Nov[r] last,[2] but that could not affect your writing at the end of Oct[r]. The "further instructions" therein spoken of were sent to you and are another matter and will have been afterwards rec[d] in due course; viz — to send me remittances forthwith; which if you have neglected, may cause us to die of want.   Yr's truly

                                                                        CB

Have the kindness to remember me &c [3]

· 157 ·

TO FRANCIS LIARDET AND HENRY KING [1]

ALS: Keats House, Hampstead.

To Capt. Liardet R.N. and Capt King R.N.   [March 11, 1842]
Gent[n],

Mr Cutfield [2] has taken the particular pains of informing me that both of you have applied the words "ungentlemanly and insulting" to my conduct towards him. I am surprised you did not perceive that by attempting to stigmatise another's character without hearing his statement of previous facts, you must inevit-

[2] An entry in Brown's logbook provides the gist: "16 Nov[r]. The whole of the above [an order for quantities of fishhooks, tobacco pipes, "men's slop shirts," and other merchandise] annulled, and directions given not to remit any thing, either in goods or otherwise, till further instructions from self or son."

[3] Another entry summarizes a postscript to this or a later letter: "28 Feb[y] 1842 in PS. Directions to remit money not to the firm, but to Cha[s] Brown alone."

[1] A draft preserved in Brown's logbook. The final state of the text is somewhat in question. Brown wrote, successively, the first, fourth, third, and second paragraphs, and then seems to have reversed the order of the middle two. Commander Henry King (1783–1874), who had arrived with Carlino in September, was chief commissioner of the New Plymouth colony until superseded after a few months by Captain Francis Liardet (1798–1863), who himself departed to return to England in February.

[2] George Cutfield (1799–1879), King's brother-in-law, was storekeeper and immigration agent for the colony, and a justice of the peace. Subsequently he twice opposed Carlino for the superintendency of Taranaki (1857, 1861), the first time successfully.

ably be unjust — which is a term I could less endure than being called ungentlemanly and insulting.

I avail myself of this opp^y of inquiring from either or both of you, gentlemen, who is "the Resident Officer of the Plyth C^o of N.Z. for sale of Lands in N P"? — as such an Officer is unknown to every one in the Colony, at least to a great many whom I have asked to tell me, including Comp$^{y's}$ Agents, while I possess land Orders with a P of A [3] from C, — I knowing that the whole of the land purchased by any Corres^t is liable to be forfeited should the Land Orders not be presented within a limited period to the said "Resident Officer", whose name is either unknown or kept a profound secret from me, to the probable loss of my Cor$^{t's}$ property

It is not for me to imagine what designation you will be pleased to bestow on one who sent me an assurance before a Magistrate that Mr Chilman [4] was, on 25 Jany last, the Postmaster of New Pl when the assurance was immediately and absolutely denied by Mr Chilman himself, and who, on my writing to him for an explanation, would not answer; — a circumstance of great importance to me with my correspondents, and to whom I can return only the fact and his extr^y silence as my exp^n to them.

Never have I been so foolish as to defend myself to those who have chosen to prejudge me; but we may suppose the case of a person having, under his own hand, forfeited his title to veracity (not including the above apparent deception, still unexplained); [5] then, should you, aware of the forfeiture, continue to behave to-wards him as if still within the pale of honour, such conduct can never, however high the example, be followed by

Gentlemen,

11 March 1842.   Your most obed^t hum Servt CB

[3] Power of attorney.
[4] Richard Chilman (1816–1877), then clerk to Cutfield.
[5] The words "not . . . unexplained" are written above the line and in the right-hand margin. The parentheses are an editorial addition.

INDEX

INDEX